Caring for the Developing Child

Second Edition

Patricia E. Marhoefer
Pomona Unified School District • Pomona, CA

Lisa A. Vadnais
Baldy View Regional Occupational Program • Claremont, CA

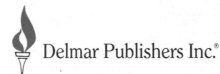

Delmar Publishers Inc.®

NOTICE TO THE READER

Cover photos: *Courtesy of Paul E. Meyers*

Photograph Credits:
Photo figures courtesy of Julie Hooke: 1-3, 1-11, 2-6, 4-1, 4-7, 4-8, 5-2, 5-3, 6-0, 6-3, 6-9, 6-11, 6-15, 7-0, 7-1, 8-0, 8-1, 9-10, 12-9, 13-5, 14-2, 14-3, 14-8, 15-1, 16-5, 16-13, 18-6, 18-7, 18-8, 18-9, 18-17, 19-6, 21-0, 21-1, 21-2, 21-3, 22-0, 22-2, 22-4, 23-17, 23-18, 23-21, 24-4.
Photo figures courtesy of Patricia Marhoefer: 2-5, 10-21, 12-2, 13-4, 14-10, 19-1, 20-4.
Photo figures courtesy of Bettman Archive: 11-1, 11-2, 11-3, 11-4.
Photo figures courtesy of Lisa Vadnais: 9-5, 20-0.
Photo figure courtesy of the American Nanny Plan, Inc.: 2-9.
All other photographs that appear in Caring for the Developing Child, courtesy of Richard Miller.

Delmar Staff
Administrative Editor: Jay Whitney
Associate Editor: Erin Peek
Project Editor: Laura Gulotty
Production Coordinator: Bruce Sherwin
Senior Production Supervisor: Larry Main
Art Supervisor: John Lent
Art and Design Manager: Rita C. Stevens

For information address Delmar Publishers Inc.
2 Computer Drive West, Box 15-015
Albany, New York 12212

10 9 8 7 6 5 4 3

Printed in the United States of America
Published simultaneously in Canada
by Nelson Canada,
a division of The Thomson Corporation

Library of Congress Cataloging-in-Publication Data

Marhoefer, Patricia E.
    Caring for the developing child / Patricia E. Marhoefer, Lisa A.
Vadnais. — 2nd ed.
        p.   cm.
    Includes index.
    ISBN 0-8273-4681-6.
    ISBN 0-8273-4682-4 (instructor's guide)
    1. Child care—United States.   2. Day care centers—United States.
3. Child development—United States.
I. Vadnais, Lisa A.
II. Title.
HQ778.7.U6M37   1992
305.231'—dc20   91-4938
                                                                CIP
ISBN 0-8273-5043-0 (workbook)
ISBN 0-8273-5044-9 (Teacher's Resource Book)

CONTENTS

PREFACE

Caring for the Developing Child answers the need for a comprehensive text covering all the basic topics of child care. Caregivers must have a fundamental understanding of these areas whether working with infants, toddlers, preschoolers, school-age children, or children with exceptional needs. Because of the increasing demand for quality children's centers and quality caregivers, this text was developed.

Students interested in beginning a career in the field of child care will find this book of particular value. Others who wish to have a formative understanding of children, such as social workers, medical personnel, parents, and caregivers already working in centers, will find information to increase their comprehension and knowledge.

ARRANGEMENT OF SECTIONS

The text is divided into sections so the reader can easily locate the area of interest.

Section I, General Information, discusses the responsibilities and jobs of the staff and defines the child care programs available today. It also explains how good environments for children are established including a section on learning centers. It embodies precise safety guidelines for indoors and the play yard. A new feature "In the Home Care" has been included in several appropriate chapters to address issues relative to family day care and Nanny Programs.

Section II, Health, discusses the importance of maintaining good health practices in a children's center and lists community resources available for referral. It gives specific first aid information concerning possible injuries and poisoning. Another chapter explains the symptoms and characteristics of communicable diseases and includes Fifth Disease and Lyme Disease. Reviews of current CPR information is also given in detail. Child abuse is defined and examples of different types of abuse are explained, as well as how-to information on education, detection, and intervention. Good nutritional training for young children and adults, including recent facts on the Five Food Groups is outlined. New information on recipes and menus is included.

Section III, The Four Basic Areas of Child Development, gives an overview of the major theorists in the field (Sigmund Freud, Jean Piaget, Arnold Gesell, Erik Erikson, B.F. Skinner, Abraham Maslow, and Burton White). Included is their contribution to the understanding of how children develop. Separate chapters on each area of development (physical, social, emotional, intellectual) are thoroughly discussed. Case studies are used to illustrate major growth patterns for each age group. Because observation of children, staff, and facilities is used to evaluate growth, observation methods are taught in the final chapter of this section through examples and explanations.

Section IV, The Ages of Child Development, gives precise information on prenatal care, infants and toddlers, preschoolers, and school-age children. Daily schedules, self-help tasks, and the caregiver's role for each group are covered in depth. A separate chapter discusses gifted children and children with physical or mental impairments. Mainstreaming is emphasized as a means to incorporate exceptional children into the established classroom.

Section V, Classroom Management, stresses the need to establish fair and concise guidelines for a classroom or center conducive to learning. This section discusses respect for children, freedom to discover, positive reinforcement, ethnic differences, and the importance of an anti-bias curriculum, as well as meeting the individual needs of each child. The management of typical methods of discipline is also covered.

Section VI, Curriculum, gives detailed information on subject areas that should be presented to children. Arts, crafts, music, science, math, social studies, motor development, nutrition, and language arts are explained and illustrated. How-to information is given for each age group. Two types of lesson plans are also demonstrated along with lists of themes and special days or events.

SPECIFIC POINTS OF INTEREST IN THE TEXT

Objectives are stated at the beginning of each chapter to familiarize the student with the subject matter to be presented. Key terms are listed at the beginning of each chapter and are highlighted in the text discussion to enhance learning. A glossary of all key terms is included at the back of the book. Case studies throughout the text lend interest and understanding. Each illustrates a specific major point of reference as do the numerous illustrations and charts. A brief summary emphasizing the main points is added at the end of each chapter. Review questions in "Things to Do and Discuss" sections reinforce learning and give practical application of the chapter material.

To strengthen the text, an *Instructor's Guide, Teacher's Resource Guide* and *Student Workbook* are offered as supplementary materials. The *Instructor's Guide* includes answers to quizzes, "Things to Do and Discuss," and extra credit activities. The *Teacher's Resource Guide* includes annotations and teaching suggestions, an overview of each chapter, transparencies, and curriculum themes. A bibliography and suggested films and videos are also included. The *Student Workbook* contains chapter overviews, questions from "Things to Do and Discuss," group and extra credit activities, and a Final Test with space for answers. An additional feature is pertinent handouts pertaining to the chapter which are excellent resources to enhance learning.

ABOUT THE AUTHORS

Patricia E. Marhoefer has spent twenty-five years in the area of child care. Beginning as a substitute aide and progressing to director of a cooperative preschool, she is currently instructing students from infants through adults.

Her title is the Child Care Specialist for the Career and Continuing Education Department of Pomona Unified School District in Pomona, California. In this capacity, her duties include teaching high school and adult students in the field of Child Care Occupations Course for the San Antonio Regional Occupation Program, as well as the Teen Parenting Skills Course, Adult Parenting Courses, providing workshops in child development and parenting, and for the SOLO project for women reentering the workforce. She is responsible for establishing the Laboratory Schools and Infant/Toddler Program on the high school campus as well as being in charge of the Drop-In Center for the children of students enrolled in the Adult Education Program. She is involved in consulting in the early childhood field and does numerous teacher in-services for various schools. She holds a Vocational Teaching Credential from California State University at San Bernardino and the California State Children Center Permit. Mrs. Marhoefer lives in California with her husband Jim and two sons, Jon and Ken.

Lisa A. Vadnais has been involved in the field of Child Care for eighteen years. She has acted as a teacher for ages two through adult. She held the position of director of an early childhood program for five years and is currently a Regional Occupation Program Vocational Child Care Instructor for high school students and adults. She teaches a child growth and development class at a Nanny College in Claremont and is a consultant in the field of child care. She has received her B.S. degree in Child Development from the University of La Verne and is currently working on obtaining her master's degree. She holds a Vocational Teaching Credential from the University of California in Los Angeles. Mrs. Vadnais lives in California with her husband Ed and two daughters, Trisha and Amy.

ACKNOWLEDGMENTS

We have been extremely fortunate to have many people and schools help us in the writing of this book. We wish to thank all of you for your valuable support. A special warm thank you to Richard Miller for spending many hours providing his professional services as photographer. We also wish to thank the staff and children of the numerous schools who allowed us to photograph them and their facilities—Drop-In Center (Pomona Unified School District, Career and Continuing Education, Pomona, CA), Pomona High School Child Development Center (Pomona, CA), Claremont Presbyterian Children's Center (Claremont, CA), Valley View Infant Center (Ontario, CA), Calvary Christian Preschool (Ontario, CA), and Pebbles Christian School (Rancho Cucamonga, CA).

DEDICATION

This book is dedicated to and would not have been possible without the encouragement, love, and support of our families: Jim, Jon, and Ken Marhoefer; and Ed, Trisha, and Amy Vadnais. Thank you. A special dedication to our mothers who had always encouraged us in each new endeavor: Alma B. Polk (Patricia Marhoefer's mother) and Delores Criffield (Lisa Vadnais' mother).

PATRICIA MARHOEFER
LISA VADNAIS

General Information

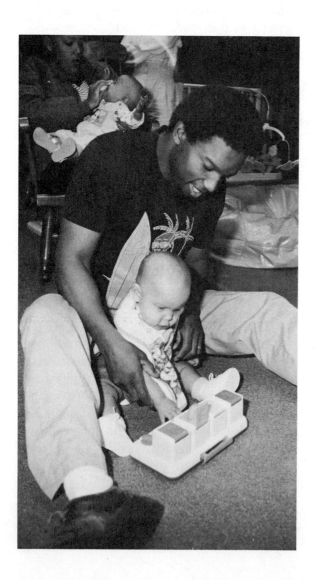

OBJECTIVES

After completing this section, you will be able to:

1. identify the separate responsibilities of the director, the teacher, and the aide;
2. identify the different types of center programs;
3. discuss good room and yard environments for young children.

SECTION I

In this section we discuss the fundamentals of the child care center. Before you begin training as a caregiver, you must understand the jobs of the director, teacher, and aide. Together these people work as a team. They provide a stable environment in which children feel comfortable, happy, and successful as individuals, yet can function in a group.

Working with young children is hard, but it can be rewarding and fun. The attitudes of the staff members affect the atmosphere of the school. In a cheerful environment, the children flourish and respond to learning, eagerly looking forward to the school day.

There are many different types of school centers, and each is unique in its responsibilities for staff members and its goals for children. In this section you, as the caregiver, should be able to find a center that will meet your needs.

CHAPTER 1
Responsibilities of the Staff

Caregivers should nurture.

KEY TERMS

communication
curriculum
development
facilitator
imitative
initiative
learning centers
observing
open classroom

personnel
philosophy
professionalism
proprietors
role models
self-help skills
structured classroom
supervision
teacher

OBJECTIVES

After completing this chapter, you will be able to:
1. list and discuss three responsibilities of the director;
2. list and discuss three responsibilities of the teacher;
3. list and discuss three responsibilities of the aide.

DIRECTOR

Role modeling, communicating, organizing, observing, nurturing: These key terms represent only a few of the responsibilities that a director faces each day. The director, or administrator, is the central, most important person in the daily operation of a child care facility. The director's knowledge, philosophy, attitude, and managerial ability make a successful or unsuccessful program.

Philosophy

The director establishes the school's goals and philosophy with help from the school board or *proprietors* (owners). The *philosophy* is a statement of the teachings and beliefs guiding the school. It usually includes the types of programs, individual care, and opportunities given to all children. Below is a philosophy that might be found in a parent handbook:

> The Children's Center reflects our sense of community, its support and reinforcement of the family, and its concern for the individual. Our center provides an enrichment environment, offering a variety of activities to advance the child socially, emotionally, physically, and intellectually. Our focus is to develop an environment in which children are respected, accepted, and allowed to develop their potential for growth.

Following are some goals that might be found in a parent handbook:

> The goals of the Children's Center are:
>
> 1. to respect children as individuals;
>
> 2. to give children opportunities for stimulation and growth within their abilities;
>
> 3. to treat children in a positive manner in order to enhance their self-esteem.

General Supervision

The director sets the tone for the school. By being cheerful each morning, spending quality time with each person, and showing genuine concern throughout the day, the director helps ensure a quality program. Directors should be available and have open communication policies with students, parents, and staff.

By setting an example of *professionalism* (education, ethics, and experience), the director encourages good attitudes, appear-

Figure 1-1: This director discusses the menu with the cook.

ance, and relationships with staff members. The *supervision* (watching over the work of others) of all people working at the child care facility is the main responsibility of the director. The list includes teachers, aides, volunteers (parent helpers, community helpers, and vocational training students), secretaries, cooks, and maintenance staff. The director interviews, hires, observes, trains, evaluates, and terminates if needed, all of the above staff, in order to maintain a quality program.

A warm and pleasant atmosphere should be encouraged so the staff enjoys working at the center. The director must maintain fair policies and rules. Daily *communication* (dialogue) among staff members helps to create a positive attitude and high morale. More formal communication is provided by holding regular staff meetings. These allow the director to stay informed of any staff concerns or problems and to develop new projects and incentives. Sharing ideas helps keep the staff energized.

Personnel

The director must employ the most competent staff available to meet the needs of the children. Compliance with city, county, state, and federal requirements is a major concern of the director. Part of the task includes keeping all staff records, work schedules, adult-to-child ratios, health and immunization records, and in some states, disclaimers of felony arrests. Fingerprinting of staff members is required in most states.

A list of qualified substitute teachers and aides is also kept on file. Regulations regarding staffing vary from state to state. Figure 1-2 gives an overview of standards in California, Illinois, and Connecticut.

When interviewing potential staff members, directors look for maturity, experience, education, a responsible attitude, and good moral character. All *personnel* (people employed by the facility) must be able to interact with the students and other staff members and serve as good *role models* (people others wish to copy or emulate).

The director must meet with new staff members and student teachers for orientation before they are placed in the classroom. Orientation should include review of the staff

handbook on the school's philosophy, goals, responsibilities, dress code, procedures, and expectations. Constant review of staff performance is essential to making a more positive learning environment for students and staff.

Record Keeping

The director must keep all files on personnel and students current and accessible to appropriate authorities. The records must be completed and filed from the first date of enrollment or employment.

Student records vary from state to state, but an identification form, an emergency form, immunization form, and record of physical examination usually are required. A tuition and policy agreement, field trip consent form, and hospital emergency form may also be filed.

Staff records usually include a personnel application form, an emergency form, a physical examination form, tuberculosis test verification, transcripts, educational records, and fingerprint clearance. Some states require a signed statement showing no prior felony arrest, and clearance by a child abuse registry. Personnel records must be reviewed regularly to ensure that the staff remains current with educational methods and professional standards.

Planning, Designing, and Maintaining the School Plant

All child care facilities are planned differently and allow creativity on the part of the director. Centers can be housed in a church building, community center, converted house, or a privately owned building constructed specifically for child care. All of them allow the

State Regulations for Personnel

Teacher Qualifications

State	Education	Experience	Age
California	12 semester units of E.C.E.	6 months	18
	6 semester units plus 2 units per year thereafter	None	
Illinois	2 years of college with 6 semester units of E.C.E.	None	19
	1 year of college	1 year	
	C.D.A. Credential		
Connecticut	C.D.A. Credential or 12 units of E.C.E.	1 year	20
	No E.C.E. Education	2 years	

Director Qualifications

State	Education	Experience	Age
California	12 semester units of E.C.E.	4 years	—
	3 semester units of administration		
	2 years of college	2 years	
	B.A.	1 year	
Illinois	2 years of college with 18 semester units of E.C.E.	None	21
	1 year of college with 10 semester units of E.C.E.	2 years	
	C.D.A. Credential		
Connecticut	C.D.A. Credential	1 year	20
	12 semester units of E.C.E.	2 years	

Figure 1-2: State Regulations for Personnel chart.

director to plan the classroom and play yard. Equipment, furniture, and developmental supplies must be carefully planned, purchased, and presented in a pleasing manner, always keeping in mind the budget.

The conscientious director and teacher seek a balance between high-activity and low-activity toys and learning centers (*learning centers* are areas of the classroom designated for a particular learning environment; i.e., blocks, housekeeping, table games, music, arts and crafts, science, and language development). Together the staff members arrange the classroom and play yard for the ages of their students, allocating space attractively, efficiently, and effectively. The successful director is able to blend color, pattern, and design to create a stimulating and inviting atmosphere for the children and staff of the center.

The director inspects the equipment daily to be sure it is properly maintained and safe, often making the small repairs. Equally important are the offices, kitchen, and bathrooms, which must be equipped properly and maintained according to health and safety regulations. They must be kept sanitary yet appealing. Similarly, the grounds outside the play yard, which include a grassy area, sidewalks, and a parking lot, should also be maintained in a safe condition.

Curriculum

Directors must also ensure that the school's *curriculum* (planned program of activities) meets the developmental needs of the children. By checking the lesson plans and activities in each classroom, they encourage the children to grow socially, emotionally,

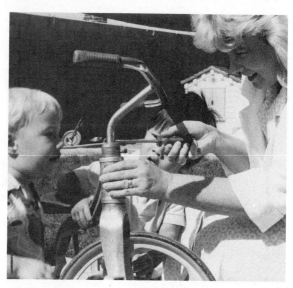

Figure 1-3: This director fixes a tricycle with help from her friends.

physically, and intellectually. Often a director will meet with staff to discuss weekly and monthly themes and to plan the activities in each area. (Themes can be holidays, seasons, community helpers, health, safety, animals, or family.) From the broad theme title, the director can set a guideline that matches the school's philosophy to help the teachers and aides build a balanced learning program.

The director can also arrange for classroom visitors, such as a nurse to discuss good nutrition, or a police officer to share safety rules. Field trips, locally and at a distance, can also be arranged to fit within the theme.

Parent Education and Interaction

The director is a leader to the staff and parents, and is a resource to the community.

Parents look to the director for the most current information on parenting skills and child rearing. To keep current, professional directors extend their knowledge and skills by taking courses and attending local, state, and national conferences and conventions, directors' group meetings, and legislative forums. The director is usually a member of the local, state, and national organizations for child care and education.

The National Association for the Education of Young Children (1834 Connecticut Avenue NW, Washington, D.C. 20009), and The National Parent-Teacher Association (700 North Rush Street, Chicago, Illinois 60611) are excellent resources. They have current listings of most organizations throughout the United States. They also list current legislation affecting the education of children, licensing of facilities, and requirements for staff members. Local information can be obtained through state departments of education, state departments of social services, school districts, or children's centers.

The director is a role model and represents the school to the community. By communicating the school's goals and objectives to parents, and by being a strong, positive motivator, the director encourages parent participation and education.

The director is the school's referral person. A director must know how to talk constructively with parents about their children's progress. Parents and teachers should feel free to talk with the director about any school-related problems. A list of community resources and professional services can be made available for more in-depth assistance.

Parent involvement is the backbone of a quality child care center. The director and staff must tell parents about the progress of their children. By 1988 the number of licensed child care centers increased to approximately 60,000 with an additional 161,000 licensed family day care providers in the United States (Kutner, 1988). These facilities generally are open from 6:00 A.M. to 6:00 P.M. Children sometimes spend 10 or more hours a day in a center. These statistics clearly show the need to inform parents about their children's activities.

To keep parents informed about what happens at school, the director often writes a

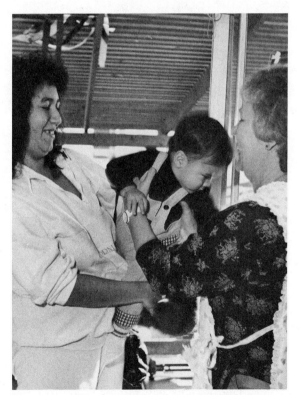

Figure 1-4: This director welcomes children and parents each morning.

A Day Care Director's Typical Day

7:00 A.M.	Find substitute teacher for the four-year-old class.	
7:30 A.M.	Check with the kitchen staff to ensure breakfast is ready.	
8:00 A.M.	Greet children and parents.	
8:10 A.M.	Discuss daily routine with sub.	
8:25 A.M.	Continue greetings.	
9:05 A.M.	Join the children in the morning flag salute and song. Conduct morning group time, outlining the day's program.	
9:30 A.M.	Plan an agenda for staff meeting on Wednesday.	
9:45 A.M.	Comfort a child and perform first aid on bloody knee.	
9:55 A.M.	Help prepare the morning snack (a student aide was absent and did not call).	
10:15 A.M.	Conference with parents about their child's excessive bed-wetting.	
11:00 A.M.	Order more paint and construction paper.	

11:15 A.M.	Check classrooms and help teachers.
11:40 A.M.	Help the cook serve lunch.
12:15 P.M.	Eat lunch.
12:40 P.M.	Answer a phone call concerning enrollment of a new child.
1:00 P.M.	Continue to outline agenda for the staff meeting.
1:30 P.M.	Check nap rooms.
1:45 P.M.	Research curriculum ideas for Valentine's Day.
2:30 P.M.	Welcome extended day care.
3:00 P.M.	Help serve the afternoon snack.
3:30 P.M.	Share in afternoon group time, sing with the children.
4:00 P.M.	Leave for the day.
6:30 P.M.	Evening call from a parent concerning a child's aggressive behavior with a sibling.
7:30 P.M.	Attend evening school board meeting.

Figure 1-5: A Child Care Director's Typical Day chart.

weekly or monthly newsletter. Notes also can be left in the child's file or cubbie concerning anything of personal or immediate importance. Bulletin boards are often available in a convenient location for posting general information about upcoming events.

The director is generally ready to greet each child and parent every day, taking time to address questions about school policies, curriculum, social events, and the child's progress. This is a transition time for the child and the parent. It must be handled with warmth and understanding for the ease and comfort of all involved.

The director must get involved with the children by getting to know them and their families personally and by being aware of their stages of growth and development. Each child needs to feel loved and valued.

In some schools the director may also take all or partial responsibility for teaching a class. Therefore, administrative duties must be finished before or after class time.

Community Relations

Sending newsworthy articles or interesting pictures of students to the area newspapers introduces the school to the community. This helps to maintain an awareness of the facility and increase the enrollment (without spending money on advertising).

The director may be on community committees representing the school. Building trust and respect for the school within the community maintains the school's reputation.

The tasks and duties of the director never end, but they are certainly rewarding. The successful director takes pride in the accomplishments of all the staff and the children.

TEACHER

Let's begin this section by discussing the role of a teacher. We can define a *teacher* as someone who guides, instructs, and trains students, providing knowledge and insight. To go a step further, we can say that a teacher counsels, directs, supports, assesses, encourages, and respects the students. The job is most complex and the tasks are many. This quality is confirmed throughout this textbook as the young child is discussed. In every chapter the teacher is directly involved in each

child's growth and *development* (progressive growth).

Education of Children

The teacher is the *facilitator* (provider of the methods of instruction) of the classroom. Always aware of the age and developmental level of the children, the teacher uses this knowledge to provide an enriching and satisfying environment. With basic supplies and with a bit of creativity, the teacher can develop a stimulating atmosphere. This lets children learn through all their senses and acquire a desire to keep learning.

Daily lesson plans are the key to a successful classroom. The professional teacher begins each day with a master plan, setting the goals for each child as well as the group. The materials are placed where children can easily reach them, toys and manipulative games changing periodically to ensure challenge and to avoid boredom. The choice of activities should be appropriate for the developmental level of the group, without causing frustration, denial, or negative feelings. Activities should be just difficult enough to give the children a sense of discovery, challenge, and accomplishment.

Whether in a *structured classroom* (one where all children follow a set schedule) or an *open classroom* (one where children are free to choose among learning centers), the teacher must provide activities to enhance the whole child. Throughout each day the teacher provides games, toys, learning centers (such as a science table, language arts area, or housekeeping area) and discoveries that encourage the child physically, socially, emotionally, and intellectually.

Classroom Environment

Teachers have the responsibility to arrange the classroom environment to fit the needs of their children. The arrangement of large pieces of furniture and equipment is primary to children's development. Traffic patterns, noise levels, types of activities, and supervision all should be considered.

Teachers, along with directors and aides, should help choose and purchase age-appropriate materials and supplies. The repair and maintenance of classroom equipment is a teacher's responsibility. Either by handling repairs alone or reporting them to the director, the teacher should keep all equipment ready for the children.

Schedules of daily activities should also be arranged to best suit the needs of the children. Other classroom schedules are considered during planning to guarantee a free flow of play areas.

Discipline

Teachers help set the discipline policies in the classrooms. Considering the school philosophies, teachers determine the best ways to encourage positive self-esteem and proper behavior in the children. By being alert to possible problems, teachers can redirect the children to positive goals. Maintaining a setting that allows children to experiment and explore, to interact with others, and to express their feelings is the goal of discipline in the classroom.

Communication

Direct, positive communication between teacher, director, and aide provides a pleasant

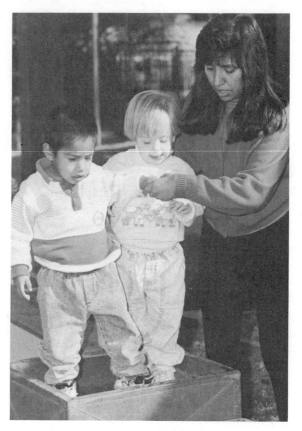

Figure 1-6: Teacher and children are interacting.

environment at the center. At the weekly staff meetings a formal time should be set aside to discuss lesson plans, field trips, speakers, school policy, community activities, and attitudes and behaviors of the children. Caregivers should feel able to discuss any positive or negative concerns about their classes.

Ongoing communication with parents is an important task of the child care worker. Parents must be reassured of the safety and care provided to their children at the center, whether it is full-day care or a three-hour morn-

A Teacher's Lesson Plan

Theme: The Beach

7:45 A.M.   Arrive, check in with the director.

7:50 A.M.   Discuss the day's lesson plans with the teacher's aide. Prepare curriculum materials and arrange learning centers.

8:45 A.M.   Greet children and parents— free choice of outside activities, water table activities.

9:00 A.M.   Salute the flag, sing patriotic song, and morning greeting.

9:15 A.M.   Circle time to discuss theme, learning centers, calendar, and weather.

9:30 A.M.   Introduce learning centers— beach puzzles, float and sink table, playhouse area. Craft— paper plate fish.

10:15 A.M.   Cleanup, toileting, and hand washing.

10:30 A.M.   Serve snack—Strawberry-banana shake, fish crackers.

10:45 A.M.   Outside time—Sand and water play, float styrofoam sailboats from yesterday in water table.

11:15 A.M.   Inside circle time—sharing time. Book: "Seashore Noisy Book (Brown)," Music: Row, Row, Row Your Boat.

11:45 A.M.   Pick-up time and dismissal; discuss the events and accomplishments of the day with parents.

12:00 A.M.   Cleanup, put away activities inside and out, prepare for tomorrow.

Figure 1-7: Teacher lesson plan chart.

ing preschool. Developing a close, friendly relationship with parents from the start helps to relax them about leaving their children with a caregiver. Greeting parents and children each morning and sharing the day's experiences at the end of day help to build a solid relationship between family and school.

When planning a lesson, keep in mind simplicity, sensory materials, and *fun* for the children and the teacher. Remember play is work for children, and it is the best way for

them to learn. Notice how the teacher in Figure 1-7 ties in learning objectives with each activity, yet keeps in mind the central theme.

AIDE

The aide, or assistant, works with the teacher to help run a classroom smoothly and effectively. An important member of the child care staff, the aide is responsible for meeting

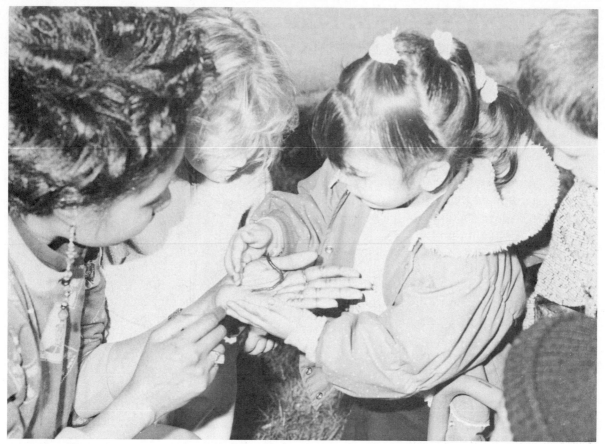

Figure 1-8: Examining an earthworm on a nature walk is exciting to children.

the goals and objectives defined by the director and teacher. The daily duties are many, and may include preparing activity and learning centers; communicating with staff, parents, and children; and providing a healthy and safe environment that is also clean and attractive. Assisting the head teacher with record keeping, *observing* (watching) the children, and relating information about their health, development, and behavior are parts of the daily communication.

Classroom

The teacher's aide usually arrives early in the day to talk with the teacher about the lesson plan, snacks, and activities. Setting up and straightening the room and yard are daily responsibilities of the aide. Other duties, such as mixing paint, gathering materials for arts and craft projects, preparing snacks, and putting up bulletin boards, contribute to the learning opportunities at the child care center.

Knowledge of the routines and an ability to work quickly are important attributes for the aide. Working as a team with the head teacher and other staff members, the aide is responsible for helping to supervise the children in the classroom and in the play yard. The aide must be a reliable, mature person with good judgment to handle both routine and crisis situations.

Routine activities that the aide performs include greeting and talking with parents and children, which helps everyone feel at ease at the center. Others include assisting with nutrition time (preparation, service, and cleanup) and helping the children to learn good social skills and table manners. The aide helps with nap time by setting out and putting away cots, supervising and soothing restless children, and providing a quiet, dimly lit atmosphere for more comfortable nap periods.

The aide also helps the children clean up. Hand washing, toileting, and picking up the play areas inside and out are important ways to teach children *self-help skills* (tasks that they can do by themselves for themselves). Talking quietly, distinctly, and slowly, and listening attentively, the aide uses this opportunity to communicate with the children.

In infant and toddler programs, the aide frequently:

- arranges bulletin boards
- assists with setup and cleanup
- changes diapers, bed linens
- charts behavior
- feeds children
- hands out supplies

Figure 1-9: The aide and child work together.

- helps with activities inside and outside
- launders sheets and other center linens
- mounts pictures
- rocks, cuddles, and talks to children
- sanitizes cribs and cots
- supervises children
- teaches social skills and manners

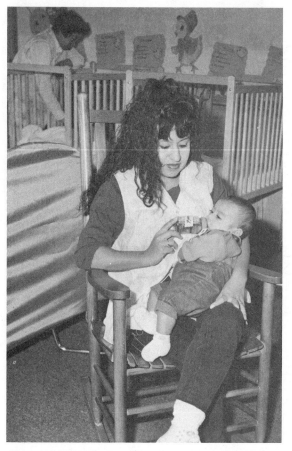

Figure 1-10: *Nurturing an infant is an important task of the aide.*

Figure 1-11: *These children enjoy the computers set up by the Instructional Aide.*

- washes bottles
- washes toys

In preschool programs, the aide frequently:
- arranges bulletin boards
- arranges learning centers
- assists with setup and cleanup
- hands out supplies

- helps with activities inside and outside
- launders
- mounts pictures
- operates audiovisual equipment
- prepares, serves, and cleans up food
- sanitizes cots

Figure 1-12: The aide enjoys supervising water play on a warm day.

- supervises children
- teaches social skills and manners
- types and files

In school-age programs, the aide frequently:

- arranges bulletin boards
- assists with setup and cleanup
- duplicates materials

- hands out supplies
- helps with activities inside and outside
- helps with homework
- keeps records
- makes inventories
- mounts pictures
- operates audiovisual equipment
- organizes learning centers

- supervises children
- teaches social skills and manners
- types and files

Role Model

Aides also act as role models, and children look to them for leadership and guidance. Personal attitude, professionalism, and grooming of an aide reflect upon the children, staff, and community. By displaying cooperation and support in the classroom, the aide shows appropriate behavior. Dependability and good attendance are important aspects of employment, for the aide is a vital part of the teaching team.

Although the aide's job is usually an entry-level position and may not require college education, the person applying for the position should have many of the personal qualities of the teacher. An aide must show genuine concern for the welfare of each child, as well as enthusiasm for the group. An aide should listen to the children and interact with the group, then provide the teacher with ideas and materials to enhance the children's growth and development. Attendance at staff meetings and updating on new rules or regulations issued by the center are usually required. College classes or vocational training programs are excellent ways to get the most current information on the care and guidance of young children. Often these courses lead to advancement to a position of greater responsibility.

The aide shares responsibility with the other staff members by using initiative and encouraging children in their activities throughout the day. Aides enjoy watching children grow and discover their world.

ATTITUDES AND BEHAVIOR

There are many separate duties for the director, teacher, and aide, but it is important that they all work together smoothly and efficiently. Teamwork ensures a welcoming environment conducive to the learning and development of the child.

The director's, teacher's, and aide's attitudes and behavior concerning their careers are reflected in the classroom and with the children they teach. These motivated people are eager and excited to be working with young children, and they look forward to each day's experiences. Working with young children can be a rewarding career.

Caregivers provide an atmosphere in which children can explore freely to discover their world and thereby discover themselves in the process. Caregivers must remember what childhood is like in order to plan activities that help the children grow and develop. They must enjoy children and their enthusiasm in discovery, while remaining mature adults.

Patience

Caregivers need tremendous energy to maintain patience when working with a large group of children. Sometimes a classroom with perfectly attentive children is often not the best environment to stimulate learning. An innovative caregiver channels the energy displayed by the children into a positive learning experience. To help maintain patience, caregivers should learn why children act unruly or upset, and keep in mind the goals and objectives for their lessons.

An Aide's Typical Schedule

11:00 A.M.	Discuss the day's activities with the teacher; set up the room, and gather materials.
11:30 A.M.	Kindergarten children arrive; greet and listen to them about their morning.
11:45 A.M.	Prepare the lunch area, help with hand washing.
12:00 A.M.	Eat lunch with the children, model social skills and manners.
12:20 P.M.	Supervise cleanup and toileting.
12:30 P.M.	Supervise sharing and story time; set out the rest mats.
1:00 P.M.	Supervise rest time, comfort restless children, prepare bulletin boards and learning materials as time permits.
2:30 P.M.	Supervise wakeup time, toileting; put away the mats.

	Children grades one through six arrive; greet and listen to them about their day.
2:45 P.M.	Supervise outside play; organize group games and activities.
3:15 P.M.	Prepare the snack.
3:30 P.M.	Supervise hand washing; serve the snack.
3:50 P.M.	Supervise the play yard.
4:00 P.M.	Take a coffee break.
4:15 P.M.	Supervise the outside cleanup.
4:30 P.M.	Bring the children inside; supervise and help with homework.
5:00 P.M.	Set up and help with table games and the craft area.
6:00 P.M.	Supervise cleanup time, prepare for arrival of parents.
6:30 P.M.	Sign out.

Figure 1-13: An aide's typical day at an afterschool care program.

Understanding growth and development, and getting background information on the children by visiting their homes and talking with their parents, allow caregivers to be more understanding about problem behaviors that may arise during the day. The more information and understanding caregivers acquire, the more patience they can show.

Consistency

Keeping a regular routine helps to establish a sense of trust. Children know what is coming next and what is expected of them. The rules of the center should be the same for all (including caregivers) and be the same from one day to the next.

Trust

Parents and children need to know that the caregivers are reliable and dependable. Caregivers must maintain fairness and control in all situations. They must not allow prejudices to interfere with the welfare of the children. They should have the general welfare of all firmly in mind at all times.

Respect

Caregivers should treat each person they contact with politeness and concern for individual differences. Again, they should keep in mind the welfare of all.

Interest

Caregivers must show interest in the daily activities of the children in their class. They must be open to suggestions concerning their classes and be ready to implement those ideas which will benefit their students. Their enthusiasm helps parents feel a part of their child's education.

Courage

It takes courage for caregivers to defend their principles and practices. It is important for caregivers to have firmly in mind the motives for their actions. Sometimes they need to review their motives to see if they have value. Change takes courage.

Confidentiality

It is important to keep confidences private. Discussions with parents or children about others involved in the program (staff members or families) should be restricted to ordinary occurrences.

Motivation

Motivated caregivers are enthusiastic about their students, classrooms, goals, and objectives. They enjoy using their *initiative* (self-starting ability) and discovering new or different teaching methods by interacting with other child care workers.

Growing caregivers are growing people. They study and want to keep current with the latest information on young children. They often attend classes, workshops, conferences, and conventions to learn new techniques, get curriculum ideas, and understand current issues. Interested caregivers take time to visit other school programs and are active in professional groups concerned with the welfare of young children. They also represent their schools at various functions.

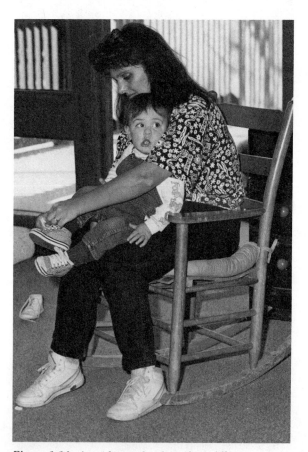

Figure 1-14: An aide ties the shoe of a toddler.

Health

Good health is essential when working with children. Irregular attendance due to poor health is not only hard on the remaining staff, but it disrupts the children's routine. Consistent illness and poor health can also cause poor performance by the caregiver, and eventually it affects the children's development.

Role Model

Children are *imitative* (that is, they copy the actions of others) and learn from what they see and hear. Therefore, a caregiver's professional appearance is most important. Caregivers should be well-groomed, confident, mannerly, and well-disciplined. They must respect themselves and others, and expect the same treatment in return. Loyalty, dependability, honesty, and high ethical standards are several character traits needed to excel in a child care career.

Caregivers serve as role models to their students, parents, and coworkers. A role model is a person whom someone can copy or emulate. Professionalism, knowledge, moral character, peer interaction, discipline, and parenting skills are traits that others may learn by observation and communication with caregivers.

In addition to knowledge and skills, caregivers need to have personal qualities that help to achieve a successful rapport among themselves, the children, and their parents. The successful caregiver must have patience, consistency, trust, respect, interest, courage, confidentiality, motivation, enthusiasm, empathy, strength of character, and a nurturing disposition.

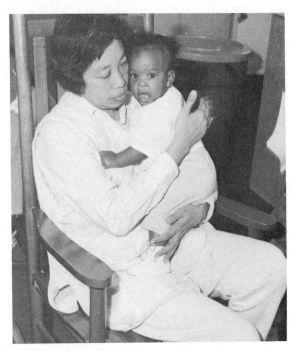

Figure 1-15: Each child deserves individual attention.

Enthusiasm

Caregivers should be excited about coming to work and watching their students' progress. Their excitement shows an enthusiasm for school and learning.

Empathy

Caregivers must show an understanding of others and their problems. They should be ready to listen and to help with suggestions on parenting skills, or be able to refer the person to other professional help in the community.

Strength of Character

Caregivers must put aside their personal emotions and problems, keeping the welfare of the children first in mind. They must be secure in their knowledge of child development and the needs of the individual child. They should exhibit a willingness to work with others in a cooperative manner.

Nurturing Disposition

The most important attribute displayed by good caregivers is a nurturing disposition—a feeling of warmth and caring toward students, parents, and other staff members. They can show concern for their students' welfare through affection, kindness, and care. Caregivers should help others to develop a positive self-concept.

OTHER CAREERS

The most common jobs available in this field are the director, teacher, and aide. However, many other careers are open to the student of child development. Depending on the student's level of education, interest area, and ambition, the following list offers possible occupations in this field.

1. Administrator of Children's Centers—supervises the staff and facilities of many programs; can be public or private institutions.

2. Child Care Specialist—an expert in the field of child development, usually employed by a school district or franchise school corporation; acts as a consultant and teacher to professionals in the field; available as a guest speaker to parents and community groups.

3. Child Development Consultant—helps communities, school districts, private schools, and industry to set up and start children's centers; available to help preexisting schools solve problem areas with children, staff, and facilities; available as a guest speaker on children's issues.

4. Child Development Teacher—teaches on the high school and college level; trains others in the field of child development; may also conduct parenting classes.

5. Children's Librarian—in charge of the children's section of community and school libraries; helps to select books; set up youth reading groups and contests; encourages children to enjoy reading.

6. Child Psychologist—deals with emotional problems of parents and children; does long-term studies to understand the development of children; often acts as a consultant.

7. Counselor—works at the elementary, junior high, middle school, high school, or college campus; helps students arrange classes; helps students solve problems.

8. Day Camp Facilitator—usually works with school-age children during vacation times; plans activities and projects; supervises children.

9. Elementary School Administrator—in charge of an individual school or department; oversees staff and facilities of public or private schools.

10. Elementary School Teacher—has the responsibility of the classroom organization, discipline, and curriculum.

11. Family Day Care Provider—self-employed individual who has charge of various-age children in the home; provides nutrition, activities, and discipline.

12. Instructional Aide—usually employed by a school district; assists the teacher; may also handle lunchtime and recess duties.

13. Marriage, Family, and Child Therapist—counsels and helps to solve problem areas dealing with severe family issues; generally long-term therapy.

14. Nanny—professional child care worker in a private home; cares for the needs of the children in the family.

15. Resource and Referral Agencies—helps members of the community to find adequate child care; assists family day care providers; operates job banks; keeps community and professionals updated on current legislation and child care issues.

16. Social Worker—generally employed by government departments dealing with welfare, Medicare, adoption, abuse cases, and placement in foster and youth homes; deals with family issues.

17. Special Needs Teacher—works with both gifted and children with impairments; provides individual instruction and care depending on the needs of the child.

18. Youth Counselor—usually works with school-age and teenage children in youth group homes; supervises, disciplines, and provides counseling.

IN THE HOME CARE

Whether it is a family day care home or a professional nanny, the caregiver has certain responsibilities to the children and their parents.

Along with those responsibilities mentioned in this chapter, the caregiver in the home must be responsible for:

- communication with the child, parents, family members, and community
- completing training courses and updating all child development education
- encouraging social development by allowing children to participate in neighborhood and community functions
- health and safety
- keeping parents current and involved with their child's daily curriculum plan
- maintaining current licensing of the family day care home

- organizing and supervising a variety of daily activities to keep children enthusiastic to the learning process

- providing nutritious meals and snacks

- providing opportunities for the physical, social, emotional, and intellectual growth of the child

- role modeling—consistency, trust, patience, motivation, and respect for all the children in the caregiver's home

- the general welfare of the child

SUMMARY

As you consider a position as a caregiver, it is important to understand the job descriptions of the various positions available to you. Staff members must be able to carry out their individual responsibilities and work together as a team to provide the children with a stable and nuturing environment.

The director is the administrator of the facility, and the director's main duty is to ensure the smooth operation of the center. Helping to establish the philosophy, setting short- and long-range goals, supervising, directing personnel, and maintaining all records to meet city, county, and state regulations are a few of the duties of the director. Others include repair and maintenance of facility equipment and grounds, reviewing curriculum materials, maintaining parent and child interaction, and providing community relations. The director may also be a classroom teacher.

The teacher's responsibilities focus on the classroom. With their knowlege of children's maturation and learning levels, teachers prepare daily lesson plans to ensure a creative environment, where children practice skills, explore, experiment, and develop a good self-concept. The classroom environment is created to allow maximum use of all materials.

The teacher is also responsible for the communication and discipline methods used in the classroom. After considering the philosophy of the school and the needs of the children and families enrolled, a policy that encourages self-esteem and proper behavior is established.

The aide works with the teacher to help meet the goals and objectives of the classroom. Helping to prepare the room for the daily activities, supervising small and large groups of children, maintaining discipline, and encouraging the growth of a good self-concept for each child are other responsibilities of the aide.

Staff members must work together to provide an atmosphere that meets the needs of the children and their families. The attitudes and behavior of staff members encourage social, emotional, physical, and intellectual growth. Good caregivers should be healthy, should communicate well, and should know how to be role models for children and parents. Caregivers should have patience, consistency, trust, respect, interest, courage, confidentiality, motivation, enthusiasm, empathy, strength of character, and a nurturing disposition.

Review Questions

1. What is a philosophy?
2. Define supervision.

3. List effective methods of communication with parents.

4. List the forms kept in the records for staff and children.

5. Define learning centers and why they are necessary to the classroom environment.

6. What is N.A.E.Y.C.?

7. What is the difference between structured and open classrooms?

8. What is the teacher's responsibility in setting up the classroom environment?

9. List 10 duties of the aide.

10. What is a role model?

Things to Do and Discuss

1. If you were a director in a day care center, what qualities would you look for when hiring a teacher or an aide?

2. What information would you include in a monthly newsletter for parents?

3. List five important duties of the director and the teacher.

4. What tasks does the aide perform?

5. If you had to choose a child care center for your child, what qualities would you look for in a teacher?

6. When looking for a job in the child care field, what center characteristics would best meet your needs for employment?

CHAPTER 2
Types of Child Care Programs

This is the inside view of an infant center.

KEY TERMS

absenteeism
characteristics
comprehensive care
custodial care
developmental care

enrichment
full-day care centers
half-day care centers
model curriculum
sliding fee scale

OBJECTIVES

After completing this chapter, you will be able to:

1. explain the differences between the three types of child care: custodial, comprehensive, and developmental;
2. list three characteristics for each style of child care center.

Figure 2-1: The outside view of a Child Care Center.

INTRODUCTION

One hundred other countries in the world have national policies regarding maternity leave, security of jobs upon return, and child care. However, the United States has no legal policy, and working mothers and single parents are having a hard time finding adequate child care facilities (American Broadcasting Company News Department documentary, "After the Sexual Revolution," 1986). There is now a great need for more secure, developmentally appropriate environments for children of all ages.

Fortunately, parents in the United States can choose the type of care facility to best fit the varying needs of children and families. Twenty five years ago, only 15 percent of women with children under the age of six were employed outside of the home (Carlson and Stenmalm-Sjoblom, 1989). By 1995, an estimated three-fourths of school-age children and two-thirds of preschool children will have mothers in the work force (Fuqua and Shieck, 1989). By 1990, twelve million children were attending child care facilities because both of their parents worked (American Broadcasting Company News Department documentary, "After the Sexual Revolution," 1986). Because these parents will be working a variety of jobs and hours, different types of child care programs are available. Each child care center is unique. Centers vary in size, shape, and type of program to suit the age level of the children for whom they care. Each school has its own philosophy and quality of staff.

When you become a child care worker, it is important to be familiar with different kinds of child care programs. While exploring the field, you may find that one type of program serves your style better than another. Many states require all programs to be licensed to ensure child care centers that provide healthy and safe environments.

Within the many programs serving children are various time frames. Parents can choose a facility with operating hours and type of care to best serve their needs.

TYPES OF CHILD CARE

There are three types of child care: custodial, developmental, and comprehensive.

Custodial Care

A center offers *custodial care* when it provides a safe environment for children and meets the minimal standards of licensing. Such programs can be established in a home or other facility. They usually offer free play, snacks, meals, naps, and some developmental tasks. The equipment and opportunities vary with the enthusiasm, knowledge, and resources of the proprietor.

Examples of custodial care facilities include special needs programs for people with impairments, residential care for people who live at a facility either part- or full-time, and baby-sitting.

Developmental Care

Developmental care is a planned program within a safe and organized environment. The program is formulated to stimulate the physical, social, emotional, and intellectual growth of the individual child, but custodial care is also provided. Parent involvement is often encouraged to unite the home and school. Developmental care programs include laboratory child care centers, Montessori schools, nursery schools, and cooperative schools. Programs may be private, public, or church sponsored.

Comprehensive Care

Comprehensive care is care that includes the *characteristics* (qualities that define a person or thing) of custodial care and developmental care plus health and social services for the child and family. The services may include physical examinations, immunizations, dental care, psychological counseling, nutrition, and parenting classes. Such programs often offer a *sliding fee scale* a rate schedule where families pay what they can afford, based on income and number of dependents. Comprehensive care

Figure 2-2: Snack is a favorite time of the morning.

programs are usually funded by the state or federal government, but they can be research or experimentally oriented. Examples include state preschool, Head Start, and some special needs programs.

TIME FRAMES

Now that we have discussed the three types of care available, be aware that there are differences between full-day care and half-day care centers. Keep in mind that, within these time frames, many different styles of programs are offered. These are described later in the chapter.

Full-Day Care Centers

Full-day care centers are facilities that are open more than four hours each day but fewer than twenty-four hours. The hours are convenient for the average working parent. The most general hours are 6:30 A.M. to 6:30 P.M. However, centers may choose any hours that suit the community needs. Family day care homes, industry-sponsored care, school district children's centers, and franchise schools generally provide full-day care. Centers may enroll children from three weeks of age through sixth grade, depending on the size and arrangement of their facility.

Full-day care centers generally include:

- custodial, developmental, or comprehensive care
- fees that vary with the area and income of parents
- meals and snacks
- nap and sleeping arrangements
- safe and healthy environment
- service for children who live with legal parents or guardians
- services that are provided on a regular schedule (open daily except for major holidays)
- social services
- staffs that meet individual state requirements

Half-Day Care Centers

Half-day care centers are facilities that operate for six hours or less per day. They gen- erally offer a developmental program, emphasizing individualized learning, and variety of activities. Common hours are 8:30 A.M. to 11:30 A.M. These are hours when children are alert and learn best.

Enrollment ages of children may range from eighteen months to sixth grade, depending on the size and arrangement of the facility. Most centers, however, concentrate on a specific age group.

Half-day care centers generally include:

- custodial, developmental, or comprehensive care
- fees charged for services
- healthy and safe environment
- parent involvement
- rest or quiet times
- service for children who live with legal parents or guardians
- services that are provided regularly relative to the public school calendar
- snacks
- social services
- staffs that meet local and state requirements

PROGRAMS

The following discussion is to help acquaint you with the variety of programs from which to choose, within the full- or half-day care center format. Each program is unique and developed to help meet the needs of individual families.

Franchise Care

Franchise care is provided by profit-making, privately owned schools. Parent companies generally provide the buildings, equipment, supplies, and familiar names. Contracts state that services are sold to an individual or group by corporations. In most cases, franchise schools serve large numbers of children of all ages for the full day. Franchise care can be custodial, comprehensive, or developmental, depending on the philosophy, criteria and standards of the parent company.

Employer-Sponsored Child Care

Employer-sponsored child care was established at the Kaiser plant in Seattle, Washington during World War II. Women were needed to work in the war plants while the men were fighting. The centers, however, lasted only during the war. Later they were closed so that the mothers would quit their jobs and stay home, thus providing jobs for the returning servicemen.

Today, employers are again establishing child care centers for the children of their employees. In 1986, only 150 companies in the United States offered child care on the site (American Broadcasting Company News Department documentary. "After the Sexual Revolution," 1986). In 1989 the number jumped to 4,100 (Galinsky, 1989). As more mothers join the work force, day care becomes a higher priority. When on-site child care is offered around the clock, it can eliminate transportation problems, because children can travel to work with the parent. On-site care provides parents with peace of mind about the care of their children and allows them to visit their children during breaks. This incentive has been proven to enhance an employee's loyalty to the company, improve working habits, and lessen *absenteeism* (not being present on the job). Sick-child care is also generally provided.

Full or partial financial support is usually established by the company as an employee benefit. Quality care is the rule, because there are enough funds to hire an excellent, professional staff and to equip the facility with the finest supplies. Developmental or comprehensive care is usually provided.

Laboratory Child Care

Laboratory child care centers are usually at a high school, college, or vocational education site. The care is usually partially funded by the sponsoring school or research group and generally has a sliding fee scale. Enrollment is open to children of students or staff members first, with children from the community added as space allows. Parental participation in the classroom is often required.

Schools may provide developmental or comprehensive care with a *model curriculum* (a program where latest theories and techniques are explored). Model curriculums offer opportunities for student teachers to observe and work under the supervision of experienced teachers.

Montessori School

Maria Montessori, for whom the schools are named, was born in 1870 in Italy. She was the first woman in Italy to complete medical training.

Figure 2-3: Inside view of a Laboratory Child Care Center.

Figure 2-4: A youngster is working with counting beads.

Maria Montessori became interested in the intellectual development of mentally deficient children. Through her laboratory school "Casa Dei Bambini" (Children's House), she found that children of normal intelligence also benefited from her teaching methods. She theorized that a child's intelligence is greatly influenced by environment. She believed that children learn best through the use of their senses in relation to the world. Maria Montessori valued self-motivation and the ability to seek out learning tasks in the environment.

An orderly, quiet, and aesthetic environment including child-sized equipment is important in a Montessori program. The program also features a structured learning atmosphere and a step-by-step process of application. An example of the process is the learning of pouring. Children are first given a tray that has a cup and pitcher filled with rice. They are allowed to practice the skill of pouring until they are successful. Then they must replace the cup and pitcher precisely back on the tray and return them to the appropriate place on the shelf.

They are then given a tray with a cup and pitcher filled with water. They are allowed again to practice pouring until they are successful. Again, they must replace all materials to the correct shelf. Children learn by firsthand experience, observing and learning practical skills including dressing, preparing food, and cleaning.

Maria Montessori also designed attrac-

Figure 2-5: Montessori equipment.

Figure 2-6: The family day care home provides many opportunities for children of various ages.

tive and easy-to-use manipulative equipment that is a staple in all Montessori centers. The equipment was developed to enable children to use their senses either in totality or separately. For example, if a child is learning shapes, the equipment is of uniform size and color, so that the child can concentrate on the shape.

Montessori programs in this country can be either half-day or full-day. The schools are profit-making. Teachers are required to have two years of specialized training in Montessori Training Centers. Children may be enrolled from infancy through high school.

Church-Related Child Care

Church-related child care generally occurs in a private, nonprofit, church-sponsored facility. Religious training is often provided. Enrollment is open to children of church members first, with additional enrollment from the community as space allows. Church members often serve on the school board. They provide input on the philosophy, goals, and objectives.

Classrooms are often used as Sunday school rooms and for other church-related activities. Such use takes the cooperation of both the school and church staffs.

Nursery and Preschool Care

Nursery and preschool care are developmental programs usually in operation for four or fewer hours per day. Children ages two to prekindergarten can attend sessions two, three, or five days per week. Classes are generally small, and there is usually a good adult-to-student ratio. The professional staff is educated in child development and is aware of individualized learning. Parent involvement is encouraged. Nursery and preschool care may be either profit or nonprofit, depending on the style of school.

Cooperative Care

In cooperative care, parents own a share of the school and hire a professional staff to administer and teach. Parents serve on the school board and committees. They are also responsible for a majority of the maintenance.

Cooperative care centers are nonprofit. Parents' fees and fundraising events are the only sources of funds. Parents are required to serve as aides to the teacher on a regular schedule. This helps to keep expenses low and allows parents to be actively involved in their children's education.

Cooperative care lets parents have direct input to the philosophy, goals, and objectives of the school. Parent education, including parenting skills, first aid, and CPR, are important aspects of this style of school.

Head Start

Head Start is federally funded, and it has a sliding fee scale for tuition. The program was established in 1965 for low-income families. Comprehensive care is provided along with experimental programs emphasizing *enrichment*

(exposing children to new ideas and knowledge) and developmental skills. Individualized curriculum meets the needs of the surrounding community and follows federal guidelines. Head Start was intended to compensate for inadequate early-life experiences and to better prepare children for school.

Children's ages range from nine months to five years. The program may be a half- or full-day care. Classes are small, and parents work closely with a professional staff. Parent education is a strong component of this program. Well-balanced meals (breakfast, snack, and lunch) are provided under the Food for Minors Act. Surplus food is also offered to the families.

State Preschool

Funded by federal, state, and local monies, these programs are similar to Head Start. They have the same requirements for family income levels. Programs provide either half-day or full-day care. Ages served include infants through kindergarten.

Infant and Toddler Care

Infant and toddler care is defined differently in various states. Care may be custodial, developmental, or comprehensive. Children from the age of three weeks until they are toilet trained may be enrolled. Special attention is given to charting, feeding, changing diapers, toilet training, and naps. The adult-to-child ration is small, generally one adult to four children, so this care is expensive. Programs may be either profit or nonprofit.

Figure 2-7: *The Infant/Toddler Center is clean and contains appropriate equipment.*

Parks and Recreation Programs

Parks and recreation departments of city government operate Mommy and Me classes (mother and child attend together) for children from one year old to prekindergarten age. Little Tots programs serve preschool children (without mothers attending). Afterschool day care is provided for school-age children. The programs offer recreational activities, ranging from sports to crafts.

Generally meeting minimum adult-to-student ratio requirements, the programs can be of any time duration. A play group environment emphasizing socialization is common.

Adult Education Programs

Adult education is sponsored by local school districts or community colleges. Programs offer parent and child participation and parenting education. High school or college credit may be obtained for enrollment. A small fee is charged for tuition.

As in the Mommy and Me program, parent and child attend class together. Classes are small, with a high adult-to-student ratio. Developmental care is offered under the supervision of a professional staff.

Extended Day Care

Extended day care, before and after-school care, and latchkey program are titles used for supervision of school-age children either before or after the regular elementary school day. Programs may be either district operated or privately owned. They are usually established to aid working parents, so transportation is often provided to and from school.

A professional staff supervises homework and plans a variety of activities. Extracurricular endeavors may include scouting, sports, dance, and music. Generally an unstructured, homelike atmosphere offers an environment different from the structured classroom setting. An afterschool snack is provided.

Child care professionals are identifying many problems associated with children left home alone while parents work. In 1984–85, one million school-age children claimed that they took care of themselves after school (Education Week, 1987). One city, San Francisco, California, has passed a city ordinance concerning all new construction of high-rise buildings. New high-rises must provide a day care facility within their boundaries or contribute to the city-operated child care programs. More cities are following this format.

Special Needs Programs

Special needs programs are located in hospitals, schools, and homes. They may be for

Figure 2-8: School-age children in an extended day care program.

either gifted or handicapped children. Under the supervision of a state-qualified staff, children receive specialized care. A small adult-to-child ratio is important. Parent education is intrinsic to these programs. Many of the facilities offer a sliding fee scale.

IN THE HOME CARE

Family Day Care

Family day care is child care located in a private home for a profit. Most states require family day care centers to be licensed. Family day care providers usually serve a small group of children of various ages, abilities, or special needs. The operating hours are flexible, depending on the requirements of the families. The operator is generally a homemaker and the main—or only—caregiver; therefore, there may be less money and space for equipment and supplies. Whether care is custodial or developmental, each child is given personal attention in a homelike environment.

Residential Care

Residential care is a licensed program provided for more than twenty-four continuous hours. Staff may work on shifts to maintain around-the-clock care. Sleeping arrangements and meals are included. Generally, custodial care is provided. A flexible fee scale is usually arranged. Residential care may be given to a special needs child or an average child in a foster home.

Nanny Program

The Nanny Program is an up-and-coming style of custodial care for all of the children in a home. It is modeled after the British nanny concept. Contracts between the nanny and the family to be served include the hours, pay structure, and whether room and board are included. Benefits such as travel and dental and health insurance may also be offered. An advantage for the family is that small-group care is offered by a trained individual within a familiar environment (the home).

Case Study #1:
Leo

Leo awakens early to get ready to attend his extended care center. He arrives at 7:00 A.M. so his mother can get to work on time. Leo is served breakfast. He enjoys inside free play time. At 8:00 A.M., he is escorted to his third-grade classroom.

When school is finished at 2:30 P.M., he rejoins his day care center friends. There, he enjoys playing in the big play yard, and enters a game of kickball. He looks forward to the 3:15 snack of milk and cookies.

At 3:30, Leo plays on the climbing equipment. He is king of the pirates and captures many prisoners. Miss Wilson blows the whistle at 4:00 to signal cleanup time. After putting away the equipment, Leo must go inside.

After cleanup, he knows Mr. Orozo will help him with his homework, learning his fives multiplication table. After finishing his homework at 4:45, Leo still has time to play computer games before his mother arrives at 5:30. Dinner, a bath, and bedtime await Leo at home. He can hardly wait to tell his mother about being a king.

Case Study #2:
Michelle

When Michelle turned three years old, her mother, Mrs. Todd, felt that Michelle should attend a child care program for a few hours several days a week because Michelle had never spent time with any caregivers but her family. She needed to learn how to relate to other adults and to children in a group setting. Mrs. Todd looked at many schools and chose one that exhibited a warm, friendly environment and had a developmental program to reinforce Michelle's social skills and intellectual needs.

Michelle arrived the first morning, hanging firmly onto her mother's hand. The teacher, Miss Betty, invited them into the room and settled them at the housekeeping center. After fifteen minutes, Michelle left her mother's side to join another girl at the puzzle table. There they talked and played, laughing occasionally at their stories.

Miss Betty suggested to Mrs. Todd that she have a cup of coffee in the office and come back in ten minutes. After telling Michelle where she was going, her mother left. Michelle began crying, so Miss Betty reassured her that her mother would be back in a few minutes. She held Michelle on her lap and suggested that they read a book together. Michelle quieted down as she became interested in the story about the Berenstain Bears. When Mrs. Todd returned, she found her daughter contentedly playing with her new friend Cindy from the puzzle table.

Mother then told Michelle that she needed to go home and do the dishes and would be back in an hour to pick her up. Apprehensively, Michelle watched her mother leave. Miss Betty, however, quickly began playing musical games with the children, and Michelle decided to join in. Later, Michelle especially enjoyed preparing her own snack of cheese and crackers and drinking grape juice, her favorite.

Outside time soon followed. The new equipment was an adventure. The water table had boats and sprinkling cans. The water felt cool on such a hot day. Michelle was having so much fun that it seemed only a few minutes before it was time to go back inside.

Miss Betty had prepared an especially enjoyable flannel story, "The Big, Big Turnip," and Michelle soon joined the other children in performing the actions. When Mrs. Todd appeared to take Michelle home, Michelle wanted to stay longer. Mother promised that she could come back another day. After giving Miss Betty a big hug, Michelle went home for lunch and a nap.

Figure 2-9: *The nanny profession is expanding in America because it offers many different opportunities. Photo courtesy of the American Nanny Plan, Inc.*

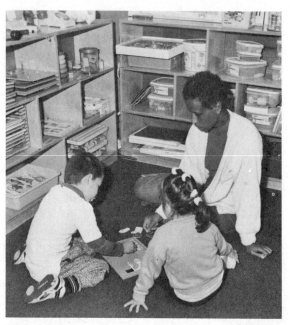

Figure 2-10: *These two preschoolers enjoy working on a puzzle together.*

SUMMARY

As you can see, there are a variety of child care programs from which to choose employment. You should carefully investigate each one to find the child care center that meets your needs as a caregiver.

Three types of child care are offered: custodial, developmental, and comprehensive. Care may be full-day or half-day. A variety of programs fit within the day care format: franchise care, employer-sponsored care, laboratory child care, Montessori school, church-related child care, family day care, nursery and preschool care, cooperative care, Head Start, state preschool, parks and recreation programs, adult education programs, extended day care, special needs programs, residential care, and the Nanny Program. Each center offers unique opportunities. By observing and learning, you can decide which program fits your requirements as a caregiver.

Review Questions

1. Define custodial, developmental, and comprehensive care.

2. What are the general hours for a full-day care program?

3. What ages of children are served in a half-day care program?

4. What are the advantages of enrolling a child in an employer-sponsored center?

5. From where does the laboratory school receive the majority of its funding?

6. Where did Maria Montessori establish her school?

7. Why would parents choose to place their child in a family day care center?

8. What year were Head Start Programs established?

9. What are the other names for extended day care?

10. Where would you find a Nanny employed?

Things to Do and Discuss

1. Observe and then discuss the advantages and disadvantages of the three types of child care available.

2. Explain the difference between full-day and half-day care programs.

3. Observe three different program styles and then discuss why you would choose one style of care over another. List your reasons.

4. Visit a family day care center and list the advantages and disadvantages of placing a child in this facility.

5. Research Maria Montessori's life and theories. Write a research paper explaining her methods.

6. Discuss how changes in society affect the child care profession.

7. Investigate the policies of other countries regarding child care.

CHAPTER 3

Good Environments for Children

Blocks and cars are favorite toys for preschoolers.

KEY TERMS

appropriate
conducive
positive reinforcement

resilient
spatial awareness
versatile

OBJECTIVES

After completing this chapter, you will be able to:
1. state the components of a good indoor environment;
2. state the components necessary for a good yard environment.

INTRODUCTION

Child care programs come in many types for many ages. They provide a variety of services. Now we concentrate on the ingredients to make a successful classroom and play yard. What must we do to enhance the growth, development, and motivation of young children? There are many factors to consider when setting up and operating indoor and outdoor learning environments. This chapter includes *most* of these factors. However, remember that the most important factors in any classroom are the teacher, the aide, and the children. Without these, a program cannot be successful.

ROOM ENVIRONMENT

When Michelle's mother, Mrs. Todd, decided to find a preschool program to help develop Michelle's social skills, she observed several facilities in her community. She was most interested in three facilities. At each, she observed the staff, size, and location. She particularly noticed the activities and equipment available to the children. She was curious about what the different learning centers offered. She looked at the amount of space provided to enhance physical development, the durability of equipment, and the safety precautions taken.

After several visits and hours of evaluating programs Mrs. Todd decided on the school that provided a well-rounded curriculum, allowed a choice of activities, and was most aesthetically pleasing. The children were involved in various learning centers, and the teacher, Miss Betty, was warm and encouraging. The classroom that Michelle was to be in was inviting, pleasant, and obviously stimulating to a child's individual development.

When working in the classroom you, the child care worker, will be responsible for setting up an environment *conducive* (contributing) to learning. As Mrs. Todd observed, there are many important factors to consider when enhancing the child's developmental needs.

Room Arrangement

The ideal classroom is large, bright, airy, attractive, clean, and inviting. It has room for learning centers, storage, and movement. Unfortunately, not all facilities are like this, but

Figure 3-1: Teachers and children working at an art learning center.

you can still make good use of the space that is allotted.

Classroom furniture and materials are usually purchased and arranged by the classroom teacher and the school director. The age and developmental level of the children should be considered as well as the number of children in the class. Manipulative materials (for fine motor activities), books, science projects, art materials, records, and toys should be *appropriate* (suitable).

Planning a classroom helps to prevent accidents and disturbances. Arranging and rearranging furniture, learning centers, and toys help caregivers envision the traffic patterns and atmosphere for the daily routines. Another way to plan is to use paper and cutouts of furniture and large equipment.

Proper lighting and ventilation are necessary for alertness. A room that is too stuffy can cause children to be lazy and uncaring. Conversely, a room that is too cool can interfere with motivation.

There should be planning for both quiet and noisy areas. Quiet areas should let children have time to themselves. The areas include a reading and book corner, a manipulative corner, an arts and crafts area, and a concept corner for math and science projects. When such areas are attractively designed, they entice the children to participate and discover without a great deal of teacher input. The caregiver, however, is available to answer questions or suggest experiments.

Fine art, whether painting by the masters, classical music, or pieces of sculpture, helps to make children aware of culture. Providing such materials in an aesthetically pleasing area lets children see them as important.

Noisy areas should be large. These are areas for blocks, cars, housekeeping, music, and movement. Place them away from the quiet areas because they often attract large groups of children.

Periodically rearrange the furniture and equipment to introduce new and interesting learning centers. Changes also keep the room from becoming boring.

The following areas and equipment are typical for an infant and toddler room:

Quiet Area (Separate Room, with Viewing Windows)

- changing table
- cribs

- mobiles
- rocking chairs
- sink with running water

Noisy Area

- high chairs
- rocking chairs
- small, padded climbers
- small tables and chairs
- toys and mirrors

Extra Equipment

- adult kitchen
- bulletin boards
- child-size sink
- easel
- individual cubbies
- low shelves for toys
- pictures
- potty chairs

The following areas and equipment are typical for a preschool room:

Quiet Area

- aquarium
- art materials
- books and display

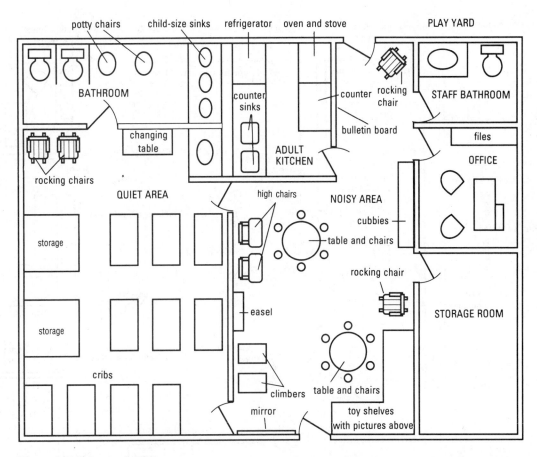

Figure 3-2: Infant and toddler room.

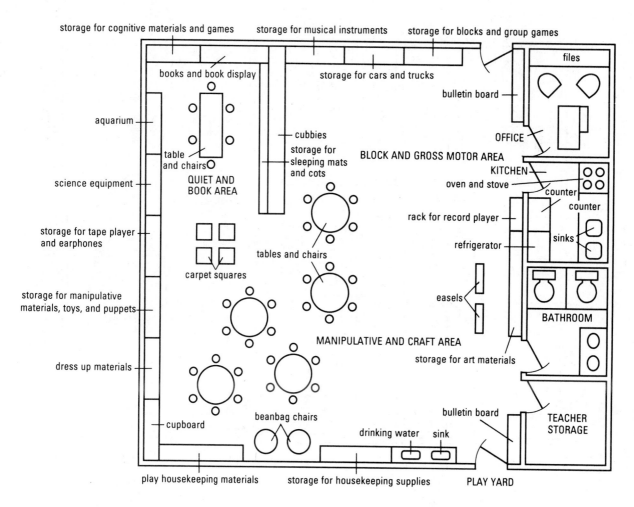

Figure 3-3: Preschool room.

- book table and chairs
- bulletin boards
- carpet squares
- cognitive materials
- easel
- manipulative materials
- puppets
- puzzles
- science equipment
- tabletop games
- tape player and earphones
- toys

Noisy Area

- blocks, large and small
- cars and trucks
- group games
- housekeeping supplies
- musical instruments
- record player
- tables and chairs

Extra Equipment

- beanbag chairs
- cupboards
- individual cubbies
- portable gross motor equipment
- sleeping mats or cots

- teacher storage
- toy shelves

The following areas and equipment are typical for a school-age room:

Quiet Area

- books, magazines, and table
- cognitive materials
- computers
- homework area
- manipulative games
- rug
- tape recorders

Noisy Area

- craft center
- group games
- kitchen
- movie projector and screen
- record player
- television and videocassette player

Extra Equipment

- individual cubbies
- sleeping mats (if appropriate)
- storage shelves
- tables and chairs
- toy shelves

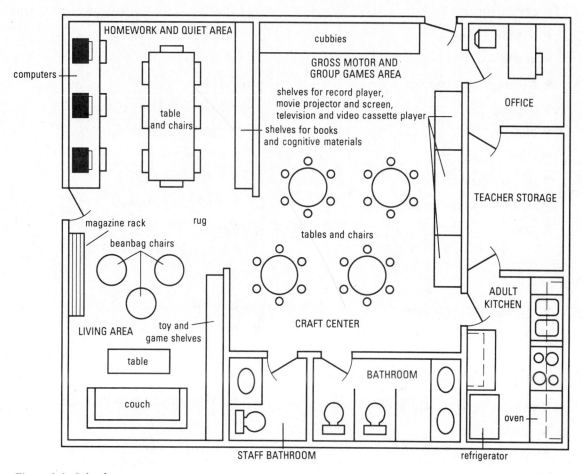

Figure 3-4: School-age room.

Learning Centers

Learning centers are particular areas in the classroom or play yard that encourage specific instruction or behavior. They are arranged in order to motivate and stimulate an interest on the part of the student. As the student demonstrates an interest, they will look for answers to questions aroused by their curiosity and increase their intellectual development. They can be set up for any age student with variations of supplies. Materials need to be age-appropriate. Listed below are some of the materials necessary to set up learning centers. Remember that any learning center that can be set up in the classroom can also be set up in the play yard.

Arts and Crafts Center

- area for drying projects
- clay and play dough, rolling pins, and cookie cutters
- collage materials
- easel
- glue and paste
- hand washing and cleanup area
- paint, crayons, chalk, pencils, markers, brushes, sponges
- paint shirts
- scissors, staplers, paper hole punches
- table and chairs
- variety of paper
- waste paper basket

Dramatic Play Center

- doll furniture
- family and animal figures
- floor mat of city streets
- large airport
- large gas station
- large playhouse
- small cars, trucks, airplanes, and trains

Gross Motor Center

- creative movement materials
- dancing materials
- large cars, trucks, airplanes, and trains
- large wooden and cardboard blocks
- record and cassette player
- records and tapes

Housekeeping Area

- boxes for special occasions
  birthday party
  fire personnel
  medical personnel
  office worker
  police officer
  school
  storekeeper
  wedding
- broom, sweeper, dustpan, mop
- cradle, pillow, blankets

- dishes, silverware, placemats, pots, and pans
- doll stroller
- dolls and doll clothes
- dress up clothes, plastic hats, shoes, accessories (jewelry, ties, scarves)
- kitchen set (stove, refrigerator, sink)
- several telephones
- table and chairs

Library or Language Center

- cassette and record player, with earphones
- easy chair, soft pillows, mattress, or bean bag chairs
- flannel story and finger play materials
- good lighting and ventilation
- mirror
- puppets
- table and chairs
- variety of books including fiction, nonfiction, and reference books
- writing materials

Manipulative Center (Fine Motor Activities)

- board games
- dress-up dolls
- lacing activities
- puzzles

- stringing beads
- table and chairs
- tabletop blocks

Math Center

- balance scale
- board games
- clock
- color blocks or cards
- counting scale
- deck of cards
- dominoes of different types
- fraction puzzles
- geometric shapes
- matching, sorting, classification, seriation, spatial, and temporal games
- objects to count
- rulers, pencils, and erasers
- small blackboard, chalk, and eraser
- table and chairs
- thermometer
- water play and objects that encourage measuring

Music Center

- colorful scarves and dancing outfits
- musical instruments
- record and cassette players with earphones
- variety of records and cassettes

Science Center

- aquarium, pets
- balance scale
- boxes of special interest
  - animals
  - birds and nests
  - desert
  - electricity
  - forest
  - insects
  - life cycle
  - magnets
  - seashore
  - universe
  - water cycle
- magnets, all sizes and types
- magnifying glass
- microscope
- pictures
- reference books
- table and chairs

Water and Sand Center

- buckets, shovels, different size containers, large trucks
- measuring cups and spoons, dishes
- sifters, funnels, sand molds
- squirt bottles, different size containers, basters
- water table

Woodworking Center

- authentic, small tools
  - clamps
  - hammers
  - nails
  - saws
  - screwdrivers
  - screws
- glue and paint
- sturdy table (waist-high)
- wood and styrofoam pieces, sawdust, shavings

Equipment

Equipment (housekeeping furniture, shelves, tables and chairs, manipulative toys, blocks) in the quiet and noisy areas should be appropriate to the age of the group. Equipment should be *versatile* (usable in more than

Figure 3-5: While supervising, the caregiver and children enjoy playing with the blocks.

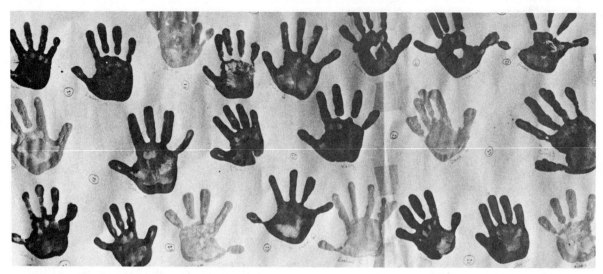

Figure 3-6: Children used their hands to create this mural of object art.

one way). An adequate amount of equipment is essential to the classroom. Caregivers must provide colorful, clean, and attractively displayed equipment and materials that are consistently maintained. This encourages participation and stimulates learning on the part of the children. Proper height and depth of storage areas and equipment help to ensure safety.

Supervision

Caregivers should be able to view all areas of the room without obstruction to be aware of any unsafe or inappropriate activity by the children. *Positive reinforcement* ("Hands are for holding," instead of "Stop hitting!") preserves a pleasant atmosphere. Because chil-

dren feel secure in such an environment, they can explore and experiment freely.

Bulletin Boards and Room Decorations

Bulletin boards and room decorations can be fun for caregivers and children. When aesthetically pleasing, these decorations often invite language development and cognitive learning. Keep displays at the children's eye level. They should be interesting to and appropriate for the age. Balance the work of caregivers and children, and display both. Remember, self-esteem increases when children feel that their work is valued.

YARD ENVIRONMENT

Play yards and equipment are as important to children as the classroom. Good play yards stimulate activity, allow for different groups of children to form, and promote good physical growth and social development. Play yards are structured for the climate, terrain, size, and location of the facility. The staff should be creative when it sets up and facilitates activities in a yard. Movable equipment, such as the water table, picnic table, and the obstacle course, is versatile. It encourages enjoyment and exploration.

Safety

Equipment (slides, climbing structures, playhouse, tables and chairs, bicycles) should be clean, attractive, and appropriate for the children. Equipment must be the proper height to be safe and fun. Inspect equipment daily. All repairs and maintenance should be done immediately. Nonmovable equipment, such as swings and climbing structures, must be securely fastened to the ground. Surface areas should be checked for dangerous objects, such as nails, glass, and rocks. Sharp edges and exposed nuts and bolts should be fixed. Provide adequate equipment for the children, so that all can play safely and satisfy the desire for learning.

Safety rules for both staff and children should be strongly enforced. When rules are few, they are more easily remembered. Too many rules can confuse children.

Figure 3-7: This child uses his imagination while playing on the large equipment in the play yard.

Variety of Equipment

A variety of equipment encourages children to use all of their muscles and to acquire coordination. Wheel toys, climbing structures, a playhouse, and sand digging toys are basic equipment in a play yard.

Figure 3-8: How many surfaces are shown in this picture?

Children can learn socialization skills by playing and sharing with others. When climbing and riding bicycles, they can learn *spatial awareness* (awareness of the relationship of the body to other objects) and develop balance.

Inexpensive materials make for interesting, imaginative play. Large boxes, wooden crates, tires, and boards can lead to a pirate's ship, a soldier's fort, or a stage for a performance.

Areas and Surfaces

The play yard, like the classroom, should be divided into areas. Carefully plan space for many different kinds of physical activities, such as running, climbing, and digging. A large tree or covered area provides shelter from the sun. It can also provide a quiet and relaxing atmosphere. A playhouse also offers relief from the sun, and it can stimulate socialization and problem-solving skills.

Many surfaces are required to provide safety and exploration on the part of the children. *Resilient* (flexible) material, such as sand, cushioned mats, wood chips should be placed under all climbing equipment. Grass is wonderful for running and playing games. Asphalt and cement make good roads on which to ride tricycles.

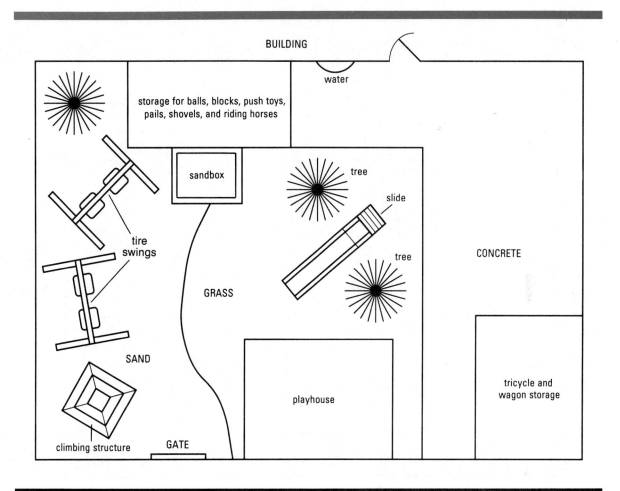

Equipment

- balls
- blocks
- push toys
- riding horses
- sandbox
- shovels and pails
- small climbing structure
- small slide
- small tricycles and wagons

Figure 3-9: Infant and toddler play yard.

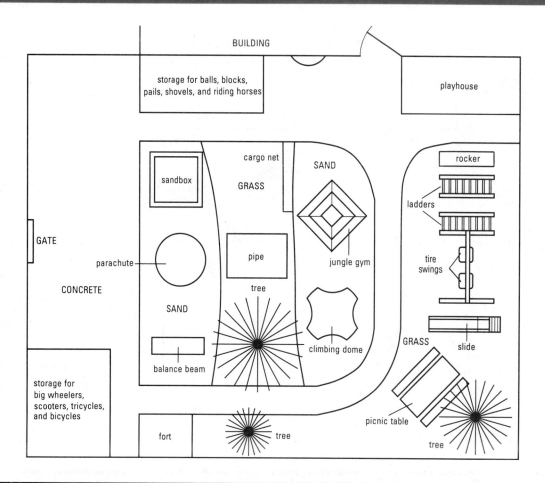

Equipment

- balance beam
- balls
- big wheels
- blocks
- cargo net
- climbing dome
- fort
- jungle gym

- ladders
- pails and shovels
- parachute
- playhouse
- riding horse
- rocker
- sandbox
- scooters
- slide
- tire swings
- tricycles and bicycles
- wagons

Figure 3-10: Preschool play yard.

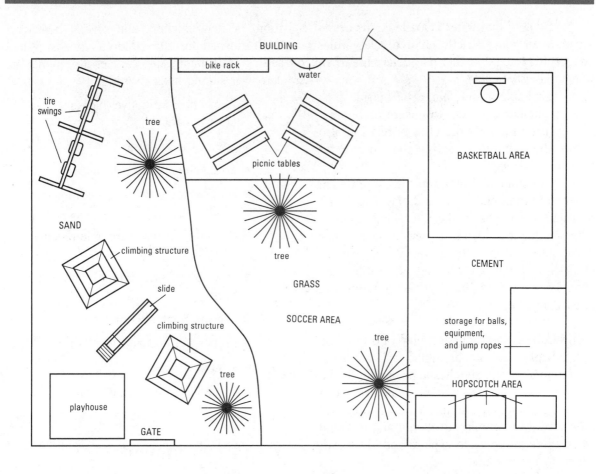

Figure 3-11: School-age play yard.

Equipment

- balls (variety for baseball, basketball, football, and soccer)
- equipment for baseball, basketball, football, and soccer)
- hopscotch
- jump ropes
- large climbing structures
- playhouse
- slide
- tire swings

Be sure that water is available for drinking and for play. Strictly enforce safety rules concerning water. Weather may determine when water play is possible.

Scheduling and sharing of outside time and equipment can help to ensure a cooperative transition among the classes. Sharing also allows the children to satisfy their desire for learning and play.

Professional caregivers take pride in organizing their classroom and play yard. Each morning, they check their learning centers. They frequently introduce new objects. They make sure that everything is neat and orderly, and that materials for teaching are readily available. They are ready to greet the children in a relaxed manner.

To enhance growth, development, and motivation, a classroom and play yard must be carefully planned, prepared, and facilitated. Using equipment and supplies appropriate for the children served plus creativity, caregivers can provide a stimulating atmosphere. Children will look forward to coming to school and learning when there are areas to explore and ideas with which to experiment.

IN THE HOME CARE

Room Environment

Large house or small, one story or two, city or country, most any home can be licensed to provide child care for one or more children. Caregivers usually set aside specific rooms for the children to inhabit during the day, although all rooms are licensed. Most often a living room or den, kitchen, and several bedrooms are furnished for the children's needs. When setting up a family day care environment, the caregiver should keep in mind:

- Aesthetics; attractive, pleasant environment
- age of the children
- arrangement of the furniture
- comfort for both the children and family
- durability of furniture, equipment, walls, floors
- easy supervision from all areas of the room
- learning materials and toys
- proper lighting and ventilation
- safety
- versatility; purchasing furniture that can be used in several ways

Yard Environment

All licensed day care homes should provide a play yard with enough space and equipment to enable children to use their muscles. Although most equipment is not expected to be as sophisticated as a day care center, a home should try to supply a variety of equipment that is:

- age appropriate
- durable
- conducive for children in using gross and fine motor development skills, as well as spatial awareness

- safe and clean
- versatile and can be used in more than one way

If possible, different surfaces (grass, concrete, sand) should enhance the yard. Several large trees provide a shady area for play, picnics, and quiet time for both the children and the caregivers. Pools, spas, and any areas containing water should be securely covered and fenced at all times when not in use. Most states require that all play yards be fenced with secure locks. Supervision is most important for both indoor and outdoor activities.

Suggested equipment for family day care is listed below.

Indoor

- art materials
- books
- chalk board
- group games
- inexpensive area rugs
- large clothes hamper or toy box to store small toys
- manipulatives
- plastic drop cloths
- plastic table cloths
- record player
- rocking chair
- rocking horse
- room gates
- sleeping mats or cots
- VCR and TV

Outdoor

- balance beam
- balls
- climbing dome
- jump rope
- pail and shovels
- sandbox
- tire swings
- tricycles and bicycles

SUMMARY

The proper room environment sets the tone of the children's center. Proper lighting, ventilation, cleanliness, room arrangement, activity areas, and areas for movement allow children to explore and experiment with the materials provided. Caregivers should provide for safe participation and suitable supervision of all areas. Rooms should be aesthetically pleasing. Decorations should display both caregivers' and children's work.

The play yard environment should have many of the same components as the room. The equipment, activity areas, and areas for movement should be arranged for maximum use, creativity, safety, and supervision. Cleanliness, a variety of surfaces, and water should be included.

In both the room and the play yard, the maturation level of the children is important. When choosing equipment, remember the age and size of the children. Proper repair and maintenance of all equipment prevent accidents.

Review Questions

1. Why is it important to have age appropriate materials?

2. What is the importance of good ventilation?

3. Why is it necessary to have proper supervision in the classroom at all times?

4. Why is it important for equipment to be versatile?

5. What learning centers are necessary in a classroom?

6. What types of equipment allow children to practice spatial awareness?

7. What materials are considered to be resilient under large equipment?

8. Why is it necessary to have water available in the play yard?

Things to Do and Discuss

1. Observe a classroom. List the learning centers and specialized areas. Sketch the room arrangement.

2. Observe a play yard. List the specialized areas and yard arrangements. Make a sketch.

3. Discuss your "ideal" classroom and play yard.

4. Discuss how you would change a classroom and play yard for the infant and toddler, the preschooler, and the school-age child.

5. Design a bulletin board using both teachers' and children's work.

6. Pretend you have $2,000. Set up a classroom learning center. Use store catalogs to price equipment.

CHAPTER 4
Safety

Children are having fun while riding a tricycle.

KEY TERMS

coordination
CPR
evacuation plan

stop, drop, and roll
  technique
ventilation

OBJECTIVES

After completing this chapter, you will be able to:

1. describe good safety precautions in the classroom, in the play yard, and on a field trip;
2. define a good emergency plan for fires or a major natural disaster.

INTRODUCTION

Every day we are confronted with signs to help us be aware of safety. *Stop, caution,* and *warning* are examples of common words used to protect us from danger.

When working with young children, our first concern should be for their safety and welfare. Young children are curious. They lack experience and *coordination* (muscles working together). They are often unaware of dangers, therefore, caregivers must be alert to prevent accidents. Classrooms, play yards, and field trips must be made as safe as possible. A safe setting contributes to a more enjoyable and relaxed atmosphere.

Figure 4-1: These children are being taught safety signs firsthand.

ROOM SAFETY

In the last chapter, we discussed room environment and touched on the importance of safety for an atmosphere conducive to learning. In this chapter, we more clearly define safety elements.

The healthy classroom is clean—floors are swept and washed as needed, carpets are shampooed regularly, trash is disposed of daily, shelves and toys are washed periodically, and the air smells fresh. The room is free from litter. Exits are accessible at all times. The arrangement of the room helps establish a traffic pattern and the places for equipment. Enough room for movement prevents crowding of children and supplies.

Toys and equipment should be checked daily. They should be sanded and painted. There should be no broken pieces or sharp corners. Budget constraints make it necessary to repair toys and equipment if possible, rather than replace them. Toys that can easily shatter or that have loose parts should be carefully considered before being purchased. Are the toys appropriate for the age of the children? Do not purchase toys

Figure 4-2: *The two boys are arguing over one toy.*

with pieces small enough to fit in the ears, noses, or mouths of infants, toddlers, or preschoolers. Will the toys remain in good condition after constant use by groups of children? Toys purchased should be strong and durable. They should be versatile. Will they withstand time? Inexpensive equipment generally does not last long.

To prevent arguments and struggles over toys and equipment, you must have adequate amounts of each. Every child should have the time and opportunity to explore and use the materials. A toy with many pieces may be divided among the children who wish to use it. However, if the toy can be used by only one person, four to six items of the same toy may be purchased, depending on the projected popularity of the toy and the number of children in the center.

Teacher supplies such as paints, paper, and resource materials must be stored in a cabi-net to prevent access by the children. Cleaning supplies and poisons must always be stored in a *locked* cupboard away from the children.

All storage shelves and heavy pieces of equipment should be anchored securely to walls and the floor to prevent falling. When purchasing furniture, keep in mind the size of the children. Sanding and painting provide both safety and aesthetics to the classroom. Proper maintenance and repair of furniture and equipment is essential.

Safety Rules

Safety rules and measures must be adopted and enforced by the staff and parents to protect the children. Each environment that a child may encounter throughout the day should have rules governing safety.

Rules should be few in number so that children can remember them. Provide for positive reinforcement and a sense of following directions correctly. What rules would be important to you as the child care worker in the classroom? Suggested safety rules in the classroom include:

1. We walk inside.

2. Toys and equipment must be used in an appropriate manner.

3. Toys and equipment must be placed in appropriate storage areas after use. (Low shelves for toys help children to learn responsibility and facilitate cleanup.)

4. Spills must be cleaned up quickly and thoroughly.

5. The rights of others must be respected.

Figure 4-3: *The family child care provider is careful about sanitary conditions when preparing meals.*

Safety Checklist

General rules for the indoor environment have been adopted into the following safety checklist. Observe the entire room for the welfare of the children.

1. Is there a minimum of thirty-five square feet of usable space per child?

2. Is there good *ventilation* (air circulation)?

3. Are windows and doors screened?

4. Are heating and air conditioning units in good working order?

5. Is the room temperature between 68 and 80 degrees Fahrenheit?

6. Are there two exits in all rooms?

7. Are carpets and draperies fire-retardant?

8. Are rooms well-lighted?

9. Are glass doors and low windows constructed of safety glass, and do they have decals to prevent children from running into them?

10. Are there bathrooms?
    a. Are toilets and washbasins in good working order?
    b. Is there one toilet and washbasin for every ten to twelve children?
    c. Are potty chairs provided for toilet training?
    d. Is the water temperature no greater than 120 degrees Fahrenheit?
    e. Is powder or liquid soap provided for hand washing?
    f. Are paper towels provided?
    g. Are fixtures scrubbed daily?
    h. Are diapering tables or mats disinfected after each use?
    i. Are wastebaskets provided for trash?

11. Are unused electrical outlets covered with safety caps?

12. Are extension cords in good repair and taped down?

13. Are smoke detectors in appropriate places, and are they in good working order?

14. Are pathways to doors kept free of furniture and other objects?

15. Are exits clearly marked?

16. If stairways are used:
    a. Are there handrails at the children's height?
    b. Are the stairs kept free of toys and other objects?
    c. Are the stairs well-lighted?
    d. Are the stairs covered with a nonslip surface?

17. Are fire extinguishers in convenient places? Are they checked annually? Do they meet local regulations?

18. Are the premises free from insects and rodents?

19. Is food preparation kept to strict sanitary standards? Are workers trained in sanitary food service?

20. Are first aid supplies convenient? Are they checked regularly?

21. Is at least one child care worker trained in first aid and *CPR* (cardiopulmonary resuscitation)?

22. Are all medications stored in a locked cabinet; even medications that require refrigeration?

23. Are fire and disaster drills conducted once a month?

24. Do fire alarm systems meet local regulations?

25. Is emergency information for the staff and children near the phone?

YARD SAFETY

Make the physical welfare and safety of the children your first consideration on the play yard as well as in the classroom. Keep eyes "behind your head!" Look, listen, and observe at all times. In the play yard, physically active children do not often stay in one group for long. They run, jump, climb, and sometimes travel quickly. Astute caregivers position themselves in a central area in the yard so that they may see and supervise all play areas. Space the adults supervising the yard evenly apart. Refrain from conversation with other caregivers unless absolutely necessary. This provides more time to observe and interact with the children. Never leave children alone!

The play yard should be totally fenced. Have a childproof gate with the latch at adult height. Check the gates periodically to see that

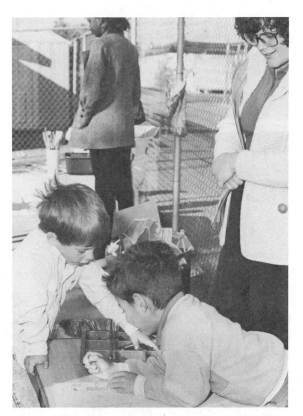

Figure 4-4: Caregivers look, listen, and observe the children.

Figure 4-5: The caregiver observes all children in the yard.

they are closed, for most young children like to explore. At least two exits from the play yard are necessary in case of emergency. Fencing should be made of a durable material and built to prevent climbing.

Storage sheds and large pieces of equipment should be anchored securely to the ground. They are usually grouped together for easy supervision and play opportunities.

Located next to the building, play areas give easy access to the classroom and bathrooms, as well as to drinking water. Play areas must have good drainage to prevent the accumulation of water or slippery mud.

Make daily checking of all outside equipment and areas for cleanliness and maintenance a habit. Eliminate trash, sweep sidewalks, keep the grass mowed, and repair or remove broken equipment each morning.

When observing a play yard look for:

- adequate equipment and centers
- adequate room for easy movement
- area free from insects and rodents
- balance of shady and sunny areas
- chemicals, insecticides, paints, and gasoline stored in a locked cabinet
- cushioned surfaces under play structures
- equipment that is age-appropriate
- no poisonous plants, shrubs, or trees in the area
- no sharp edges, nails, or broken toys
- sand area covered when not in use
- trees and plants trimmed and grass cut
- variety of play surfaces—grass, concrete, and sand
- wading or swimming pools fenced and always supervised
- water drained when not in use
- water tables always supervised

Safety rules are essential for all people involved in the child care facility, including the staff, parents, volunteers, and students. Again, keep rules few in number and easy to remember. Everyone should follow established rules consistently.

Some Common Poisonous Plants

Vegetation	Poisonous Part	Complications
Autumn crocus	Bulbs	Vomiting, nervousness
Bittersweet	Berries	Burning sensation in mouth, nausea, vomiting, dizziness convulsions
Black locust tree	Bark, leaves, pods, seeds	Nausea, weakness
Buttercup	All parts	Nausea, vomiting
Castor bean	Pods	Fatal
Cherry tree	Leaves, twigs	Fatal
Daffodil, hyacinth, narcissus	Bulbs	Nausea, vomiting, diarrhea — fatal
Daphne	Berries	Fatal
Dieffenbachia	All parts	Burning and irritation to mouth and tongue
Iris	Underground roots	Digestive upset, nausea, diarrhea
Larkspur	Young plants, seeds	Digestive upset, nervous excitement, depression — fatal
Laurels, azaleas, rhododendron	All parts	Fatal
Lily of the valley	Leaves, flowers	Nausea, digestive upset, mental confusion
Mistletoe	Berries	Diarrhea, irregular pulse
Oak tree	Acorns, leaves	Kidney failure
Oleander	Leaves, branches	Digestive upset — fatal
Poinsettia	Leaves	Fatal
Rhubarb	Raw leaves	Convulsions, coma — fatal
Sweetpea	All parts	Shallow respiration, convulsions, paralysis, slow pulse
Wisteria	Seed pods	Diarrhea, collapse
Yews	Berries, foliage	Fatal

Figure 4-6: Some common poisonous plants chart.

Rules for play yard safety may include:

1. Climb up the ladder for the slide. Slide feet first down the slide.

2. Drive carefully on the tricycles or bicycles.

3. Hold onto the swing with two hands.

4. Keep sand close to the ground and in the sand area.

5. Place litter in the trash.

6. Treat toys with respect.

7. Watch for children swinging, and walk clear of the area.

The staff should:

1. Accompany any child leaving the play yard, such as to retrieve a ball.

2. Consume any drinks or snacks in the teacher's lounge.

3. If leaving the yard for any purpose, notify another adult.

4. Take your share of the responsibility.

5. Wear durable, easy-to-move-in shoes.

6. Wear sensible clothes, professional but washable.

FIELD TRIPS

Field trips, whether they be a walk around the block or a drive to the nearby pumpkin patch, must always include safety measures for everyone. Trips to local community facilities should be fun and memorable. They should be learning experiences for the children and staff. Safety rules should be few in number and strictly enforced.

Safety

Caregivers should see that all children are dressed appropriately for the weather, wearing comfortable clothes and shoes. Name tags should be safety-pinned to the back of each child. This will prevent the child from tugging at and losing the label. Only the name and phone number of the school should be written on the tag. Never put the child's name on the tag—this information could be used to lure the child away from the group.

Walking Field Trips

Often transportation is unavailable, but walking trips around the block or to a nearby area can be fun and educational. Safety regulations regarding these trips must be carefully planned. Caregivers should walk the route beforehand to check for obstacles and to determine the length of the trip. They can also determine if any additional safety precautions are necessary.

Consider weather when planning a walking field trip. On hot days, make the distance shorter, and carry water if necessary. On cooler days, jackets or sweaters may be needed.

The caregiver in charge of the trip should carry signed parent permission slips and emergency information forms for each child. Take a portable first aid kit for the occasional skinned knee or scratch.

Safety rules for walking field trips may include the following.

1. Cross streets in crosswalks, looking both ways first.

2. Everyone must walk on the sidewalk.

3. Take care to follow all traffic laws.

Case Study #1:
Mrs. Todd

Figure 4-7: Michelle and Miss Betty are enjoying a few minutes with Sunshine, the rabbit.

When Mrs. Todd was observing child care centers, she checked for extensive safety precautions. Cleanliness was an obvious concern, although she realized that a productive center would at times be messy and well used. Mrs. Todd looked for cleaned and polished floors where Michelle would be sitting for a number of hours a day. She looked at the bathroom facilities to be sure that they were sterilized daily. She looked to see if soap dispensers were used instead of bar soap to prevent the spread of germs. The kitchen facility had to be organized, clean, and free of hazards, to protect any child who might wander inside.

Mrs. Todd looked to see if unused electrical sockets were covered and electrical cords or wires were taped to the floor to prevent tripping. She checked to see if the heaters had a protective covering.

Mrs. Todd along with Michelle walked through each doorway in the facility to see where it led and how many rooms were connected. She asked the director how often fire drills were practiced, and then she looked for posted exit routes for each classroom.

On the play yard, Mrs. Todd was conscious of the supervision of the children and the alertness of the staff. She looked to see if each major play area, climbing structure, sandbox, bike path, and water table were separately supervised. Did the adult interact with the children, or was the adult just acting as a monitor?

Mrs. Todd then walked around each climbing structure, into the outside playhouse, and behind the equipment shed. She checked for possible debris, broken glass, and old, unused toys. She knew that Michelle was very inquisitive and might stumble upon these areas and get hurt.

Michelle giggled as she and the director approached the bunny, Sunshine. Mrs. Todd was impressed with how healthy and well-kept the rabbit appeared. He obviously was accustomed to children because he snuggled in Michelle's arms. Sunshine's cage appeared clean. It contained fresh water and food. Apparently his droppings had been cleaned away before the children arrived. Michelle enjoyed feeding Sunshine a carrot before she had to leave for the day.

Mrs. Todd's choice of a school was based largely on the safety practices of the staff working with the children.

4. There should be a caregiver who leads, children walking between, and another adult assigned to the end position.

5. There should be at least one adult (caregiver or parent) for every four children.

Vehicle Trips

When traveling in private vehicles, or school-owned vehicles, the vehicle and driver must be insured. The driver needs to be capable of operating the vehicle, have a valid driver's license, and meet state regulations. All vehicles must be in good operating condition. Proof of the license and insurance should be recorded by the director to meet legal standards.

When traveling on public transportation or rented buses, insurance policies and driver certification are handled by the district or bus company. Adequate adult supervision, however, is still important.

Each child attending the field trip should have a signed permission slip from a parent or legal guardian. The form should specify the place, date, and time of the trip. The staff person in charge should carry hospital consent forms for each child plus a statement of insurance for each driver. The caregiver should call roll before leaving the center and again before leaving the field trip site.

When traveling, all children should be in a car seat or wearing a seat belt. All adults must also be belted for safety. A fire extinguisher and first aid kit should be in each vehicle. Other safety rules in vehicles may include:

1. Children must keep their hands to themselves.

2. Children must remain seated.

Figure 4-8: Michelle fastens her seat belt before going on a field trip.

3. Children must remain seated until all vehicles come to a complete stop.

4. Children must use quiet voices.

5. Only the driver opens doors and windows.

EMERGENCY PLANS

Fires

A prearranged fire *evacuation plan* (a plan to empty a room or area of people) is required. You should have two exits from each room and a written copy of the plan posted by each door. All personnel and visitors should be aware of the evacuation plan. One person on the staff is designated to call the fire department (usually 911) and give complete informa-

Case Study #2:
Leo

Leo is excited about going to the pumpkin patch with his class. He has a dollar in his pocket to buy his own pumpkin. His mother says that they will carve it into a jack-o'-lantern that evening when his father gets home.

Leo's mother is going to drive on the field trip. She brings to school her car insurance information to give to the principal. She also remembers to sign the permission slip for Leo. Without these papers, neither she nor Leo can go on the trip. Miss Davis, Leo's teacher, already has a hospital consent form in her file.

Before leaving on the trip, Miss Davis goes over the safety rules for the trip, explaining carefully, so that everyone (students and parents) understands. She explains to the parents that the cars will follow one another in case of car trouble and so no one will get lost.

Miss Davis also explains the safety rules concerning the pumpkin patch. Everyone must stay together in a group within the boundaries of the patch, and everyone must walk at a safe speed. Now they are ready to leave.

Miss Davis gives the drivers a list of names of the children who will be riding in each car. The children walk to the cars and get in, fastening their seat belts. The drivers check to make sure each child is secure.

Figure 4-9: Leo likes to dress up at Halloween.

When they return to their elementary school later in the day, everyone compares pumpkins and agrees that they have had a successful and safe trip. The children are discussing what kind of faces to carve on their pumpkins.

tion. This information must include name, address, approximate location of fire, and whether or not anyone is still inside the building.

Each caregiver is responsible for assembling a group of children and leading them out of the building, turning off the lights, and closing the doors. A list of the children in each group should be kept by the caregiver in charge. The director is responsible for taking a flashlight and the emergency cards of each child and staff member out of the building.

Once outside, everyone should meet in a designated location, as far from the buildings as possible, but clear of the street and fire hydrants. Roll should be taken to ensure that everyone is out of the building. *Do not go back into the building for any reason!*

A route from the play yard should be included in your evacuation plan. Again, two exits should be defined.

Conduct fire drills at least once a month. Some drills should be unannounced. Be sure to practice alternate routes and to drill at different times of the day. Infant and toddler centers place children in cribs and roll them to safety. In a large facility, using a stopwatch to time drills helps to make everyone conscious of the time needed to evacuate. Such consciousness may help reduce the amount of time needed.

Before holding a fire drill, discuss good fire safety practices with the children. Some possible safety rules follow:

1. Do not return to building until the director gives the signal.

2. Feel closed doors for signs of heat before opening them.

3. Keep your hands to yourself. Avoid pushing and shoving.

4. Learn the *stop, drop, and roll technique* (if your clothes catch fire, stop moving immediately, drop to the ground, and roll on the ground until the flames are put out).

5. Leave whatever you are doing and walk to the door quietly.

6. Remain quiet in order to be able to listen to instructions.

7. Select an alternate route if a hallway or stairway is filled with smoke.

8. Stay close to the floor to avoid heat and poisonous gases.

9. Take roll to account for everyone.

10. Walk carefully to a prearranged meeting place.

Disasters

Wherever you live, you must be prepared in case of a natural disaster—tornado, earthquake, hurricane, or tidal wave. Disaster plans include many of the same elements as fire evacuation plans, but they must also contain long-term elements. Copies of the emergency slips, blankets, candles, food, water, first aid kits, and in some cases shelters should be stockpiled.

Identify the safest place for the children and staff members to go in case of a natural disaster. Once a month, practice drills for both inside and outside emergencies.

Give each caregiver and each family a copy of the disaster plan. A prearranged meeting place where parents can pick up their children should be included in the plan.

As you can tell, safety is a major concern when working with young children. The

(continued on page 76)

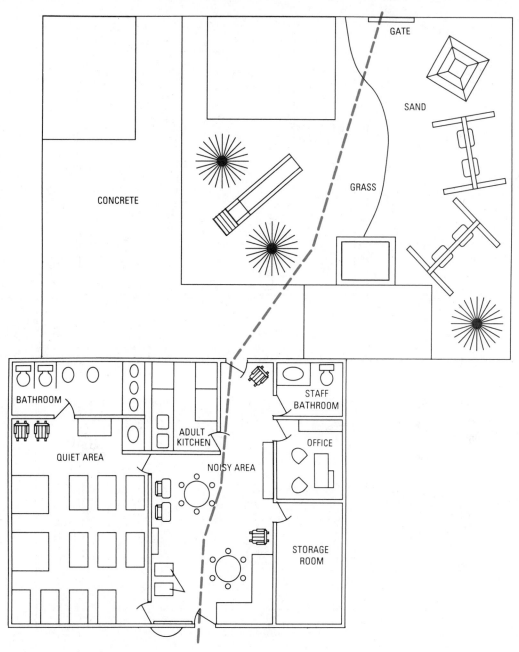

Figure 4-10: Infant and toddler evacuation plan.

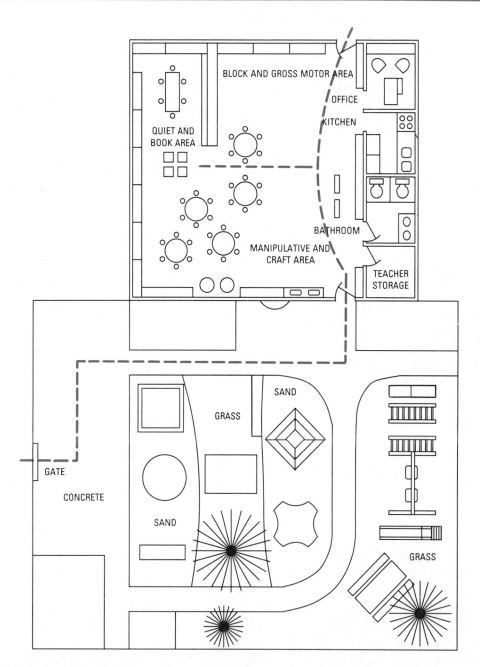

Figure 4-11: Preschool evacuation plan.

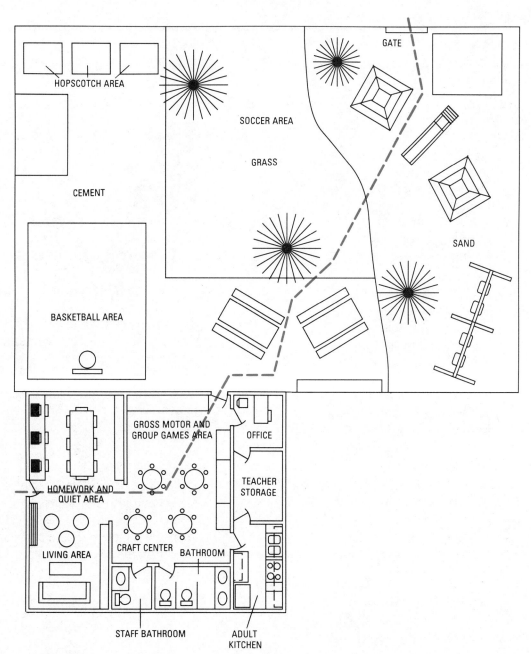

Figure 4-12: *School-age evacuation plan.*

Fire Facts

I. Causes
  A. Vandalism
  B. Arson
  C. Carelessness

II. Requirements
  A. Air
    1. Only 14% to 16% oxygen will maintain a fire.
    2. We need the same amounts to live.
  B. Fuel
    1. Gasoline is the most dangerous fuel. It vaporizes at 45 degrees Fahrenheit.
    2. Paint thinner vaporizes at 100 degrees Fahrenheit.
    3. Only cleaning solutions that vaporize over 100 degrees Fahrenheit should be used.
    4. Flammable liquids are heavier than air and therefore accumulate near the floor.
    5. Natural gas is lighter than air. It is poisonous. It will replace air and cause suffocation. There is no odor to natural gas; however, the gas company adds a "rotten egg" odor so that you can detect a leak.
  C. Heat
    1. Kindling temperature is the point at which a substance vaporizes and then burns.
    2. *Flash point* is when a substance gives off a vapor and ignites.

III. Fire types
  A. Class A: ordinary combustibles
    1. Fires burning ordinary combustibles can be put out by water.
    2. Wood, paper, and trash are ordinary combustibles.
  B. Class B: liquids (flammable and combustible)
    1. Gasoline, paint thinner, and duplicating fluid are Class B liquids.
    2. A flammable liquid gives off a vapor below 140 degrees Fahrenheit and needs an outside heat source to ignite.
    3. Combustible liquid gives off a vapor at 140 to 200 degrees and can be self-igniting.
  C. Class C: electrical
  D. Class D: combustible metal (magnesium)

IV. Extra safety measures
  A. Christmas trees should be flameproof.
  B. Panic doors should open with fifteen pounds of pressure.
  C. Know how to turn off gas valve. Turn the handle perpendicular to the pipe with a wrench.
  D. Know how to turn off circuit breakers.
  E. All staff members should be trained in the use of fire extinguishers.

Figure 4-13: Fire facts chart.

Infants and Toddlers Enjoy	To Prevent Accidents
Rolling, wiggling, moving in their cribs	Cribs should have closely placed slats, three inches apart to prevent their heads from getting caught; firm mattresses; tight corners, and bumper pads. Never leave a child in a crib with the sides down.
Changing diapers	Never leave a child alone on the changing counter. Keep pins and other small objects out of reach.
Sucking	Keep small, swallowable objects away from babies.
Pointing	Cover unused outlets and light sockets.
Exploring	Use safety gates at doorways and the tops of stairways. Keep hot pots, liquids, and foods out of reach. Avoid hanging tablecloths. Keep breakable objects such as those made of glass out of reach. Lock and remove old refrigerators and cabinets. Keep sharp articles (scissors, knives, pens) out of reach.
Turning knobs	Drawers and cabinets should have childproof latches. Keep medications in a high, locked cabinet, and use childproof lids. Keep cleaning solutions and solvents in high, locked cabinets.
Walking	Keep objects on table tops out of reach. Cover sharp corners. Lock dangerous areas.
Water play	Supervise water play at all times. Empty, fence, or cover water when it is not in use. Water should not be more than 120 degrees Fahrenheit. Water should be fresh and clean.

Figure 4-14: Safety rules for infants and toddlers.

Figure 4-15: Infants and toddlers explore their environment.

Preschoolers Enjoy	To Prevent Accidents
Exploring	Keep all dangerous supplies in locked cabinets. Remind preschoolers to follow safety rules and stay within boundaries.
Riding a wheeled toy	Remind preschoolers to: ● go at safe speeds ● keep shoes on their feet ● stay in designated areas ● stay on the sidewalk and out of the street ● watch for obstacles
Going for walks	Remind preschoolers to: ● go with an adult ● look both ways before crossing the street ● stay in crosswalks ● walk, not run, across a street
Running	Remind preschoolers to: ● look out for sharp objects ● not chase balls into the street ● wear safe, protective shoes
Helping	Allow preschoolers to: ● carry only breakproof objects, appropriate in weight and size ● clean up spills quickly and thoroughly

Figure 4-16: Safety rules for preschoolers.

Figure 4-17: What fun to jump on hay bales!

School-Age Children Enjoy	To Prevent Accidents
Creating and following through with their own projects	Provide supervision and enforce safety rules.
Vigorous play	Use floor mats. Clean play yards, keeping them free of debris. Provide water and shade. Be sure children wear appropriate clothing. Maintain all equipment.
Exploring	Supervise trips and walks. Provide identification tags. Enforce safety rules.
Swimming	Supervise all swimming. Enforce water safety rules. Provide instruction. Be sure the pool is properly fenced. Keep the gate locked when the pool is not in use.
Hobbies	Enforce safety rules. Provide specific work areas. Supervise activities.
Helping	Let children carry objects only of appropriate size and weight. Clean up spills quickly and thoroughly.

Figure 4-18: Safety rules for school-age children.

Figure 4-19: School-age children love to fix their own snacks.

professional caregiver must constantly be aware of precautions and practices to protect children. Planning prevents accidents and provides an environment which adults and children enjoy without worry.

IN THE HOME CARE

Safety is of utmost importance when caring for children in the home. The family day care provider or nanny is responsible for providing and maintaining a safe environment indoors and out. Most community colleges and state organizations offer safety classes for home care providers. These classes are often very informative and helpful when setting up a home care environment.

Although all safety measures and rules listed in this chapter are of equal importance, several below have been specifically identified for in the home care.

Indoors

- caregivers trained in first aid and CPR
- carpets and drapes fire-retardant
- cleaning supplies, medicines, and poisons stored in a locked cabinet
- cleanliness
- decals on all glass doors and windows
- doorways and stairways gated
- electrical outlets covered
- emergency information placed near the phone
- fire extinguishers in most rooms
- heat and air-conditioning units in good working order

- smoke detectors in good working order
- well-equipped first aid kit
- well-maintained toys, equipment, and furniture
- windows and doors screened

Outdoors

- age-appropriate equipment
- area free from rodents and insects
- chemicals and poisons stored in a locked cabinet
- cleanliness
- cushioned surface under the play structures
- fenced with gates closed at all times
- grass and trees trimmed and maintained
- maintained and unbroken toys
- no poisonous plants, shrubs, or trees
- pools and spas covered and fenced separately
- proper drainage
- storage sheds and large equipment anchored securely to the ground

SUMMARY

When working with young children, your first responsibility is for their safety and welfare. Be aware of the potential for accidents. Prevent them from occurring by carefully planning and observing the room and play yard.

Major safety concerns are cleanliness, toy and equipment maintenance, proper storage of supplies, and rules that are easy for children to follow. Traffic patterns both inside and out should be kept clear of obstacles.

Field trips should be carefully thought out. Safety should be upmost in the caregiver's mind. Permission slips, emergency supplies, rules, and the route of trip must be prearranged by the caregiver. Discuss rules with everyone beforehand and enforce the rules during both walking and vehicle trips.

It is important to have a fire and disaster plan at each facility. Easy-to-read charts should be posted at each exit. Drill at least once a month so children also know what is expected. Keep supplies at hand in case of emergency. Clearly define each person's responsibility.

Although there are many rules for a safe environment, remember that school should be an enjoyable experience for both adults and children. A safe environment is a secure learning environment.

Review Questions

1. Why is it necessary to practice safety?

2. Why should toys and equipment be checked daily?

3. Where are cleaning supplies and poisons stored at all times?

4. Why is it important to encourage children to walk in the classroom?

5. How often should fire and disaster drills be conducted?

6. What temperature should the hot water be kept?

7. What room temperature is best for children?

8. How many exits from the play yard are necessary?

9. What should the adult-to-child ratio be on a field trip?

10. What long-term supplies should be kept in case of a disaster?

Things to Do and Discuss

1. Observe a child care facility, using the safety checklist in this chapter (pages 60 and 61). Are safety rules defined and enforced? What additional rules do you feel are necessary to prevent accidents?

2. Visit your local fire prevention office, gathering information concerning good safety precautions for a child care facility.

3. Discuss with a director or principal the school's safety regulations pertaining to field trips.

4. Role play how a child care worker might explain to a child good safety precautions on a slide.

5. With a budget of $1,500, plan an imaginary play yard, keeping safety in mind.

6. Write a list of safety regulations for the above play yard.

7. Visit a classroom and observe the children. Make a list of potential accident situations and how to prevent them.

SECTION II

OBJECTIVES

After completing this section, you will be able to:

1. discuss the importance of a good health plan in the child care center;
2. explain the techniques of basic first aid and emergency care;
3. discuss the importance of cardiopulmonary resuscitation;
4. identify the common communicable diseases and their symptoms;
5. identify the types of child abuse and neglect, and ways of documenting and reporting suspected abuse;
6. discuss the importance of adequate nutrition.

Health

Good health in the classroom is a major concern when working with young children. *Health* can be defined as physical and mental well-being, and freedom from pain, defect, or disease. It is the condition of one's body and mind.

Successful caregivers need knowledge and skill in basic first aid, and CPR, as well as the ability to identify common childhood communicable illnesses. It is important that caregivers know how to nurture and care for children who show any signs of abnormal health. They need to be aware of signs that indicate child abuse and neglect. They must also know when parents or other professionals should be contacted about a child's health.

CHAPTER 5
Importance of Good Health in the Child Care Center

Healthy, active children have fun while playing.

KEY TERMS

administers
amblyopia
communicable
contagious illnesses
convulsions
deaf
deviant behavior
diaper gait
dilated
disposition
dosage
failure to thrive
fainting
fatigue

health
hygiene
inflammation
isolation
knock-knee
lethargy
nausea
pediatricians
perforation
posture
premature birth
strabismus
stamina
tooth buds

OBJECTIVES

After completing this chapter, you will be able to:
1. identify the importance of good health practices in the child care center;
2. name available resources for health and social services.

INTRODUCTION

As a caregiver, one of your goals is to provide a healthy environment for your children and to promote good mental and physical development. In order for children to learn and enjoy their environment, you must protect against and be observant of any health problems. Good health practices, by the adults as well as the children, are essential to keep the environment free from the spread of disease.

GENERAL HEALTH PRECAUTIONS

Staff

Whether in a school environment or in a home, the director or principal is a role model for the staff and children. It is important to establish health standards and routines for the facility or home that enforce specific health laws as required by the city, county, and state.

Physical Examination

Working with young children requires a great deal of energy and *stamina* (ability to withstand hardship or stress), as well as continual alertness. Therefore, a complete physical examination is required of each member of staff upon employment. The exam ensures that each person is physically and mentally able to work with young children for extended periods of time. Most states require that a report of the physical examination be included in the personnel file.

A tuberculosis (TB) test is generally included in the examination, and a negative result is a precondition to employment or participation. Tuberculosis is a *communicable* (capable of being transmitted) disease. Although rarely fatal in this day, it is becoming more common. Anyone is susceptible to the disease, which is transmitted through the air. Tuberculosis affects the lungs and other parts of the body. Symptoms can include a slight dry cough, a rise in temperature late in the afternoon, sweating a great deal at night, weight loss, and chest pains. Although these symptoms can just mean a common cold, if they persist, a TB test may be in order.

Administrators rely on dependability on the part of staff members. *Contagious illnesses* (illnesses spread by contact, such as colds and flu) are more prevalent when working with young children. To prevent absenteeism, caregivers must get proper rest, eat nutritiously, and maintain good health standards.

Hygiene

All staff members need to practice good *hygiene* (the science of health and maintenance) for a clean and healthy environment, and to prevent the spread of germs. Washing hands should be a common practice after using the rest room or toileting and changing children, and before and after food preparation, eating, and cleanup. Clean body, teeth, hair, and nails are important aspects of good grooming. Clothing should be clean and neat, as well as suitable for the position. Aprons or smocks are sometimes worn to protect caregivers' clothes from spills or accidents.

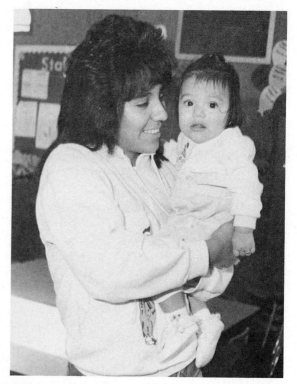

Figure 5-1: This smiling, well-groomed caregiver is a good role model.

Figure 5-2: Meagan is a healthy, happy child.

Mental Health

Mental stability is important when working with young children. A positive attitude, a sense of enjoyment, a respect for others, and an understanding nature are characteristics of good mental health for caregivers. In addition, caregivers must have an honest opinion of their abilities as well as their limitations. They should possess positive self-esteem, which is reflected in their classroom and in how others perceive them. Caregivers demonstrate control over their emotions, such as extreme anger, dislike, or sadness. Although it is all right to have these emotions, it is necessary that they not be excessively displayed.

Emergencies

A knowledge of basic first aid and CPR should be a prerequisite for employment of staff members. Each person needs to be prepared to handle an emergency.

Emergency phone numbers should be posted near each telephone in the facility as well as the phone number and address of the center (people sometimes become confused when giving out information during an emergency). Phone numbers for the police, fire, hospital, child abuse hot line, and other community services departments should be included on the list. Emergency telephone numbers for the children and staff must be readily available.

Children

Signs of Good Health

Children that display laughter, enthusiasm, and eagerness are exhibiting healthy characteristics. Busily engaging in purposeful activities, running, jumping, shouting to one another, and showing pleasure at discoveries are examples of healthy behavior. Healthy children can enjoy playing in groups or by themselves quietly, able to concentrate or dream.

Characteristics of a healthy child include:

1. appearance
   - appropriate weight and height
   - bodily cleanliness
   - bright, clear eyes
   - clean hair
   - clean teeth
   - clear complexion
   - ears and nose free of signs of infection or discharge
   - good posture and bone structure

Case Study #1:
Joey

Joey is having a bad day. He has argued with his mother about whether he should wear shorts or long pants on this rainy morning. He does not care for the pancakes that his mother serves for breakfast. He wants cereal. Next, he fights about the seat belt on the way to school. By the time Joey arrives at school, he is in a very negative mood (as is his mother).

During circle time, Joey has difficulty paying attention and is disrupting the class. Miss Betty repeatedly reminds him to remain seated and listen carefully to the story. Miss Ann, the aide, gently picks him up and places him on her lap for the rest of the story.

At snack time, Joey is still upset, and decides he dislikes the juice that is being served. This is the last straw for him. He picks up the cup of juice and deliberately throws it across the table, aiming at Miss Betty and two other children. Miss Betty is both shocked and angry. She removes him from the table, saying, "This makes me very upset. Your behavior is inappropriate. You need to use your words and tell me if you do not like the juice. Now help me wipe up the spill. Here is a sponge."

When Joey and Miss Betty finish cleaning up the area, Miss Betty takes him to a private corner and sits him on her lap, saying, "You're having a bad day. You're feeling angry. Can you tell me about it?" Because Miss Betty has empathy and a nurturing manner, Joey is

Figure 5-3: Joey doesn't like the juice being served.

able to discuss his feelings and sense that someone cares and understands.

After their talk, Miss Betty does not bring up the subject of the spilt juice again. She observes that Joey is now behaving in a more cooperative manner and seems to feel better about himself.

It is important that caregivers express their feelings, both negative and positive. However, these statements ought to be presented without embarrassing the child. Role modeling appropriate behavior and problem-solving techniques for children help them to be able to talk about their feelings rather than acting them out in an inappropriate manner. Understanding your own feelings as well as those of others is a characteristic of positive mental health.

2. behavior

- appropriate fine and gross motor skills
- curious and active
- getting along well with others
- happy and pleasant
- positive outlook

3. routines

- good appetite
- good sleep habits
- plenty of exercise

Hygiene

Children learn through observation and imitation. Caregivers and parents are role models and therefore should demonstrate good health practices. Cleanliness should be emphasized. Proper hygiene, the washing of hands before and after meals, brushing teeth, and toileting periodically through the day must be taught and reinforced.

Nutrition

Good eating habits can be encouraged by serving nutritious and attractive food, allowing plenty of time to eat, providing a relaxing atmosphere, and promoting desirable table manners. This can be practiced each day at meals and snacks. The adults should model the appropriate behaviors.

Physical Exams

Before enrollment, children should have a complete physical examination and a record placed in their files. Any abnormality or spe-

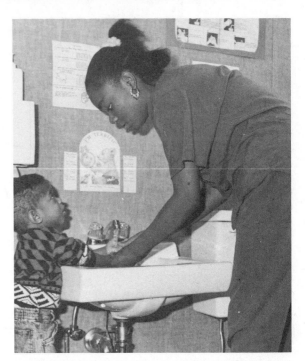

Figure 5-4: Proper hand washing techniques must be taught.

Figure 5-5: Mealtime should be relaxing and enjoyable.

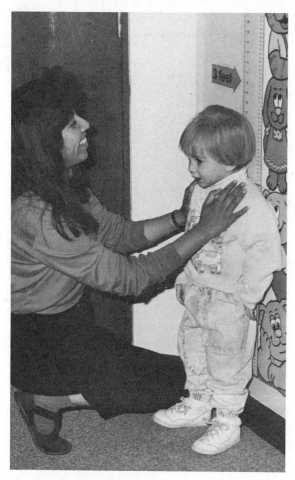

Figure 5-6: How much have I grown?

cial needs should be brought to the attention of the caregivers during orientation. At that time, special arrangements, such as for food allergies or disabilities, can be discussed.

Periodic conferences with parents concerning doctor visits help caregivers to become familiar with new instructions that affect the weight, diet, limitations, or abilities of the children. Because children are often at a center for long periods of time, it is equally important that caregivers keep parents informed about any changes concerning the children's health or developmental patterns.

It is important that parents be encouraged to arrange appointments with their children's doctor monthly for the first six months, every two months for the second six months, at three-month intervals up to age two, and then at least once a year until kindergarten. Regular medical attention helps to ensure the health of young children.

Immunizations

All fifty states and the District of Columbia now require immunizations against all preventable childhood diseases. Entrance to any licensed child care program may be delayed until immunizations are certified by a medical practitioner. Diphtheria, pertussis, and tetanus (DPT) inoculations; trivalent oral polio vaccine (TOPV); and measles, mumps, and rubella (MMR) inoculations are given to prevent the spread of communicable diseases. Exceptions to immunization may be made because of an allergy or the religious beliefs of the family. Documentation must be provided in accordance with licensing procedures and be kept in the child's file. Figure 5–7 is an immunization guide.

Mental Health

Unfortunately in today's society, children experience stress more than in previous generations. Stress and tensions can be caused by:

- birth of a sibling
- both parents entering the work force
- conflicts of child-rearing ideas

Immunization Guide

Child's Age	Immunization Needed
2 months old	DPT and TOPV
4 months old	DPT and TOPV
6 months old	DPT
12 months old	TB test
15 months old	MMR
18 months old	DPT and TOPV
4–6 years old	DPT and TOPV
12 years old	MMR
14 years old	DT (diphtheria/tetanus)

Figure 5-7: Immunization guide chart.

- death of loved one (family member, friend, or pet)
- divorced or separated parents, or single-parent households
- early separation anxiety
- illness of the child or principle caregiver
- overstimulation and hectic schedules
- peer and parental pressure
- poor diet
- relocation of families
- television or movies

Suicide rates are rising among children. Because of this fact, stress management has become a concern of caregivers. Teaching children to express their emotions, to relax, and to exercise to relieve tension are essential for promoting good mental health.

Drug and alcohol abuse are also becoming major problems for school-age children. Caregivers should be aware of signs of substance abuse. *Dilated* (wider or larger) eyes; a slowing down of activity; deterioration of grades; changes in sleep habits, peer groups, and personality; and a lack of personal grooming should be questioned.

Nervousness, depression, withdrawal, continual aggressiveness, and destructiveness are emotional problems that should be identified early. Professional help may be required. Caregivers are in the unique position to observe and evaluate *deviant behavior* (behavior different from normal) among children. Parents may be unaware of problem behaviors because these behaviors generally develop slowly, and parents do not have the advantage of comparing children of the same age.

Caregivers should discuss behavioral problems with the director or principal. Together, they can decide on a method of guiding the child to achieve success in behavior or to seek

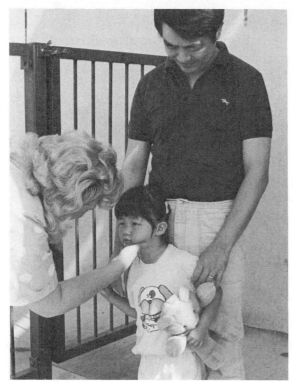

Figure 5-8: Morning health checks are required by many schools to help prevent the spread of disease.

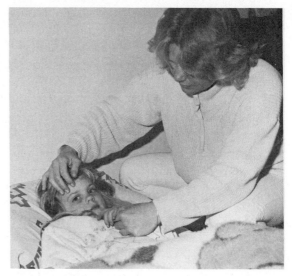

Figure 5-9: Reassurance from a friendly caregiver helps the ill child while waiting for her mother.

additional counseling. Parent-teacher conferencing is often recommended, so that the family and the school can set consistent guidelines and expectations for the child.

Daily Health Checks

Caregivers should check children daily as they arrive. They should take a few minutes and observe each child to see if there is any outward sign of illness. This procedure helps to protect the group from contagious diseases. It also provides a good opportunity for caregivers to greet the child and to give special attention to the child.

Procedures for Illness

A child may become ill quickly, having appeared fine at the morning health check. Immediate *isolation* (separation from the group) of the child, along with proper supervision, helps to stop the spread of illness. A warm, comforting area, complete with cot, pillow, and blanket and away from the noise and activity of the other children, protects the ill child until the mother or father arrives.

Medications

Medication may be given only with detailed instructions from the doctor and written permission of parents or guardians. All medicines must be kept in a locked cabinet (a locked box may be placed in the refrigerator if medication must be kept cold) and away from all the children. Usually the director or designated staff member *administers* (gives out, applies, or dispenses) the appropriate *dosage* (amount) and keeps a record of time, date, and circumstance. This record is then placed in the child's file after the course of medication is completed.

When administering medication, remember to follow these simple rules:

1. Apply ointments with an appropriate applicator, not the fingers.

2. Check the date on the label to ensure freshness.

3. Give medication at the prescribed times.

4. If a child is unable to swallow tablets, dissolve or crush them, or mix them with good-tasting food.

5. Match the medicine with the right child (always check the name on the label).

6. Never give medicine from an unlabeled container.

7. Read the label and instructions carefully before giving any medication to a child.

8. Return unused medicine to parents or pour it in the sink and wash out the container before throwing it in the trash.

9. Shake liquid medicine before measuring.

10. Use a medicine dropper for infants and toddlers.

11. Use the procedure specified in the directions when administering medicine.

Signs of Illness

Small children may experience discomfort and pain yet be unable to describe the symptoms to caregivers. *Headache* and *tummyache* may be words the children relate to illness, but the head and stomach may not be the areas affected. Due to lack of experience, children often use words inappropriately. It is important that caregivers be familiar with the daily habits and *dispositions* (emotional attitudes) of children in order to accurately discern abnormalities.

The common headache often precedes or accompanies illness. Viral infections are associated with pain in the forehead or behind the eyes. Muscle tension headache, which children can experience, is located in the back of the head, neck, and shoulders. Visual problems, eye strain, and eye muscle tension can also cause headaches. Report continual and progressively worse headaches to parents and suggest that medical advice be sought. Any pain that is experienced by children (such as an earache or a sore throat), vomiting, a rash, diarrhea, fever, and teething also should be reported immediately to the parents or guardians.

Look for the following characteristics to identify an unhealthy child:

- complaints of constant pain
- *convulsions* (spells in which the body stiffens and twitches)
- dental problems, cavities, or sores in the mouth
- dirty hair, scalp, and nails
- earaches or discharge from the ears
- excessive thinness or fatness
- excessive perspiration

- *fatigue* (tiredness)
- *fainting* (brief period of unconsciousness)
- fever, a flushed and dry face
- frequent sore throats and colds
- inability to hear
- hoarse voice and swollen glands
- *lethargy* (abnormal drowsiness, laziness, or indifference)
- *nausea* (a sense of needing to vomit)
- nosebleeds or constantly running nose
- paleness or cold skin
- poor muscle coordination
- poor *posture* (alignment of the body)
- rashes, bruises, unusual scars, or injuries
- runny, red, or crusted eyes
- *strabismus* (squinting or crossed eyes) or *amblyopia* (lazy eye)
- unclean body or clothing

Certain behaviors may also indicate an unhealthy child. Look for:

- child rubbing eyes continually
- emotional disturbances
- excessive use of the toilet
- irritability
- lack of fine and gross motor coordination
- negative attitudes
- nervousness
- restlessness
- speech defects
- trouble getting along with others

Also be aware of certain habits, such as:

- lack of physical activity
- poor eating habits
- poor sleep habits

Substance Dependency

Children born of a mother who abuses substances such as alcohol, cigarettes, or drugs will usually experience withdrawal symptoms upon birth. *Premature birth* (birth before maturity), low birth weight, irritability, excessive crying episodes, difficulty sucking or taking nourishment, and *failure to thrive* (not showing normal development) are characteristics of substance-dependent babies.

Caregivers need to be especially nurturing of such children. Spend extra time to be sure these children are receiving adequate nourishment and sleep, as well as additional activities and encouragement for physical, intellectual, social, and emotional development. Because these children are more susceptible to illness, it is imperative that the caregivers insist upon receiving current medical information. Daily communication with the parents about the children's progress can show support for the family.

ABNORMALITIES

The following descriptions of abnormalities include signs for caregivers to be aware of when working with children. These conditions can usually be corrected if detected early and treated properly. The examples included are by no means all the deviations. They are merely some of the more common disabilities with which you should be familiar.

Vision

Within a few weeks of birth, infants become more alert and responsive to their surroundings. If there is no response to light or movement of objects, infants may have defective vision. During the first three months, infants may not be able to coordinate eye movement. However, this condition usually corrects itself by six months. If eyes turn in or out regularly after this time, a doctor should be consulted immediately.

Children are usually unable to detect their own eye problems because they cannot differentiate between good and poor eyesight. Preschoolers may show signs of eye problems by holding their heads too close to the paper, squinting regularly, stumbling, or continuously exhibiting uncoordinated movements. Children in this age group should have a vision screening. Early detection of sight difficulties increases children's success rate at school.

Usually by school age, visual problems are detected and in the process of being corrected. However, a small percentage may have gone unnoticed. Children who need to move closer to the blackboard or are unable to read may need a vision screening.

Strabismus, or crossed eyes, is a problem that must be treated immediately. It is not self-correcting. This condition makes the child see two different images. In order to focus on only one image, the child will stop using one eye. The condition may become impossible to correct.

Figure 5-10: It is important to have a vision test at an early age.

In *amblyopia,* or lazy eye, one eye is dominant and the other eye is seldom used. It has been estimated that one out of every twenty-five preschool children has this defect. The defect usually develops in young children, and it must be treated while they are still young. Symptoms may include rubbing the eyes excessively, closing or covering one eye, and tilting or thrusting forward the head when looking at an object. Frowning or blinking, difficulty playing games that require good distance sight, and stumbling over small objects are further indications. Doctors usually recommend that the dominant eye be covered with a patch to force the use of the recessive, lazy eye. Exercises, glasses, or surgery may also be used to correct the vision.

Hearing

It is estimated that one out of every three thousand babies born has a hearing problem (Gardephe, *Healthy Kids*, "Hear, Hear!", 1989.) A hearing test given to a new-born can indicate if the child is *deaf* (lacks hearing) or the percentage of hearing in each ear. Rehabilitation is possible, in some cases, if hearing problems are detected early.

Middle-ear infection is often the reason behind mild to moderate hearing losses in the toddler and preschool-age child. An estimated one-third of all children experience this infection three or four times a year by the age of three. Colds, flu, and allergies are the most common situations for ear infection to occur. (White and Shelov, *Healthy Kids*, "Is Your Baby's Hearing Normal?", 1990.)

Speech defects and emotional setbacks are often the result of inadequate hearing. Young children model speech from the people around them. If they cannot hear, there is a definite communication gap. Thus they may feel frustrated and lonely.

Hearing loss can be caused by the simple accumulation of wax in the ear, *perforation* (hole) in eardrum, or *inflammation* (redness, pain, heat, or swelling). These conditions are relatively easy to remedy. Cleaning the insides of the ears by the doctor, the insertion of drainage tubes, and the removal of the tonsils and adenoids are common solutions. Severe hearing loss may require the use of a hearing aid. Caregivers should never insert anything in children's ears, even cotton swabs.

A child in your care who does not respond to noise by turning toward the sound, who always positions the head so that one ear is facing the source of sound, or who has dif-

Figure 5-11: A professional administers a hearing test.

ficulty following spoken directions may have a hearing loss. Document your observations and request a conference with the parents.

Teeth

Children who are served meals in a child care facility should be provided with a personal, labeled toothbrush. Brushing teeth should become a habit after each meal. Tooth decay, irritation of the gums, and plaque forming on the teeth can be caused by food debris. These conditions can cause a decline in the overall health of the children.

Hold infants being given a bottle. Never prop up bottles or give bottles to infants in the crib. Milk or juice can puddle around the gums and can cause permanent damage to the *tooth buds* (teeth below the gums). This condition is called bottle mouth. Always wipe the gums gently with a warm wash cloth after feeding. Note that *pediatricians* (doctors who treat children) do not recommend adding sugar or honey to water in the bottle.

For children of all ages, eliminating sugar ingredients, including corn syrup, honey, and fruit sugar (fructose) in snacks and meals helps to preserve teeth. When planning meals, avoid sweetened drinks, candies, syrups, jams, and confections. Sugar can become a hard habit to overcome.

Occasional observation of the teeth by caregivers is important. Any abnormalities should be reported at once to the parent.

Legs and Feet

Infants often exhibit toeing in of the feet and bowed legs. This is caused by the position of the child in the womb, where the infant's legs are pressed close to the chest and the feet are tucked into the body. *Diaper gait* (bowed legs) is a normal condition for toddlers as they learn to walk. This is due to the fact that the leg bones are still soft and the need to support the weight of their bodies. These conditions are usually remedied by time and exercise. If toeing in or out, bowed legs, flat feet, or tip toeing persists into the preschool years, children should be checked by their pediatrician.

Knock-knee (knees close together) is common in preschoolers. However, if the condition is not self-corrected by elementary school age, medical attention should be sought. By observation, caregivers can be aware of awkwardness of walking, running, or climbing to identify a suspected problem.

RESOURCES

It is often necessary to refer parents to an appropriate agency in order for children to receive the proper health care and attention. Each community has its own resources. Caregivers should investigate and maintain a list of referrals. Health resources may include the following:

- American Arthritis Foundation
- American Diabetic Association
- American Red Cross
- child and adolescent health services
- churches
- county and state health departments
- Department of Health and Human Resources
- developmental services
- Easter Seals
- free immunization clinics
- local school districts
- March of Dimes
- Salvation Army

Counseling resources may include the following:

- adoption agencies
- Children's Aid Society
- Family Services
- Legal Aid Society
- mental health services
- Parents Anonymous

Emergency resources may include:

- American Trauma Society
- child abuse hot lines
- hospitals
- House of Ruth (for battered women)
- rape, suicide, and drug hot lines

Abnormalities can be present in any child. Observant caregivers document irregularities and discuss suspected health problems with the director or principal. Everyday illnesses such as colds, flu, and fever are most often easy to detect and treat. Professional caregivers look beyond the obvious for symptoms of hearing or vision loss, or physical impairments.

Abnormalities in vision, hearing, teeth, and extremities can be determined and sometimes corrected at an early age. Suspected problems, such as drug and alcohol use, depression, and suicidal tendencies should be discussed with parents immediately.

Daily health checks can help detect signs of communicable illnesses such as colds, influenza, and viral infections. The isolation of ill children helps to keep diseases from spreading to others. Good health practices by staff and children help prevent the spread of disease.

It is important to maintain a file of community resources in order to refer parents or guardians to helpful services. These resources should include health, counseling, and emergency agencies.

SUMMARY

Health can be defined as physical and mental well-being, and freedom from pain, defect, or disease. It is the condition of one's body and mind. Caregivers must be observant for any health problems.

To provide security and stability to the children, the staff must stay healthy. Caregivers should avoid being absent unless they have a communicable illness. A positive attitude, a sense of enjoyment, and respect for others are some of the characteristics of good mental health when working with young children.

Happy, active children with an enthusiasm for learning are exhibiting healthy traits. Proper hygiene, good eating habits, and appropriate dress are learned most easily by example. Immunizations and physical examinations are a requirement before enrollment in school.

Review Questions

1. Why is it necessary for a staff member to have a physical examination?

2. What are symptoms of tuberculosis?

3. What emergency numbers should be kept by the phone?

4. At what specific times of the day should both staff and children wash their hands?

5. Define: DPT, TOPV, and MMR.

6. What conditions can cause stress and tension in young children?

7. What are some of the signs of substance abuse?

8. Why is it important to give daily health checks?

9. What is strabismus and amblyopia?

10. Why is it necessary to have a list of resources?

Things to Do and Discuss

1. Visit a children's center and note the hygiene practiced by the staff and children.

2. Discuss the association between health and learning.

3. Observe and note healthy characteristics of two children.

4. Research further and report on one of the following subjects (include healthy and unhealthy aspects):
   - alcohol
   - drugs
   - hearing
   - legs and feet
   - speech defects
   - suicide
   - teeth
   - vision

5. Establish a file of resources in your community. List services for health, counseling, and emergencies.

6. What would you do if:
   a. a normally happy child suddenly appeared extremely nervous, depressed and withdrawn from others?
   b. you found a fourth grader smoking in the bathroom?
   c. you observed a child in your room who squinted, rubbed his eyes, consistently moved closer to a speaker, and had illegible handwriting?

CHAPTER 6
Basic First Aid

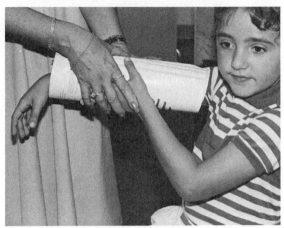

A magazine can be used to splint an arm.

OBJECTIVES

After completing this chapter, you will be able to:

1. define shock, wound, burns, poison, and common emergencies;
2. discuss symptoms and treatment for shock, wounds, burns, poisoning, and common emergencies;
3. demonstrate the application of direct pressure to stop bleeding and first aid for fractures.

KEY TERMS

abrasions
anaphylactic shock
avulsions
brachial pressure
chemical burns
comminuted fracture
compound
  comminuted fracture
compound fracture
concussion
convulsions
dehydration
deformity
direct pressure
elevate
fainting
femoral pressure
first aid

fracture
frostbite
greenstick fracture
heat exhaustion
heat stroke
hypothermia
incisions
incoherence
indirect pressure
lacerations
poison
punctures
simple fracture
shock
sprain
strain
tourniquet
wound

INTRODUCTION

This chapter highlights the basics of first aid. However, it is not meant to take the place of an official first aid course. Anyone involved in the care of young children should seek formal certification. Health departments, the American Red Cross, and hospitals offer courses in emergency care. Knowledge, and confidence in handling unexpected occurrences can possibly make the difference between life and death, temporary and permanent disability, or short- and long-term recovery.

First aid is the immediate and temporary care given the victim of an accident or sudden illness before the services of a physician can be obtained. Accidents happen without warning. As the caregiver, you need to remain calm and in control of your emotions. Be careful of your words and facial expressions. You must demonstrate to the child your willingness to help and show confidence in your abilities.

GENERAL DIRECTIONS FOR FIRST AID

The caregiver should relate to the child's mind and spirit as well as to the physical injuries. Determine the most serious injury, and treat that first. Remember to comfort the child. First and foremost—DO NOT PANIC!

When discovering an injury you should do the following:

1. Rescue the child from the dangerous situation.

2. Determine if the child is breathing. Administer CPR (cardiopulmonary resuscitation) if necessary.

3. Stop excessive bleeding.

4. Give other first aid as indicated by the injury.

5. Always treat for shock.

6. Be ready to exert yourself, and be prepared to direct others.

7. Ask another person to notify the parents, doctor, or to dial 911 for an emergency squad if the injury warrants such action.

8. Provide for supervision of the other children in the center.

Keep the victim lying down to reduce the chance of shock (see the section on shock). Do not disturb or move the child unnecessarily. Keep the body temperature from dropping by placing a warm cover over the child.

Figure 6-1: A teacher questions a child about how he became injured.

Check for severe injuries and consciousness. If the child is conscious, ask what happened and observe the reaction to the accident (determine coherency). Look for surface injuries first—fractures, lacerations, and head injuries. Internal injuries may also be present, but they are harder to detect. If you suspect internal injury, immediate medical attention is essential. Keep injured parts motionless.

To allow free breathing, loosen any clothing that may bind the child, but do not pull on the belt in case of spinal injury. Check the child's appearance. Is skin color pale or flushed? Press on the child's fingernails to determine the amount of oxygen in the blood. When pressure is released, the color should appear rosy.

Check the pulse by placing your fingertips against the carotid artery at the side of the neck. Use the tips of your index and middle fingers only. Press gently to see if blood is circulating. Observe the chest for signs of movement to indicate breathing. If the child is not breathing, start CPR immediately. Once started, you must not stop until a qualified person, such as a doctor, nurse, or ambulance attendant relieves you (see Chapter 7 for CPR directions).

Check for head injuries. Are the child's pupils of equal size? Do they appear larger or smaller than normal? Do the eyes look dull, or do they have expression? Is there any bleeding from the nose, mouth, or ears?

Next, check the child's trunk, arms, legs, and head for any open cuts or abrasions. Are there any fractures? Fractures must be kept free from any movement. To stop the flow of blood, apply pressure and *elevate* (raise) the injury. Determine if any emergency dressings are necessary.

After ensuring the child's safety, and if not endangering the child's life, wash your hands thoroughly in order to reduce the chance of infection to any injuries.

Caregivers must stay calm and be ready to give directions to others nearby. Dial 911 if emergency help is indicated (911 is the standard emergency phone number for ambulance, fire, or police). Dial 0 for operator if there is no 911 number for your area. Give the name, address, phone number, number of victims, nature of injury, and your name.

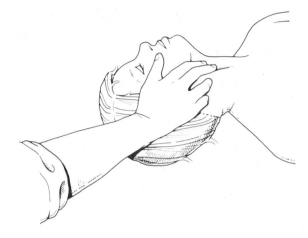

Figure 6-2: Check for a pulse by placing your index and middle fingers against the neck at the carotid artery.

SHOCK

Shock is a depressed condition of many of the body functions due to failure of enough blood to circulate through the body following an injury or trauma. This condition, by itself, can cause death. Severe injury, stress, loss of

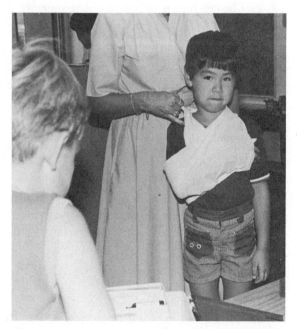

Figure 6-3: School-age students can learn first aid skills.

fluids, infection, lack of oxygen, heart attack, stroke, or poisoning may induce shock. Always treat for shock when first aid is required.

Shock may be shown by various symptoms. Look for the following symptoms of shock:

- dilated pupils
- nausea
- pale, cold, and moist skin
- shallow and irregular breathing
- vacant eyes
- weak or absent pulse

Treat shock with first aid. First aid for shock may include the following:

1. Keep the child lying down, but do not insist.
2. Elevate the head and chest if there is no injury or breathing difficulty.
3. Elevate the feet about twelve inches if blood loss is great and there is no injury to the legs or head or if breathing is difficult.
4. Cover the child with a blanket.
5. Do not give the child fluids.

Anaphylactic shock is usually caused by an allergic reaction, such as from bee stings, insect bites, or penicillin. The most apparent symptom is sudden, excessive swelling. This type of shock can occur quickly and cannot be treated by nonmedical personnel. Treatment must be obtained within fifteen minutes. Adrenalin may have to be administered to facilitate breathing. Do not treat this as ordinary shock— call for emergency help immediately.

WOUNDS

A *wound* is a break in the skin or mucous membrane. It is usually caused by external physical force (such as falls, sharp objects, tools, or machinery) and usually extends into the underlying tissue. The objective is to protect wounds from contamination and to control bleeding.

There are five types of open wounds. You should be familiar with each in order to properly give the right attention:

1. *Abrasions* are wounds made by rubbing or scraping the skin. There is usually little bleeding with abrasions.
2. *Incisions* are sharp cuts that tend to bleed freely. The two sides of the wound are clean and straight.
3. *Lacerations* are jagged or irregular wounds. They usually include much tissue damage. They can become contaminated easily. Lacerations usually bleed freely.
4. *Punctures* are deep, small holes such as those from a splinter, nail, or bite. As a very deep puncture wound will close at the top, leaving a pocket of germs at the bottom of the hole; do not remove the object until medical help is obtained. These wounds often have limited bleeding and are therefore hard to clean.
5. *Avulsions* are torn or separated tissue with extensive bleeding. For avulsions, seek medical attention if necessary. Reattachment of the tissue may require surgery.

First aid for wounds includes the following:

1. Flush the wound with warm water.

2. Wash the wound gently with a clean gauze pad. Wipe from the center of the wound to outer edge. Throw away pad after each wipe. This keeps from spreading contamination to other parts of the wound. Use a small amount of soap.

3. Flush the area again with warm water.

4. Cover the wound with a clean dressing that is larger than the wound and covers all the edges.

5. Seek medical attention if necessary.

Bleeding

Do not use a tourniquet (a device to stop the flow of blood) unless all other attempts to stop bleeding have failed and the child's life is in danger! A tourniquet stops all blood and nourishment to the wound and causes death to the tissues in that part of the body. A tourniquet can cause blood clots to form and cause shock. If use of a tourniquet is indicated, however, it should be at least two inches wide. Wrap it tightly between the wound and the heart. Do not undo the tourniquet once it is applied. Get medical attention immediately.

To stop severe bleeding, place a clean cloth over the wound and apply firm and constant *direct pressure* by placing a hand over a clean cloth. Do not remove the first blood-soaked cloth, just apply a new cloth over the old one as to not disturb blood clots. Secure the cloth with a bandage after the bleeding has slowed.

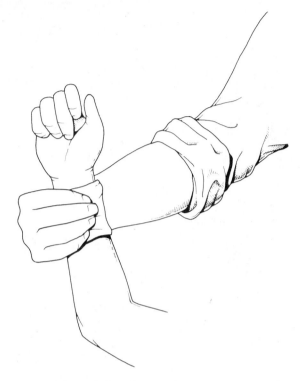

Figure 6-4: Apply firm, direct, and constant pressure against a wound that is bleeding severely.

Elevate the wound above the heart if possible. This will slow down the bleeding. Keep applying pressure.

If an artery appears to be affected by the wound, *indirect pressure* may be necessary. For severe injuries to the arms and hands, find the *brachial pressure* point on the inside of the upper arm. Place the inside flat surface of the fingers between the biceps and the triceps of the arm. Place the thumb on the other side of the arm. Press firmly and constantly until the flow of blood slows down or stops. Elevate the wound.

a)

b)

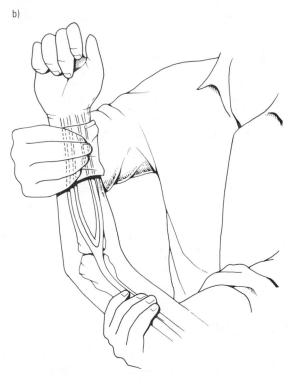

Figure 6-5: If direct pressure is not sufficient to stop severe bleeding, apply brachial pressure—grasp the upper arm firmly and compress the artery.

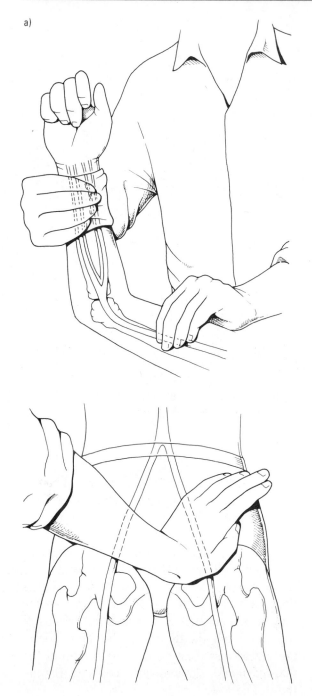

Figure 6-6: If the wound is in the leg or foot and direct pressure does not stop the severe bleeding, apply femoral pressure by placing the heel of your hand against the femoral artery.

Use *femoral pressure* at the upper thigh near the groin for severe injuries to the legs and feet. Place the heel of your hand against the femoral artery. Press firmly and constantly until the flow of blood slows down or stops. Elevate the wound.

Infections

The second danger to wounds is infection. It takes about three days from when the wound is contaminated to the onset of noticeable infection. Symptoms of infection include redness, fever, tenderness, swelling, and warmth.

Red streaks up an arm are signs of serious infection. The streaks are the veins of the lymph nodes carrying white corpuscles to fight the disease. Streaks may also be found in the underarms, along the jaw line, down the neck, and in the groin area.

If possible, wash your hands before attending to the wound. This helps to eliminate or reduce the bacteria which causes infections. Cleanse wounds by holding the limb down, pointed toward the sink. This prevents germs from flowing back into the wound. Wipe from the center of the wound outward with the gauze pad. Discard the pad and use a new pad to again wipe the wound from the center outward. Each time you wipe, use a new pad. Do not wipe in a circular motion. This will spread the contamination.

To bandage a wound, use a dry sterile dressing. The dressing should be large enough to extend beyond the wound edges. Use at least four layers of cloth over the wound. Secure the ends of the cloth firmly, but not too tightly, with dressing or tape. Avoid touching the surface of the bandage.

Bites

Whether by human or animal, bites can cause punctures, lacerations, or avulsions. They can become easily infected. Tetanus shots should be updated periodically to help alleviate the risk of infection.

The human mouth is a source of germs. If a human bite breaks the skin, thoroughly cleanse and flush the area. Cover it with a sterile dressing. If the bite is severe, get medical help immediately to avoid infection.

Animal bites can transmit rabies, a serious disease that can cause death. Suspected rabies needs immediate medical attention. Bites on the face or neck are the most serious. Restrain any suspected animal—try not to kill the animal. Treatment before the onset of the illness is 95 percent effective in preventing rabies.

INJURIES CAUSED BY ACCIDENTS

Because children like to explore and experiment within their environment, they are susceptible to falls and injuries. Even though a school atmosphere is planned with safety in mind, accidents do occur. You, the caregiver, need to know how to handle common emergencies until medical attention arrives.

A major cause of injury to infants is falling from tables or from cribs that have their sides down. Never leave an infant unattended. Always keep one hand placed firmly on a child. Falling can cause death in young children. Other safety precautions to prevent falls include:

1. Keep the stairs and landings free of clutter.

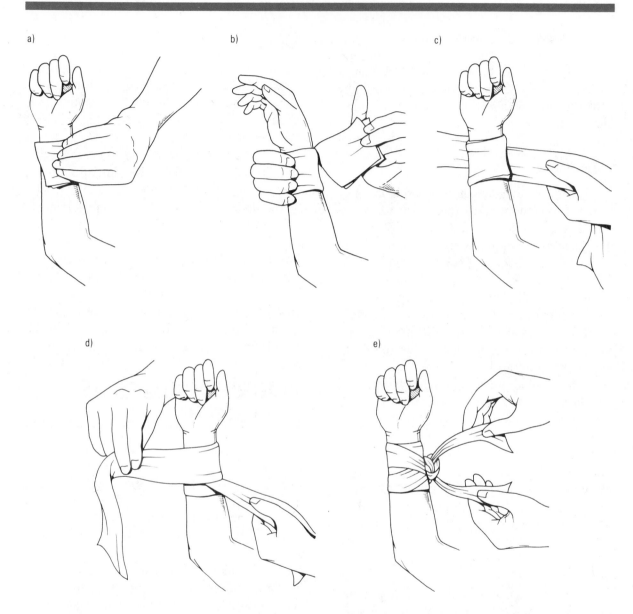

Figure 6-7: *Wrap a wound with a clean cloth or a bandage
and tie it securely.*

2. Hold on to the banister.

3. Place a gate at the top and bottom of the stairs.

4. Keep a harness or safety strap on an active baby in the carriage or stroller.

5. Never leave a baby unattended in a carriage or on a bed.

Fractures

A *fracture* is a break in a bone. The bone should not be allowed to move in order to keep the broken sections and the adjacent joints from causing more damage to the surrounding tissue.

If you are unsure whether an injury is a sprain or a break, treat it as if it is a break. Talk to the child and others who witnessed the accident and get information about what happened.

There are several types of fractures:

1. A *simple fracture* is a closed fracture that does not go through the skin.

2. A *compound fracture* is a break in a bone that also breaks through the skin. A compound fracture must be treated for both infection and bleeding. Be sure that the dressing does not cut off the circulation.

3. A *greenstick fracture* is a chip or break on one side of a bone caused by a bend on the other side.

4. A *comminuted fracture* is several breaks in a bone.

Figure 6-8: Children often want to explore unsafe areas.

5. A *compound comminuted fracture* is several breaks in a bone, one or more of which stick through the skin.

The most obvious symptom of a fracture is pain. Swelling, tenderness, and frequently *deformity* (abnormal formation or shape) often occur. Compare the area of the suspected fracture with the other side of the body to determine any difference. Touch gently to try to find the point of break. The pain should be localized. Do not ask the child if he can move the suspected fracture. You can cause a simple fracture to become a more serious injury.

First aid for a compound fracture includes controlling the bleeding by applying indirect pressure. Keep broken ends and the adjacent joints from moving by applying a splint. To splint, use any sturdy material such as a thick magazine, long blocks, or a broom handle. Tie the splint securely, placing any knots away from the break. Be careful not to cut off the circulation. Elevate the fracture to reduce swelling.

Head Injuries

Some of the major causes of head injuries are automobile accidents, heads bumping together, or impact against a wall or floor. To understand the extent of the injury, you must first determine how the accident happened. Ask others because the injured child may not know what happened.

Symptoms of a head injury include swelling, usually at the front of the head. Unconsciousness for either a short or long period of time is another symptom. Watch the child's pupils carefully for an extended period of time. Check both eyes to see if the pupils go from large to small. Make sure they react in the same way. If they react unequally, there may be a head injury.

Incoherence (inability to answer questions logically) or speech difficulties may also indicate a head injury. Look for any bleeding from an ear, the nose, or the mouth. Check to see if the child's face is flushed. Is the pulse rapid yet hard to detect? Does the child have a

headache? Is the child dizzy? Is the child unable to control the bladder or bowels? Is the child vomiting?

First aid for a head injury includes checking to see if the child is breathing. Give CPR if necessary.

Have the child lie flat. Check for any neck injuries. If there is no neck injury, then raise the head and shoulders by placing a pillow or folded blanket beneath the head. If the brain is bruised and blood rushes to the injury, the child may become unconscious.

Treat for shock. Turn the head to one side in case of vomiting. Loosen clothing. Do not allow the child to drink any liquids. If there is bleeding, apply a bandage with gentle pres-

Figure 6-9: The caregiver points to 911 while teaching a lesson on safety and first aid.

sure. While waiting for medical help to arrive, keep a close watch on the child's breathing.

Concussion

A *concussion* is a type of head injury usually caused by a violent blow or impact. This impels the brain to bump against the skull. Although no one really understands exactly what happens to the brain at this time, the child may lose consciousness for a while.

Symptoms of concussion include headache, dizziness, confusion, restlessness, lack of coordination, unresponsiveness, loss of consciousness, loss of bladder or bowel control, vomiting, or uneven dilation of the pupils of the eye.

In case of concussion, keep the child lying down. If there is no suspected neck injury, elevate the head and shoulders. Treat the child for shock.

Sprains

A *sprain* is any injury to the ligaments around a joint. Symptoms include swelling, tenderness, and discoloration. Treat a sprain as if there is a break. Keep the part immobile. Elevate the injury. Loosen the clothing around the injury. Apply cold compresses, but do not use ice. Always have an X-ray to check for a fracture.

Strains

A *strain* is any injury to muscles or ligaments due to overuse. Symptoms include pain when the part is moved and tenderness to touch. In case of a strain, restrict the movement of the area and apply warm compresses.

BURNS

Burns can be caused by many conditions, such as scalding liquids, playing with matches, spills from stoves, or chemicals. Treatment is used to stop the burning process, restrict the blood to the area, and to retard scarring. There are three degrees of burns. The treatment differs depending on the type:

1. With first degree burns, the skin is red and tender. First aid for first degree burns includes applying cold compresses or placing the part in cold water. Apply a dressing if necessary.

2. With second degree burns, there are blisters on the skin. Place the burned part in cool water until the pain stops. Apply dampened, cold compresses (pads for pressure). Then pat the place dry carefully. Do not rub it! Apply dry, sterile dressing. Do not disturb blisters or the injured area. Elevate burned arms or legs.

3. Third degree burns involve destruction of the underlying tissues of the skin. Do not remove burned clothing—this will disturb the burns. Cover the burns with sterile, dry dressings. Elevate the burned limbs above the heart. If the head is burned, elevate it and check for breathing problems. If the burned area is large, do not immerse it; rather, apply cold packs. Get medical attention immediately.

Always wash your hands before treating any burned area in order to lessen the chance of infection. Never use ice. Ice may cause the

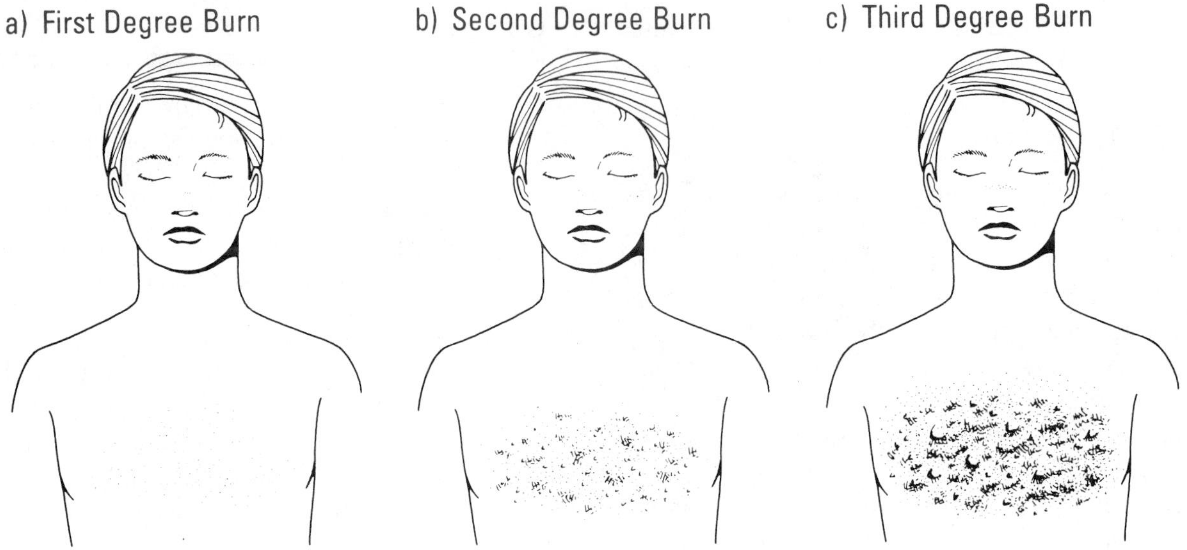

a) First Degree Burn   b) Second Degree Burn   c) Third Degree Burn

Figure 6-10: Burns.

tissue temperature to drop too quickly and thus cause damage to the surrounding tissue. Never use petroleum products or butter. They promote bacterial growth and retain heat to the injured parts. In addition, later removal of the petroleum product or butter may cause more damage to the area. Give burn victims some fluid if less than ten percent of the body is burned.

Sunburns

Sunburns are caused by the ultraviolet rays of the sun. Be aware of the danger of permitting children to play for long periods of time in direct sunlight. Sunburns are uncomfortable, and sometimes painful, for young children. People with sensitive skin should always wear a sunscreen and limit their exposure time to the sun.

Treat sunburns as you would first or second degree burns, depending on the severity. If blisters form, the child should wear a white shirt or blouse to reduce the chance of infection caused by dyes. Do not open blisters.

Chemical Burns

Chemical burns are burns that can be caused by either acids or alkalis. Both can cause severe damage unless they are treated properly. If possible, read the label of the product causing the burn to determine the type of burn.

Acid burns can be caused by many solutions used for cleaning or by gasoline. Flush acid burns with large amounts of water in order to stop the burning process. Remove any clothing contaminated with the acid. Treat the burn as a regular burn by applying cold water. Seek medical attention immediately.

For acid burns to the eye, turn the head to the side. The injured eye should be facing down. Flush it with water for at least five minutes. Be sure to wash the eye, eyelid, and face. Cover the eye with a dry, clean dressing, being careful not to rub the eye. Seek medical attention promptly.

Alkali burns can be caused by detergents and other cleaning solutions. Wash alkali burns with cold water. *However, this does not stop the burning process.* Remove any clothing contaminated with the alkali. Cover the burn with a dry dressing. Seek medical attention promptly.

For alkali burns to the eye, turn the head to the side and flush the injured eye with water for at least *fifteen* minutes. Remove any stray particles with gauze or a clean cloth. Cover the eye with a dry, clean dressing, being careful not to rub. Seek medical attention promptly.

ILL EFFECTS OF HEAT AND COLD

Extreme heat and cold can also cause ill effects. Heat can cause heat stroke or heat exhaustion. Extreme cold can cause frostbite or hypothermia.

Heat Stroke

Heat stroke is a condition caused by higher than normal body temperature and disruption of the cooling properties of the body. This can be fatal, so medical help should be given quickly. Heat stroke may happen suddenly or gradually.

Symptoms of heat stroke include a body temperature of up to 106 degrees Fahrenheit; red, hot, dry skin; a rapid pulse; delirium, convulsions; and unconsciousness. To treat heat stroke, cool the body rapidly by applying cold packs to the arms and underarms (pulse areas). Cover the child with moist, cool sheets, or submerge the child in a tub. Face the child to a fan or air conditioner. For a conscious child, slowly give salt and water orally. Get medical attention immediately.

Heat Exhaustion

Heat exhaustion is more common than heat stroke. *Heat exhaustion* is a condition caused by the lack of water in the body to replace fluids lost by sweating. Everyone is susceptible to heat problems caused by extreme exertions or exercise during very hot weather. Symptoms of heat exhaustion include thirst; cool, moist skin; heavy perspiration; confusion; tiredness; headache; cramps; nausea; and dizziness. With heat exhaustion, the person is conscious.

First aid for heat exhaustion should include giving salt and water to drink slowly. Get the person out of the sun and into a shaded area. Apply cold cloths to the forehead, neck, and wrists to lower the temperature, or give an alcohol bath (use one part alcohol to two parts water). Have the person lie down and elevate the feet.

Frostbite

Frostbite is a condition caused by extended exposure to the cold. It usually damages the extremities, such as the fingers, toes, ears, and nose. Symptoms of frostbite include dark, flushed skin at the onset. The skin becomes pale as the frostbite progresses. There is pain in the affected area. Thin blisters appear, then the part feels cold and numb. Drowsiness may occur because of the slow circulation of the blood. Unconsciousness and shock may eventually occur. Frostbite can be terminal.

When a child is suffering from frostbite, cover the child with warm clothing or blankets or submerge the body in tepid water. Warm the body slowly. After warming a part, exercise it gently. If toes or fingers are involved, place a dressing between the digits. Seek medical help quickly. Do *not* rub the affected area (this can damage the skin). Do *not* apply cold compresses, place the child near a heater, break the blisters, or have the child walk if the feet are affected.

Hypothermia

Hypothermia is a condition caused by a drop in the body temperature below 98.6 degrees Fahrenheit. Cooling the blood causes the metabolism to slow down and decreases the amount of oxygen to the tissues. Doctors often induce hypothermia when performing delicate surgery on the heart or brain. Other causes include prolonged exposure to the cold, aging, heart disease, and certain drugs.

Symptoms of hypothermia include semiconsciousness, mental confusion, slow breathing, and slow pulse. First aid consists of immersing the body in a warm bath and gentle massage. This will slowly increase the body temperature. Seek medical attention immediately.

POISONS

A *poison* is a substance causing illness or death when eaten, inhaled, drunk, or absorbed in relatively small quantities. It can be a solid, liquid, or gas. Because small children have a tendency to put objects in their mouths, they are particularly susceptible to poisoning.

Frequent causes of poisoning include lack of supervision, carelessness on the part of an adult, and plants. Many common household and garden plants are extremely poisonous. To help prevent poisoning, supervise children carefully, and keep medicine cabinets and purses under lock and key. Be sure bottles have childproof lids.

In garages and sheds, be sure substances are labeled. Do not store substances in familiar-looking bottles (such as paint thinner in a soda bottle). Remember that fumes can escape from containers with loose caps. Lye, paint, gasoline, turpentine, kerosene, and other products can cause poisoning. In kitchens and bathrooms, store detergents, bleaches, ammonia, acids, glue, and cleaning supplies out of children's reach.

In some cases, the child will inform the caregiver after taking a poison. In other cases, caregivers may observe an open or empty container or bottle. If a child complains of sudden pain or illness, has a strange breath odor, or becomes unconscious, poison may be the cause.

In case of poisoning, read the label on the container for the ingredients. Call the local poison control center, hospital, or 911 and follow the directions carefully. If the victim is conscious and not convulsing, you may be told to dilute the poison by having the victim drink

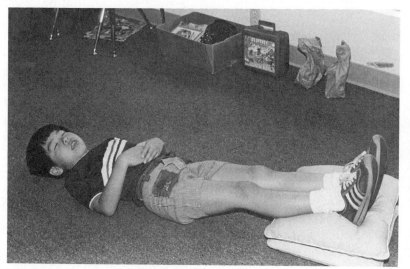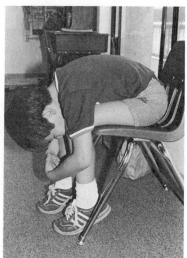

Figure 6-11: To help combat fainting, lie down and elevate your feet or place your head between your knees.

quantities of fluids. Water, milk, and tea are good choices. The most common recommended dosage is four or more glasses for an adult and eight ounces for a child. If the victim is unconscious, do not give fluids, but keep the airway open and give CPR as indicated.

Do not promote vomiting if the child is unconscious or you are unsure of the substance. Poisoning caused by a strong acid (such as carbolic acid), an alkali (such as lye), strychnine, or a petroleum product (such as kerosene, furniture polish, or petroleum jelly) can cause additional damage to the stomach and throat linings if vomiting occurs.

However, if vomiting is recommended but liquids cannot be administered, use a finger or spoon in the mouth to induce gagging. If the substance is unknown and the child vomits, take some of it to the emergency room with the child.

COMMON EMERGENCIES

Simple Fainting

Fainting is a short-term loss of consciousness due to a lack of blood to the brain. Symptoms may include paleness, perspiration, coldness of the skin, dizziness, and nausea. Treatment consists of elevating the feet to allow blood to flow freely to the brain or placing the head between the knees and lower than the heart.

Convulsions

Convulsions are the onset of unconsciousness, characterized by paleness, high body temperature, salivation, and violent jerky movements of the body. Treatment entails keep-

a)

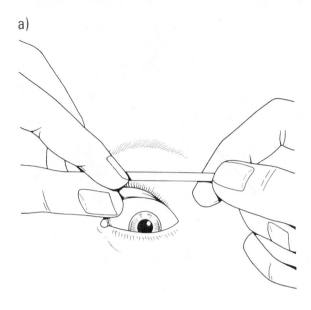

b)

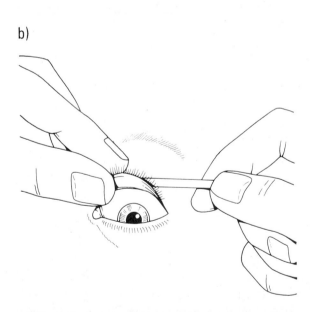

Figure 6-12: Carefully examine the eye for foreign objects. Remove any object carefully with the corner of a clean cloth.

ing the child safe by clearing all objects away from the area where the child may fall. Turn the head to the side to enable particles from the mouth to drain away from the throat. This may appear to be foam, which is a mixture of saliva and oxygen. Loss of bladder and bowel control may occur. Cover the child to avoid shock. Do not try to restrain the child or to place anything in the mouth. Watch the breathing and check the pulse. Seek medical help.

Foreign Objects in Eyes

Sand is a common irritant to the eyes. It is a problem that caregivers ought to feel confident in treating. Other small objects, such as dust and dirt, are frequent concerns because they can cause scratching to the surface or become embedded in the eye.

Tears, or watering of the eyes, often clean particles out. They are nature's way of protecting the child. Keep the child from rubbing the eye. Look closely in the eye to determine where the object is located.

Symptoms of a foreign object in the eye include redness, burning, and pain; headache; and an abundance of tears. Check gently under both lids of the eye to determine the whereabouts of the object. If the object is under the lid, carefully lift the object out with the corner of a gauze pad. Never use tissues, cotton balls, or cotton-tipped swabs. (These will leave particles that will further irritate the eye.)

Sometimes it is necessary to flush the object out of the eye. Turn the child's head to the side so that the eye is facing downward. Flush the object out by pouring water from the inner corner of the eye toward the outside of the head. If an object penetrates the surface of the eyeball, cover the eyes to keep the movement minimized and seek medical attention to remove it.

Foreign Objects in the Nose and Ears

Small children will often put small objects in their noses and ears. Food such as peas and beans, small berries, or beads are typical items. You may notice that the child is having difficulty breathing or hearing, is pulling on the ears or bothering the nose. There may be a strange odor coming from the child. Use a flashlight to check ears and nose. Do not try to remove the object or ask the child to breathe hard through the nose in order to dislodge an object. You may cause the object to become further embedded and surgery may then be needed. Instead, calm the child and seek medical attention quickly.

Obstructed Airway

Foreign objects can lodge themselves in the throat and cause the cessation of breathing. Death can follow quickly, within four to six minutes, unless action is taken.

Small children often explore and experiment by placing objects in their mouths, so be aware of small objects that are in the range of the child. Until the teeth are totally formed, it is also difficult for the young child to chew food into small enough pieces to swallow it easily. Therefore, be careful of the size of the pieces of food served.

Symptoms of an obstructed airway include violent choking, trouble breathing, grasp-ing at the throat with the hands, a blue color to the face, cessation of breathing, and unconsciousness. If the child is conscious, reassure him or her. Try to stimulate coughing by tickling the neck or placing your fingers or a spoon in the mouth. Do not give the child fluids.

If an infant or toddler is not breathing, place the infant face down over your forearm, with the child's head in your hand. Your hand should be lower than the child's heart. Give four abdominal thrusts, pushing upward with two or three of your fingers. If you can observe the object, hold the jaw down and place your little finger in the child's mouth. Sweep the object to the side, being careful not to push the object farther down the throat. If necessary, give CPR to start breathing. If CPR is not effective, start the process over until the child is breathing alone.

When a young child is not breathing, use the sweeping finger method to remove the object if it is visible. If you are unable to dislodge the object, place your arms around the child's waist. Make a fist with your thumb to the inside. Place the fist next to the child's abdomen at the bottom edge of the ribs. Place your other hand over the first and give an upward thrust. Repeat the procedures until the object is dislodged. If necessary, give CPR. The procedure is the same for older children and adults with the exception that you must give harder thrusts. After the airway is cleared, take the child to the emergency room for an X-ray.

Stings and Bites

Stings and bites from insects are among the leading causes of death in America. They

a)

b)

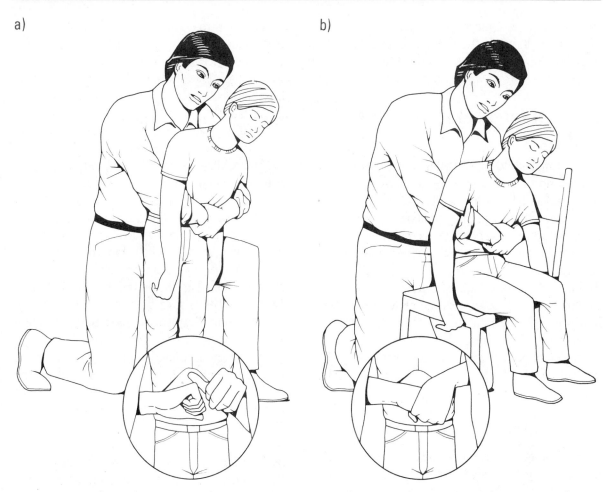

Figure 6-13: Use the Heimlich maneuver to dislodge foreign objects in the throat.

can occur from bees, wasps, yellow jackets, spiders, mosquitoes, fleas, lice, ticks, chiggers, and ants. Insect bites may transmit disease but are not usually fatal to adults. Children, however, can have an allergic reaction to the venom, and this can cause respiratory difficulties.

If symptoms include pain, redness, or swelling, apply cold compresses or soothing lotion to the area of the bite or sting. However, if the symptoms also include a large swollen area, nausea, difficulty breathing, or shock, seek medical attention immediately.

You can remove the stinger from a bee, wasp, or yellow jacket by scraping your fingernail across the area. Do not try to pull the stinger out—it has a barbed end like a fish hook, which may cause a portion to remain embedded in the skin.

Nosebleeds

Common injuries to the nose can cause it to bleed profusely. A sudden blow, high blood pressure, excessively dry or cold weather, high altitudes, or the common cold can all irritate the nose lining, tearing the blood vessels and causing the nose to bleed.

In case of a nosebleed, keep the child calm and quiet, sitting upright, and leaning slightly forward. This keeps the blood from flowing down the throat and causing choking or nausea. Pinch the nostrils with your thumb and forefinger. Hold them for at least twenty minutes. Do not release them to check the flow of blood. Apply cold compresses to the nose and face. If the bleeding does not cease, pack the bleeding nostril or nostrils with gauze. Be sure to leave an end outside the nostril in order to remove the gauze easily. If normal first aid is not effective, seek medical help.

Figure 6-14: For a nosebleed, have the child lean forward slightly and pinch the nose tightly.

Vomiting

There are three types of vomiting. It is important to know the differences in order to give correct information to medical personnel if necessary.

1. *Spitting up.* Infants will occasionally regurgitate a small, curd-like milky substance that dribbles out of the corner of the mouth. This may occur when the young child eats or drinks too quickly, ingests too much food for the stomach size, or the sphincter muscle in the upper region of the stomach is not fully developed and contracts.

2. *Vomiting.* Vomiting is regurgitation of food substances caused by spasms of the body muscles. Feeding difficulties, overfeeding, food allergies, illness, not burping after bottle feeding, or anxieties can cause vomiting. Continued vomiting can lead to *dehydration* (the loss of body fluids). The speed of dehydration depends on the size of the child. Because of small body weight, particularly watch infants for this condition. Seek medical attention immediately for infant dehydration.

3. *Projectile vomiting.* Projectile vomiting is forceful emptying of the stomach contents. It will shoot out of the mouth, sometimes landing several feet beyond. This can occur several times a

day after feedings. Upon examination of a doctor, surgery or change in the child's diet may be required.

In case of vomiting, rest the stomach by stopping all feedings for one or two hours. Observe the child for signs of illness. Then, if the child appears all right, give ice chips, sips of water, or a carbonated beverage cautiously every fifteen minutes. If the vomiting begins again, call the doctor. If vomiting does not return, give small amounts of liquids such as broths, gelatin, juices, or water. Soda crackers or dry toast may be added to the diet later.

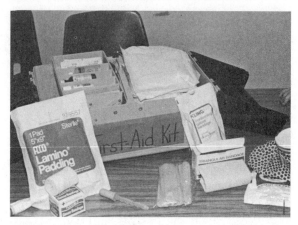

Figure 6-15: A first aid kit should be included in every classroom.

FIRST AID KIT

Every child care center must have a complete basic first aid supply kit. Supplies should be checked and updated regularly to ensure potency and quantity. A first aid book for reference is a necessity. Check your local and state licensing standards for other required items.

Supplies in a first aid kit may include the following:

- absorbent cotton, pads or balls
- adhesive tape, at least one-inch width
- alcohol
- assorted sizes of band aids
- baking soda
- blankets
- clean, sterile gauze rolls of two-inch width
- cold packs
- flashlight
- hot water bottle
- large safety pins
- liquid soap
- petroleum jelly for chapped skin
- scissors
- splints
- sterile gauze pads, two-inch square and four-inch square
- surgical gloves
- thermometers, rectal, oral, or digital
- tongue depressors
- triangular bandages for slings
- tweezers

You do not often have time to look up information on how to deal with emergency situations, yet you need to be able to react quickly and accurately when problems arise. The knowledge gained concerning first aid may make the difference between life and death. It influences how a child perceives your ability to cope with injuries and accidents. A child is often frightened when hurt or when someone else is hurt. A caring, comforting caregiver can calm a child so that the injuries may be properly attended to.

SUMMARY

First aid is the immediate and temporary care given the victim of an accident or sudden illness until the service of a physician can be attained. When discovering an injury, rescue the child, determine breathing, stop excessive bleeding, treat for shock, dial 911 (or other appropriate emergency phone number), and administer appropriate first aid.

If possible and it does not endanger the child's life, take time to wash your hands thoroughly to reduce the chance of transmitting infection. One of the major causes of the spread of disease and infection in a day care center is unclean hands.

Shock is the slowing of the body functions due to lack of blood circulation following a severe illness or injury. Keep the child warm and lying down, and check for breathing difficulties. Always look for and treat shock.

Wounds are any open break in the skin. Five types of wounds are abrasions, incisions, lacerations, punctures, and avulsions. Keep wounds free from contamination or infection, and control bleeding. Do not use a tourniquet unless all other efforts to stop bleeding have failed and the child's life is in danger.

Bites must be cleansed thoroughly to prevent serious infection. Animal bites can transmit rabies, a deadly disease. If possible, retain any suspected animal until it can be checked by the animal control department. Human bites can become easily infected if the skin is broken.

A fracture is a break in the bone. Simple, compound, greenstick, comminuted, and compound comminuted are the five types of fractures. Immobilize the area of a suspected break to keep the ends from moving. X-rays are necessary to determine severity of the break.

Head injuries are commonly caused by falls, heads bumped together, or impact against a wall or floor. Swelling and bleeding are the first indications of a head injury. Treat head injuries for shock and bleeding. Administer CPR if indicated.

There are three types of burns—first degree, second degree, and third degree. Treatment differs depending on severity. The main objective is to stop the burning process, restrict the flow of blood to the burned area, and to retard scarring. Most burns on children are caused by a lack of supervision on the part of the caregiver.

Poisoning can occur when any substance that can cause illness or death is eaten, inhaled, drunk, or absorbed. Check suspected containers for their contents and antidotes. Call the poison control center in your area for specific information. Administer antidotes or treat the child as indicated.

Common emergencies that may occur at a children's center are fainting, convulsions, objects in the eye, throat, nose or ears; bites; stings from insects; nosebleeds; and vomiting. Caregivers must know how to respond to each of these emergencies in order to safeguard the health and welfare of young children.

Review Questions

1. Why is it important to be certified in First Aid?

2. When do you call 911 after discovering a victim?

3. Where is the pulse located?

4. Under what circumstances do you treat for shock?

5. What are the five types of wounds?

6. When is it necessary to use a tourniquet?

7. Where are the pressure points located?

8. What are sources of infection?

9. Why is it necessary to keep a fracture immobile?

10. Should you remove the clothing from a burn victim and why?

11. Where is the First Aid Kit stored?

Things to Do and Discuss

1. Role play the steps necessary to treat simple fainting, an object in an eye, a nosebleed, and vomiting.

2. Take a first aid and CPR courses. Become certified.

3. Demonstrate first aid immobilization of fractures.

4. Take a person's pulse by checking the pressure points.

5. Price supplies necessary for a complete first aid kit.

6. Demonstrate the proper method of dealing with foreign objects in the throat.

CHAPTER 7
Cardiopulmonary Resuscitation (CPR)

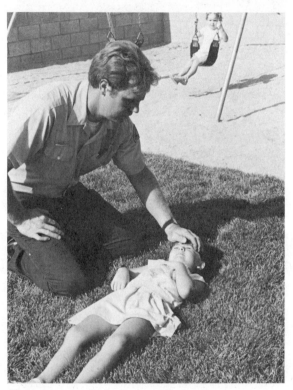

Children can easily become accident victims.

KEY TERMS

brachial pulse
cardiac arrest
cardiopulmonary
  resuscitation
carotid pulse

cholesterol
hemorrhage
respiratory arrest
suffocation

OBJECTIVES

After completing this chapter, you will be able to:
1. discuss the reasons for administering CPR;
2. explain the necessity of taking an official CPR course.

INTRODUCTION

There may only be a few times when it is necessary to perform CPR (*cardiopulmonary resuscitation*) or artificial respiratory action, but these times may save a life. It is important that anyone taking care of young children become certified by taking an official course. This chapter is offered to give you an understanding of that importance and to explain the procedure and principles. *Do not try to perform CPR unless you have passed a course and obtained certification.*

RESPIRATORY RESTORATION

Respiratory arrest is a condition that exists when the breathing stops but the blood continues to circulate. Only artificial respiratory action is necessary when this occurs. The heart is still functioning and circulating the blood to all parts of the body. Convulsions, drowning, poisoning, or severe injury may cause this condition.

Training in a professional class is strongly recommended. It is a precondition for employment in some schools or centers. The following is considered a review for persons who have already been certified and a source of introductory information for others.

To restore breathing:

1. Approach the victim and shake him or her to determine consciousness. Shout the person's name loudly to determine responsiveness. If the victim responds, then he or she is able to breathe without aid.

2. If the victim is unconscious, have someone else call the emergency number, usually 911 or 0.

3. Check for a pulse by using either the *brachial pulse* (on the upper arm) or *carotid pulse* (on the side of the neck). Permanent brain damage can occur within four to six minutes of cessation of breathing.

4. Lay the victim flat on his or her back on a hard surface if other injuries do not inhibit your ability to do so.

5. If unable to establish a pulse, begin artificial respiratory action.

6. Tilt the victim's head backwards in order to clear the passage to the lungs. Be careful of tilting the head

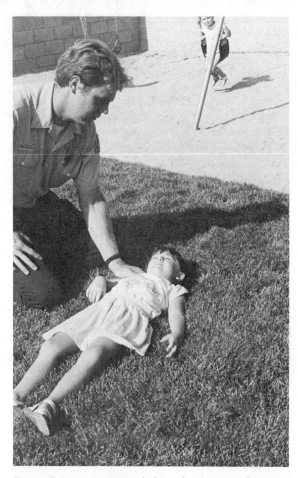

Figure 7-1: A rescuer is shaking the victim to determine responsiveness.

of an infant or small child too far back—you could obstruct the passage. Check the victim's chest to determine if the victim is breathing. Breathing causes movement. Listen and feel for breaths by placing your ear close to the victim's mouth.

a)

b)

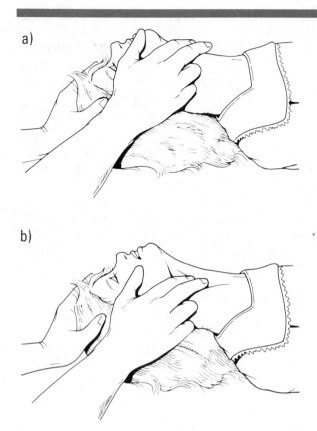

Figure 7-2: The carotid pulse is found on the side of the neck.

Figure 7-3: For the head tilt, place one hand under the neck and lift up; place the other hand on the forehead and push down to point the chin toward the ceiling.

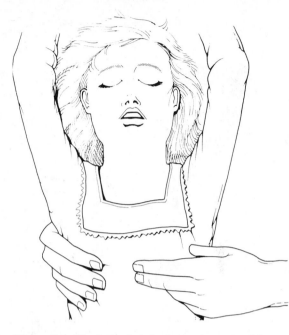

Figure 7-4: Check the victim's chest to determine if there is breathing. If the victim is not breathing, begin artificial respiration.

7. If unable to distinguish breathing in a child over eight years of age, pinch the nostrils closed with your thumb and forefingers and place your mouth over that of the child to form a tight seal. In an infant or small child, cover the mouth and nostrils with your mouth to form a tight seal. In both cases, give two quick breaths. Turn your head to the side to observe chest movement. Keep the side of your head close to the victim's mouth in order to feel air.

8. If you cannot feel air entering the victim's chest, turn the head to the

9. Check for a pulse. If one is present, continue to give one breath every five seconds for children over eight years and adults. Give one breath every four seconds for infants and small children. Each breath should last one to one and a half seconds. Keeping your head close to the child's mouth and nose, turn to observe the chest between breaths to determine if the victim is breathing without aid. Stop giving breaths only when the child's respiration is restored or medical help arrives.

10. After restoring breathing, it is essential that the victim be kept lying down and covered with a blanket to prevent shock. Elevate the feet and legs if no injuries are apparent. Raise the head if the victim has trouble breathing and no injuries are observed. Seek medical attention immediately.

Figure 7-5: After giving artificial respiration, check again for breathing by turning your head to the side and listening for air and looking for movement in the chest.

Figure 7-6: Cover the victim to prevent shock.

side and sweep the victim's mouth with your forefinger to dislodge any foreign particles. Turn the head back to its original position, tilting it back, and again give the victim two full breaths.

CARDIOPULMONARY RESUSCITATION

Cardiopulmonary resuscitation (CPR) is performed when the heart has stopped beating and breathing has ceased. Be sure that cessation has occurred for no longer than six minutes. After six minutes the condition is considered clinical death.

CPR should be started immediately in an emergency. Its purpose is to restart breathing and blood circulation by an artificial means (an outside source, usually another person). Once begun, the process is not to be stopped until emergency personnel arrive, the circulation and respiration have been restored (the victim is able to breathe without artificial support), or the person has been transported to a medical facility. Any victim receiving CPR must be taken as quickly as possible to an emergency center.

Cardiac arrest is the condition when the heart has stopped beating and circulation of the blood has ceased. Pulse and breathing have also disappeared. This is when CPR should begin. The condition may be caused by a heart attack, violent accident, electrical shock, *hemorrhage* (excessive bleeding), or *suffocation* (inability to breathe).

To restore a pulse:

1. Place victim on his or her back on a flat, hard surface.

2. Check for breathing and a pulse.

3. If absent, have someone call 0 or 911.

4. Place your body alongside the victim's and trace the ribs upward with the middle finger and index finger toward the tip of the sternum.

5. Keeping the middle finger at the tip of the sternum, place the heel of the other hand next to the index finger.

6. Place the first hand over the second hand.

7. Begin compressions, being careful to press only to the depth indicated and to maintain the proper number of compressions per minute. *For infants*, press one-half to one inch at a rate of one hundred times per minute. *For children*, press one-half to one inch at

Figure 7-7: For CPR, place your body alongside the victim's.

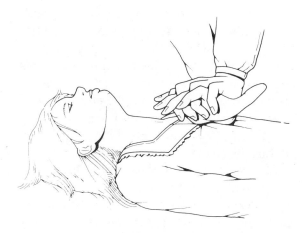

Figure 7-8: For CPR, trace the ribs upward with the middle and index fingers toward the tip of the sternum. Keeping the middle finger at the tip of the sternum, place the heel of the other hand next to the index finger.

a rate of eighty to one hundred times per minute. *For adults*, press one and a half to two inches at a rate of eighty times per minute.

8. To combine artificial respiration and CPR, use the following number of compressions and artificial respiration. *For infants and children*, give five compressions and then one breath. *For adults*, give fifteen compressions and two breaths.

9. Have the victim transported to the hospital as soon as possible.

Unless performed exactly and precisely as you have learned in an official course, CPR may be ineffective. Once begun, CPR must be continued until you are absolutely exhausted or have been relieved by medical personnel. Do not attempt to move the victim to a more convenient place because this may worsen internal injuries.

Heart failure, cardiac arrest, and heart attacks can be prevented through early education on the value of eating low-*cholesterol* (a substance that can line the blood vessels) foods and lower amounts of animal fat. Americans are noted for being overweight and indulging in passive activities, such as television watching, rather than exercising. Although we are starting to change our values and our health habits are improving through the efforts of fitness programs, children need to be encouraged to participate. Through adult example and the availability of proper foods and exercise, children learn the importance of healthy life-styles. Healthy living can reduce the chance of heart attacks and other diseases in adulthood.

Figure 7-9: School-age children exercising during a physical education class.

SUMMARY

Respiratory restoration is performed when breathing ceases and there is still blood circulation. A variety of situations may necessitate reviving a person. There are nine steps that must be followed in a precise manner.

Cardiopulmonary resuscitation (CPR) is performed when both breathing and blood circulation stop. Heart attacks and violent accidents are the most common causes of cardiac arrest.

When performing either of these rescue attempts, remember to remain calm, react in a quick and professional manner, and perform needed emergency measures in a smooth, regular, and uninterrupted sequence. Once begun, do not stop until relieved by medical personnel or you become exhausted. *Do not perform CPR unless you have taken and passed an official course!*

Review Questions

1. What do the initials CPR mean?
2. How long does it take for a victim without oxygen before permanent brain damage occurs?
3. When do you begin CPR?
4. What is cardiac arrest?
5. What can be done to prevent heart failure?

Things to Do and Discuss

1. Take a certified CPR course.
2. Discuss the reasons for performing artificial respiration and CPR.
3. Research the number of emergency cases your local paramedics, emergency room, or police perform each week.
4. Research cholesterol levels in common foods, such as potato chips, dairy products, or red meat, chicken, and fish.

CHAPTER 8
Communicable Diseases

Always wash your hands after each nose wipe.

KEY TERMS

acute
antibiotics
bacteria
communicable illness
contagious
direct transmission
feces
fungicide
incubation
indirect transmission

isolation
jaundice
lesions
low resistance
malaise
prescribed
stress
symptoms
trimester
viruses

OBJECTIVES

After completing this chapter, you will be able to:

1. identify the common childhood diseases;
2. discuss how communicable diseases are transmitted;
3. discuss the treatment of childhood diseases;
4. list the control methods for communicable diseases.

INTRODUCTION

Communicable diseases are a major problem in child care centers. Caregivers must ensure that the environment is kept as germ-free as possible to prevent the spread of diseases. In Chapter 5, we discussed the importance of the daily health check, which is given to each child upon entering the facility in order to spot the onset of illness. However, children may become ill after their arrival at school. Children often are more susceptible to disease than adults because they have not had a chance to build antibodies and immunities to resist disease. Their immature bodies allow more respiratory illness because of close proximity of their ears, nose, and throat.

This chapter identifies common communicable diseases and discusses the procedures for immediate care. You will also learn how to protect other children and staff from contamination and how to maintain the environment to prevent the growth of germs. Caregivers are not responsible for diagnosing or treating an illness, but they are responsible for keeping the child comfortable and informing the parents of the illness and a possible need for medical attention.

COMMUNICABLE ILLNESS

A *communicable illness* is an illness spread either directly or indirectly from person to person, animal to person, or object to person. Three ingredients are necessary for an illness to be transmitted:

1. *Viruses or bacteria. Viruses* and *bacteria* are microorganisms invisible

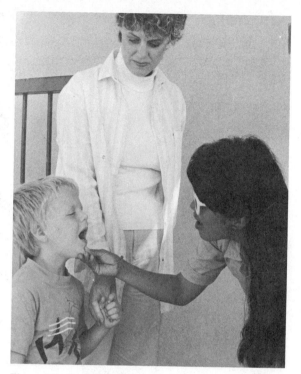

Figure 8-1: Health checks help keep communicable diseases from spreading.

to the naked eye. They can cause specific illnesses.

2. *Low resistance. Low resistance* is susceptibility to illness. It may be caused by tiredness, inadequate nourishment, a weakened condition caused by previous disease or injury, or the absence of immunization against illness. A lack of cleanliness may contribute to susceptibility.

3. *Means for transmission.* Contact with another who has the disease is *direct transmission*. It can occur through the air, or by touching the place of

Figure 8-2: A daily health check is given to the child during the morning greeting.

infection or body by-products, such as blood or feces. *Indirect transmission* is contacting materials previously handled by the infected person, such as toys, tissues, and food.

For disease to be transmitted, all three of the listed conditions must be present. The lack of one condition helps to prevent the spread of illness. Therefore, cleanliness of children, caregivers, and the environment, as well as good health habits, cuts down the distribution of germs. The most common cause of disease in a child care center is the neglect of frequent hand washing.

Progression

The progression of an illness follows a specific pattern. Exposure to an affected person or object is followed by an incubation period. During *incubation,* the disease gains strength in the body. Incubation lasts until visible symptoms are observed. Often this is a time of contamination to others. During this period, it is difficult for caregivers to detect the onset of illness. Incubation periods differ with the illness. They can last for hours, days, or weeks.

A general feeling of unwellness, including headache, slight fever, a sore throat, and irritability, may indicate the onset of infectious disease. Caregivers should pay particular attention to mild complaints by children. Such complaints are usually the first clue.

In the next stage, obvious *symptoms* (conditions that accompany an illness and aid in diagnosis) of illness, such as high fever, diarrhea, vomiting, rash, cough, earache, sore throat, enlarged glands, or a runny nose, can be observed. The child is definitely feeling ill, and the disease may be highly *contagious* (communicable). Rest, fluids, and medication may be recommended at this time.

A recovery period is necessary to allow the child's body to fight the infection and to return to normal. If the child is properly rested and nourished, recovery is automatic. It may take several days or weeks. When the disease is no longer contagious, the child may rejoin the class.

Caregivers' Health

Caregivers help to maintain their own health by eating balanced meals, which provide the proper nutrients. Caregivers' diets should be within the guidelines for their weight and height. Caregivers need to schedule enough hours of sleep and relaxation to be thoroughly rested. They should exercise, too, in order to promote physical well-being.

Mental health also should be stable. Time away from the children (such as breaks and lunch) should be programmed into caregivers' schedules in order to allow their minds and bodies to rest.

TEACHER OBSERVATIONS

Caregivers who know their children well can distinguish when a child is happy at the center and when there is a problem. Unusual behavior on the part of a child may signal the onset of illness. Clues of a probable illness include:

- bad breath
- breathing from the mouth
- breathlessness after moderate exercise
- clumsiness
- depression, unhappiness, irritability, unusual crying
- deterioration of work
- excessive tiredness

Figure 8-3: This child falls asleep while others play nearby.

- frequent scratching
- lack of interest
- loss of appetite

Caregivers who observe these symptoms should talk to the child and listen carefully to the child's answers to determine the health condition. Any deviation in behavior is cause for concern. However, signs may reflect an ongoing allergy condition or a transition at home such as moving, mother returning to work, or cousins visiting.

Isolation

Isolation is indicated when the following symptoms are noticed. They may be signs of a communicable illness:

- achiness
- coughs
- cracked lips
- dark, tea-colored urine
- diarrhea
- dizziness
- enlarged glands
- fever
- gray or white stools
- headache
- nausea
- nose or ear discharge
- open, running, or oozing sores
- pale or flushed skin
- pink eyes
- rash, spots, or lesions

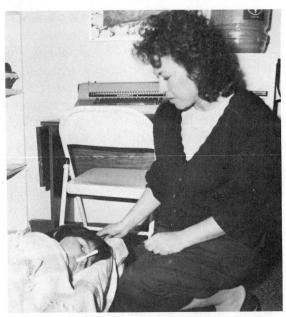

Figure 8-4: This child became ill and waits in isolation for her parents to pick her up.

- red and watery eyes
- sore throat
- vomiting
- yellow skin or eyes

Caregivers who observe these signs in a child should isolate the child to protect others from infection. Make the child comfortable on a cot, and take care of the child's immediate needs. Then call the parents or guardians.

Take the child's temperature if you suspect a fever. A normal body temperature is 98.6 degrees Fahrenheit when taken orally. Fever is considered serious if an oral thermometer registers 100 degrees Fahrenheit or above or if a rectal thermometer registers above 101 degrees Fahrenheit. Reassure the child, and inform the parents so they can assume the principal care of the child. Such care may include seeking medical attention.

Reportable Illnesses

In some counties or states, caregivers are legally responsible for reporting communicable illnesses. Such reports allow the public health officials to quantitate the numbers of people affected with the disease in an area, as well as to alert them to possible major outbreaks of infections. Some of the common reportable illnesses are:

- head lice
- hepatitis
- impetigo
- infectious mononucleosis
- mumps
- pinkeye (conjunctivitis)
- rubella (German measles)
- rubeola (measles)
- salmonella infection
- Shigella infection
- strep infection

It is the duty of any individual having knowledge of a person who has a communicable disease but has not sought medical advice to report the illness to the appropriate health official. This report should include the name and address of the ill person. It is the responsibility of the supervisory personnel of a public or private institution to report knowledge of a person who has contracted a communicable disease to the appropriate health official. Again, you should include the name and address of the affected person.

It is generally the responsibility of the director, principal, or nurse to exclude a person suspected of having a communicable disease from the facility until the contagious period has ended. If a physician, however, examines the person and deems the disease no longer communicable, that person may be allowed to return with the written permission of the doctor.

COMMUNICABLE DISEASES

There are many communicable diseases. Common ones include colds, cold sores (and fever blisters), and influenza. Other communicable diseases are less common, but you should know about them because of their seriousness. The following sections list some of the communicable illnesses you may encounter.

AIDS (Acquired Immune Deficiency Syndrome)

Symptoms

Symptoms include headache, fever, night sweating, diarrhea, rapid weight loss, unexplained bleeding from body openings, easy bruising, and a thick white coating on the tongue and throat. The AIDS virus may attack the brain cells, causing forgetfulness, impaired speech, seizures, and trembling. Pneumonia and Kaposi's sarcoma (a cancer) are later complications that result from the weakened immune system.

Incubation

Incubation may include an inactive period lasting from several months to ten years before the onset of the symptoms.

Communicability

The estimated number of children that will acquire AIDS by 1991 could reach 20,000 (Wilson, 1990). The period of communicability from contact with the virus until death is not known at this time.

Contamination

Contamination is through transference of blood and body fluids, sexual contact, and using infected needles during injections. Unborn children may contract the infection from their mothers.

Control

There is no known cure for AIDS. Therefore, it is important to avoid the exchange of blood and body fluids with people who have been exposed to the virus. Wearing surgical gloves at infant and toddler centers when changing diapers is becoming a common practice.

Chicken Pox

Chicken pox is a form of herpes simplex I.

Symptoms

Symptoms include listlessness, headache, fever, irritability, scratching, nausea, vomiting, and a rash with blisterlike heads appearing first on the trunk and body (the chest, back, and neck). There is scabbing at the later stages.

Incubation

The period of incubation for chicken

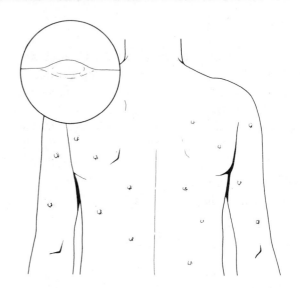

Figure 8-5: Chicken pox have white blisters surrounded by reddish areas.

pox is two to three weeks from exposure, usually thirteen to seventeen days.

Communicability

The period of communicability is usually two to five days before the beginning of the symptoms and until the blisters scab over. Moisture from the blisters is contagious.

Contamination

Contamination is from person to person, from droplets in the air, or from a recently soiled object.

Control

Control for chicken pox involves isolation of the sick child and personal hygiene. Children may return to school only after all blisters have scabbed over.

Cold Sores and Fever Blisters

Cold sores and fever blisters are also forms of herpes simplex I.

Symptoms

Symptoms include painful, clear blisters around the mouth, nose, or genitals, although sores around the genitals are usually herpes simplex II. Physicians can determine whether the infection is type I or II.

Incubation

The period of incubation for cold sores is usually two to twenty days after the virus enters the body.

Communicability

The period of communicability is usually from the development of the virus until the blister disappears.

Contamination

Contamination is from direct contact with another individual.

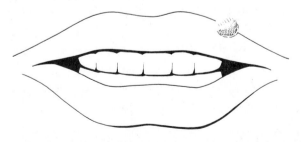

Figure 8-6: Cold sore blisters appear around the mouth. A later stage includes scabbing.

Control

There is no known cure, but an ointment *prescribed* (ordered in writing) by a doctor may lessen the severity of attacks. *Stress* (mental pressure or physical strain) or illness may cause an outbreak. The herpes virus remains in the body at all times. To control herpes, avoid contact with an infected person during outbreaks.

Common Colds

Symptoms

Symptoms of the common cold include a runny nose, slight fever, chills, red and watery eyes, sneezing, achiness, coughing, and fatigue.

Incubation

Incubation is twelve to seventy-two hours, usually twenty-four hours to the onset of the symptoms.

Communicability

The period of communicability is twenty-four hours before the onset until five days after.

Contamination

Contamination may result from contact with an infected person or indirect contact with articles freshly soiled, such as tissues and eating utensils.

Control

To control the cold, observe cleanliness —wash your hands frequently. Avoid contact if possible.

Conjunctivitis (Pinkeye)

Symptoms

Symptoms of conjunctivitis include a red cast to the white portion of the eye, swollen eyelids, itchiness, and a yellowish or watery discharge. There is a white halo effect around the iris.

Incubation

The period of incubation for conjunctivitis is one to three days.

Communicability

The period of communicability is several days to three weeks. Conjunctivitis is highly contagious.

Contamination

Contamination may result from contact with the discharge from an infected eye or contact with objects contaminated with the discharge.

Control

Control of conjunctivitis includes antibiotic ointment applied to the eyes, careful and frequent hand washing, and exclusion of the child from school until all symptoms have disappeared.

Fifth Disease (Erytghema Infectiosum)

Symptoms

Fever and a distinctive, intensely red rash that begins on the face (this disease is sometimes referred to as the "Slapped Face

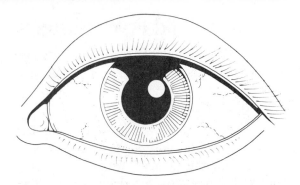

Figure 8-7: In conjunctivitis (pinkeye), the white portion of the eye turns pinkish. The pink does not touch the iris of the eye, and thus it creates a halo effect.

Disease"). After one to four days, a lacelike rash appears on the arms, trunk, buttocks, and thighs. Temperature and exposure to sunlight can intensify the rash.

Incubation

The incubation period is usually between four and fourteen days but can be as long as twenty days.

Communicability

The infected person is most contagious to others before and within a few days after the onset of the illness.

Contamination

The means of spreading the disease is unknown, however, it is thought to be spread by respiratory secretions and blood.

Control

None has yet been identified.

Hand, Foot, and Mouth Disease (Vesicular Stomatitis with Exanthem)

Symptoms

Symptoms include lesions in the mouth, and on the hands and feet. Occasionally there is a rash on the buttocks. Painful sores in the mouth can cause the child discomfort when eating or drinking. A low-grade fever may be present at the onset.

Incubation

The period of incubation is unknown. The disease is usually mild and lasts four to ten days.

Communicability

The disease generally affects children under the age of ten and especially those in preschool or lower elementary grades.

Contamination

The disease is transmitted via respiratory secretions and droplets as well as unclean hands.

Control

Good personal hygiene, including frequent hand washing especially after toileting is important. A child with the disease must be excluded from school during acute illness. Respiratory and stool precautions should be taken.

Hepatitis

Infectious hepatitis (or type A) causes inflammation of the liver.

Symptoms

Symptoms include fever, a loss of appetite, *malaise* (a vague feeling of discomfort or uneasiness), nausea, abdominal discomfort, and *jaundice* (a yellow appearance to the skin and eyes).

Incubation

The period of incubation is ten to fifty days. The average incubation period is twenty-five to thirty days to the onset of the symptoms.

Communicability

The period of communicability is from a few days before the onset of symptoms to several days after the onset of jaundice, usually not more than seven days.

Contamination

Contamination may be from person to person or through contact with respiratory droplets, *feces* (stools), blood, or contaminated food, milk, or water.

Control

Good personal hygiene is important for control of hepatitis. Feces should be properly disposed of. Infected persons should be excluded from groups and from donating blood.

Impetigo

Impetigo is a skin infection, usually appearing on the face and hands.

Symptoms

Symptoms include blisters or open, pus-like *lesions* (sores). Later the lesions become crusted and irregular in outline. They look like crusty scabs, but they spread instead of clearing up.

Incubation

Incubation of the infection is normally two to five days, but it may be longer.

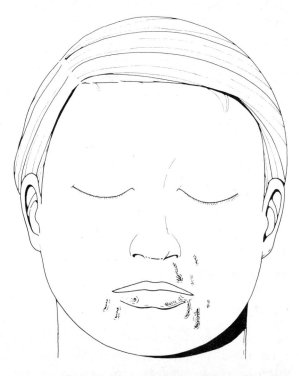

Figure 8-8: In an impetigo infection, irregular scabs appear with an oozing yellowish discharge.

Communicability

Communicability is from the eruption or appearance of blisters until they are healed.

Contamination

Contamination is by direct contact with the discharge from the sores or with articles soiled by the discharge.

Control

Antibiotics (medications that inhibit the growth of bacteria) are used to get rid of the lesions. Children should be excluded from a group until the lesions are gone. A frequent difficulty of impetigo is reinfection from soiled materials.

Influenza (Flu)

Symptoms

Symptoms of the flu include achiness, chills, fever, nausea, headache, runny nose, cough, and sore throat.

Incubation

The period of incubation is one to three days.

Communicability

The period of communicability is one day before the onset until five days after the onset.

Contamination

To avoid contamination, avoid contact with an infected person and soiled articles.

Control

Observe good personal hygiene. Exclude infected persons from groups. Many types of influenza may be avoided by immunization. Antibiotics may help the victim avoid other infections as a result of the weakened condition caused by the influenza virus.

Lice

Lice are wingless parasites.

Symptoms

Symptoms of lice infestation include scratching of the head and body, especially behind the ears and around the back of the neck. Tiny white eggs (nits) may also be visible in the hair.

Incubation

Nits hatch in one week and reach sexual maturity in two weeks.

Communicability

Lice may be spread until all lice and nits are destroyed.

Contamination

Contamination is through direct contact with an infected person or indirect contact with contaminated articles such as combs, brushes, clothing, or hats. Lice cannot fly or jump, but they may live from two or three weeks in beds, furniture, car seats, or clothing.

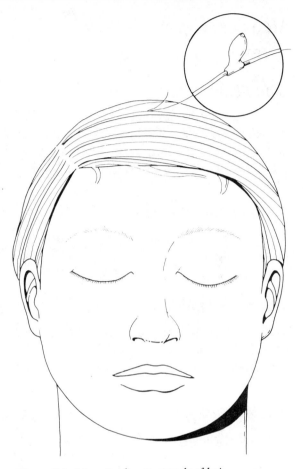

Figure 8-9: Lice nits cling to strands of hair.

Control

To control lice infestations, exclude the infected person from groups. The infected person must use a medicated shampoo and remove the lice and nits through inspection of the head and body and combing of the hair. It is also important that the person's environment be cleaned thoroughly.

Measles, German (Three-day Rubella)

Symptoms

The symptoms of German measles include malaise, listlessness, headache, fever, watery and puffy eyes, a runny nose, swollen glands, and a rash on the face and neck.

Incubation

The period of incubation is fourteen to twenty-one days.

Communicability

The period of communicability is one week before the onset of symptoms until five days after.

Contamination

Contamination is by direct contact, coughing or sneezing, and contact with soiled articles.

Control

The best control for German measles is immunization. Good personal hygiene is important to prevent spreading the disease. Gamma globulin is sometimes used to treat infected persons. Infected individuals should be excluded from groups. Note that German measles contracted by a woman in the first *trimester* (three months) of pregnancy can cause extensive damage to the fetus.

Measles (Rubeola, Two-week Measles)

Symptoms

Symptoms of rubeola include fever, runny nose and eyes, eyes sensitive to light, and a dark, red, blotchy rash over most parts of the body.

Incubation

The period of incubation is eight to thirteen days. A rash develops approximately fourteen days after exposure.

Communicability

Communicability is from the onset of symptoms until four or five days after the rash appears.

Contamination

Contamination may occur from direct contact, coughs, sneezes, and contact with soiled articles.

Control

The best method of control is immunization. However, infected persons should be excluded from groups for at least five days after the rash of rubeola appears.

Meningitis

Meningitis causes inflammation of the membranes of the brain and spinal cord. It is the result of an *acute* (having severe and sudden symptoms of short duration) bacterial or viral infection.

Symptoms

Symptoms include sudden fever; intense headache; nausea; vomiting; a stiff neck; irritability; a rash of small, round, purple spots; and delirium. A deep unconsciousness may result.

Incubation

The period of incubation is fourteen to twenty-one days.

Communicability

Communicability usually lasts until twenty-four hours after administration of an antibiotic for the bacterial variety.

Contamination

Contamination may be from direct contact with an infected person or a carrier.

Control

Infected individuals should be excluded from groups. They also normally receive antibiotics. If you encounter an infected person, be sure to use good personal hygiene.

Mononucleosis

Mononucleosis causes an abnormality in the blood cells.

Symptoms

Symptoms include malaise, fever, sore throat, swollen glands, tiredness, loss of appetite, and headache.

Incubation

The period of incubation for mononucleosis is one to two weeks for children and two to eight weeks for adults.

Communicability

The period of communicability is unknown.

Contamination

Contamination is normally from direct contact with the saliva of an infected person.

Control

Infected persons should be excluded until after the acute phase, normally six to ten days.

Mumps

Symptoms

The symptoms of mumps include fever followed by swelling of the salivary glands under the jaw and in front of the ears.

Incubation

Incubation is from twelve to twenty-six days, commonly eighteen days.

Communicability

The period of communicability is seven days before the onset of the symptoms until nine days after the swelling occurs.

Contamination

Contamination is by direct oral contact with an infected person or with soiled articles.

Control

Immunization is the best control for mumps. Peak outbreaks of mumps occur in the winter and spring. Infected individuals should be excluded from groups until all the symptoms have disappeared.

Pinworms

Pinworms are parasites that infest the intestines and migrate to the rectum and anus.

Symptoms

Symptoms include itching of the rectal area, irritability, restlessness, loss of appetite, loss of weight, nausea, and vomiting.

Incubation

The period of incubation is the life cycle of the worm, which is three to six weeks.

Communicability

The period of communicability is two to eight weeks or as long as the worms are present.

Contamination

Pinworms are spread by contaminated hands, bedding, food, clothing, or swimming pools.

Control

Infected individuals should be excluded from groups. Personal hygiene is very important. Toilet seats should be disinfected and the environment should be cleaned. Exposure to heat over 132 degrees Fahrenheit will kill pinworms.

Ringworm

Ringworms are parasitic fungi.

Symptoms

Symptoms of ringworm infection include lesions; chapped, rough skin; head and body scratching; and small pimples that spread in a circle, healing from the center outward. Ringworm can appear as athlete's foot.

Incubation

Incubation is from two to fourteen days.

Communicability

Communicability is for as long as lesions are present.

Contamination

Contamination is from direct or indirect contact with infected people or animals.

Control

Infected individuals should be excluded from groups. The treatment is to use a *fungicide* (medication that kills fungus infections). Lesions may return if some of the fungus is not killed.

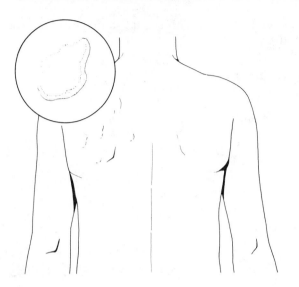

Figure 8-10: In ringworm, small blisters form around a healed area (in the middle).

Roseola (Infant Measles)

Symptoms

The symptoms of roseola include fever, loss of appetite, listlessness, and a rash lasting one or two days. The rash covers the trunk, arms, and neck. Roseola usually occurs in infants and toddlers.

Incubation

Roseola incubates in ten to fifteen days.

Communicability

Communicability is from one or two days before the onset of symptoms until two days after the rash disappears.

Contamination

The method of contamination is unknown.

Control

Infected individuals should be excluded from groups.

Scabies

Scabies are parasitic mites that burrow under the skin.

Symptoms

Symptoms include intense itching and linear tracks under the skin at the finger webs, wrists, elbows, armpits, and thighs.

Incubation

Incubation is from one or two days to several weeks.

Communicability

The period of communicability is until all mites and eggs are destroyed by treatment.

Contamination

Contamination results from contact with an infected person or contact with contaminated undergarments or bedding.

Control

Infected individuals should be excluded from groups until treated. Control involves frequent bathing with a prescribed soap, application of a prescribed ointment, and clean clothing and bedding.

Scarlet Fever and Strep Throat

Symptoms

Symptoms include fever, sore throat, swollen glands, nausea, vomiting, a fine rash on the neck and chest, and a "strawberry" tongue.

Incubation

Incubation is from one to five days.

Communicability

With adequate treatment, communicability is eliminated within twenty-four hours of the treatment. In untreated cases, communicability may last from two to three weeks.

Contamination

Contamination may occur from direct contact with an infected person or carrier. Strep throat may also be contracted from contaminated milk or food.

Control

Antibiotic treatment is used to control strep throat. Infected individuals should be excluded from groups until twenty-four hours after treatment begins. Personal hygiene is important.

Tuberculosis (TB)

Symptoms

The symptoms of tuberculosis include fatigue, weight loss, loss of appetite, a chronic cough, fever, night sweats, and symptoms of the common cold.

Incubation

The period of incubation from infection to primary lesions is four to six weeks.

Communicability

Communicability is for as long as an active infection persists.

Contamination

Contamination may occur from exposure to persons with the active disease. The infection may be airborne.

Control

Tuberculosis can be controlled, but it cannot yet be cured. Skin tests and X-rays are used to determine contamination. Special drugs normally can control the disease in infected individuals. Good hygiene and proper nutrition help to prevent the disease.

NONCOMMUNICABLE DISEASES

Noncommunicable diseases are those that are not spread by direct contact with an infected person. They include encephalitis, Lyme disease, Rocky Mountain spotted fever, and tetanus.

Encephalitis

Encephalitis is inflammation of the substance of the brain.

Symptoms

Symptoms include high fever, convulsions, sudden headaches, confusion, a stiff back, and a coma.

Incubation

The period of incubation is five to fifteen days.

Contamination

The disease is transmitted by bites from disease-carrying ticks and mosquitoes.

Control

Control includes public information, the use of insect repellents, and the destruction of mosquito breeding areas.

Lyme Disease

Symptoms

A spreading red, blotchy, circular, expanding rash, accompanied by flulike symptoms, fever, and aches are the early signs of Lyme disease. Later complications include disorders of the heart or nervous system. Months to years later, patients may develop arthritis. Symptoms may persist, change, disappear and reappear intermittently for several weeks.

Incubation

The disease usually occurs three to thirty days after the bite of the infected tick.

Contamination

Lyme disease is an infectious disease transmitted by the bite of a tick.

Control

Prompt removal of ticks may prevent the disease. Apply antiseptic to bite area and wash hands thoroughly.

Rocky Mountain Spotted Fever

Symptoms

The symptoms include fever, joint and muscle pain, nausea, vomiting, a white coating of the tongue, and a rash.

Incubation

The incubation period is two to fourteen days.

Contamination

The disease is transmitted by ticks.

Control

Control is by removal of the tick and antibiotics.

Tetanus

Tetanus is caused by bacteria that enter the body through a wound.

Symptoms

Symptoms include muscular spasms and stiffness, a locked jaw, convulsions, and an inability to breathe. Death is often the result of a tetanus infection.

Incubation

The period of incubation is four days to two weeks.

Contamination

Tetanus spores may be found in dirt, dust, or human and animal feces. The spores enter the body through an injury such as a cut or burn.

Control

Immunization should occur every five to ten years or if a person is injured.

PREVENTION OF DISEASE IN THE CENTER

Professional caregivers must remember three steps to providing a healthful atmosphere in the center. First, they should maintain their own health. Second, they should teach nutrition and hygiene by providing good role models. Third, they should keep the environment clean and sanitary.

Children need to be taught good hygiene practices. They learn by observing caregivers and listening to their instructions concerning toileting, hand washing, eating, covering their mouths when they cough or sneeze, disposing of soiled tissues, and general cleanliness of the environment. Continuous, daily hygiene routines allow the children to become accustomed to these practices.

In some states, centers are required to meet the same health and sanitary regulations as restaurants. The areas used for storing, preparing, and serving food and drinks must be cleaned before and after preparation. They must be kept separate from other areas. Washing hands before and after preparing food or eating should become a habit for both staff

Figure 8-11: The aide prepares a morning snack for the children.

and children. Children should be taught not to share food, utensils, cups, and plates.

The facility environment also must be kept clean and sanitary to prevent the spread of disease. It is desirable for the air temperature to be between 68 and 72 degrees Fahrenheit. Ventilation and circulation of fresh air are also important to the health of the children. Not crowding the children during meals, activities or naps (placing them head to foot) also decreases the passing of germs.

Case Study #1:
Leo

Leo arrives at school, happy and eager to see his friends. Miss Wilson talks to Leo about his new bike and the difficult math homework he finished last night. While talking to Leo, Miss Wilson observes for any noticeable signs of illness. Leo appears to be his normal, excitable self.

About 10:00 A.M., Leo becomes quiet and seems to lack energy. Miss Wilson is concerned about his unusual behavior. She quietly speaks to Leo about how he is feeling. Leo says that he is very tired and wants to go to sleep. Miss Wilson suggests that Mr. John take Leo to see the school nurse to have his temperature taken. Leo's face appears flushed, and his eyes are watery.

The nurse takes his temperature, and it registers 101 degrees Fahrenheit. By this time, Leo is complaining that his stomach hurts too. When the nurse checks his chest and under his arms, she notices that small bumps are beginning to form. She has enough experience to suspect that Leo is coming down with chicken pox.

She calls Leo's mother and asks her to come to school and pick him up. Meanwhile, the nurse makes Leo as comfortable as possible on a cot in the office. She covers him with a blanket to prevent chills and gives him some water to drink. She also reads him a story to help keep him from worrying about how he feels.

Leo is glad to see his mother when she arrives. He wants to go home to his own bed and room. His mother, however, calls the doctor's office and makes arrangements to stop there on the way home.

Dr. Barbara checks Leo's stomach, back, and groin. She confirms that Leo does have the chicken pox. She recommends that he be given a warm bath, drink liquids, and rest until his temperature goes down to normal. He must stay home until all the chicken pox are covered with scabs.

After a week, Leo's blisters have scabbed over and he is able to return to school. Leo missed his friends and tells them about all the gelatin and ice cream he ate. He also tells them about how much the chicken pox itched and the special care he had to take to not scratch them. His mother had to give him baths in water with baking soda. Then she put lotion on the pox to help keep them from itching. Leo makes the chicken pox seem fun, but nobody else wants to have the itching and scratching.

Case Study #2:
Michelle

Today is the day the children at Michelle's preschool are going to prepare stone soup. Miss Betty has brought a special clean stone to place in the pot. Each of the children is to bring a favorite vegetable. Michelle decides to bring carrots to add to the soup. The vegetables are all placed near the sink in the kitchen.

When it is time to begin, Miss Betty calls the children together and explains carefully the steps to prepare stone soup. All the children must wash their hands before beginning. The sink and counter will be washed before the vegetables are cleaned. After everything is ready, the children begin to scrub their vegetables, one at a time. Then they cut the vegetables into pieces to place them into the pot.

Michelle's turn finally arrives. She carefully follows each step of the directions. Miss Betty is standing next to her to offer assistance if Michelle needs it. Michelle scrubs her carrots. Handling the knife correctly, she cuts the carrots into pieces. Next she places them into the pot.

After two hours, the room smells delicious. Everyone's tummy is growling. The children wash their hands again and scrub the tables. Each child is responsible for setting his or her own place at the table. At last, the soup is ready to eat. Everyone is eager to try it because they made it themselves.

There are onions, rice, celery, potatoes, tomatoes, carrots and zucchini in the soup. Miss Betty passes out the milk and bread to go along with the meal. Most children ask for seconds.

The children have learned good hygiene and cooking practices as well as good nutrition. They have followed directions, worked, had a good time, and cooperated to produce the delicious soup. They have also used all their senses (smell, taste, touch, hearing, and seeing), and learned about vegetables.

Because small children place many objects in their mouths, model and practice cleanliness in order to keep the spread of germs to a minimum. All items at an infant and toddler center should be disinfected daily or more often if needed. These objects include cribs, changing tables, tables, chairs, toys, doorknobs, water faucet handles, toilet seats, shelves, and floors.

Disinfect these surfaces with either a commercial disinfectant or make a solution of one-fourth cup bleach per gallon of water. Keep these supplies out of the reach of the children and locked up when not in use.

Changing diapers and soiled clothing takes particular care and attention. Place all soiled clothing and diapers in plastic bags. Tightly close the bags and send them home with the child. Do not attempt to wash such articles at the center because this promotes the spread of disease. Wash both your hands and the child's hands thoroughly.

The most important way to prevent the spread of germs or disease is by washing hands frequently. When washing hands:

1. Use plenty of soap and water.

2. Rub hands together quickly to generate friction to loosen dirt and germs.

3. Include all surfaces, such as the backs of hands, between each finger, under the nails, and the wrists.

4. Use a brush or blunt orange stick under and around the nails if needed.

5. Rinse well, under running water. Point hands downward toward the sink to keep germs from running down the arms.

6. Use a paper towel only once to dry hands.

7. Use a paper towel to turn faucets off.

Figure 8-12: This is the way we wash our hands.

SUMMARY

Communicable diseases are common to children in group settings. It is important that caregivers recognize the means of transmitting illness in order to keep them at a minimum.

Germs are either viral or bacterial micro-organisms that invade a body with low resistance. They are spread by direct or indirect means. People becoming ill experience an incubation period, a time for the illness to complete its course, and a recovery period.

Caregivers can eliminate many of these occasions by keeping the environment clean and free of germs. Prevention of disease in the center is a major concern for caregivers. Cleanliness of the room and the people who occupy it helps to stop the spread of germs. Children should be taught the proper techniques of washing hands, preparing food, and toileting.

Caregivers must know and observe the children. They should be aware of any deviations in their behavior. Caregivers often are the first ones to know when a child is feeling ill. Children who become ill should be isolated from the others, and their parents should be called to take them home. Some diseases must be reported to the local health department to avoid an epidemic.

Review Questions

1. What is a communicable illness?

2. What conditions must be present for an illness to be transmitted?

3. When is a child placed in isolation?

4. Who is responsible to report a communicable illness to the county or state?

5. When are chicken pox the most communicable?

6. You can determine conjunctivitis by observing the _____ effect around the iris.

7. What three steps can caregivers take to prevent the spread of illness?

8. Why is washing hands so important?

Things to Do and Discuss

1. Discuss the ingredients necessary for the transmission and the progression of disease.

2. Find pictures of children to illustrate the onset of illness. Write a description of the symptoms.

3. Call your local health department to discover which diseases must be reported.

4. Write an extended report on a communicable disease of your choice and report to the class.

5. Observe a child care center to determine if health precautions are being practiced. List the precautions followed. In a separate list, tell what precautions are not followed.

6. Make a hand washing chart for children. Be sure to include all aspects of proper hygiene. Send the chart to your local child care center.

7. Write a report on the development of vaccinations to prevent smallpox or polio. Present the report to your class.

CHAPTER 9
Child Abuse and Neglect

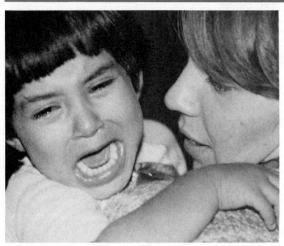

Listening to young children is an important responsibility of caregivers.

KEY TERMS

abandonment
abuse
child abuse
child molestation
child neglect
coercion
cruel and unusual
  punishment
emotional neglect
excessive physical
  punishment
fetus
fondling
genitals
hyperactivity
hyperextension

hypervigilant
hypoactivity
immersion
incest
liable
masturbation
mental abuse
neonatal care unit
phobias
physical abuse
physical neglect
pornographic
  materials
postnatal
prenatal

OBJECTIVES

After completing this chapter, you will be able to:

1. identify signs of child abuse and neglect;
2. demonstrate documentation and reporting techniques for child abuse and neglect.

INTRODUCTION

Did you know:

- Over two million cases of child abuse are reported yearly in the United States.

- Over one out of twenty families are affected by child abuse.

- One out of three girls and one out of four boys are molested by age eighteen—ninety percent of these cases by someone they know and trust.

- Most people who abuse others were abused themselves as children. (State of California, San Bernardino Sheriff's Department, 1987)

Seventy percent of all people who abuse children grew up in a home where abuse was common. When adults become frustrated or angry they often rely on discipline methods or show love in the ways that were used when they were children. No adult decides, "Today I'm going to abuse a child." Rather, he or she is caught up in the "cycle of abuse." People who abuse others need to receive therapy and re-training in order to relate to children in appro-priate ways. Some of these people receive help through private and group counseling and by attending parenting classes. These sessions are often arranged through the civil court system.

Child abuse and neglect are major areas of concern. They affect all races, ages, cultures, and economic statuses. There is no way to iden-tify the "typical" abuser or molester. It could be a neighbor, a parent's best friend, or a rela-tive. Children, because of their small size and because they are taught to respect and follow directions of an older person, are particularly vulnerable and often become victims.

In the United States there is a great effort to educate young children concerning their rights in protecting themselves from un-wanted advances. They are no longer taught to be "seen but not heard," to remain quiet, or not to talk about adults. Children are being listened to and taught to say no when a situa-tion feels uncomfortable to them.

Caregivers play an important role in the protection of children from abuse. Because they have knowledge of normal mental and physical development and because they see the children on a continuing basis, they are in a unique position to observe any unusual behav-ior. The detection of a series of small injuries or low self-esteem may provide clues for chil-dren to obtain help and preventative action. This may save them from permanent physical and emotional injury or death.

CHILD ABUSE

To *abuse* is to hurt or to treat badly. There are several types of abuse, and caregiv-

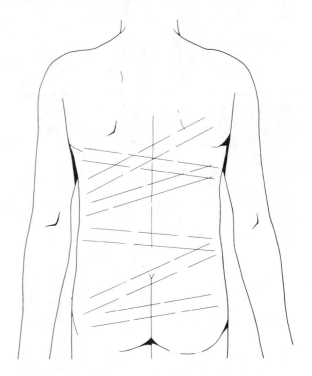

Figure 9-1: Beating marks may be a cluster of welts.

ers need to become familiar with the physical and behavioral symptoms of each. It is impor-tant to listen to children when they tell about an unhappy incident and to reassure them that you will help. Keeping communication lines open to any kind of discussion helps children feel free to talk to you. Although typical three and four year olds like to use bathroom words in order to evaluate the shock effect to adults, you must learn to differentiate between experi-mentation and a call for help.

Child abuse is defined as the lack of an act or the incorporation of an act that endan-gers a child's health and development either physically or mentally. These may include one or more of the following descriptions.

Signs of Abuse

Physical Signs

1. *bruises or welts* of specific shapes, such as belts, buckles, electrical cords, ropes, hangers, hands, or knuckles. Look for:

   - clustered forming patterns — several bruises in the same area

   - bruises or welts that appear regularly, especially after weekends, absences, or vacations

   - bruises or welts that appear on the parts of the body covered by clothing — torso, back, buttocks, or thighs (injuries caused by normal falling are generally on the front of the child, who usually falls forward, not backward)

   - a multitude of bruises in varying colorations — indicates that injuries have occurred at different times. Different stages of healing follow:

     up to 24 hours.. bright red to red blue
     48 hours .... blue black, fading margins
     48 to 72 hours.. yellowish green
     5 to 7 days....... uniform fading, yellowing
     7 days............. deep discolor gone, fading

2. burns

   - generally of a specific shape, such as cigarettes, cigars, a burner of the stove, or an iron — found especially on backs, buttocks, palms, and soles

     - *immersion* (placing) into hot liquid — causes socklike or glovelike burns on hands or feet; can also appear on the genitals or buttocks

3. fractures

   - spiral in nature (indicating twisting of limbs) and multiples in various stages of healing (indicating repeated abuse, usually to the skull, nose, or facial structure)

4. lacerations or abrasions

   - usually to mouth, lips, gums, eyes, or external *genitals* (male and female reproductive organs)

Behavioral Signs

- extreme aggressiveness or withdrawal

- unwillingness to go home (by staying longer or coming too early to the school)

- clinging to parent in public (to keep from angering parent and provoking further abuse)

- fear of parents or other adults

- apprehensiveness when others cry

- uncommunicative behavior

- frequent tardiness or absence

Figure 9-2: Signs of abuse chart.

Immersion Burns and Object Burns

Immersion Burns

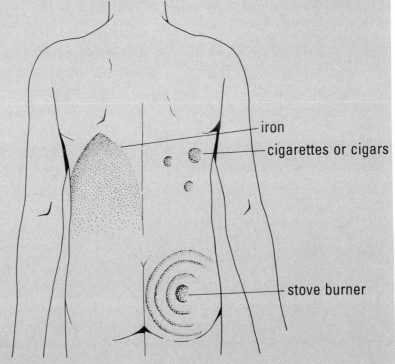

sock effect   mitten effect

Object Burns

iron

cigarettes or cigars

stove burner

Figure 9-3: Immersion burns and object burns chart.

Physical and Mental Abuse

Physical abuse is any physical action that injures, such as hitting, pushing, biting, punching, slapping, or burning. Some signs are visible, such as scratches, burns, or welts. Others may be internal, such as broken bones, hemorrhaging, or other damage to the organs.

Cruel and unusual punishment is inappropriate or extreme punishment for an action. Age, abilities, or behavior are not considered by the adult. Examples are placing child in a locked closet, tying a child to the bed, or having the child wear the potty chair after an accident.

Excessive physical punishment is any physical punishment that results in injuries to the child. Excessive spanking (with hand, belt, belt buckle, or another object), and kicking or hitting the child in vulnerable areas such as the face, stomach, back, or genitals are examples. This treatment borders on physical abuse.

Mental abuse is verbal barbs used to damage self-esteem. Name-calling, belittling a child's efforts, or constant put-downs by others can cause mental suffering.

Drug-exposed Children

In today's society we are seeing a great increase in the number of infants born drug-exposed. According to the National Institute on Drug Abuse, 375,000 drug-exposed infants are born each year. Experts estimate that half a million to four million drug-exposed children are expected in the United States by the year 2000. (Jackson, CTA Action, "Crack babies are here! Can you help them learn?" California Teachers Association, November, 1990.)

Drug-exposed infants are born to mothers who have been substance abusive during pregnancy. Alcohol, cigarettes, PCP, crack, cocaine, methamphetamines or crystal, marijuana, heroin, over-the-counter drugs, and prescription drugs are only some of the substances that can cause life-long difficulties for children. For women of child-bearing age, cocaine is usually the drug most often used. It is used generally in combination with other drugs.

There are many community and hospital rehabilitation programs to help mothers to lead a clean and straight existence during and after pregnancy. However, many of these women are receiving little or no *prenatal* (before birth) care. Often the physical dependency on the drug overshadows the needs of the *fetus* (the baby before birth). Poor diet, poor medical care, poor decision making, and poor health of the mothers can cause the infants to have low birth weight, failure to thrive syndrome, to suffer severe withdrawal symptoms, damage to brain cells, and multiple health problems.

Some *postnatal* (after birth) symptoms for children include sleeping for short and infrequent periods of time, exhibiting extended crying episodes, having jerky motion of limbs, are *hypervigilant* (always watching or staring), having *hyperextension* (wide-spread and stiff) of fingers, hands, toes and feet, poor ability to relate to caregivers, and poor ability to suck or take nourishment. Infants are placed in *neonatal care units* (special department of the hospital for infants at risk) until medical attention can intervene to help the infants. The extent of the lifetime damage is hard for medical personnel to determine.

Because of the mothers' drug dependencies and their inability to cope with their infants' abnormalities, many of these children are subject to further physical and mental abuse. Children who are born drug-exposed are often placed in foster care home situations. In some states, mothers are being arrested for child abuse and held responsible for the health condition of their newborn children. The extent of the father's drug dependency on the fetus is now being ascertained. Some data is supporting the rationale that the sperm are affected.

Drug-exposed infants need early intervention, special care, patience, and nurturing by caregivers. More time, more exposure to planned hands-on experiences and curriculum, smaller classroom size, consistency in their lives, forming a partnership between home and school, and more caregivers are required to help drug-exposed children. As these children mature, learning disabilities, behavioral problems, attention deficiency disorders, and inabilities to get along with others become common problems. The long-term effect of the multitudes of children in schools and centers with this condition has not been determined, nor has its effect on society as these children become adults.

Child Molestation

Ninety percent of the victims of child molestation personally know and trust the person responsible. Many of the victims are told that they share a secret and may not tell anyone else. These children often feel that it is their fault. They feel guilty, alone, helpless, shamed, and confused. They develop low self-esteem. Sexual molestation can involve anything from *fondling* (handling in a caressing manner) of private body parts to long-term *incest* (sexual relations between close relatives).

Child molestation is the use of force or *coercion* (making one do something against one's will) to induce a child into sexual actions that are physically or socially inappropriate. Forms of force or coercion include tricks, threats, and the showing of pornographic materials. *Pornographic materials* are materials that depict action of the type considered unacceptable by the community. Pornographic materials may be written, visual, or auditory.

Remember the following facts about sexual abuse:

1. The stigma of sexual abuse falls on the child as well as the abuser.

2. Children have long-lasting emotional difficulties after abuse, even after fondling.

3. In the majority of sexual abuse incidents, the abuser is known to the child.

4. All social and economic sectors of society have sexual abuse victims, not just low-income families.

5. Boys, as well as girls, are victims.

6. Other family members are often aware of sexual abuse or incest but are afraid to report it to the authorities.

7. Often, abusive adults are not prosecuted, convicted, or sentenced. Thus, there is further abuse. (Child Abuse Prevention/Intervention/ Education Program, 1986)

All abuse leaves scars that can affect the child for life. Usually, some form of psychological counseling is needed to overcome feel-

Signs of Sexual Abuse

Physical Signs

1. difficulty in walking or sitting
2. torn, stained, or bloody underwear
3. pain, swelling, or itching in genital area
4. poor sphincter muscle tone (frequent urination)
5. genital injuries
6. vaginal or penile discharge
7. venereal disease
8. pregnancy

Behavioral Signs

1. abrupt change in personality
2. excessive crying
3. regression
4. exaggeration
5. advanced sexual knowledge and behavior
6. truancy
7. alcohol abuse
8. attempted suicide
9. bodily complaints
10. depression
11. withdrawal
12. fantasy
13. clinging behavior
14. self-destructive behavior
15. drug abuse
16. running away
17. poor self-image
18. fear of certain people or places
19. sleep disorders
    - nightmares
    - bed-wetting
    - fear of sleep
    - tiredness
20. excessive *masturbation* (handling one's own genitals for sexual gratification)
21. role playing incident with dolls
22. unwillingness to participate in physical education class
23. eating disorders
    - loss of appetite
    - obesity
    - difficulty swallowing
    - anorexia or bulimia
24. excessive bathing
25. unwillingness to change clothes

Figure 9-4: Signs of sexual abuse chart.

ings of being unloved or unwanted. Abused children often feel guilty for not being good or feel that they have done something horrible to justify this treatment.

Children trust the adults in their lives to protect and care for them. They may come to think abusive treatment is normal and is a sign of being loved. They are afraid to talk about or report abuse for fear of what will happen to them or their parents. Often, they have never known any other kind of family life. Unfortunately, abused children who never receive treatment often grow up to become abusive parents themselves. This is just one more reason to learn the signs of abuse and what you, as a concerned caregiver, can do to stop the cycle.

Case Study #1: *Ruthie*

Figure 9-5: Ruthie is pulling away from her caregiver.

Ruthie, age six, arrives at school appearing withdrawn and quiet. This is unusual behavior. Mr. Barker, her teacher, tries to talk with her to find out what is the matter. He places his hand on her shoulder, but she quickly pulls away.

Later in the morning, while playing in the housekeeping corner, he notices that Ruthie is very angry with her doll, flinging it around and treating it in a threatening manner. While observing Ruthie, Mr. Barker also watches her fondling the doll's bottom.

These actions are enough to raise suspicions in the mind of Mr. Barker. He decides to talk to the school nurse, Mrs. Davis. He asks Mrs. Davis to help Ruthie in the bathroom. Mrs. Davis notices that Ruthie's underwear is stained and that she has difficulty urinating.

The nurse brings Ruthie to her office. Together, she and Mr. Barker question Ruthie calmly. Ruthie begins crying and appears fearful of her teacher. Mr. Barker then returns to his class and Mrs. Davis comforts her. After a long time, Ruthie starts to talk. She tells the nurse about the boy next door, Michael, who is fifteen.

While babysitting, Michael had told her they would play a game, but it was a secret game. No one else could be told. She showed Mrs. Davis where Michael had touched her.

Reassuring Ruthie that she has done nothing bad and that Mrs. Davis will protect her, Mrs. Davis gives her some hugs. She then calls the child protective agency, who sends an investigator to talk with Ruthie. She also calls Ruthie's mother to come to school.

Ruthie's mother has no knowledge of the incident, but she is understandably upset. She is, however, very warm, protective, and comforting to her daughter. She, too, reassures Ruthie. The authorities, after hearing Mrs. Davis and Mr. Barker's observations, leave to talk to Michael.

It is strongly suggested to Ruthie's mother that she seek a medical examination and counseling for Ruthie to help alleviate any long-lasting emotional problems. Several resource agencies in the community are recommended. Michael confesses to child molestation when confronted. He is now on probation and receiving appropriate counseling.

CHILD NEGLECT

Child neglect is failure to provide the care, love, and support necessary for a healthy and nurturing existence. The adults in children's lives are responsible for meeting the needs of the children.

Physical neglect is the withholding of physical necessities to a degree that endangers the child's health or well-being. Examples are improper nutrition, clothing, housing, and medical attention.

Abandonment, the leaving of a child to fend alone at too young an age or the leaving of a child in a potentially dangerous situation (such as in a car unattended), is also considered neglect.

Physical Signs

1. consistent hunger or undernourishment
2. unmet physical and medical needs
3. lack of supervision
4. falling asleep easily in class
5. poor personal hygiene
6. inappropriate dress for weather
7. abandonment

Behavioral Signs

1. begging or stealing food
2. consistent fatigue
3. delinquency (such as theft or truancy)
4. staying at school longer than necessary
5. alcohol and drug abuse

Figure 9-6: Signs of physical neglect.

Emotional neglect is any action that negatively affects a child's sense of self. An adult may emotionally neglect a child through noncommunication, absence of nurturing, or withdrawing emotionally from the child.

Physical Signs

1. speech disorders
2. *hyperactivity* (a condition characterized by a short attention span, restlessness, and impulsive and disruptive behavior)
3. nervous skin disorders
4. inability to control urine discharge
5. obesity or underweight
6. *hypoactivity* (a condition characterized by passive or compliant behavior)
7. nervousness
8. failure to thrive physically, emotionally, socially, or intellectually

Behavioral Signs

1. habit disorders — excessive sucking, rocking, or biting
2. extreme emotional reactions — hysteria, *phobias* (fears), compulsions
3. suicide or attempted suicide
4. inappropriate conduct — destructiveness, disruptiveness, or hyperaggressive or antisocial behavior
5. neurotic traits — inhibition from playing or sleeping
6. extreme behavior — either compliant and passive or aggressive and demanding
7. extreme need for displays of affection
8. uncommunicative behavior

Figure 9-7: Signs of emotional neglect.

Case Study #2:
Sally

Sally is ten years old. She is in charge of her three younger siblings—Josh (five years old), Billy (three years old), and Sarah (sixteen months). Her parents divorced when she was eight. Sally's mother sometimes works eight to ten hours a day. She often comes home tired and irritable. She spends many nights out with friends because she is lonesome.

Sally's mother has gotten up late again and is hurrying to get to work. Sally gets up early each day to fix breakfast for her brothers and sister. This morning she goes to the refrigerator and finds that there is no milk for the cereal, so she gives the other children yesterday's donuts and some soda pop to drink. At least they won't be hungry.

She rushes to get them all dressed so that she won't be late arriving at her own school. The washing hasn't been done, so Josh and Billy have to wear yesterday's clothing again. She hopes that the neighbor who sits for Billy and Sarah has extra diapers. On her way to school, Sally drops the younger children off and tells Josh to run to catch his bus.

During school, Sally has a hard time concentrating on her work. The teacher observes that she is often listless and overly tired. Sally's clothes are rumpled and unclean. Her hair also needs washing. When trying to communicate with Sally, her teacher finds her unresponsive. Sally, she notices, is often aggressive on the play yard with her schoolmates.

A few weeks ago, the teacher observed what appeared to be clusters of welts on Sally's legs. When asked how this happened, Sally said that she had fallen off her bike at home. This week, the teacher notices a handprint on the side of Sally's face. Sally explains that she had made her brother angry and they had gotten into a fight.

The teacher becomes suspicious of all the signs of neglect, so she sends Sally to the school nurse. The teacher has also kept a diary of indications of child abuse. Later, the nurse and teacher meet to discuss their observations.

After school, Sally needs to get home quickly. Billy and Sarah have to be picked up from the sitter, and Josh has been home alone for several hours. (He hates being left by himself because he gets frightened.) Maybe she has time to do some wash and to do the dirty dishes in the sink. She hopes her mother will bring home something for dinner.

When her mother gets home, she brings a frozen pizza and some milk. She has had a bad day at work and is too tired to eat. She is furious when she finds the washing hasn't been finished. She yells at Sally that she is lazy and stupid, and can't ever do anything right! She loses her temper and strikes Sally and Josh (for not helping Sally) several times with her belt. Mother tells Sally that she cannot go to bed until the wash is done. Sally finishes the wash about 9:30. Once again, she is too tired to finish her homework, although she isn't too interested, since she doesn't understand it anyway.

Meanwhile, the teacher, nurse, and principal review the situation. They decide to call a social worker to investigate Sally's home condition. There are too many indications of child neglect and physical abuse. Sally's mental attitude also concerns them because Sally doesn't get along with her peers and has poor study habits.

The social worker visits the home and speaks with the mother, who is very upset. He feels that the mother does love and care for her children, but she is under a great deal of pressure. After much discussion about the problems affecting the family, the social worker offers some plans for solving the situation. Sally's mother will take a job training course to enable her to obtain more satisfying and better-paying employment. The social worker also finds a child care center for all the children. The family will be charged on a sliding fee scale. The center also provides bus service to pick up the older children after school.

Because the mother now has some workable solutions to her many problems, she begins to feel better about herself. She is able to have more patience and time for her children. She also enrolls in a parenting class to learn more effective child rearing. Josh is no longer home alone, and Sally has time to be a little girl.

EDUCATION

Educating young children to protect themselves has become the responsibility of both parents and caregivers. Specific programs teach small children their rights and how to handle problems. The programs are taught in a manner that does not frighten children but rather gives information. The age and maturity of the children are taken into consideration. Many books, films, and games are designed for this purpose.

Education programs teach young children the following:

1. Some touching is good, such as hugs and kisses, if it makes you feel comfortable. Touching is bad if it makes you uncomfortable or you don't like it. It is all right to tell the person to stop. Tell another adult about bad touching and they will help you.

2. The area of your body that is covered by your bathing suit is private. If someone touches you there, yell "No!" Tell another adult about the touching and they will help you.

3. Some secrets are good, such as birthday and Christmas gifts. Secrets are bad if they make you feel uncomfortable. Tell another adult about bad secrets and they will help you.

4. Some picture taking is good, such as on a vacation or for holidays. Picture taking is bad if someone asks you to take off your clothes or makes you uncomfortable. Tell another adult about bad picture taking and they will help you.

Figure 9-8: *The caregiver gives instructions to his first grade class.*

5. It is nice to help others, but most adults do not come to children for help—they ask other adults. Never go with an adult (in a car, for a walk, or into a home) unless you have your parents' permission. Tell another adult about requests for help or bad invitations and they will help you.

6. It is fun to receive gifts and money from your family or friends, but do not take them without your parents' permission. Tell another adult about the gifts and they will help you.

7. If you are scared or uncomfortable when visiting relatives or friends, call home (teach each child his or her name, address, and phone number), 911, or the operator 0. Some communities have a hot line for children to call. The phone number can be placed near the phone. If you need help, call, and another adult will help you.

8. Looking at photographs or pictures is fun. But it they are about sex or make you uncomfortable, tell another adult about the pictures and they will help you.

9. If home alone, never answer the door or tell someone on the phone that you are alone. If you are scared, call another adult you trust and they will help you.

10. Reassure children that you, the caregiver, will always listen to them, believe them, and help them. (Children rarely lie about abuse and molestation!)

WHAT TO DO IF...

Unfortunately, you may be confronted with child abuse or neglect. Look carefully for the signs, evaluating carefully all instances. Discussions with the child and any suspicions that you may have should be relayed to the school director or principal. Document discussions, listing observations, signs, the date, the time, and a description of the child. Remember that abuse can include social and emotional distress as well as physical harm.

Following, you will learn how to deal with suspected cases of abuse or neglect, how to report suspected cases to the proper authorities, and what you can do to help the child who is the victim.

Look for the following indications of abuse or neglect:

1. Does the child have too much money or too many new possessions that do not fit into the normal pattern for the family?

2. How does the child spend free time? With whom? Does the child appear comfortable with them?

3. Does the child have strong feelings (either positive or negative) concerning an adult—teacher, friend, clergy, or baby-sitter?

4. Does the child not want to go with a certain adult or pull away from him or her? Does the child refrain from physical contact, such as hugs and kisses, with this person?

5. Is there a change in the child's overall physical development, attitude, or behavior?

6. Are there observable symptoms, physical or behavioral, of abuse or neglect?

Caregivers must always be prepared to listen when children express concern, appear frightened, or appear uncomfortable. Allow the children the opportunity to discuss problems. Caregivers also must be able to recognize the signs and indications associated with child abuse.

If you suspect abuse or molestation, take the following steps:

1. Talk with the child in a private and quiet place. Believe the child. Children seldom lie about abuse or molestation.

2. Commend the child for telling you about the experience. Reassure the child that you will protect him or her and that you are sorry that it happened.

3. Convey your support for the child. A child's greatest fear is that he or she is at fault and responsible for the incident. Alleviating this self-blame is very important. The child is not to blame; rather, the child is a victim.

4. Remain calm—don't overreact! Recognize that your opinions and acceptance are critical signals to the child. Your greatest challenge may be to not convey your own horror about the abuse.

5. Respect the privacy of the child. Do not discuss the situation with others in the child's presence.

6. Report the suspected abuse to a social services agency, the child abuse agency, or the police, as indicated for your community.

7. Have a referral file of agencies that evaluate or counsel victims and their families. Referrals may be to hospitals, child abuse clinics, or professional counselors.

8. Remember that taking action is imperative. If nothing is done, other children may be at risk, too.

9. We teach the child to tell someone when situations are uncomfortable and that we will help; therefore, caregivers are responsible for protecting each child.

Reporting Abuse

To report suspected cases of abuse or molestation, take the following steps:

1. Observe and document any abnormal indicators, such as radical behavior changes, suspect bruises or welts, general health and body condition, or conversations relaying abuse.

2. Arrange for a private meeting with your director or principal to discuss your concerns (include all documentation of your observations).

3. Most states have legal statutes stating that anyone *suspecting* a case of child abuse or molestation must report it to the local social services department or police. If you do not report a suspected case, you may be personally held *liable* (legally responsible).

Although it is necessary that every child be made to feel special and confident, the abused or neglected child needs additional nurturing and understanding.

Helping the Abused Child

To help the abused or molested child, take the following steps:

1. Make the child feel secure and safe. The abused or molested child needs to rebuild a sense of trust in adults. Do not touch the child without the child's permission, gossip about the problem, or in any way cause the child embarrassment. Greet the child warmly each day, and make the child feel an important part of the group.

Figure 9-9: The director must report a possible child abuse case.

2. Structure helps to build security. Consistent rules and schedules help to give the child feelings of belonging and direction while recovering from the experience. Schedules let children predict the upcoming events of daily life.

3. To rebuild a sense of identity for the child, give the child specific information. Praise the child openly and frequently about the positive qualities demonstrated.

4. Displaying the child's work and putting the child's name on the desk or cubbie help the child to feel accepted and to have a personal place within the group.

5. Share positive events from your life with the child. Develop a personal relationship. It is best not to touch a sexually abused child, for a touch may cause flashbacks. After establishing a warm interaction with the child, ask permission to touch a shoulder or hold a hand. The child needs to relearn trust of some adults.

6. Validate the child's behavior by showing signs of approval. A wink, a warm smile, a friendly tone of voice, and a written note are methods of positive communication.

7. Show empathy by verbalizing the child's feelings, such as "If that happened to me, I would be afraid, too." Provide opportunities for the child to express feelings through words, drawing pictures, and sculpting with clay.

8. Make the child feel worthwhile and likable as an individual.

SUMMARY

Child abuse is the action or lack of action that endangers a child's health and development. Child abuse and neglect are major areas of concern. They affect the whole nation and cross all boundaries.

Physical abuse, cruel and unusual punishment, excessive physical punishment, physical neglect, emotional abuse and neglect, mental suffering, and sexual molestation are all types of child abuse. Teaching young children

protective measures and their rights helps to give them strength and a means to withstand unwanted advances. Believing children and reassuring them of their worth are functions of the nurturing caregiver.

Drug-exposed infants and children are becoming an increasing concern of all caregivers. Because these children have many physical, social, emotional, and intellectual difficulties, homes, schools, and centers have to be ready to help them to adjust to society.

Professional caregivers play an important role in detecting and reporting abuse. They also educate and protect children. Helping a child recover from abuse and rebuilding trust and self-esteem are of equal importance.

Figure 9-10: Allowing children to display their work gives them a feeling of acceptance and self-worth.

Review Questions

1. Who is the most affected by child abuse?

2. What signs would indicate that a child may have been physically abused?

3. How could you determine that a child may have been mentally abused?

4. What determines incest?

5. What is the "cycle of abuse"?

6. What is neglect?

7. Who is responsible for educating children about abuse?

8. List the steps in reporting abuse.

9. How should the caregiver conduct an interview of a child who has suffered abuse?

10. How would you help the abused child?

Things to Do and Discuss

1. Role play a caregiver's response to different types of abuse, including the mental and physical aspects. Act out the caregiver's reactions to the situations.

2. Research child abuse statistics in your area. What is your community doing to combat this problem?

3. Research reporting laws and documentation for child abuse in your state.

4. Compile a referral list of agencies in your area that provide counseling, medical treatment, and hot lines dealing with child abuse and molestation.

CHAPTER 10
Nutrition

A healthy child at play.

KEY TERMS

anemia
amino acids
beriberi
calories
carbohydrates
cell
connective tissue
deficiency
DNA
energy
epithelial tissues
fats
fat soluble vitamins
goiter
lactation

metabolism
muscular tissue
nucleus
nutrition
pellagra
proteins
protoplasm
RNA
rickets
scurvy
synthesizes
vitamins
water soluble
   vitamins

OBJECTIVES

After completing this chapter, you will be able to:

1. explain the value of good nutrition;
2. discuss the factors to consider in purchasing, preparing, and serving food to young children;
3. plan and prepare a well-balanced menu for a school setting.

INTRODUCTION

Bugs on a log, space candy, stone soup —*nutrition* is the taking in and using of food for growth and energy. Studying nutrition can be fun as well as healthy and educational. Caregivers should make meals pleasant for all. Mealtime is an opportunity for enjoyable conversation, good manners, sharing ethnic backgrounds, and learning about how bodies are enriched by foods.

Emotions are often tied to foods. When you're feeling happy and excited, do you celebrate by going out to dinner or having a scrumptious dessert? When you're depressed, do you eat something special to make yourself feel better? Did your mother ever tell you, "Eat everything on your plate! Think of the starving children in the world"? Have you heard from your friends, "Liver and spinach are yukky"? These quotes are familiar to us as children, and they reflect eating habits and cultural influences. We tend to eat and treat food as we were taught as children. We learn from our families, peers, and teachers.

THE IMPORTANCE OF GOOD NUTRITION

Nutritious diets are essential for children. Centers need a healthy diet to offset the large amounts of fast foods that we have become accustomed to eating. Some of the most popular over-the-counter foods in the United States are also among the least healthy.

Many times, these foods are eaten in a hurried atmosphere, with little attention to the nutritional content or surroundings. Fast foods have high fat and salt content, often as much or more than the total daily allotment for an adult.

What We Are Made Of

We are made of individual cells that combine to form tissue. The cells and tissues contain water. Tissue, cells, and water help our bodies to grow. In order to give our bodies the best treatment possible, we need to understand how we are built.

Tissues

There are four types of tissues:

1. *Bone, blood, and nerve tissue.*

2. *Connective tissue* includes groups of cells that bind different parts of the body together or support the body.

3. *Epithelial tissues* are the coverings. Examples are the skin (covering the outside of the body) and membranes that line the body cavities that open to the outside. Glands are also comprised from this type of tissue.

4. *Muscular tissue* is made of cells that can contract and then relax again. By this action, they move parts of the body and move materials through the body.

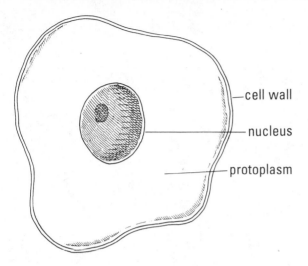

Figure 10-1: Animal cells have irregular shape.

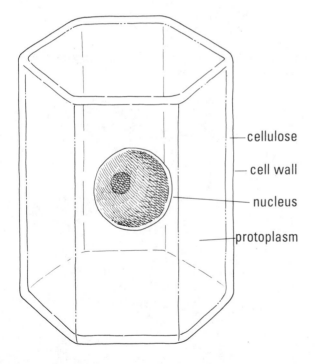

Figure 10-2: Plant cells have straight edges.

Cells

We are made up of millions of cells. A *cell* is a small unit of protoplasm, usually with a nucleus and a membrane or cell wall. *Protoplasm* is a mixture of proteins, fats, and other complexes suspended in water and providing the living materials of cells. The *nucleus* is the central portion of the cell. The nucleus is responsible for the growth and division of cells.

All plants and animals are made up of one or more cells. Ninety-eight percent of tissues and cells are made up of the following elements:

- carbon
- hydrogen
- nitrogen
- oxygen

Water

Every living thing consists mostly of water. The body is made up of two-thirds water. Plants and animals must take in nutrients. Water helps to dissolve these particles and carry them to all parts of the body. Through chemical change, the body turns the nutrients into energy or materials it needs to grow or to repair itself. Such changes can occur only in a watery solution. Water also helps to carry away the waste products and to cleanse the system. In addition, it helps to regulate body temperature. People can only live three or four days without water. You need eight glasses daily, some of which can be in the food you eat.

Minerals

Minerals are inorganic nutrients necessary to the body. They help regulate body functions and help to build body tissue. The remaining two percent of tissues and cells are made of minerals. The following minerals are vital to our existence and must be replenished daily:

- calcium
- iron
- magnesium
- phosphorus
- potassium

Essential minerals include iron, iodine, sodium, potassium, calcium, magnesium, phosphorus, zinc, manganese, copper, chromium, and nickel.

Iron

Iron appears in the organs of the body where the blood cells are formed and destroyed. It is necessary in the muscles and other tissues. The largest part of the iron in the body (fifty-five percent) is found in the red blood cells, where it forms an essential part of hemoglobin.

Women need more iron than men because their bodies are preparing for birth. Iron *deficiency* (lack of something needed or required) in children is a common concern. By checking under the bottom eyelid to determine if it is red and meaty, you can distinguish if the body is consuming a normal amount of iron.

Iron is the only mineral in the body that combines with oxygen. Therefore, it helps in the circulation of oxygen in the blood system. Extra iron is stored in the intestines. Iron

Figure 10-3: Foods rich in iron include meats, prunes, seeds, eggs, and green vegetables.

Figure 10-4: Foods rich in iodine include fish, sea salt, and salt with iodine added.

can be found in meats, yeast, wheat germ, prunes, raisins, seeds, leafy dark green vegetables, and egg yolks.

Iodine

Iodine is important to the body because it allows the thyroid gland to secrete a hormone, thyroxine, which controls the body's rate of physical and mental growth. Adequate amounts of iodine prevent the development of the condition called *goiter* (a condition of the thyroid gland). Sources of iodine include sea salt, seafood, and commercial table salt with iodine added.

Sodium

Sodium, or salt (sodium chloride), is an important mineral in our diets, but many times we use it too much and too often. Large amounts tend to cause high blood pressure and lead to retention of water in our systems. Hypertension is also a by-product of too much sodium, and sodium can delete potassium from the body. Excess stress can cause a craving for more salt. More than enough salt is available in our foods without adding salt while cooking or eating. Most salts have been totally eliminated from commercially processed baby foods, and they should be eliminated from the foods served at schools.

Sodium is essential for neuromuscular development and function (such as keeping the heart beating and eliminating palpitations). It helps to maintain the balance of fluids and minerals. Sodium is found in the bodies of animals, in plants, and in the oceans, salt lakes, salt deposits, and rocks. It never occurs in a pure state—it must be refined.

Figure 10-5: Large amounts of sodium (salt) can cause high blood pressure and water retention.

Figure 10-6: Potassium is found in bananas, oranges, cheese, nuts, and seeds.

The average daily allowance of sodium for children is:

- 1 to 3 years of age...325 to 925 milligrams
- 4 to 6 years of age...450 to 1,350 milligrams

Zinc

Zinc prevents eczema, acne, dwarfism, and delayed healing of wounds. Sperm has the most zinc in the body. Sources include oysters, whole grains, seeds, brewer's yeast, liver, meat, and nuts.

Potassium

Potassium is found in foods that are yellow and orange in color, for example, bananas, oranges, nuts, seeds, and cheese. Potassium is necessary for good digestion. Low levels can lead to colic, constipation, fatigue, irritability, listlessness, and depression.

Calcium

Calcium strengthens bones, teeth, muscles, nerve function, and blood clotting. Bones store calcium with the help of vitamin D. Vitamin C helps in the absorption of calcium. Charley horses (muscle cramps) and convulsions may suggest a lock of calcium in the body. In some children, hyperactivity is helped with an increase in calcium.

Sources of calcium include nuts, beans, oysters, soybeans, wheat germ, cabbage, and turnip greens. Milk products also are high in calcium, but recent medical authorities are divided on the amount of milk necessary for good nutrition.

Magnesium

Magnesium is for teeth and bones, along with calcium. Sources are seafood, nuts, whole grains, green vegetables, apricots, figs, and dates.

Phosphorus

Phosphorus helps calcium and vitamin D to be absorbed. Bonemeal is the best source.

Manganese, Copper, Chromium, Nickel, and Other Trace Minerals

Manganese, copper, chromium, nickel, and other minerals are also necessary in minute amounts.

Figure 10-7: Calcium is readily found in milk products, nuts, beans, oysters, cabbage, and turnip greens.

Vitamins

Twenty-five different vitamins are needed. *Vitamins* are complex substances that are essential to the human body for health and growth. The best way to obtain them is to eat foods in which they occur naturally. Vitamins are usually categorized in two types, fat soluble and water soluble.

Fat Soluble Vitamins

Fat soluble vitamins are those that can be dissolved in fat. The body does not excrete overdoses of these vitamins. Instead it stores them in fatty tissue. Overdoses can therefore cause serious damage. Supplements of these vitamins should be taken only on the recommendation of a physician.

1. *Vitamin A* aids in the building and growth of body cells essential for the growth of children and for normal development of babies before birth. It is also needed for bone growth and normal tooth structure. A lack of vitamin A has been found to cause small bumps on the skin, night blindness, respiratory infection, cavities, and ear and skin infections. Stress lowers the ability of protein to move vitamin A throughout the body.

   Sources of vitamin A are spinach, turnips, beets, lettuce, parsley, carrots, sweet potatoes, squash, apricots, and peaches. Liver, eggs, and some dairy products also have vitamin A.

2. *Vitamin D* is produced from certain sterols found in plants and animals exposed to ultraviolet light (sunlight).

Figure 10-8: Vitamin A is found in spinach, turnips, beets, lettuce, carrots, sweet potatoes, squash, apricots, peaches, liver, and dairy products.

Extra amounts are necessary during infancy, adolescence, pregnancy, and *lactation* (nursing). Lack of vitamin D can cause serious bone changes and *rickets* (a disease that causes bone malformation). Sources are sunlight, butter, eggs, beef liver, fish, and cod liver oil.

Water Soluble Vitamins

Water soluble vitamins can be dissolved in water. They are readily found in the cooking water left over from preparing vegetables. The

Figure 10-10: *Thiamine (vitamin B$_1$) is found in beef heart, pork, cereal, grains, peas, green vegetables, and avocados.*

Figure 10-9: *Vitamin D is found in sunlight, butter, eggs, liver, fish, and cod liver oil.*

water soluble vitamins are best in raw vegetables. The body excretes any overdose of these vitamins.

1. *Vitamin B-complex* is a group of more than fifteen vitamins necessary for the conversion of foods to energy. B-complex vitamins are also helpful during times of added stress, pregnancy, and growth. The nerve tissue, skin, eyes, hair, mouth, and liver are the parts of the body dependent on the vitamin B-complex.

   We discuss only five of the most essential vitamins associated with the B-complex. The others are readily found in the same foods.

   Thiamine (B$_1$) prevents and cures *beriberi,* a disease of the nervous system. Thiamine tends to lift depressions, relieve hyperactivity, and decrease fatigue. It helps in the metabolism of carbohydrates to energy. Sources include beef heart, yeast, pork, whole-grain and enriched cereals, soybeans, nuts, peas, green vegetables, and avocados.

Riboflavin (B_2) helps growth, healthy skin, and proper functions of the eyes. It promotes the utilization of oxygen. Vitamin B_2 helps in the metabolism of carbohydrates, fats, and proteins into energy. Lack of riboflavin may show up in cracks in the skin at the corners of the mouth, inflamed lips, a sore tongue, scaliness of skin at the nose and ears, and sensitivity to light. Sources include cheese, eggs, and oysters.

Niacin (B_3) helps prevent *pellagra,* a chronic disease causing gastrointestinal disturbances, acne, and nervous disorders. It is essential for growth and the proper use of oxygen. Niacin also metabolizes carbohydrates, fats, and proteins into energy. Sources are seafood, dairy products, legumes, mushrooms, fowl, and pork.

Pyridoxine (B_6) helps to prevent premenstrual symptoms and *anemia* (lack of iron in the red blood cells). It

also helps control irritability, tremors, and convulsions in infants. It *synthesizes* (combines parts to make a whole) protein and fatty acids, helps red blood cells, and helps in nerve transmissions. Sources are brewer's yeast, meats, whole grains, legumes, and leafy vegetables.

Cobalamin (B_{12}) helps in producing good red blood cells; reduc-

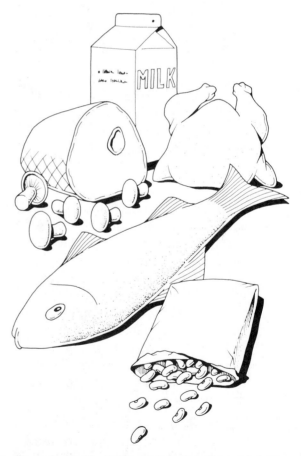

Figure 10-12: Niacin (vitamin B_3) is found in seafood, dairy products, legumes, mushrooms, poultry, and pork.

Figure 10-11: Riboflavin (vitamin B_2) is found in cheese, eggs, and oysters.

Figure 10-13: Pyridoxine (vitamin B$_6$) is found in yeast, meats, grains, legumes, and leafy green vegetables.

Figure 10-14: Cobalamin (vitamin B$_{12}$) is found in meats and dairy products.

ing anemia; lessening fatigue, weakness, stress, and allergies; and increasing appetite. It synthesizes the *DNA* (chemical found in the genes and dealing with hereditary traits when combined with another's genes) and the *RNA* (chemical in the cells). It also helps in the formation of the fatty coverings of nerve cells and the metabolism of carbohydrates. Sources are animal protein such as meats, and dairy products.

2. *Vitamin C*, or ascorbic acid, is not stored in the body. A supply is necessary daily. Vitamin C is essential for healthy blood vessels, sound bones,

Figure 10-15: Vitamin C is found in citrus fruits, tomatoes, cabbage, strawberries, cantaloupe, green peppers, broccoli, cauliflower, and spinach.

and teeth. A deficiency can cause *scurvy* (a disease causing bleeding of the gums), as well as general fatigue and hemorrhaging under the skin. Vitamin C helps the adrenal glands to combat stress. It also aids in the absorption of iron and calcium in the body. Sources are citrus fruits, tomatoes, raw cabbage, strawberries, cantaloupe, guavas, green peppers, broccoli, cauliflower, and spinach.

The intake of too many commercial vitamins can be harmful. The body finds it easier to break down vitamins to fulfill the necessary functions when the vitamins are taken as part of the regular diet in the form of foods. By watching what we eat and how it is prepared, we should be able to include all the vitamins and minerals necessary for good health. Vitamins and minerals are needed in only small amounts.

Three Classes of Food

The three classes of food are carbohydrates, fats, and proteins. All foods are listed under these categories.

Carbohydrates

Carbohydrates provide living things with much of the energy needed to operate muscles and nerves and to maintain optimum performance of plant and body tissues. They break down into simple sugar. Carbohydrates are stored in the small intestines and are readily accessible for energy. Insulin from the pancreas combines with the sugar, which is then used for energy, burning up the sugar but leaving the insulin.

Figure 10-16: Carbohydrates are found in rice, wheat, beets, vegetables, fruits, and juices.

Carbohydrates are made during *photosynthesis* (a process by which plants make carbohydrates) in green plants. They are the most readily available food and can be found as complex carbohydrates in the raw state in rice, wheat, beets (and all vegetables), fruits, and juices. They are easily stored in the body. With the increase of refined sugars (such as in desserts, sodas, and white bread), the supply of good nutrients and carbohydrates to the body has decreased. Excess sugar as glucose is stored around the liver and hips. Four calories equal one unit of energy.

Fats

Fats furnish more than twice as much fuel and energy for the body as the same amounts of proteins or carbohydrates. This is because fats contain more carbon and hydrogen. Fats contain nine calories per gram. Many foods from animal sources, including dairy products, eggs, and meats, have a high cholesterol level.

Recommended Daily Allowances[a]

Age (years)	Weight[b] (kg)	Weight[b] (lb)	Height[b] (cm)	Height[b] (in)	Protein (g)	Fat-Soluble Vitamins Vitamin A (µg RE)[c]	Vitamin D (µg)[d]	Vitamin E (mg α-TE)[e]	Vitamin K (µg)
Infants									
0.0–0.5	6	13	60	24	13	375	7.5	3	5
0.5–1.0	9	20	71	28	14	375	10	4	10
Children									
1–3	13	29	90	35	16	400	10	6	15
4–6	20	44	112	44	24	500	10	7	20
7–10	28	62	132	52	28	700	10	7	30
Males									
11–14	45	99	157	62	45	1,000	10	10	45
15–18	66	145	176	69	59	1,000	10	10	65
19–24	72	160	177	70	58	1,000	10	10	70
25–50	79	174	176	70	63	1,000	5	10	80
51+	77	170	173	68	63	1,000	5	10	80
Females									
11–14	46	101	157	62	46	800	10	8	45
15–18	55	120	163	64	44	800	10	8	55
19–24	58	128	164	65	46	800	10	8	60
25–50	63	138	163	64	50	800	5	8	65
51+	65	143	160	63	50	800	5	8	65
Pregnant						60	800	10	10	65
Lactating 1st 6 months						65	1,300	10	12	65
2nd 6 months						62	1,200	10	11	65

[a] The allowances, expressed as average daily intakes over time, are intended to provide for individual variations among most normal persons as they live in the United States under usual environmental stresses. Diets should be based on a variety of common foods in order to provide other nutrients for which human requirements have been less well defined. See text for detailed discussion of allowances and of nutrients not tabulated.

[b] Weights and heights of Reference Adults are actual medians for the U.S. population of the designated age, as reported by NHANES II. The median weights and heights of those under 19 years of age were taken from Hamill et al. (1979) (see pages 16–17). The use of these figures does not imply that the height-to-weight ratios are ideal.

[c] Retinol equivalents. 1 retinol equivalent = 1 µg retinol or 6 µg β-carotene. See text for calculation of vitamin A activity of diets as retinol equivalents.

[d] As cholecalciferol. 10 µg cholecalciferol = 400 IU of vitamin D.

[e] α-Tocopherol equivalents. 1 mg d-α tocopherol = 1 α-TE. See text for variation in allowances and calculation of vitamin E activity of the diet as α-tocopherol equivalents.

[f] 1 NE (niacin equivalent) is equal to 1 mg of niacin or 60 mg of dietary tryptophan.

Figure 10-17: Recommended daily allowances designed for the maintenance of good nutrition of practically all healthy people in the USA. Recommended Daily Dietary Allowances, 10th ed. Washington, D.C.: The National Academy of Sciences — National Research Council, 1989. Reprinted by permission.

	Water-Soluble Vitamins						Minerals						
Vitamin C (mg)	Thiamine (mg)	Riboflavin (mg)	Niacin (mg NE)[f]	Vitamin B_6 (mg)	Folate (µg)	Vitamin B_{12} (µg)	Calcium (mg)	Phosphorus (mg)	Magnesium (mg)	Iron (mg)	Zinc (mg)	Iodine (µg)	Selenium (µg)
30	0.3	0.4	5	0.3	25	0.3	400	300	40	6	5	40	10
35	0.4	0.5	6	0.6	35	0.5	600	500	60	10	5	50	15
40	0.7	0.8	9	1.0	50	0.7	800	800	80	10	10	70	20
45	0.9	1.1	12	1.1	75	1.0	800	800	120	10	10	90	20
45	1.0	1.2	13	1.4	100	1.4	800	800	170	10	10	120	30
50	1.3	1.5	17	1.7	150	2.0	1,200	1,200	270	12	15	150	40
60	1.5	1.8	20	2.0	200	2.0	1,200	1,200	400	12	15	150	50
60	1.5	1.7	19	2.0	200	2.0	1,200	1,200	350	10	15	150	70
60	1.5	1.7	19	2.0	200	2.0	800	800	350	10	15	150	70
60	1.2	1.4	15	2.0	200	2.0	800	800	350	10	15	150	70
50	1.1	1.3	15	1.4	150	2.0	1,200	1,200	280	15	12	150	45
60	1.1	1.3	15	1.5	180	2.0	1,200	1,200	300	15	12	150	50
60	1.1	1.3	15	1.6	180	2.0	1,200	1,200	280	15	12	150	55
60	1.1	1.3	15	1.6	180	2.0	800	800	280	15	12	150	55
60	1.0	1.2	13	1.6	180	2.0	800	800	280	10	12	150	55
70	1.5	1.6	17	2.2	400	2.2	1,200	1,200	320	30	15	175	65
95	1.6	1.8	20	2.1	280	2.6	1,200	1,200	355	15	19	200	75
90	1.6	1.7	20	2.1	260	2.6	1,200	1,200	340	15	16	200	75

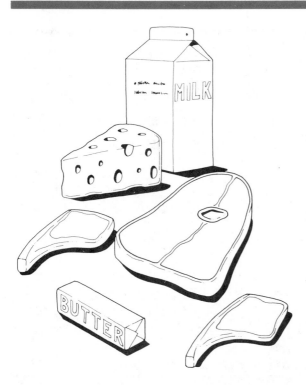

Figure 10-18: Fats are found in meats and dairy products.

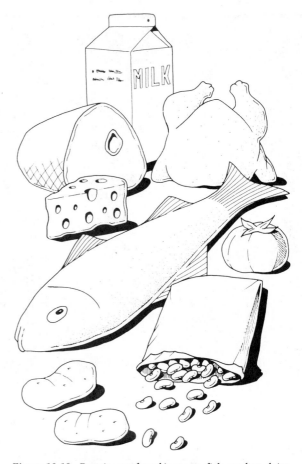

Figure 10-19: Proteins are found in meats, fish, poultry, dairy products, legumes, and vegetables.

Too much fat is a leading component of heart disease and cancer.

The average daily allowance of fat intake recommended for children is 480 calories, or 50 to 55 grams. Since fat is so abundant in our diets, usually fat intake must be reduced to about a third of the total calorie count. Fats are hard to digest and are finally broken down into fatty acids in the small intestines. Because of this, they can keep a person from feeling hungry for a longer period of time than non-fatty foods.

Fats serve as a source of heat and as an insulation against cold. All fat not used to fuel energy or growth is stored in the tissues as body fat (in the arms, back, hips, and liver, and under the eyes). Fat is also used as a shock absorber and as a protective layer around the kidneys.

Proteins

Proteins are chemical compounds that are an essential part of every cell. They are digested in the stomach and break down to twenty different *amino acids* (components that aid the heart, dilate the air passages, and are essential to living cells). They are then absorbed into the blood and carried to all organs and tissues. Proteins are used to build new cells and for growth. They make up one-third of the muscle structure and one-fifth of bones, blood, cells, and enzymes. They supply four calories per gram.

Foods high in protein value include lean meat, fish, cheese, nuts, eggs, milk, legumes, vegetables, and poultry. These foods not only are high in proteins but also contain all the amino acids needed by the body. Complementary foods, such as rice and beans, contain amino acids so that the body can make protein. This is often a cost-effective and low-fat method of supplying protein to the body.

Energy

Energy is the ability of the body to do work. *Calories* are units of food energy. The number of calories necessary to maintain a healthy body is individual and depends on *metabolism* (how much energy we use and store), the body size, and the rate of body growth. Eating more than the body needs results in weight gain. Remember the following facts about calories:

1. Girls and women need fewer calories than do boys and men.

2. Inactive people need fewer calories than do active people.

3. Older people need fewer calories than do teenagers.

4. Young children need fewer calories than do teenagers.

NUTRITION IN CENTERS AND SCHOOLS

For bodies to remain healthy, we must provide balanced diets. Supplying diets that include the nutrients children need to repair and maintain their tissues is a responsibility of caregivers. To encourage eating, portions of food should be small and attractive. Children should have some freedom to choose foods and to eat in their own way. It is important that caregivers remain relaxed and enjoy children during mealtimes. All of these actions help children have a happy meal. Children are more interested in how foods taste, look, and feel than in their nutritional value.

Caregivers are concerned about the eating habits of children, but avoid confrontations over eating certain foods. Begin by teaching

Figure 10-20: Active children need good nutrition.

Figure 10-21: Children talk and socialize during lunch.

the benefits of a healthy body to the children. Discuss the advantages of maintaining a healthy body through a balanced diet. Help to choose and prepare food aesthetically, and provide a nurturing environment during meals.

The Five Basic Food Groups

Secretary of Agriculture Clayton Yeutter stated that Americans have "never been more concerned about their diet and health. Diet directly influences the health of every age group, ethnic group, and region in the country." The United States Department of Agriculture established 1990 Guidelines for good diet and health. The main points are:

- Eat a variety of foods.
- Maintain a healthy weight.
- Choose a diet low in fat, saturated fat, and cholesterol.

- Choose a diet with plenty of vegetables, fruits, and grain products.
- Use sugar only in moderation.
- If you drink alcoholic beverages, do so in moderation.

When planning meals and snacks for young children, it is important to understand the five basic food groups. Using these food groups as a guide simplifies meal planning. Three meals a day plus snacks are recommended to refuel the body as it uses energy. The following groups are listed according to the United States Department of Agriculture, the Health and Human Services Department:

- Breads, Cereals, and other Grain Products
- Fruits
- Vegetables
- Meat, Poultry, Fish, and Alternates (eggs, dry beans and peas, nuts, and seeds)
- Milk, Cheese, and Yogurt

Be sure to choose at least the minimum number of servings recommended from each group every day. Many women, older children, and most teenagers and men need more.

Breads, Cereals, and other Grain Products

This group includes most foods made from grain and flour, for example: bread, crackers, English muffins, bagels, tortillas, biscuits, rice, pasta, noodles, and cereal. However, most sweets made from flour, such as cookies, cakes,

The Five Basic Food Groups

Milk Group

Vegetable Group

Fruit Group

Bread and Cereal Group

Meat Group

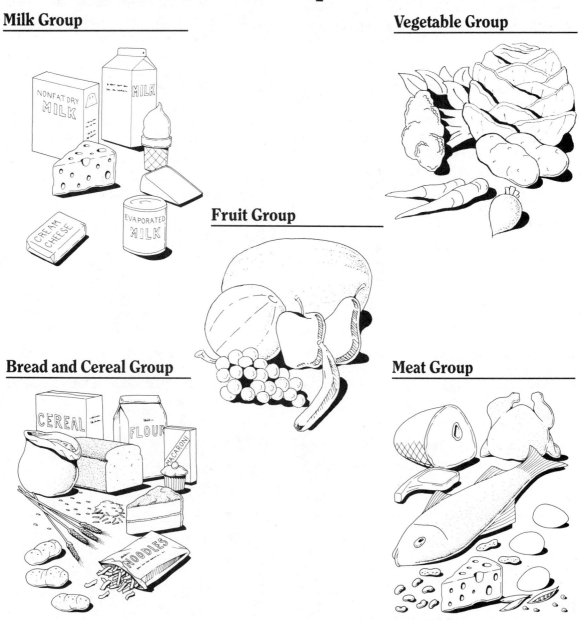

Figure 10-22: Five basic food groups chart.

and doughnuts, are not considered basic foods and do not fit in this group. This group provides thiamine, niacin, and iron. Six to eleven servings (equal to one slice of bread) are recommended daily.

Fruits

This group includes all oranges, grapefruit, melon, berries, tomatoes, and other fruits that are a source of vitamin C. Two to four servings (a whole, medium-size banana, apple or orange; one-half cup of berries) are recommended daily.

Vegetables

This group includes dark-green leafy, deep-yellow, dry beans and peas (legumes), starchy, and other vegetables. Excellent sources of vitamin A are lettuce, broccoli, spinach, mustard greens, carrots, sweet potatoes, and winter squash. Sources of vitamin C include green peppers and potatoes. Three to five servings (equal to one-half cup of cooked or chopped vegetables) are needed.

Meat, Poultry, Fish, and Alternates

This group includes all kinds of meat, poultry, and fish, as well as alternates of eggs, nuts, seeds, peanut butter, dried beans, refried beans, baked beans, and split or dried peas. These foods supply protein, iron, some fat, copper, sodium, potassium, magnesium, phosphorus, zinc, and vitamins (A, B-complex, and D). Two to three servings (five to seven ounces of lean meat, poultry or fish; one egg, one-half cup cooked beans, or two tablespoons of peanut butter equal one ounce of meat) per day are recommended.

Milk, Cheese, and Yogurt

This group includes milk and products made from milk, such as cheese, cottage cheese, yogurt, custard, pudding, and ice cream. These foods provide calcium, protein, and riboflavin. (Butter, whipping cream, and sour cream are only one-part milk and do not fit into this group.) Two servings (one cup of milk or one and a half ounces of cheese) per day from the entire group is recommended. (Three servings for women who are pregnant or breast-feeding and for teens; four servings for teens who are pregnant or breast-feeding.)

Extra Foods

Foods that do not fit into a specific group include sugar, salt, fat, and those used mainly for flavoring. These foods supply the body with energy and add flavor and variety to our diets. However, these foods often contain many calories and few nutrients. If eaten in excess, they can add unwanted pounds. Spices and some flavorings add little fat, salt, or sugar and few calories.

Foods with high fat content include:

- butter
- cakes
- chips
- cookies
- cream
- doughnuts
- gravies
- margarine
- pies

- sauces

Foods with high sugar content include:

- beer
- cakes
- candy
- catsup
- cookies
- cough drops
- doughnuts
- gelatin
- gum
- honey
- jams
- jellies
- liquor
- mints
- molasses
- pies
- popsickles
- soft drinks
- sugars
- syrup
- wine

Foods with high salt content include:

- broths
- butter
- catsup
- chips

- gravies
- margarine
- mayonnaise
- most seasonings
- mustard
- relishes
- sauces

Planning Menus

Plan your daily menus to include at least the minimum servings in each food group. Keep the age, sex, body size, activity level, season of year, food allergies, medical problems, and the cultural or ethnic background of the people in mind. Religious prohibitions against certain foods and their preparation, and vegetarianism should be considered and respected. Toddlers and young children need the same variety as adults but smaller portions are necessary due to their size and age. Provide nutritious snacks such as fruits and vegetables instead of cookies and sweets.

1. Avoid too much fat, saturated fat, and cholesterol.

2. Avoid too much sodium (salt).

3. Avoid too much sugar.

4. Eat a variety of foods.

5. Eat foods with adequate starch and fiber.

6. If you drink alcohol, do so in moderation.

7. Maintain ideal weight.

When planning menus, have you remembered to include fun? Are the children involved in the planning and preparation? Are the foods easy and simple so that children may participate? Do the children practice self-help skills by washing fruits and vegetables, setting the table, and helping to clean up? Do you take this opportunity to discuss the nutritional values of the foods? Have you thought of how the foods will look when served (colors and arrangement)? How will the combination of foods taste (sweet, sour, or spicy)? Do the foods have different textures or feels (crunchy, soft, or crisp)? If you can answer these questions positively, you will have a successful meal.

If the opportunities are presented, children can learn many concepts while helping in food planning and preparation. Besides nutrition, they learn basic math skills such as shapes, measurement, numbers, and fractions. Good health practices are acquired by washing hands and scrubbing the table before and after eating. Children also learn socialization (manners), language arts (conversation), and social science (different cultures). Children can learn science (where and how foods grow). Sensory experiences are present when children taste, hear, see, smell, and feel the foods.

When they are involved, children are apt to look forward to snacks and meals. New foods are more often enjoyed and accepted when children have a chance to help prepare them.

Snacks

Snacks make up twenty-two percent of all the foods preschoolers eat every day (Rothlein, *Young Children*, "Nutrition Tips Revisited...", 1989). At least two of the five basic food groups, as well as juice, should be included in the preparation of snacks. Juices should be made from natural fruits and vegetables. No sugar should be added. Carbonated drinks and fruitades are not good for young children because they have few nutrients and too much sugar. Children have small stomachs and snacks provide nutritional value and energy between meals. Space snacks evenly between meals and at least two hours apart. Figure 10–23 contains recipes that are simple and easy for the children to help to prepare.

Snacktime is also an opportunity to present good table manners, a clean environment, a properly set table (including napkins, utensils, and cups), and a pleasant atmosphere. Remember, children imitate. You must demonstrate an appreciation for food well-served, sample all foods presented, and use good manners.

Snacks

Bugs on a Log
- celery cut into two-inch pieces
- filled with peanut butter
- topped with raisins (a raisin for each year)

Space Candy
- 1/2 cup peanut butter
- 1/2 cup honey
- 1 cup powdered milk

Mix, roll into balls. *Note:* Honey should not be served to children under the age of one, due to the danger of botulism.

Figure 10-23: Simple recipes for children.

Meals

Meals should include all five of the basic food groups plus a nutritious drink. The same principles that were discussed for snacks also apply to meals. Pay special attention to portion sizes and the amount of time allotted for eating. Most young children are tired after strenuous play or study, so mealtime should be relaxed and unhurried. Figure 10–24 (page 184) contains examples of nutritious and easy-to-prepare meals.

Elements of establishing positive eating habits include:

- a pleasing atmosphere

- food attractively served

- food offered in the expectation that the meal will be eaten and enjoyed

- freedom to choose some of one's own food

- introduction of new foods one at a time with the suggestion to try it, you might like it

- learning self-help skills

- manners taught by role modeling

- relaxed and pleasant caregivers

- small servings (allow children to ask for seconds)

- spills treated lightly (encourage children to help clean up)

- the satisfaction of serving oneself

- utensils appropriate in size and number

Food intake can be regulated by remembering:

1. Allow a child to be fully awake (at least half an hour before serving food).

2. Children need five to six small meals a day (including snacks).

3. Each meal should include one-third or less of total caloric intake.

4. Sweets cause cavities in the teeth.

5. Too many carbohydrates at snacks can cause a decrease in appetite at meals.

Meals are generally planned by the director or the dietician of the school. Each meal should meet one third or less of the servings recommended by the United States Department of Agriculture. Meals must be safe. They must be of sufficient quality and quantity to meet the nutritional needs of the children. Remember that nutritional needs vary with age.

All states have laws governing the food service in centers, schools or family day care homes. Figure 10–26 (page 186) shows an example of the California State Guidelines for food service. The person in charge must follow all the state and local laws. These include personnel and kitchen facilities, as well as the nutritional value of the food.

WELL-NOURISHED CHILDREN

How can you tell when children are well-nourished? You will first be aware of their general appearance. They are able to function within the normal span for their age and development. Their eyes are clear and bright. Their

Sample Meals

Stone Soup

- 1 large soup pan filled with water
- 1 clean stone
- 1 large onion
- 1 eight-ounce package of noodles
- 2 bouillon cubes
- Clean and cut-up vegetables (supplied by each child—have them bring their favorites)
- water

  Add the vegetables to the water. Cook for two hours.
  Serve the soup, whole-grain crackers or bread, milk, apples, and cheese.

Tuna Sandwich

- 1 can of water-packed tuna
- 2 stalks of diced celery
- 1/4 cup diced sweet pickles
- 2 tablespoons light mayonnaise
- whole wheat bread

  Serve the sandwich with carrot sticks, apple slices, and milk.

Figure 10-24: Sample meals chart.

Sample Menu

Breakfast

- orange juice
- Vienna sausage wrapped in a biscuit
- scrambled egg
- milk

Midmorning Snack

- cheese and crackers
- grape juice

Lunch

- oven-fried chicken
- roasted potatoes
- green beans
- ambrosia
- cornbread and butter
- milk
- pudding

Afternoon Snack

- snack mix (raisins, coconut, nuts, seeds, granola)
- apple juice

Figure 10-25: Sample menu chart.

hair is smooth and glossy. Their skeletal structures are straight. Their chests are full and round, and give a solid sound when thumped. Their teeth fit their mouths without crowding and are free of cavities. Their gums are firm around the teeth and do not bleed when brushed.

Children need to look padded and well-rounded without excessive fat under the eyes and at the small of the back. The inside of the mouth and under the bottom of the eyes should be nicely red. The muscular systems should be developed so that children can manage most skills appropriate for their age. These skills may include hanging on to a bar, working a paper punch, or riding a bicycle.

The bodily functions of healthy children operate normally. Healthy children have good appetites and regular bowel movements (at least once every three days). They have regular sleep patterns and sleep eight to twelve hours a day. With a little rest, they can wake up promptly and recover from their naps.

Healthy children show excitement about learning. They ask questions and enjoy the fun of discovery. They are alert, have good endurance, and are emotionally stable in coping with ordinary daily activities. They get along well with their peers and teachers, and they are generally cooperative.

POORLY NOURISHED CHILDREN

What are the signs of poorly nourished children? Their general appearance is strained. They may look as if they are trying too hard.

Their eyes may have dark circles or bags underneath and may lack luster. Their legs may be bowed. Poorly nourished children may have barreled or sunken chests and overlarge joints. Their muscles may appear flabby under the arms. Their coordination may be poor or not up to their development level. Their gums may bleed easily, and their teeth may have several cavities.

Such children may have pale, loose, and dry skin. The mouth linings and the undersides of the bottoms of the eyes may also be pale. The bodily functions may be disturbed by poor appetite, constipation, or diarrhea. Such children may be listless, irritable, or hyperactive. They are poor sleepers (light and short). They recover slowly from naps and illnesses.

Poorly nourished children are often underweight and short for their ages. General decreases in appetite may have been caused by too little sleep, lack of outdoor play, too much exercise, infectious disease, poor teeth, or worms.

Why aren't some children well nourished? There are several reasons, which can appear singly or together. There may be a breakdown in the body functions, failure to utilize nutrients, or a failure of the diet to supply the required nutrients. Children may have poor eating habits. Poor eating habits can be caused by psychological problems created by:

- food served in an unhappy atmosphere
- hurried and irritable caregivers
- introducing too many new foods at one time
- insisting the child eat all food at one setting

- negative presentation of food
- too large portions served
- too much emphasis on good manners

A lack of awareness on the caregiver's part concerning nutritional needs and good health habits can lead to poor nourishment. A balance of activities is important. Outdoor play, inside play, quiet time, and noisy time are essential for the child to develop well. These items help to build a good appetite.

SUMMARY

Nutrition is a responsibility of the children's center or school. Children need to be provided with a sound diet to offset the large amounts of fast foods consumed in this country.

The four types of tissues include epithelial; muscular; connective; and bone, blood and nerve. Both animals and plants are made up of millions of cells, which make up all components of the body. Water is two-thirds of our total structure. It helps to dissolve nutrients and carry them to all parts of the body.

Caregivers should have a basic knowledge of nutrients supplied by foods, including minerals and vitamins. Minerals help to regulate body functions and to build body tissue. They are inorganic nutrients. Vitamins can be either fat or water soluble. They are essential for health and growth.

The three classes of foods are carbohydrates, fats, and proteins. Carbohydrates provide energy to work the muscles and nerves. They also help maintain tissues. Fats supply the body with twice as much fuel and energy as carbohydrates or proteins. However, consuming too many fats can lead to heart disease and cancer. Unused fats are stored in the tis-

State of California

(a) In facilities providing meals to clients, the following shall apply:
  (1) All food shall be safe and of the quality and in the quantity necessary to meet the needs of the clients. Each meal shall meet at least 1/3 of the servings recommended in the USDA Basic Food Group Plan — Daily Food Guide for the age group served. All food shall be selected, stored, prepared, and served in a safe and healthful manner.
  (2) Where all food is provided by the facility, arrangements shall be made so that each client has available at least three meals per day.
    (A) Not more than 15 hours shall elapse between the third meal of one day and first meal of the following day.
  (3) Where meal service within a facility is elective, arrangements shall be made to ensure availability of a daily food intake meeting the requirement of (a) (1) above for all clients who, in their admission agreement, elect meal service.
  (4) Between meal nourishment or snacks shall be available for all clients unless limited by dietary restrictions prescribed by a physician.

Figure 10-26: State of California requirements.

Food Service Licensing Requirements

(5) Menus shall be written at least one week in advance and copies of the menus as served shall be dated and kept on file for at least 30 days. Menus shall be made available for review by the clients or their authorized representatives and the licensing agency upon request.

(6) Modified diets prescribed by a client's physician as a medical necessity shall be provided.

    (A) The licensee shall obtain and follow instructions from the physician or dietitian on the preparation of the modified diet.

(7) Commercial foods shall be approved by appropriate federal, state and local authorities. All foods shall be selected, transported, stored, prepared and served so as to be free from contamination and spoilage and shall be fit for human consumption. Food in damaged containers shall not be accepted, used or retained.

(8) Where indicated, food shall be cut, chopped or ground to meet individual needs.

(9) Powdered milk shall not be used as a beverage but shall be allowed in cooking and baking. Raw milk, as defined in Division 15 of the California Food and Agricultural Code shall not be used. Milk shall be pasteurized.

(10) Except upon written approval by the licensing agency, meat, poultry and meat food products shall be inspected by state or federal authorities. Written evidence of such inspection shall be available for all products not obtained from commercial markets.

(11) All home canned foods shall be processed in accordance with standards of the University of California Agricultural Extension Service. Home canned foods from outside sources shall not be used.

(12) If food is prepared off the facility premises, the following shall apply:

    (A) The preparation source shall meet all applicable requirements for commercial food services.

    (B) The facility shall have the equipment and staff necessary to receive and serve the food and for cleanup.

    (C) The facility shall maintain the equipment necessary for in-house preparation, or have an alternate source for food preparation, and service of food in emergencies.

(continued on next page)

(13) All persons engaged in food preparation and service shall observe personal hygiene and food services sanitation practices which protect the food from contamination.

(14) All foods or beverages capable of supporting rapid and progressive growth of microorganisms which can cause food infections or food intoxications shall be stored in covered containers at 45 degrees F (7.2 degrees C) or less.

(15) Pesticides and other similar toxic substances shall not be stored in food storerooms, kitchen areas, food preparation areas, or areas where kitchen equipment or utensils are stored.

(16) Soaps, detergents, cleaning compounds or similar substances shall be stored in areas separate from food supplies.

(17) All kitchen, food preparation, and storage areas shall be kept clean, free of litter and rubbish, and measures shall be taken to keep all such areas free of rodents, and other vermin.

(18) All food shall be protected against contamination. Contaminated food shall be discarded immediately.

(19) All equipment, fixed or mobile, dishes, and utensils shall be kept clean and maintained in safe condition.

(20) All dishes and utensils used for eating and drinking and in the preparation of food and drink shall be cleaned and sanitized after each usage.

(A) Dishwashing machines shall reach a temperature of 165 degrees F (74 degrees C) during the washing and/or drying cycle to ensure that dishes and utensils are cleaned and sanitized.

(B) Facilities not using dishwashing machines shall clean and sanitize dishes and utensils by an alternative comparable method.

(21) Equipment necessary for the storage, preparation and service of food shall be provided and shall be well-maintained.

(22) Tableware and tables, dishes, and utensils shall be provided in the quantity necessary to serve the clients.

(23) Adaptive devices shall be provided for self-help in eating as needed by clients.

(b) The licensing agency shall have the authority to require the facility to provide written information, including menus, regarding the food purchased and used over a given period when it is necessary to determine if the licensee is in compliance with the food service requirements in the regulations in this Division.

(1) The licensing agency shall specify in writing the written information required from the licensee.

Figure 10-26 continued

sues. Proteins are needed in order to build new cells and for growth. Many sources other than meat can supply our bodies with protein.

There are five basic food groups—Breads, Cereals, and other Grain Products; Fruits; Vegetables; Meat, Poultry, Fish, and Alternates; and Milk, Cheese, and Yogurt. Caregivers must carefully plan to include all the basic food groups in their daily menus. If the proper food is provided, children will consume all the basic nutrients necessary for good growth and health.

Well-nourished children have rosy skin, clear eyes, glossy hair, and straight skeletons. Their personalities are pleasing and cooperative. They have good self-esteem and muscular coordination. Caregivers' attitudes and expectations about meals contribute to well-nourished children.

Poorly nourished children may have pale skin, dull eyes, flabby muscles, and underdeveloped coordination. They are listless and irritable, and they may have low self-esteem. They are often underweight and short for their ages. Psychological problems during mealtimes can lead to poor eating habits.

Review Questions

1. How do emotions reflect your eating habits?
2. Why is it important to avoid too much "fast food"?
3. Why is it important to drink eight glasses of water daily?
4. What are some sources of iron?
5. What is the difference between fat and water soluble vitamins?
6. What is anemia?
7. Why are carbohydrates necessary for the body?
8. Why is it necessary to have proteins in our diet?
9. List the five food groups.
10. Why is it important to include fun when planning menus?
11. Why do some children suffer from poor nourishment?

Things to Do and Discuss

1. Keep a weekly diary of your meals. Explain the nutritional value of your eating habits.
2. Plan a one-day menu for a child care center. Include breakfast, morning snack, lunch, and afternoon snack. Go to the market and check the prices. Read labels to determine nutritional value. (Keep in mind, budgeting is an important factor.)
3. Find recipes for three snacks that children can participate in preparing and serving and that they will enjoy eating. Keep nutrition, creativity, and fun in mind.
4. Research your state laws and regulations concerning food service for the age group in which you are interested.
5. Read your local newspaper. How many articles can you find about good nutrition for young children?
6. Research the statistics concerning the percentage of poorly nourished children in your community and state.

SECTION III

OBJECTIVES

After completing this section, you will be able to:

1. explain the basic concepts of Freud, Piaget, Erikson, and Gesell;
2. define and discuss physical, social, emotional, and intellectual development;
3. discuss and record observations of children, staff, school, or center.

The Four Basic Areas of Child Development

The following section discusses gaining an understanding of how children develop. This will help you to determine normal and abnormal growth patterns. Children develop independently according to their maturation level and abilities.

There are four basic areas of development that caregivers need to be aware of. Physical development includes motor skills, health characteristics, and growth. Feelings, decision making, problem solving, and independence are parts of emotional development. Social development includes self-esteem, responsibility, personality, and interaction with others. Intellectual and cognitive development include reason, concept learning, senses, creativity, and language. These developmental areas are not listed in order of importance. Children develop in a combination of areas, which often overlap. For example, in a span of a few min-utes Jimmy climbs on the play structure (physical development) and interacts with his playmates (social development). He appears happy and relaxed (emotional development). He counts to ten (cognitive development) as he waits for his turn on the sliding pole.

Each child is a unique person. Caregivers must observe the child to determine the next step in the developmental process. Caregivers need to have this basic knowledge to recognize signs of the four basic areas of development. With this knowledge, they can structure the learning environment and provide materials to meet the individual needs.

This section details the proper methods of observing the children, the staff, the school, and the center. Written observations allow caregivers to plan for the future. Several examples are included to give you an understanding of various methods to enhance your skills.

CHAPTER 11
Theorists

One child enjoys sliding, while others wait their turn.

KEY TERMS

chronological age
ego
id
maturation level
subconscious mind

superego
theorists
theory of cognitive
    development

OBJECTIVES

After completing this chapter, you will be able to:
1. describe the importance of Freud, Erikson, Piaget, Gesell, Skinner, Maslow, and White:
2. explain how cognitive and psychosocial stages of early childhood combine in the process of development.

INTRODUCTION

Theorists are experts who develop theories by observation and reasoning. They do extensive testing to confirm an original assumption. There are theorists in many aspects of child development, including social, emotional, physical, and intellectual development. The basic goal for this chapter is to let you learn how theories can work in the developmental process of young children. As caregivers, you should look at children as complete individuals and understand that they must develop in a well-rounded manner.

Theorists are important because they develop standards by which to measure normal development. You need to remember that normal can fall into a wide category. Children develop at different rates. Following are four of the major theorists of importance to understanding the development of young children. Many others have also contributed to our knowledge.

SIGMUND FREUD

Sigmund Freud (1856–1939) is considered the father of personality theory. He is noted for writing the *Psychosexual Theory of Man*, on the *subconscious mind* (mental processes of which the individual is not aware) and how it influences behavior. Freud believed that the early experiences of children affect the behavior and personality that they exhibit in later life.

He divided the personality into three parts—the id, the ego, and the superego. The *id* is present at birth, is concerned with the pleasure principle, and functions on the unconscious level of motives and desires. The id seeks immediate gratification. The *ego* (meaning "I" in Latin), however, develops soon after birth and is the part of the mind associated with reason and common sense. It functions on the reality principle and is willing to wait for gratification. The *superego*, or conscience, does not develop until the age of four or five. It encompasses morals and identification with the parent of the same sex. Although Freud was not concerned with the educational field, educators use his theories to help explain the development of the child.

JEAN PIAGET

Jean Piaget (1896–1980) is important in understanding child development from birth to adulthood. He wrote *The Origins of Intelli-*

Figure 11-1: Sigmund Freud. Photo courtesy of Bettman Archive.

Figure 11-2: Jean Piaget. Photo courtesy of Bettman Archive.

gence in Children, among many other volumes, and established the *theory of cognitive development*. Piaget believed that children's thinking processes are fundamentally different from those of adults. He used open-ended questions (such as "What do you think will happen?") to test the intelligence level of children, thus permitting the children to answer in their natural manner.

Cognitive development, as Piaget theorized, depended on *maturation level* (the stage of development as the child progresses and learns) and experiences (environment). He felt that all learning follows a predictable pattern, although each person progresses at a different rate. As children gain new knowledge, they combine it with previously learned information. Thus, it is important that children be able to interact with all their senses with various materials (experience a sensorimotor stage) and be creative with the use of materials. He also felt that children need large blocks of time in order to make decisions and reach conclusions based on their own work during the sensorimotor stage.

ARNOLD GESELL

Arnold Gesell (1880–1961) was concerned with how the body grows and influences child development as the child interacts with the environment. He thought that the chronological age (the age of the child counted in years) was not as important in determining the child's progress as was the maturation level. He established a series of behavior tests (the School Readiness Test) that measure maturation levels of children. These are still considered norms of how children grow and develop. The tests cover four areas of behavior — motor, adaptive, language, and personal-social. Although these tests were devised in 1928, they have withstood time with only minor changes.

ERIK ERIKSON

Erik Erikson (1902-   ) was a student of Freud, and he expanded on the theories of psychosocial development. In the *Eight Ages of Man*, published in 1950, Erikson stated that individuals must go through eight stages, or crises of behavior, in order to develop a strong social and emotional life. He believed that a child's self-esteem and social conscience were based on their relationships with others and their ethnic background. Each stage must be completed and the crisis solved before individuals can go on to the next stage. How each stage is met and how the crisis is resolved determines the future development of the child.

Figure 11-3: Arnold Gesell. Photo courtesy of Bettman Archive.

Figure 11-4: Erik Erikson. Photo courtesy of Bettman Archive.

Figure 11-5 gives a breakdown of the above theories in the order of the development of the child. This has been done to give you, the caregiver, an overview and an understanding of how children develop.

OTHER WELL-KNOWN EXPERTS

Abraham Maslow

Abraham Maslow (1908–1970) believed that all people have a set of basic needs (i.e., food, water, shelter, clothing). These must be fulfilled before going on to higher needs (i.e., achievement, approval, and fulfillment of goals and potentials in life). If all needs are met and satisfied, Maslow stated that a person will reach self-actualization (self-initiated striving to become what one is capable of being). As a humanistic theorist, Maslow emphasized self-knowledge (knowing oneself) and the process of achieving a positive self-concept. The child moves toward self-actualization by being provided a healthy and safe environment, loving parents and caregivers, and positive peer interaction.

Maslow's "Hierarchy of Needs" includes:

1. Physiological Needs: food, water, air, shelter, warmth, pain avoidance, sex

2. Safety Needs: protection, security

3. Love and Belonging: friends, social groups, acceptance, intimacy

4. Self-esteem: respect, competence, approval, achievement, recognition, prestige

5. Aesthetic: beauty, order, symmetry, justice, truth

6. Self-actualization: fulfillment of our potential, completion, individuality, self-sufficiency

Burton White

Dr. Burton White is considered one of the country's foremost authorities on the development of the infant and toddler. He is the cofounder and director of the Center for Parent Education (1978). Through thirty years of research, Dr. White has acquired volumes of firsthand information on how children develop during their early years and how parents can help their children get the best possible foundation in life.

(continued on page 202)

Theorists: Chronological Stages

ERIKSON (Psychosocial)

Infancy: Trust vs. Mistrust

Creating trust through sensitive and consistent care of infants' needs — physical and emotional.

1½–3 Years: Autonomy vs. Shame and Doubt

Developing a sense of self, doing more for self, and learning self-esteem.

3½–5 Years: Initiative vs. Guilt

Establishing a conscience, being curious, having feelings, and discovering self.

5½–12 Years: Industry vs. Inferiority

Increasing need to interact with and be accepted by peers. Developing a feeling of importance — I can do. Desiring tasks — can carry through to completion. Needing recognition.

12–18 Years: Identity vs. Identity Diffusion

Development of a strong ego. Sense of self — Who am I? and Who can I be? Establishing a role in society.

FREUD (Psychosexual)

Infancy: Oral

Attains most gratification from sucking, biting, and swallowing. Id is dominant during this stage.

1½–3 Years: Anal

Sources of sexual gratification include expelling feces and urinating, as well as retaining feces. Id and ego.

3½–5 Years: Phallic

Child becomes concerned with genitals. Pleasure from manipulating genitals. Id, ego, superego.

5½–12 Years: Latency

Loss of sexual interest. Identification with like sexual parent. Id, ego, and superego.

12–18 Years: Genital

Concern with adult modes of sexual pleasure. Masturbation is common. Strong attachments to others of same sex gradually superseded by heterosexual relationships. Superego becomes more flexible.

Figure 11-5: Theorists: Chronological stages.

PIAGET (Cognitive)

Infancy: Sensorimotor

Learns about world through activities by using senses — taste, smell, touch, sight, and hearing. No language and no thought in the early stages. Object permanence — if an object is gone from sight, it has disappeared.

2½–4 Years: Preconceptual

Acquiring language. Self-centered (egocentric). Able to use symbols to represent objects, places, and people. Thought is more flexible but is still not mature in the adult sense.

4–7 Years: Preoperational

Capable of more complex thought based on immediate understanding rather than logical, rational thinking. Limited ability to put objects and thoughts in proper order. Egocentric. How the individual sees objects dominates the individual's thinking.

6–12 Years: Concrete Operations

Becoming efficient at classifying, seriating, numbers, and principles of conservation. Can handle several ideas at the same time. Egocentrism is diminishing.

12 Years–Adult: Formal Operations

Thought becomes as logical as it ever will. Capable of hypothetical reasoning.

GESELL (Maturation Level)

4 Weeks

Cannot sit, stand, creep or walk. When on stomach, most can lift head slightly.

28 Weeks

Can lift legs high while on back and can roll onto stomach; most can sit erect momentarily.

1 Year

Can reach and grasp objects. Can transfer from hand to hand. Can creep. Can stand alone. May walk with assistance. Can stack blocks. Can pick up small objects.

2½ Years

Able to stand on one foot. Can stack a tower of ten blocks. Can hold a crayon with fingers.

3½ Years

Walks on tiptoe two or more steps. Begins skipping with one foot. Can descend stairs with alternating feet. Can use blunt scissors and make expert and precise marks with crayon.

6 Years

Stands on one foot. Walks on tiptoes five or more steps. Broad jumps thirty-two inches. Prints first and last names. Can count ten or more objects correctly.

Developmental Theories

Developmental Research Tells Us:

Teachers Can:

1. Growth occurs in a sequence.

- Think about the steps children will take when planning projects.
- Know the sequence of growth in their children's age group.

2. Children in any age group will behave similarly in certain ways.

- Plan for activities in relation to age range of children.
- Know the characteristics of their children's age group.

3. Children grow through certain stages.

- Know the stages of growth in their class.
- Identify to family any behavior inconsistent with general stages of development.

4. Growth occurs in four interrelated areas.

- Understand that a person's work in one area can help in another.
- Plan for language growth, while children use their bodies.

5. Intellectual growth:
Children learn through their senses.
Children learn by doing; adults learn in abstract ways, while children need concrete learning. Cognitive growth occurs in four areas:

- Have activities in looking, smelling, tasting, hearing, and touching.
- Realize that talking is abstract; have children touch, manipulate, act out what they are to do.

Figure 11-6: Developmental research tests theories of growth and learning to find out about children and childhood. Reprinted from Beginnings and Beyond: Foundations in Early Childhood Education *by Gordon and Browne. Copyright 1985 by Delmar Publishers. Used with permission.*

Developmental Research Tells Us:

Teachers Can:

perception (visual, auditory, etc.)

- Provide materials and activities in matching, finding same/different, putting a picture with a sound or a taste, or with a symbol.

language

- Provide opportunities to find and label things, talk with grown-ups, friends, tell what it "looks like," "smells like," etc.

memory

- Know that by three, a child can often remember two to three directions.

- Know that memory is helped by seeing, holding objects and people.

reasoning

- Recognize that it is just beginning, so children judge on what they *see*, rather than what they reason they should see.

- Be sure adult explanations aid in understanding reasons.

- Practice finding "answers" to open-ended questions such as "How can you tell when you are tired?"

(continued on next page)

Developmental Theories

Developmental Research Tells Us:

6. Social growth:
   The world *is* only from the child's viewpoint. Seeing is believing.

   Group play is developing.

   Independence increases as competence grows.

   People are born not knowing when it is safe to go on.

   Adult attention is very important.

   Young children are not born with internal mechanism that says "slow down."

Teachers Can:

- Expect that children will know their ideas only.
- Be aware that the rights of others are minimal to them.
- Remember that if they cannot see the situation, they may not be able to talk about it.
- Provide free-play sessions, with places to play socially.
- Understand that group play in structured situations is hard, because of "self" orientation.
- Know that children test to see how far they can go.
- Realize that children will vary from independent to dependent (both among the group, and within one child).
- Understand that children will need to learn by trial and error.
- Know the children individually.
- Be with the child, not just with the group.
- Move into a situation before children lose control.

Figure 11-6 continued

Developmental Research Tells Us:

Teachers Can:

7. Emotional growth:

   Self-image is developing.

- Watch for what each person's self-image is becoming.
- Give praise to enhance good feelings about oneself.
- Know that giving children responsibilities helps self-image.
- Talk to children at eye level. Children learn by example.
- Model appropriate behavior by doing yourself what you want the children to do.

8. Physical growth:
   Muscle development is not complete.
   Muscles cannot stay still for long.
   Large muscles are better developed than small ones.

   Hand preference is being established.

- Not expect perfection, in either small- or large-muscle activity.
- Plan short times for children to sit.
- Give lots of chances to move about, be gentle with expectations for hand work.
- Watch to see how children decide their handedness.
- Let children trade hands in their play.

   A skill must be done several times before it is internalized.

- Have available materials to be used often.
- Plan projects to use the same skill over and over.

   Bowel and bladder control is not completely internalized.

- Be understanding of "accidents."
- If possible, have toilet facilities available always, and keep them attractive.

As a student studying under Abraham Maslow, most of Dr. White's philosophy and research techniques have been modeled after that of Maslow and Piaget. Dr. White contends that if a child is performing at above-average levels in intelligence and social development by the age of three, he will most likely succeed in school years to come. If a child is developmentally delayed in these two areas by age three, it is likely that he will find it difficult to keep up academically in the following school years. He stressed the importance of parental involvement and sensitivity to the social, emotional and intellectual needs of the child.

B. F. Skinner

Behavioral Psychologist, B. F. Skinner (1906–1990) introduced the concept of reinforcement and emphasized how a child's surroundings influence learning. He maintained that people, as well as animals, behaved in certain ways because they were reinforced in doing so. He concluded that positive behaviors should be rewarded and negative or aggressive behaviors should be modified by refusing to reinforce them. Another name for this theory is behavior modification.

Case Study #1:
Jane and Diane

Jane and Diane are both four years old. They are in the same preschool class.

Jane comes from a family that places emphasis on physical capabilities and is accustomed to gross motor activities. Her physical abilities are at a six-year-old level. She enjoys all outside play. She excels in bicycle riding, jumping rope, and gymnastics. Her cognitive abilities are not so well developed because she is not interested in identifying colors, identifying shapes, or counting.

Diane, however, comes from a family that takes pride in intellectual activities. She enjoys working on her numbers and colors. She enjoys matching and sorting games. She can recite and identify the alphabet, and do simple arithmetic. Her interests do not include most gross motor activities. When outside, she prefers the paint easels and sandbox to the climbing structures.

Although each girl excels in one particular developmental area, there is no reason to be concerned that either is delayed in her developmental process. The conscientious caregiver encourages each child to use all of the materials and equipment to develop to full potential and have a full learning experience.

SUMMARY

The expert theories of Sigmund Freud, Jean Piaget, Arnold Gesell, Erik Erikson, B. F. Skinner, Abraham Maslow, and Burton White are essential to the understanding of the field of child development. They developed theories of how children mature from infancy through adulthood. Because of their research, caregivers can now understand child development. We also can better recognize the children that need special help, whether they be delayed or gifted in their maturation. We are able to comprehend how children emerge as whole beings —physically, socially, emotionally, and intellectually. By using the above theories, curriculum can fit the individual needs of children.

Review Questions

1. When is the id and the superego in conflict?

2. Who established the theory of cognitive development?

3. According to cognitive development, how do children gain new knowledge?

4. Define the sensorimotor stage.

5. Gesell's "School Readiness Test" covers what four areas?

6. Who wrote the *Eight Ages of Man*?

7. Define "autonomy."

8. According to B. F. Skinner, how much attention should be given for negative or inappropriate behavior?

9. Define "self-actualization."

10. Under whom did Burton White study and base his philosophy?

Things to Do and Discuss

1. Research the life of a theorist in the field of child development. Report to the class on your findings. Theorists in the child development field include:

   ● Albert Bandura

   ● Jerome Bruner

   ● David Elkind

   ● Erik Erikson

   ● Sigmund Freud

   ● Arnold Gesell

   ● Eleanor Maccoby

   ● Abraham Maslow

   ● Jean Piaget

   ● B. F. Skinner

   ● Lendon Smith

   ● Burton White

2. Observe a child in a school setting to determine the child's maturation level. Devise a curriculum to further the child's development. Explain your rationale.

3. Discuss why it is important to consider all aspects of the child when preparing curriculum.

4. Role play a child and the caregiver's reactions to the child during each period of Erikson's eight ages.

CHAPTER 12
Physical Development

The child is practicing his gross motor skills on the climbing structure.

KEY TERMS

ambidextrous
bonding
cooperative play
creative movement
diaper gait
fine motor
  development
games with rules
gross motor
  development
growth in
  body structure
handedness

integrated movement
internalize
kinesthetic sense
manipulatives
motor development
motor skill
parallel play
pincer hold
primary movement
secondary movement
sensorimotor activity
solitary play
symbolic play

OBJECTIVES

After completing this chapter, you will be able to:

1. describe the importance of good general physical development:
2. discuss the three characteristics of the growth patterns of infants and toddlers;
3. distinguish between gross and fine motor development;
4. discuss the statement "Play is learning";
5. discuss ways to enhance creative movement by using the five senses.

INTRODUCTION

Maria is crawling, Pat is running, Jim is throwing a ball. These are examples of physical development. Within this chapter we discuss the components of the physical aspects of children—health, growth, motor skills, creative movement, and sensory integration. The importance of play as an element of learning is also discussed.

HEALTH

Health means more than mere absence of illness or disease. Health is the general condition of the body or mind with reference to soundness and vigor (*Random House College Dictionary*, 1984). The overall health of children is important for physical development. Some good health characteristics are:

1. Bright, shiny, and clear eyes

2. Cleanliness—frequent baths and absence of odor

3. Clean hair—free of lice and cradle cap

4. Clear complexion—firm, unblemished with skin soft and smooth

5. Curious and active—inquisitive attitude and active involvement with the environment

6. Good bone structure—strong and nonbreakable

7. Good diet—sufficient intake of nutritious foods from the five basic food groups

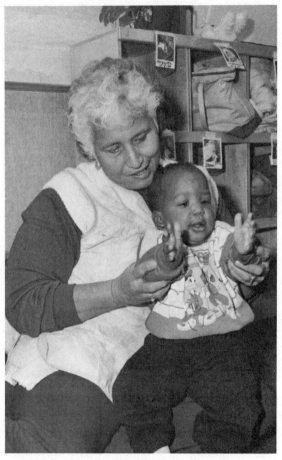

Figure 12-1: The toddler is bonding with the caregiver.

8. Good disposition—pleasant, happy, free from depression, positive outlook, get along well with others

9. Good posture—erect and straight back, shoulders, and head

10. Good skin color—rosy and vibrant

11. Good teeth—brushed daily and free of cavities or abnormalities

12. Proper height and weight for age

It is caregivers' responsibility to provide a healthy environment to promote good physical development. This includes planning a nutritious menu; providing a clean, safe environment; balancing active and quiet activities; and supplying adequate sleeping arrangements. Caregivers should also design appropriate tasks and activities, offer bonding opportunities (*bonding* is interacting with another to form a warm, secure closeness), and recognize any physical impairments.

GROWTH

Growth in body structure is the physical change that occurs as children mature. It can be influenced by socioeconomic factors, heredity, environment, nutrition, and general health. Physical, social, emotional, and intellectual stimulation are other factors to consider in growth.

Usually all infants and toddlers develop in three stages:

- *Stage I: Development from top to bottom.* Infants learn first to use the upper body, such as lifting the head before sitting. They rock on hands and knees before crawling.

- *Stage II: Development from body center to outer parts.* Infants move their arms for the sheer joy of movement, without purposeful thought, and advance to observing an object and purposefully grasping it with their hands.

- *Stage III: Development from using two sides to using one side.* Toddlers

Figure 12-3: Infant using purposeful thought in order to grasp an object.

develop from catching a ball with two hands to catching it with one hand or from jumping with two feet to hopping on one foot. Likewise, they develop from reaching for blocks with both hands to reaching with only one.

Infants

At no other time do children grow and develop as rapidly as during the first year of life. At birth, the average child weighs seven to eight pounds and is twenty inches long. Birth weight usually triples by the end of the first year. As an example, a child weighing seven pounds at birth should weigh approximately twenty-one pounds at twelve months. Length increases fifty percent at twelve months.

In the first year of infancy, the head is large in proportion to the rest of the body due to the rapid growth of the brain. The circum-ference of the head should be measured periodically. It should be close in size to the chest circumference by the end of the year.

Did you know that babies' eyesight is the least developed sense at birth? Babies cannot distinguish objects clearly. Their uncoordinated muscles allow their eyes to blink separately and to cross. By six months, the infant's eye coordination and the ability to see clearly have improved greatly.

Babies' hearing is acute even before birth. A baby is accustomed to hearing the mother's voice in the womb. Therefore, the baby feels reassured by that sound after birth. This is the beginning of the bonding process between mother and child.

By the end of twelve months, other physical changes include four upper and lower teeth, and hair. The eyes are coordinated and can focus on an object. Hearing has become more acute. Babies are able to distinguish different noises. As the voice and the muscles of the mouth develop, infants can repeat commonly heard vowel sounds. They have a vocabulary of about ten words.

Toddlers

Infants become toddlers when they begin to walk. They often walk with what is known as a *diaper gait* (movement with the legs spread for comfort and balance). From ages one to three, physical growth slows to half the rate of the first year. At age two, weight is one-fifth of the weight at age eighteen. Height development also slows to half that of the first year. Toddlers have a full set of twenty temporary teeth. The average vocabulary increases to 200 words by the age of two. In six more months, toddlers can use 450 words.

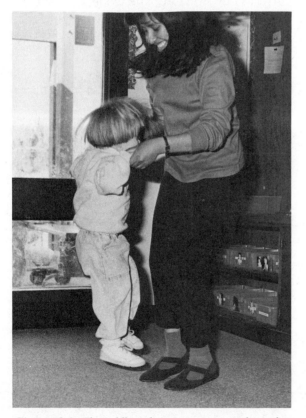

Figure 12-4: The toddler is learning to jump with two feet.

Due to toddlers' mobility, they develop a sense of independence. Their legs and arms have grown longer, and their bodies have lost their look of plumpness. Heads appear smaller and more in proportion to the rest of the body.

Preschoolers

From age two and a half to five, pre-schoolers' growth slows down considerably. Weight increases by four to five pounds. Height increases by approximately three inches. The body lengthens and straightens, with children appearing slimmer and more erect. Balance and coordination improve significantly. Vocabulary is 900 to 2,100 words, with an understanding of 20,000 words.

School-age Children

School-age children are between the ages of six and twelve and are enrolled in elementary school. Six year olds move quickly and are constantly in motion. Girls tend to have more control over their precise movements, while boys are more interested in strong muscles. Seven-year-old boys and girls generally even out physical accomplishments such as more complicated exercises (jumping jacks and balancing on one foot with eyes closed).

Eight and nine year olds have refined their eye-hand coordination and can participate in most team sports. However, boys exceed girls in jumping, running, and throwing. This trend continues through age twelve.

School-age children have another period of rapid growth at the onset of puberty. Girls' physical development occurs earlier than that of boys. Girls begin puberty at approximately age ten to twelve. Therefore, they are generally taller at this age. Boys' growth spurts occur generally between ages fourteen and sixteen. They then usually surpass girls in height.

School-age children are often awkward because their extremities (hands, arms, feet, and legs) have grown to adult size, while their torsos will continue to develop over several more years. Temporary teeth are mostly replaced by the thirty-two permanent teeth.

Caregivers need to keep in mind the individuality of each child. There are great variations in body sizes and types, ranging from short to tall and fat to thin. There is no one correct body structure. The uniqueness of each of us is the result of heredity, environment, nutrition, health, and other factors.

MOTOR DEVELOPMENT

Motor development is the actual physical movement and control of the body. *Motor skill* is the ability to use muscles to control movement.

Physical Movement

Movement is important in the physical development of young children. It helps to develop muscle tone, coordination (control of the body muscles), circulation of body fluids, and the senses. Experiences and success in physical movement enable children to feel good about themselves and to be more confident and cooperative.

Stages

The three developmental stages of motor development are primary, secondary, and inte-

HEAD CONTROL	LOCOMOTION	SITTING BALANCE	STANDING BALANCE	WALKING
PRONE — lifts head & chin (1 mo.)	ROLLING — back to stomach (5 & 6 mos.)	EQUILIBRIUM REACTIONS — balance (6 mos.) sits in high chair	BOUNCES — takes fraction of own weight (7 mos.)	WALKS WHILE TWO HANDS ARE HELD (12 mos.)
HEAD & SHOULDERS DEV. — on elbows (3 mos.)	stomach to back (5 & 6 mos.)			
arms straight (5 mos.)	CREEPING — stomach on ground (7 mos.)	beginning sitting leans forward on hands/sits alone (7 mos.)	pulls to feet (10 mos.)	WALKS WHILE HOLDING ONE HAND (13 mos.)
	on all fours (7-9 mos.)			
head held steady while being pulled into a sitting position (begins at 3 mos., completed at 5 mos.)	creeps (10 mos.)	completed — also going from sitting to prone (10 mos.)	stands momentarily (14 mos.)	WALKS ALONE (15 mos.)

Figure 12-5: Baby's developmental sequence. Reprinted from Children in Your Life *by Radeloff & Zechman. Copyright 1981 by Delmar Publishers. Used with permission.*

grated movement. *Primary movement* is the use of large muscles for gross motor activities, such as walking, running, and jumping. *Secondary movement* is the use of small muscles for fine motor activities, such as writing, stringing beads, and buttoning. *Integrated movement* is the combination of primary and secondary movements for activities such as running and jumping to catch a ball in an organized game of baseball.

Figure 12-6: Toddlers walk with a diaper gait.

Infants

Children learn through doing. First they learn through physical movements. Then they learn through mental activity. The maturation of the muscle, bone, and nervous systems combined with the freedom of movement puts infants on their way to gross motor development. As stated previously, development starts with the lifting of the head. This action is not taught—it develops as the muscles in the neck are strengthened. It is practiced until the next

level of skill (lifting the upper trunk) is performed. Babies usually cannot do one activity without having mastered the movements in the previous stage.

Stimulation of the infant's senses and muscles is encouraged by the caregiver. Simple movement exercises, mobiles, and soft toys, encourage infants to reach, turn, lift, and scoot, therefore developing their muscles. While engaging in *solitary play* (playing by oneself), infants begin to adapt to their environment. They are learning to look, listen, and enjoy the accomplishments of themselves and others.

Although some researchers now question the concept that chronological age should determine when children are taught skills, it is still agreed that children progress through a sequence of developmental stages. Children usually sit before they stand, stand before they walk, and walk before they run.

Toddlers

Toddlers are able to do more on their own (autonomy). Their large muscles in the shoulders, legs, and back are more defined and flexible than before. The control of the small muscles such as those in the fingers and ankles begins. Toddlers can turn the pages of a book, (usually several at a time), scribble with a crayon across paper, and cut fringe with scissors. They also can construct towers by stacking several blocks. They use wide-open hands for grasping but have difficulty releasing small objects. Their eye-hand coordination improves.

Toddlers are interested in using their larger muscles for activities such as climbing, running, tumbling, pushing, and pulling. Their

Figure 12-7: The toddlers love to feel, smell, and even taste
the shaving cream, a sensorimotor activity.

Figure 12-8: School-age children jumping rope.

coordination and balance are not yet well defined, which causes them to fall suddenly and to bump into things. Toddlers enjoy rhythm instruments and dancing to music. Rolling a ball is a challenge because their aim and release are poor. They enjoy going up and down stairs, placing both feet on a step before ascending or descending.

At this age, children are sometimes referred to as going through the "terrible twos." This is a poor description of the fascinating and exciting learning process. "Terrific twos" is a better description. They have tremendous physical energy, budding independence, and movement. They are quick, enthusiastic, curious, and mostly interested in free, active play. Toddlers like the company of others but usually engage in *parallel play* (playing next to someone else) rather than *cooperative play* (playing with someone else). Their excitement over each new discovery is fun to watch.

Case Study #1: *Trisha*

Upon coming home from the hospital, Trisha sleeps all but four hours a day. During wakeful periods, her automatic reflex of sucking enables her to satisfy her nutritional needs from the bottle or breast. Physically, she can turn her head from side to side, see objects clearly eight to twelve inches from her eyes, and automatically grasp objects placed in her palms. She can also hear and respond to her caregiver's voice.

At about three to six months, Trisha is more responsive to her environment. She scoots on her stomach, smiles, and laughs at others. She rolls over from her stomach to back and back again. She reaches with both hands to grasp objects (this is the beginning of eye-hand coordination).

From six to nine months, Trisha sits alone, crawls, stands with support, and feeds herself with finger foods. She is curious and learns the meaning of the word *no* by experimentation. Trisha also frequently squeals with joy and pleasure.

At nine to twelve months, Trisha stands alone, walks while holding on, likes picture books to be read to her, and begins to manipulate and enjoy toys and other objects in her environment. Her eye-hand coordination improves tremendously. She begins to imitate verbal sounds. Trisha becomes more of an individual, and her caregiver enjoys Trisha's uniqueness.

Case Study #2:
Amy

Amy is twenty-two months old, of average build, fair, and delicate. She is very inquisitive and into everything. Amy is fascinated with musical toys, instruments, and anything that makes noise. Her sense of rhythm is becoming well developed. Intricate objects capture her imagination as she exercises her small muscles. She likes to experiment putting little things into little openings.

Amy also runs, jumps, and tumbles as she stretches her large muscles. Her attention span is very short, approximately five to ten minutes in duration. She jumps from toy to toy and runs from room to room and from person to person.

The last year has been one of measurable maturation. She does more for herself, so the task of the caregiver becomes different. Amy can eat the same food as her family. She enjoys feeding herself, as well as drinking from her own cup. She also bathes in the family tub, attempts to dress and undress independently, and is working on toilet training.

Amy's vocabulary is approximately 150 words, with *no-no, hot, dirty, please, pretty,* and *good* being very popular. Her favorite expression is "Me do!" which shows her budding independence and the beginning of sentence structure. Amy practices her language skills by constantly jabbering to herself.

Figure 12-9: Amy is twenty-two months old.

Amy is assertive, observant, and quite often frustrated. When her caregiver says, "Come here," she playfully runs the other way, testing the limits and developing a sense of humor.

Observing Amy reveals that she is a much loved and nurtured child. She comes from an environment that stimulates her not only physically, but also socially, emotionally, and intellectually. She has good self-esteem!

Preschoolers

Never again are children as active and free-spirited as they are in the preschool years. These happy, carefree times have few boundaries and limitations. This is a time of unlimited curiosity and learning, when three to five year olds are given opportunities to explore and experiment within safe limits.

Preschoolers do their best work at play. Their larger muscles, shoulders, torso, arms, and legs are well developed. They love to run, jump, tumble, and climb, and they do so easily and smoothly. They can ride tricycles with speed and skill.

Preschoolers can alternate feet as they go up and down stairs. They love music and march and keep time to a rhythm, as well as being able to make sliding and skating motions. Young children can balance on one foot and, with practice, walk across a balance beam. Throwing and catching a ball with accuracy is a new accomplishment for preschoolers. They are very proud of their new abilities and are eager to demonstrate their skills at any time.

Fine motor skills increase as preschoolers have more opportunities to practice. They can cut shapes with the scissors, using one hand to hold and turn the paper. They can control pens, pencils, and paint brushes easily, using a *pincer hold* (the correct way to hold an object such as a pencil between the forefinger and thumb).

Craft projects with gluing, pasting, coloring, and tracing are sources of enjoyment. Simple puzzles of up to thirty pieces are a challenge. Children will do them repeatedly, until they have a sense of satisfaction and completion. Preschoolers have good imaginations.

They enjoy putting manipulative toys together in many different combinations. While working with clay, young children make representational objects, such as animals, cookies, and snakes.

Enhancing both fine and gross motor development, preschool children enjoy *symbolic play* (role playing). This may occur in the playhouse area, when dress-up and imitation is welcomed and encouraged, or in the play yard where cardboard boxes are transformed into fire trucks and police cars.

Preschoolers can dress with success. Choosing their own clothes and managing the buttons and zippers help children develop a good self-concept. Preschoolers can also feed themselves with a spoon and a fork. They are able to pour a drink into a cup, although sometimes they make messes as they practice. Self-

Figure 12-10: Preschool-age children using fine motor activity in play.

Figure 12-11: *School-age children enjoy the competition of playing sports.*

help tasks (routine tasks that one can do for one's self) become important as they develop more independence.

The attention span of four to five year olds is short, and their attention is fickle, which explains why one minute they are tossing a ball and the next minute they are riding tricycles. This age group begins to play with other children (cooperative play) but needs occasional supervision to help keep order and to smooth conflicts.

School-age Children

School-age children spend large amounts of time sitting at a desk and using their mental abilities. After school, they need the release of physical activity. They are capable of enjoying games that allow them to test their well-developed muscles, skills, strength, and endurance. Games with rules, such as team games, relays, baseball, and soccer, are favorites. Individual competitive efforts, such as races, jumping rope, and riding a bicycle, are popular, too.

School-age children have tremendous amounts of energy. Organized activities help to channel this energy into an acceptable outlet. In order to meet the individual needs of all children, caregivers need to offer a variety of activities.

Fine motor development is more sophisticated at this stage. Eye-hand coordination is advanced. Arts and crafts and handiwork are common. Children like to be involved in all stages of activities, such as the planning, the collection of materials, and the execution of plans.

Figure 12-12: Amy and her friend Beth enjoy musical instruments and dancing.

Interest areas are developing. Children imitate adult activities. Hobbies such as sewing, stamp collecting, and baseball card trading are major considerations. Large amounts of their free time is used in collecting, discussing, and researching. Public figures, such as musicians, movie stars, and sports players, are often role models.

PHYSICAL DEVELOPMENT THROUGH PLAY

Play is young children's work. Play is how they learn best. It promotes exercise and good health. Children gain knowledge when education is combined with play. The environment should be set up to encourage exploration and creativity in the classroom and on the play yard. Caregivers should set goals and plan a variety of learning centers and activities to let children choose an activity at their own levels. Choices stimulate and help children to build on their existing skills. Choice enables children to feel comfortable and to build self-image in a nonthreatening environment. In this atmosphere, children enjoy a toy or activity to the fulfillment of their own satisfaction.

Stages of Play		
Solitary Play	playing alone	infant
Parallel Play	playing side-by-side, little interaction	toddler
Cooperative Play	two or more children playing together	preschool
Symbolic Play	imitating, role-playing	preschool
Games with Rules	organized games, specific set of rules	school-age

Gross Motor Development

The play yard is most often planned to enhance *gross motor development* (developing the large muscles, such as those in the arms, legs, and torso). Children need a variety of stimulating equipment to properly exercise all their muscles. Equipment that allows children to experiment with different modes of locomotion and that challenges their muscles and creativity is important. Examples of skills are climbing, crawling, balancing, swinging, lifting, hauling, shoving, throwing, and catching. Children also need enough space to run and move freely. Opportunities for rhythmic activities, such as bouncing, jumping, and swinging, also should be offered.

When planning a play yard, remember that many common materials can be used to make play equipment. Swings can be made from old tires and ropes and hung from a sturdy limb or crossbar. Sawhorses and boards can be made into balance beams. Large blocks can be used to build the child's own creations. Balls and tires are fun to roll.

You can find or make equipment by using your imagination. Other sources for ideas are catalogues, school supply stores, parks, construction yards, rummage and yard sales, and city schools.

Caregivers should be aware of safety and maintenance of the equipment used in the yard. Equipment built or purchased must be extremely sturdy. Stationary equipment such as swings must be securely anchored in the ground. One young child does not have large body weight, but several children using the equipment at a time can strain and stress the equipment.

Figure 12-13: Preschool-age children practicing a pincer hold.

Caregivers should consider themselves facilitators. They should be aware of what additional equipment and materials would enhance the play. Sand, water, and even dress-up clothes add to the creative opportunities for play. Keep an open mind about how the children are using the equipment. Allow them as much freedom as safety permits. Provide a large, uninterrupted time span for play so that children have a sense of satisfaction from completed play. Also be aware of children who need help to successfully enter into play.

Working with young children can be a noisy adventure as well as a dirty one. Caregivers can enjoy this time if they interact and they observe children stretching their muscles, learning new skills, and playing cooperatively.

Children need repeated opportunities to successfully learn a specific skill. By being observant, caregivers are better able to identify new ideas suggested by the children. These ideas give clues to the next step in the child's learning process.

Fine Motor Development

In the school environment, *fine motor development* (developing the small muscles and eye-hand coordination) is just as important as gross motor development. *Manipulatives* (materials for activities that provide opportuni-ties to increase small muscle control) should be offered to the children.

Catalogues and department stores are filled with various types of manipulatives. Among the favorites for preschoolers are pegboards, puzzles, sewing cards, string and beads, building blocks, Tinkertoys, and stacking and balancing cups. Activities to include are block building, pouring, and spooning. Art materials should include crayons, paints, clay, and scissors.

Many materials can be homemade (such as puzzles and pegboards) or purchased inex-

Case Study #3: *Tim*

Tim, age three, sits at the table working independently on a fifteen piece puzzle of a Tyrannosaurus rex. After concentrating for several minutes, he becomes frustrated and throws the pieces on the floor. Marie, the caregiver, quietly puts her hand on his shoulder and asks if she can help. Tim says, "The dumb pieces won't fit!" Marie suggests that they pick up the pieces together and that she work with Tim to finish the puzzle. After successfully completing the puzzle and praising Tim, Marie suggests that he help Peter in the block area.

Marie's understanding of Tim's frustration and the calm manner in which she helps him complete the puzzle enable Tim to feel good about himself and to be more confident in problem solving in the future. Because a variety of activities are offered, Tim can successfully change areas.

Figure 12-14: Tim is working on a puzzle and increasing fine motor skills.

pensively from yard and rummage sales, thrift shops, and community stores. Some businesses are generous with supplies or provide advice about how to acquire materials inexpensively. Do not be afraid to use your imagination.

When presenting fine motor activities, keep in mind several things. First, each child has a different level of skill and attention span. Within a large group of four year olds, the degree of comprehension, emotional control, and fine motor development is individual. To challenge each child, it is vitally important to set out a variety of manipulative activities.

The materials and the amount of time allotted are also important to consider when providing fine motor activities. Due to a short attention span, children should not be expected to sit for long periods of time at any given task, especially activities that require a considerable amount of self-control. Therefore, several choices of activities should be available to children. Children need to be able to get up and walk freely around the room to investigate another activity. Be alert for any signs of frustration on the part of the children.

CREATIVE MOVEMENT

Have you ever seen children's self-esteem suffer because they are the last ones chosen for the team? Have you seen children who are frustrated because they cannot keep up with their friends? Children in such situations need special help developing physical skills.

Creative movement is the combination of gross motor skills, fine motor skills, and imagination. It occurs as children explore different methods of moving. Children have to *internalize* (feel from within) how their bodies move. They learn to distinguish up from down, front from back, right from left, and crossing the midline of the body.

Caregivers usually notice that children who experience trouble learning can be helped by practicing moving their bodies in space. Movements help children develop spatial awareness. Being observant of children, caregivers can plan activities to meet their individual needs. All children need time for free play and to become involved in movement activities. It is fun to experiment with movement. Figure 12–15 lists physical actions and activities in developmental sequence.

The ability to move successfully through space and to effortlessly change directions is the goal of creative movement. Encourage children to use and discover how their bodies are able to move. Creative movement can occur either inside the classroom or outside, on the play yard.

Caregivers can facilitate learning from creative movement by planning activities that encourage children to move on each side of their bodies. Caregivers also can plan different levels of movement, such as standing, sitting, and walking on tiptoes. Encourage children to move backward and sideways as well as forward. By asking children to unexpectedly change direction or to stop, you allow them to practice following directions as well as feel how their bodies move in space.

Caregivers need to plan for adequate space for each child to move safely and comfortably. It may be necessary to move chairs and tables out of the way for indoor movement activities. Music can be used inside or outside to enhance the experiences.

Physical Actions and Activities

Action	Activity
Rolling	1. Roll the child's whole body front to back and back again. 2. Roll to music. 3. Roll downhill.
Crawling and Creeping	1. Go frontward and backward. 2. Crawl under, over, around, and through (using furniture, boxes, tunnels, and tires). 3. Imitate animals (snakes, lizards, and turtles).
Walking	1. Hold on to objects. 2. Walk quietly or noisily. 3. Tiptoe, walk on heels, and go barefoot. 4. Imitate a giant, an elephant, a duck, and a bear. 5. Use hands and feet together like a crab. 6. Walk barefoot through textures — rough, smooth, paint, shaving cream, grass, water, sandpaper, and styrofoam.
Climbing	1. Climb ladders, ropes, and rungs. 2. Climb hills and ramps. 3. Climb stairs. 4. Climb poles.
Running	1. Run to specific areas. 2. Run fast, slowly, quietly, and noisily.

Figure 12-15: Physical actions and activities chart.

Action	**Activity**
(Running continued)	3. Run in time to music. 4. Run on tiptoes. 5. Imitate a tiger, a butterfly, and the wind. 6. Play games such as tag. Race.
Jumping	1. Jump in, on, through, over, and under. 2. Jump rope. 3. Jump a designated number of times. 4. Imitate a grasshopper or a jumping bean.
Hopping	1. Imitate a rabbit or a kangaroo. 2. Hop on one foot. 3. Hop on two feet.
Skipping	1. Skip using alternate feet. 2. Skip forward and backward. 3. Skip to rhythm.
Galloping	1. Imitate a horse. 2. Gallop sideways.
Balancing	1. Balance on a beam, a string, or a line on the floor. 2. Balance on one foot. 3. Balance with eyes open or closed. 4. Balance bean bags on hands, head, back, and shoulders. 5. Balance carrying water in a cup.

Kinesthetic sense (sensation of movement) is enhanced by allowing children to move while their eyes are closed. Children experience this awareness as they use their muscles and balance in space. Always keeping safety in mind, plan creative movement to be short in duration, to be fun, and to combine quiet as well as energetic activities.

SENSES

Since everything we learn is first perceived by using our senses, it is important when planning activities for motor development to remember to stimulate touch, smell, taste, sound, and sight. In order for children to perform even the simplest motor skill, their sensory abilities must function.

Making popcorn, which children enjoy, is a *sensorimotor activity* (an activity that combines the use of the senses and the muscles). Children can first see the popcorn uncooked and later cooked; they then can hear and smell it popping. Finally, they get the treat of touching and tasting it.

Ingenious caregivers can include a large motor, creative movement activity (imitating the popcorn popping), a science activity, and a nutrition activity with the popcorn lesson. Children love using their imaginations to pretend being kernels of corn, shaking their bodies as the corn is cooked, and popping up as the moisture in the kernel changes to steam. As you can see, children can learn several concepts from one lesson.

Figure 12-16: Collections are a favorite pasttime for school-age children.

HANDEDNESS

Handedness is the dominant use of one hand over the other. It usually is the one that children are comfortable using most often. By the age of two, children generally show a preference for one hand. Usually by age six, children have developed a consistent habit of using one hand over the other.

Because we live in a mainly right-handed culture, left-handed people often experience difficulties. Caregivers can be sensitive to the special considerations necessary to make left-handed children comfortable. They can supply left-handed scissors and seat these children at the left end of the table to allow for more elbow space.

Ambidextrous people are ones who can use both hands equally well. They can cut, eat, or hit a ball with either hand. There are few people who are truly ambidextrous.

It is best to not attempt to change a child's handedness. Such a change can cause learning disabilities in reading or writing. It can also disrupt equilibrium, causing physical disabilities. Frustration and anger can be other side effects. Allow children to determine their own handedness.

IN THE HOME CARE

When parents choose a nanny or a family day care provider for their child, they are doing so for several reasons:

- flexibility of hours and schedule
- homelike environment
- personal attention for their child
- small group of children

Therefore, the home or nanny that they hire is expected to have such qualities.

Although physical, social, emotional, and intellectual development is important to enhance in the home, the caregiver has more time and flexibility to concentrate specifically

Case Study #4:
Marc

As a parent of a sixteen month old, I wanted my son, Marc, to be in an environment much like ours at home. I had to go back to work part-time, five hours a day, and I didn't want to place him in a child care center due to the cost, (having to pay an all day fee), and the impersonal attention that I felt he would receive at such an autonomous age.

After observing several homes, I chose one that had only two other children, ages twenty-two months and thirty-six months. The caregiver really seemed to be concerned for the welfare of each child. She had a daily schedule that was followed. This included mealtime, naps, specific daily activities, outside play, and even an occasional trip to the park or shopping mall. The children in her home all seemed to be happy, clean, and well cared for.

I guess my intuition about this home paid off because my son, now four, is still in Mrs. Wilson's home. Marc has made many new friends, has developed into an intelligent little boy, and has acquired a good feeling about himself and others.

on each child. Also, some tasks are more appropriate for the personal care at home. These tasks include the following.

Physical Development

Hygiene

Set time aside each day to concentrate on proper hand and face washing, teeth brushing, and hair care. Reinforce proper toileting habits. A wash cloth, towel, and specific toothbrush may be placed at the right height in the bathroom to aid the independence of each child.

Play Time

Children must be given instructions about inside and outside rules. Doors must be opened and closed quietly. Constant running in and out of the house is not permitted. Running and loud noises should be left for outside play only. Quiet games and activities are encouraged inside.

Housekeeping

Children should be taught to clean their play area when they are finished with their toys. Small brooms, sponges, and clean dust rags can be supplied to encourage children to clean up after spills, meals, and play. Beds can be made after nap, and tables can be cleared after mealtime. Older preschool children can occasionally help prepare simple meals such as sandwiches and desserts. These tasks not only encourage learning and participation but give a child a feeling of accomplishment.

Naps

Any child of preschool age or younger should have a period of the day designated for a nap or rest time. This time is most often after lunch. A story before nap is often very helpful and can produce a quiet mood.

Social Development

Manners

Children learn from the examples that their role models exhibit. "Please," "Thank You," and "Excuse Me," should be said and expected in the home regularly. Children should be taught not to interrupt when someone else is talking. Also, whispering in the presence of others is rude. Everyone in the home, children and adults, should be respected and treated fairly. If a door to a bedroom is closed, children must knock before entering. Privacy is important! Answering the telephone in the family day care home by young children should be prohibited. Proper telephone etiquette may be taught as children get old enough to understand.

TV Time

Television should be a treat and not part of the routine schedule. Too much television for young children may cause them to become lazy and unmotivated. Programs should be age-appropriate and educational as well as entertaining. Certain programs at certain times may be enjoyable as long as the attention span can be maintained.

Emotional Development

Conferences

Home care providers should always discuss the child's problems in privacy away from other children and adults. Confidentiality is important and problems should not be discussed with other parents from the group.

Intellectual Development

Learning Activities

Specific time can be set aside each day for learning activities. Caregivers can establish monthly or weekly themes to base their activities around. Learning centers, science experiments, and story telling are just a few examples of daily activities that can be planned. (See Chapters 23 and 24 for more curriculum ideas.)

SUMMARY

The overall health of children is important for physical development. It is the caregivers' responsibility to provide a safe, clean, and inviting environment. Growth is the physical change that occurs as the body matures. The three stages of growth are well-defined from birth to school age. Height, weight, and abilities differ from child to child.

Most physical development follows a prescribed pattern. As children are better able to control their bodies, motor development becomes more advanced. Gross motor development is the mastering of control of the large muscles of the body. Fine motor development is the skilled use of the small muscles of the body and eye-hand coordination.

Play is how children work and how they learn to perceive the world. Caregivers should be facilitators and be aware of what equipment or creative ideas can enhance the play.

Creative movement is a combination of gross motor skills, fine motor skills, and imagination. It is the ability to successfully use most of the muscles of the body.

Senses pertain to touch, sight, sound, taste, and smell. Sensorimotor activity is the combination of the senses and the use of the muscles for learning. Handedness is the dominant hand used by the child, whether it be right, left, or both (ambidextrous).

Review Questions

1. List and define the three stages of growth.

2. What are the most-developed senses and the least-developed senses at birth?

3. What is the difference between motor development and motor skills?

4. List the stages and ages of play.

5. What is a pincer hold?

6. At what age do children enjoy team games?

7. Define and give examples of gross and fine motor development.

8. What are manipulatives? Give three examples.

9. Why is it necessary to include creative movement in your daily plan?

10. What are the five senses?

11. When is a child ambidextrous?

Things to Do and Discuss

1. Discuss the traits that characterize a physically healthy child.

2. If you were to interview an infant's primary caregiver, what questions would you ask concerning the infant's physical development and whether the infant is developing in the normal range?

3. If you had a budget of $1,200 to purchase gross motor equipment, what would you buy? Identify the age group for which you are purchasing the equipment.

4. If you had a budget of $700 to purchase fine motor equipment, what would you buy?

5. Describe five creative movement activities for inside the classroom and five creative movement activities for the play yard.

6. Use your imagination. Be creative and develop a lesson plan using all the senses.

7. Assist caregivers in a child care center with fine and gross motor activities with infants, toddlers, and preschoolers.

CHAPTER 13
Social Development

As children learn to interact with others, they develop social skills.

KEY TERMS

autonomy
games with rules
peers
self-concept

self-esteem
social development
symbolic play

OBJECTIVES

After completing this chapter, you will be able to:

1. define and discuss methods of enhancing positive self-esteem;
2. list three ways of developing problem-solving skills in relationships;
3. explain how caregivers serve as role models in the classroom.

INTRODUCTION

Children playing together, children arguing, children talking to the teacher — As children learn to interact with others, they are developing socially. They are able to explore on a trial and error basis or by observing different methods of getting along with their *peers* (children of similar age, sex, interests, and intellectual ability) and with adults.

Every part of a child's day is affected by social interaction. Getting up in the morning, children associate with their family members. As they arrive at the day care center, they interact with other children and adults. During school hours, they are a part of play, group learning experiences, and meals with different groups of people. After school, they may join a scout troop or sports team. Later, they are reunited with their families. All parts of the day have been involved with other members of society.

Children need to learn social skills in order to feel confident in today's world. They must be able to get along with different members of society and to be self-reliant in their relations with others. Children who fail in this important skill can be outcast from their peers.

SELF-ESTEEM

Children need to feel good about themselves and to have confidence in their abilities. This is the definition of *self-esteem*. The first step to socialization and self-esteem is the interaction of children with their mothers, fathers, and other family members.

Caregivers have a responsibility to children to enhance their concept of self at every opportunity. You can do this by recognizing that children want to gain your attention by their actions. by emphasizing and commenting on the positive aspects of their behavior, you enable children to learn the principles of positive social development. Children must also learn what is not acceptable behavior and to control their behavior if they are to retain the esteem of others.

Self-concept is how children view themselves. This can be either negative or positive. Caregivers can influence the concept that the children develop of themselves and of others by the way they react to children.

Self-concept begins as children interact with their parents and caregivers. A sense of *autonomy* (independence) is important to self-worth. Children value themselves in various

Figure 13-1: The caregiver enjoys some quiet time with a student.

Figure 13-2: The caregiver and children enjoy the Flannel Board Story.

Figure 13-3: The caregiver is paying special attention to her student's art project.

ways—how they perceive themselves, how they perceive others, and how they perceive they compare with others.

Means by which caregivers can help children establish a healthy self-esteem and a sense of autonomy include:

1. Allow children to independently accomplish a task.

2. Allow them to solve their own problems.

3. Allow them to learn by their mistakes.

Caregivers often need to wait patiently while children attempt to carry out duties or to figure out a means to solve a problem. It is important that you do not rush in. Allow children sufficient time to accomplish their tasks.

This enables children to learn self-confidence in their abilities, their independence, and their dealings with others.

Like all of us, children make mistakes. Astute caregivers exhibit patience and offer reassurance so that children will feel confident in their abilities to attempt tasks. Learning is often accomplished by making mistakes.

The positive or negative responses that children elicit from the adults in their environment help to form the picture they have of themselves. If children are treated as loved, accepted individuals, they begin to envision themselves in that manner. If they are perceived as intrusions or problems, they begin to believe that they are not worthy.

Caregivers need to be careful of the signals that they send to children. Respect for individual differences and enjoyment of special qualities and abilities allow children to feel confident when trying new skills or entering in social relationships. By focusing on the good or positive aspects of children, we reinforce the behaviors we want them to exhibit.

Put yourself in the child's place. Imagine how you would feel if you were put down in front of your peers. Would you like to be belittled? Would you like someone to talk about your lesser traits to others? Do you like to be embarrassed?

Instead, imagine how you would feel if you were praised for doing a good job. Would you like someone to talk about your outstanding abilities to others? When someone describes your efforts to you, you can tell they have noticed your accomplishments.

Of these examples, which would make you want to work harder? Which would boost your efforts to succeed? Which would make

Case Study #1:
Leo

Leo enjoys helping Mr. John; however, every day when the equipment must be taken outside, Mr. John chooses one of the bigger and stronger boys to help him. When Leo asks to help, Mr. John says, "Leo, let Ralph take out the net. He's bigger than you." Leo is getting discouraged about ever being able to help with the equipment.

Later in the evening, Leo's mother asks him to take out the trash. Leo tells her, "I'm too little. Mr. John says I need to grow bigger before I can lift heavy things."

His concept of himself is of a small, inadequate boy. He feels unable to do heavy tasks. After all, Mr. John told him he would have to get bigger. He has accepted the adult's impressions of his size and therefore does not try to accomplish the task.

Case Study #2:
Leo Revisited

Let's turn this case study around and see if we can change Leo's concept of himself. Leo enjoys helping Mr. John. Today when it is time to take the equipment outside, Mr. John says, "Leo, please help Ralph take the heavy net to the play yard. You can each take an end." Leo struggles to carry his end of the net but manages to get it out to the play yard.

Later that evening, when his mother asks him to take out the trash, Leo jumps up and says, "Sure, Mom, I can lift heavy things! Mr. John said I have big muscles, and he let me take out the giant net."

Because Mr. John allowed Leo the opportunity to carry out the net, Leo's concept of worthiness added to his self-esteem. Even though Leo struggled with the net, he was given the advantage of trying to succeed. He was encouraged to participate in a task in which he was interested.

you feel better about yourself and your abilities? Remember, putting yourself in the child's place often helps you to use the positive approach when interacting. By being supportive, you offer encouragement to children and enable them to feel secure.

Figure 13-4: Tying shoes is hard work for preschoolers.

Figure 13-5: The caregiver observes as this student puts on her own jacket.

RELATIONSHIPS

Infants and Toddlers

Social development begins during infancy, as young children start to interact with their principal caregiver. They are totally dependent, unable to exist on their own. They therefore must learn to communicate their needs. Their cries have different meanings, and caregivers soon learn to recognize what must be done to help.

Tones of voice used by caregivers enable children to respond. If a pleasing, warm tone is used, children react in a positive manner. Conversely, a harsh, unpleasant tone indicates a negative feeling. Babies soon recognize the voice of familiar caregivers. They often smile, coo, or giggle when familiar caregivers are near. Of course, caregivers react by greeting them in return in a positive manner. Children soon learn that their actions encourage caregivers to give them favorable attention. Their needs are met quickly and to their satisfaction.

While in the infant stage, children engage in solitary play (playing by themselves). They may spend time on the floor with various toys placed around them. Young children have not learned to share. They enjoy being entertained by others and consider only their own wants or needs.

As children become toddlers, many of the skills they have learned from their parents or caregivers are carried over to their relationships with peers. Because they have established a positive sense of autonomy, they are able to successfully deal with others. Through playing with others, they learn acceptable behavior that cannot be taught by any other means. Shar-

Treat Children With

- respect
- understanding
- equality
- individuality
- kindness
- consideration

Figure 13-6: Developing self-esteem.

Figure 13-7: This infant is engaging in solitary play.

ing toys and equipment, taking turns, and learning the rights of others are aspects of this development.

Two-year-old children are not so self-centered as infants and toddlers. They enjoy parallel play (play beside another with little interaction). They like having company. They still do not share willingly. Their main interests are in their own activities. They often want whatever other children possess.

Preschoolers

Family is less important in the preschoolers' social world. Although preschoolers are still egocentric, they seek the company of friends. They can communicate well, letting others know their likes and dislikes. At this age, children leave most of the self-centered attitudes behind. They begin to learn that each friend is an individual. Friends differ in color,

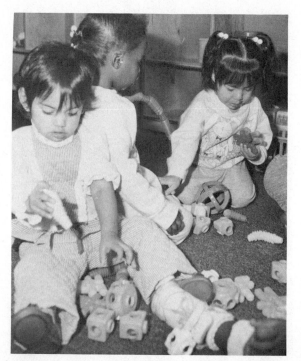

Figure 13-8: These toddlers are engaging in parallel play.

size, family, culture, abilities, likes, and dislikes. Preschoolers enjoy *cooperative play* (playing together) and learn to respect others. They like to share ideas and toys, whether practicing leadership or following another's directions.

Symbolic play (imitation or role playing) occurs during this age. Children like to dress up and act out problems. This can happen at school in the housekeeping area, as they pretend to be family members such as Daddy or Mother. A child may even decide to be the big brother who sometimes picks on the little brother.

Many times, children act out their aggressions or frustrations in play situations. When new babies are brought home, older siblings often have feelings of resentment. Caregivers can help children work through problems by offering alternative methods. Suggestions on how the children can help at home, listing the advantages of being older, can give children a clue to solving their problems.

Children are eager for approval. They often seek out adults to validate their actions. Being unsure, they practice many modes of behavior. They are still learning appropriate behavior. When problems arise, they still need comfort and reassurance from their caregivers.

Figure 13-9: Preschoolers enjoying cooperative play with blocks.

School-age Children

School-age children begin to play sophisticated *games with rules* (organized games, such as baseball, board games, and tag, with specific rules). They can understand and follow directions governing the games. The games are usually long in duration and have complicated sets of rules (many rules are made up as the game goes along). Group activities, such as sports, scouts, and clubs, are fun for children at this age.

Involvement with peers requires many social skills. Cooperation, problem solving, assertiveness, self-discipline, and appreciating the rights of others are just a few of the skills children need to learn. When interacting with others, it is important that children feel confident in their social abilities.

Peers are of paramount importance. School-age children are very concerned about

Figure 13-10: These preschoolers are engaging in symbolic play.

Figure 13-11: School-age children playing an organized game and following rules.

what their friends say and do. Appearance and similar clothing are a must. They become interested in fads. Long telephone conversations and secrets with friends develop. Privacy, closed doors, and modesty are high priorities. Awareness of the opposite sex begins.

CAREGIVERS AS ROLE MODELS

Children emulate the adults in their environment; therefore, caregivers must portray themselves as caring and concerned. They must show respect when dealing with others, whether adults or children. They must set a good example for the children by displaying appropriate behavior.

Children perceive moral development

from the reactions of caregivers. They need to learn that they are responsible for their own actions and the consequences that result. Learning right from wrong, fairness, honesty, and consideration for others, children begin to realize that everyone has rights and should be treated with respect.

Caregivers must be conscious of assigning duties in an equitable fashion. Thus, at snack time, they should allow each child to have a turn at a responsibility, such as passing out napkins or cups. After all children have washed their hands, they sit at the table. They may pour their own juice and pass the snack, being careful to take only one portion at a time. Encourage conversation and use proper manners while at the table.

Children witnessing the fairness of the duties and the division of the snack feel confident in their abilities to participate at snack

Figure 13-12: Playing house is fun for caregivers and toddlers.

time. They know that "please pass the tray" and "thank you" are expected. They then observe the caregivers' relaxed manners and enjoyment of the snack. Later, as the caregivers remove their trash to the basket, the children copy their behavior and clean up their places too. However, they may occasionally need to be reminded of their duties or proper behavior.

By watching and observing adults, children learn expected and acceptable behavior. They try to win positive attention by imitating what they see. The self-identity or self-awareness of each child depends on the role or birth order in the family, cultural heritage, and the value paced on the type or kind of work that people do.

SUMMARY

Social development is the process of interacting with others. Family is the first place that children develop social skills. Soon other adults and peers become important.

Children who have a positive self-esteem are able to relate easily with others and to feel good about their abilities. Self-concept is influenced by caregivers' reactions. A sense of autonomy begins as children learn self-control and independence. Caregivers help children develop autonomy by letting them feel a sense of accomplishment, by allowing them to solve their own problems, and by allowing them to learn from their mistakes.

As they mature, children become socialized through various stages of play. Beginning with solitary play, they progress to parallel play, cooperative play, symbolic play, and games with rules. Peers gain importance as the social world expands and children get older. Peer pressure influences many of their decisions.

Caregivers must model appropriate social behavior. Children can imitate the ways they solve problems and interact with others.

Review Questions

1. Why are some children considered "outcasts" by their peers?

2. What is the first step to socialization?

3. How can caregivers influence a child's self-concept?

4. What are the three ways to encourage autonomy?

5. How do babies communicate their needs to caregivers?

6. At what age does the child learn to share and play together with other children?

7. At what age does awareness of the opposite sex begin?

8. Why is it important for caregivers to be good role models for children?

Things to Do and Discuss

1. Observe a classroom of any age. Focus on the social characteristics displayed by the children. Make a list of signs of socialization.

2. Write a diary of your own social interactions for one day. Be sure to include everyone with whom you socialize.

3. Role play how to give a child a positive self-concept and how to give a child a negative self-concept. Refer to case studies in the chapter.

4. Observe a group of children of different ages. Describe and compare the types of play they are exhibiting.

5. Make a list of qualities the caregiver should display in order to be a good social role model.

6. Discuss how you would handle situations such as a child stealing a personal item from another child or a child lying to get his way.

CHAPTER 14
Emotional Development

Caregiver nurturing an unhappy child.

KEY TERMS

aggression
assertive
emotions
empathy
environment
heredity
negative emotions

self-fulfilling
    prophecy
sibling rivalry
stereotypes
sympathy
venting

OBJECTIVES

After completing this chapter, you will be able to:

1. recognize signs of emotional stability;
2. discuss means of providing a healthy emotional environment;
3. explain the difference between positive and negative emotions.

INTRODUCTION

Emotions are internal feelings. Children experience a wide range of emotions. Their emotions are often short-lived, quick to show and quick to leave. Children's emotions may easily shift from happiness to fear to anger and back again to happiness.

On the first day of school, children feel happy that they are big enough to go to kindergarten. They are with their mothers. That presence makes them feel secure. When it is time for the mothers to leave them with a strange adult, however, they become fearful. They may throw tantrums at being made to stay at school. As the teacher reassures them and welcomes them into the group, they begin to feel happy and secure again.

This is only one example of how children can quickly shift from one emotion to

Figure 14-1: On his first day of school, the teacher is greeting the toddler and his mother.

another. Caregivers should distinguish between the emotions that the children exhibit and reinforce appropriate behavior. They can do this by watching for problems and adjusting their programs to accommodate emotions.

EMOTIONS

Emotions are feelings that make children happy or unhappy, satisfied or dissatisfied. They can include anger, fear, despair, jealousy, sadness, disgust, affection, love, joyfulness, and curiosity. They often are intense feelings. Caregivers can help children to understand and to cope with emotions by realizing that all feelings are real and that they have importance. There are no 'bad' emotions. By naming the emotion ("I can see that you are really angry!"), caregivers allow children to learn that it is all right to have these feelings and that there is an appropriate method for handling and controlling them. Children also learn that caregivers understand and are willing to help them.

Fear

What fears did you have as a child? To understand children, it helps to remember the feelings that we had when we were younger. We all have fears.

1. Julie, age one, is afraid of loud noises. Her older brother thinks it's fun to suddenly appear from around corners and shriek at her in a loud voice. (This can be the result of *sibling rivalry*—competition among children in a family.)

2. Mark, age four, is afraid of dogs. When he was younger, his mother warned him repeatedly to stay away from dogs. She would say, "They may bite you!" (She may be transferring her own fear to her son.)

3. Susan, age five, is afraid of the dark. She thinks there may be monsters under her bed and in her closet. She needs the reassurance of a night light and understanding caregivers. (Children at this age often fantasize scary situations to seek solutions to problems.)

4. Jeremy, age nine, fears strangers. He has heard many stories of being kidnaped, molested, or hurt by people he doesn't know. He is wary of anyone with whom he is not familiar. He hangs back with his caregiver in new situations. (Although children need to be warned about strangers, they also need to be reassured about the benefits of new experiences.)

Figure 14-3: A visit from a fire fighter discussing fire safety.

Figure 14-2: A fearful toddler is being comforted by the caregiver.

Caregivers can help children overcome fears by listening carefully to their descriptions of their feelings and by giving careful and thoughtful answers. Treating fears lightly or discounting them does not help children solve their problems. Their fears are real to them.

It is important that caregivers be careful about displaying their own fears to children in new situations. Encouraging children to explore within safe boundaries is beneficial. Often caregivers can prepare children by giving prior information about upcoming events. If children know what to expect, their fears are diminished.

Figure 14-4: This child is learning traffic safety.

Some fears are helpful. Fears can protect us from dangerous situations. Preschool children may be careful of climbing to the top of the jungle gym for fear of falling. This fear may have come about because one of their friends lost his balance and fell yesterday. The emotion will probably persist until the preschoolers have the coordination and feel confident enough to try to climb to the top.

School-age children may learn the fear of using drugs from the neighborhood police officer during a school assembly. This may prevent them from experimenting with drugs and alcohol when offered by a peer.

Anger

Young children display anger in various ways. They may kick, scream, cry, throw temper tantrums, or refuse to cooperate. They may appear extremely hostile.

1. Julie, age one, often cries excessively when her needs or wants are not immediately satisfied. She has little patience when her breakfast is not readily available. (She has not yet learned to consider that the caregiver is in the process of preparation and Julie will be fed in a few moments.)

2. Mark, age four, is angry because Billy took his truck, which he just left for a moment. He begins to pull the truck from Billy's hand, kicking and yelling at the same time. Billy becomes angry and starts to cry. He runs to the caregiver for help. (Children handle anger in different manners. The self-confident child may be more openly aggressive, while the insecure child often cries and relies on the adult for help in solving the problem.)

3. Susan, age five, is in the housekeeping corner of her day care center. She wants to be the mother. However, Audrey also wants to be the mother and is already putting on the apron. Susan displays her anger by saying, "I want to be the mother! If you don't let me be it, I won't invite you to my birthday party. You're mean!" (As children become older and they show anger, they learn to use words that can hurt feelings in place of physical violence. She has

Figure 14-5: Young children sometimes express anger by having a temper tantrum.

Figure 14-6: Playing baseball can help to alleviate anger and frustration.

learned this method from observing others who threaten, call names, or scold.)

4. Jeremy, age nine, missed catching the fly ball during the noon baseball game. All his friends made fun of his abilities. Jeremy responded by saying, "I don't care! Who wants to play baseball anyway! You're all a bunch of sissies." (School-age children often use exaggerated expressions to show anger as well as indirect revenge. They try to conceal their feelings and act as if they do not care what others think.)

Caregivers can demonstrate appropriate methods of handling anger. Of course, you cannot let children repeatedly injure others; however, children do need to have their feelings confirmed. Angry children need positive means of *venting* (getting rid of) their anger. One method is to talk about the anger, using words instead of actions with the offending party. Children may need support and understanding to accomplish this.

If anger persists, punching a bag hung from a tree limb, hammering nails, or pounding clay may give a constructive outlet for frustrations. Caregivers should be aware of the duration of the episode and be ready to redirect children to another activity if necessary.

Caregivers model appropriate expressions of anger. By not being physical or attacking self-esteem, they demonstrate that talking over a problem calmly and coming to a mutual solution is the desirable method of handling anger.

Sometimes anger is good. Children need to be *assertive* (to stand up for their rights) when dealing with others. Anger can also spur children into striving to accomplish a goal. They need to learn appropriate methods of dealing with frustration and anger early in their lives before *aggression* (combative behavior) becomes a habit.

Jealousy

Jealousy between siblings is common in childhood. Fear of being replaced or a need to compete for parents' love can become a matter of rivalry. Tattling, criticizing, and lying are methods of showing jealousy. Bed-wetting, thumb sucking, or going back to the use of baby talk often accompanies the arrival of a new baby into the family. Reassurance and the showing of affection can help to alleviate jealousy.

Figure 14-7: Caregiver and child discuss the necessity of sharing.

Eliminating comparisons between siblings or friends also dispels jealousy. Remarks such as "Why can't you clean your room like your sister?" or "Tommy gets such good grades. Why can't you?" can lead to feelings of jealousy and revenge.

Jealousy is an emotion which generally peaks in the preschool years. Then it rapidly declines, when children's social experiences grow to include outside relationships.

Affection

One positive emotional response that one feels towards another person or object is affection. Affection is usually spontaneous. It occurs with little stimulation. Infants show affection to the person who takes care of their needs, satisfying their hunger, changing their diapers, or entertaining them. This is a beginning of a sense of trust.

Young children learn warmth, caring, and sympathy by experience. Children develop affection toward those who show them the same feelings. Pleasant experiences encourage the development of healthy emotions. Parents are the first teachers of positive interaction for children. The more often children receive smiles, the more they will smile in return.

Children choose to be with others who make them feel good or give them attention. Other children and adults who display pleasure at their company or enjoy their activities are ones with whom they will associate. Caregivers can stimulate this response by greeting children with a warm smile and genuine concern. By giving positive reinforcement for actions and by gentle discipline and direction, caregivers state their affection for the children.

Figure 14-8: One sign of affection is sharing a good book together.

Thus, caregivers model the attitude that the children are worthwhile individuals. Such actions enable the children to build a positive self-concept. Children display affections to the objects and people which bring them emotional satisfaction.

Love

Love is a stronger emotion than affection. Children learn to love from their principal caregivers. Love suggests a deep attachment to another. Advantaged children have love as part of daily living. They are shown love through verbal signs of approval and outward signs such as hugging and kissing, thus enforcing a sense of security. When love is given unconditionally, self-esteem is enhanced. Children feel valued and worthwhile. In return, they demonstrate love to others.

Other Emotions

Other positive emotions are happiness, joyfulness, and curiosity. Looking at the world in a positive way, feeling that they are in a good environment and that they are accepted, reflects these emotions.

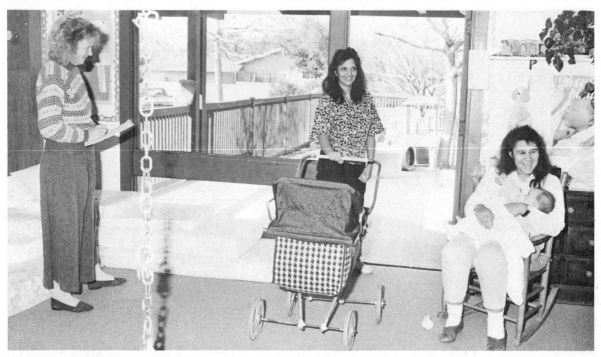

Figure 14-9: The director observes her staff as they enjoy themselves at work.

PERSONALITY

Many components make up personality. These include sex, temperament, heredity, and environment.

Sexual Differences

Both cultural and biological influences determine the sex roles assigned to children. Caregivers often assign appropriate behavior. Girls are usually expected to be nurturing, while boys are often thought of as aggressive. Cultural background often indicates the way children will behave. For instance, girls may be referred to as "pretty, sweet, and cuddly," while boys may be referred to as "rough, tough, and hardy."

Although children of both sexes generally choose the same types of toys, girls tend toward activities and toys that require fine motor control (writing, puzzles, matching cards). Boys often choose toys and activities that involve gross motor control (blocks, chase games, bicycling). Society tends to dictate what boys and girls should be as adults and reinforce these traits.

In the past, books, role models, and

Figure 14-10: Daddy and Ken are taking a rest.

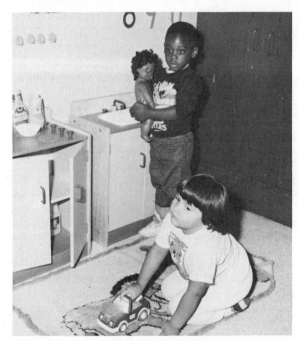

Figure 14-11: Children making a choice of activities; a boy playing with a doll and a girl playing with a truck.

toys depicted *stereotypes* (cultural expectations of appropriate role) of adult behavior. Nurses were always girls; doctors were always boys. Mothers stayed at home; fathers went to work. Today, educators place less emphasis on stereotypes. Now, both boys and girls are encouraged to take part in all aspects of life. Boys may become nurses; girls may become doctors. Boys may stay home and nurture children, and girls may hold down full-time jobs.

Research (from *Understanding Child Development* by Charlesworth. Copyright 1987 by Delmar Publishers. Used with permission) supports that girls are:

- ahead in early motor development
- less likely to have school problems
- less vulnerable as infants
- more compliant to adult demands
- superior in verbal ability

The same research supports that boys are:

- better in math
- eventually better at eye-hand coordination
- more aggressive and more often the victims of aggression
- more likely to have difficulties in school
- more variable in their response to directions from adults
- more vulnerable during prenatal and infancy periods
- superior in muscular capability (about age nine)

Do you feel these traits are inborn or cultural expectations? Do we expect boys to have more difficulties in school and therefore cause them to have difficulties? Do we expect girls to be more verbal and therefore talk to them more? Children often exhibit the behavior that adults expect them to demonstrate (a *self-fulfilling prophecy*).

Anti-bias Approach

Anti-bias is defined as an active approach to challenging prejudice, stereotyping, bias, sexism, racism, and handicappism (Derman—Sparks, 1987). Every child deserves the right to be respected regardless of color, gender, or nationality. Research reveals that children begin to notice differences in people at a very young age and the societal impact of stereotyping and bias affects children's attitudes toward others (Derman—Sparks, 1987).

Caregivers can create an environment that teaches children daily about each others' culture so they can learn to respect and appreciate one another. Caregivers often only focus in on a specific culture when celebrating a holiday. Chinese New Year is an example of a holiday when Asian life is introduced. The caregivers' celebration mainly consists of only several days of displaying foods, dress, dance, and crafts of that particular culture. Known as the tourist curriculum, this method only allows the child to visit other cultures temporarily instead of accepting the likenesses and differences of people into their everyday lifestyles.

If a Child Says:	You May Respond:
"I don't want to stand next to him, he's black."	"I like children that are black and it hurts me when I hear you say that about my friend."
"I don't want to touch your hand because its too dark and it looks dirty."	"My hands aren't dirty. You can touch them if you like, it will not rub off."
"If I speak Chinese will my eyes be funny like Yuko's?"	"No, Yuko's eyes are a different shape than yours and mine and they are beautiful."
"Emil's hair feels like a wire brush."	"I like the way Emil's hair feels. Touch my hair and tell me what my hair feels like."
"Grandma, your face is so wrinkly."	"You may touch my face, it's real."
"You're not an Indian or else you would have feathers on."	"I only wear feathers on special occasions. They are respected and valued."
"I don't want to go near Marissa because she drools and talks funny."	"I like her. Come with me and we will get to know her together."

Thanks to Consuelo Rodriquez—Chaffey College

Section IV THE AGES OF CHILD DEVELOPMENT

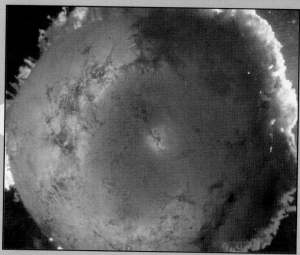

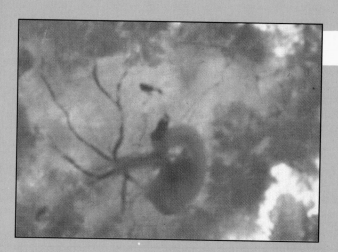

During the fourth and fifth weeks of pregnancy, the eye, heart, arms, and legs develop. An expectant mother must be careful what she consumes during these weeks, because it greatly affects her unborn child (see pages 298 - 300). Smoking during pregnancy has been linked with low birth-weight. Drug use during the embryonic period may cause limb malformation and postbirth addiction. Tranquilizers and even aspirin may be unsafe for the developing fetus.

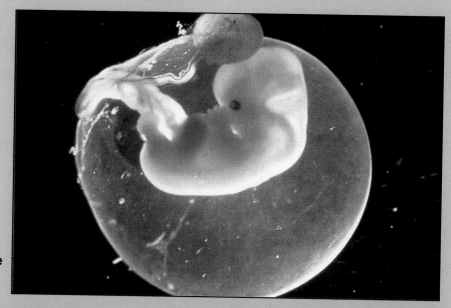

During the sixth week of pregnancy the ears and the teeth develop.

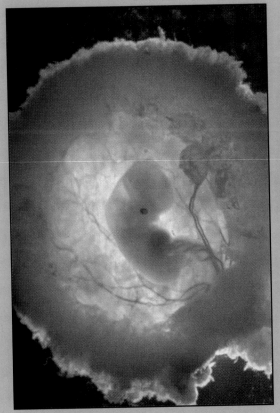

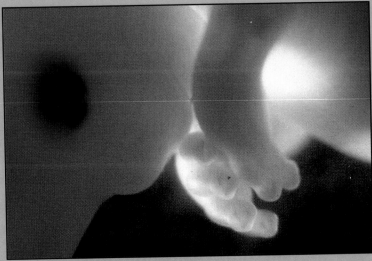

The palate develops in the seventh and eighth weeks of pregnancy. This first stage (the embryo stage) of pregnancy is critical, because it is during this stage that 95% of the body parts appear or develop (see pages 298-299). During the eighth and ninth week, external genitalia also develop.

The second pregnancy period is the fetal period. This period begins at about nine weeks and extends until birth. The child now begins to look like a human being. The head becomes proportional to the rest of the body and the limbs are more clearly differentiated during the fetal period.

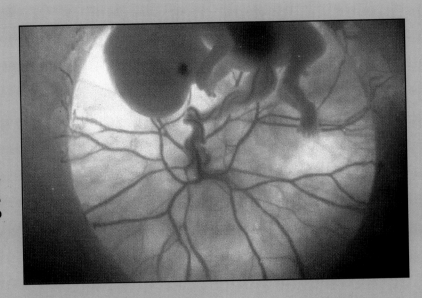

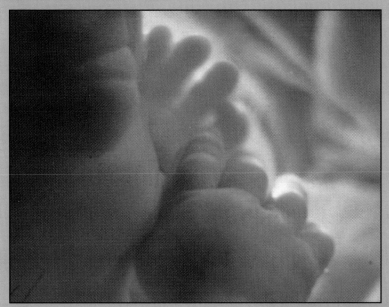

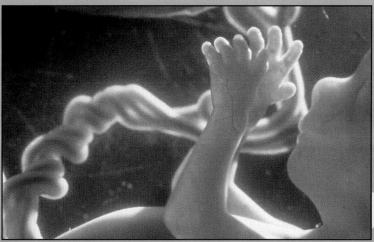

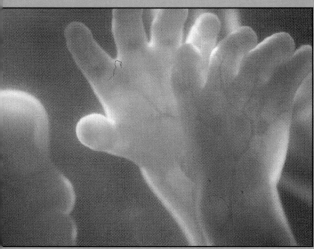

Between twenty and thirty-six weeks, the brain develops. By the twenty-first week the fetus may be able to survive outside of the uterus. By the twenty-fourth week the fetus has eyelashes and eyebrows and the eyelids are opened.

The umbilical cord connects the fetus and the placenta. The placenta is the vehicle through which the fetus receives nutrients and oxygen and disposes of waste.

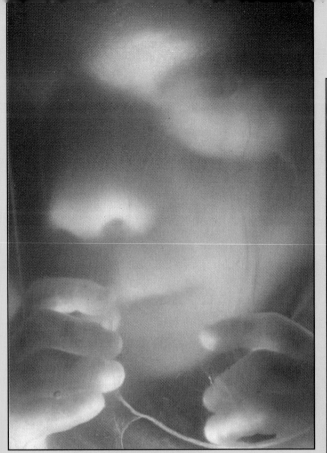

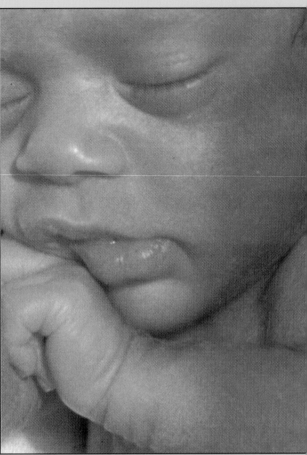

Toenails and fingernails are completely formed by forty weeks of gestational age (shown here at six months' gestation prior to development and at eight months' gestation with fingernails developed). The full-term fetus (thirty-eight weeks' gestation) will begin to drop down into the pelvis, ready for birth.

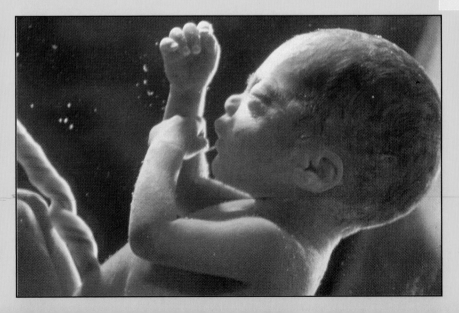

SECTION III THE FOUR BASIC AREAS OF CHILD DEVELOPMENT

The four basic areas of child development are physical, social, emotional, and intellectual. Preschoolers and school-age children experience different levels of development in gross motor skills. The average 3- to 4-year-old should be able to:

- pedal a tricycle ten feet
- complete a forward somersault (aided)
- jump to the ground from 12 inches
- step on footprint pattern

**The average 4- to 5-year-old should
be able to:**

- kick a 10-inch ball towards target
- catch a ball
- bounce a ball under control

**The average 5- to 6-year-old
should be able to:**

- kick a rolling ball
- skip alternating feet

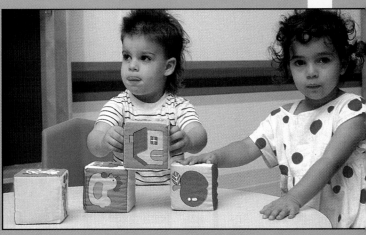

Preschoolers and school-age children experience different levels of development in fine motor skills. The average 3- to 4-year-old should be able to:

• **build a three-block bridge**

The average 4- to 5-year-old should be able to:

• **copy figure X**

The average 5- to 6-year-old should be able to:

- trace around hand
- cut interior piece from paper
- reproduce letters

Two areas of development other than physical are emotional and social development. An awareness of emotional development stems from an understanding of emotions. Emotions are internal feelings. Some emotions are fear, anger, jealousy, sadness, disgust, affection, love, happiness, joy, and curiosity. On this page and the following page are photographs of the various emotions a child can experience.

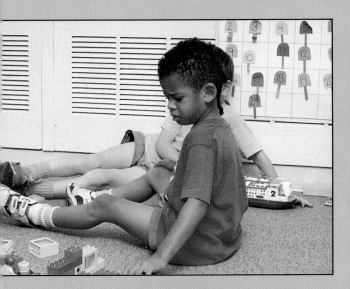

As a child progresses through the different stages of social development, he or she partakes in various levels of play. The various levels of play are solitary, parallel, symbolic, cooperative, and games with rules.

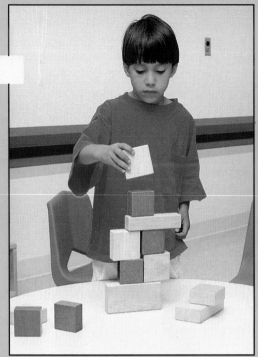

An important part of personality development is an understanding of self-concept. On this page, photographs show how this process is brought about as children relate with themselves, other children, and their teachers.

SECTION IV THE AGES OF CHILD DEVELOPMENT

Special needs children partake in many of the same activities as regular children. These children are enjoying puzzles and painting.

Occupational therapy
and physical therapy
are essential elements
in the exceptional
child's day.

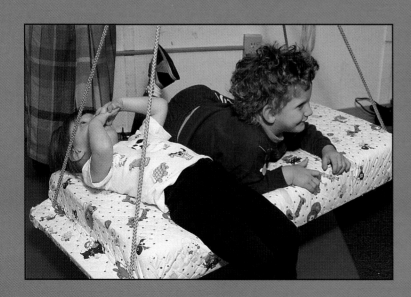

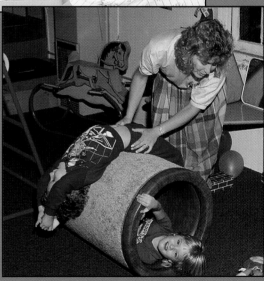

Special needs children enjoy playtime and storytime.

A sampling of the various technological advancements available to the special needs child today.

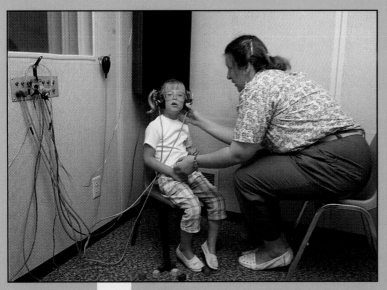

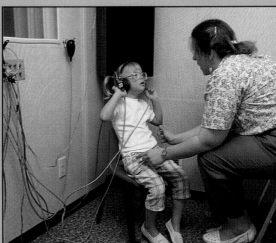

Ways of creating an anti-bias environment are:

1. Attractively display photos of all the children and their families.

2. Display artwork of various cultures including dolls that reflect all major cultures in the United States, both male and female, and dolls with disabilities.

3. Display photos of diverse family lifestyles; single parents, gay and lesbian families, interracial families.

4. Display photos of old people as well as young people.

5. Display various photos of different ethnic backgrounds, people at work and play.

6. Include books and records that reflect all different racial and cultural backgrounds, gender roles, special needs, different ages, and occupations.

7. Photos of people engaging in all types of work: blue collar (factory workers), pink collar (beauticians, sales), and white collar (doctors, lawyers).

Temperament

Every child has a different temperament. One child may be easy to get along with, enjoy new situations, generally be cheerful, and have good self-esteem. Another child may be hesitant to enter new groups and situations. That child needs to observe for a while before feeling comfortable joining a group or trying a new skill. A third child may have difficulties entering a group, finding transitions between activities hard. The child may resist new skills and may experience intense reactions to any new situation.

Each child has a basic temperament at birth. This temperament will remain fairly consistent throughout life. However, children who receive positive feedback can be made to feel calm and reassured about new situations. Children who come from a calm, relaxed, and loving environment are more able to exhibit as easy temperament. Children who live in an argumentative, unstructured environment often learn to be fearful of new situations and to be insecure.

As you know, family members are the first teachers of infants. Although children are born with a basic temperament, they are influenced by the people around them. If they are greeted each morning with love and a smile and their needs are met, they will look forward to each day as a part of the family group. However, if they are allowed to cry for long periods, are propped up with bottles instead of being held, and the family atmosphere is quarrelsome, they will soon learn to dread each morning.

Environment and Heredity

Environment and heredity are factors that help to develop emotional reactions. Children may inherit the tendency to be easy, hesitant, or difficult, but they learn from the environment how to react to situations. Children learn self-confidence and positive reactions if these are demonstrated to them by their caregivers.

Case Study #1:
Gary and Marie

Gary has low self-esteem. He has heard his mother tell other adults that he is always into trouble and that he can never do anything right. Gary is told over and over to straighten up! He is told, "Stop doing that!" and "Why can't you be as well behaved as your brother Jerry?" Because Gary often hears that he is unable to behave or do anything right, he begins to believe that he is incapable of behaving in an appropriate manner. Thus he demonstrates a self-fulfilling prophecy and develops low self-esteem. Gary lives up to his mother's expectations.

Marie, however, is told repeatedly that her mother likes her well-behaved manner. Marie is encouraged to try new experiences. She often overhears her mother explaining the good aspects of her personality to other adults. Because of these positive reinforcements, Marie tries to demonstrate the behavior that is encouraged. Her self-esteem is high, and she too exhibits a self-fulfilling prophecy, living up to her mother's expectations.

Environment

Environment (surroundings) is a great influence to the developmental process of the child. A variation of experiences with different people, places, and things all combine to make up the environmental process. Parental child rearing practices, the quality of life in the home, culture (food, dress, habits), and peer interactions, all make up the child's environment. The surrounding in which a child is raised is often a contributing factor to the emotional satisfaction that the child will attain throughout life. Children growing up in poverty stricken, disadvantaged homes, lacking proper nutrition and supervision, often develop a low self-concept, therefore, delaying their normal developmental process.

Heredity

Have you often been told that you look just like one particular parent? Is your temperament more like your mother's or your father's? These qualities and traits transmitted from parent to offspring define *heredity*. A person is conceived by the union of the ovum from the mother and the sperm from the father. Both the ovum and the sperm each contain forty-six chromosomes in twenty-three pairs. These chromosomes contain genes. Each gene contains a substance called DNA which contains genetic information derived directly from each parent. This genetic information determines if a child will be a boy or girl, their hair and eye color, height, and personality traits.

Figure 14-12: Children displaying easy, hesitant, and difficult temperaments.

THE CAREGIVER'S ROLE

Caregivers should establish a climate conducive to the emotional well-being of children. They should enable children to feel secure and nurtured by remaining calm, professional, and warm during times of stress. Planning the environment can encourage positive interaction between children and their classmates. In order for caregivers to be positive role models, they must display consistency, a sense of trust, and strength of character.

Consistency

When dealing with the children in their care, caregivers should be consistent. School rules should be few, well-established, and understood by all. The rules are for everyone, including caregivers, to follow. They are the same each day. Caregivers must be careful to treat each child fairly and with consideration.

Daily schedules must be closely adhered to in order for children to have a sense of routine. Thus, children learn what is coming next in the day, establishing a sense of security and stability.

Moods of good caregivers are also consistent from day to day. Caregivers should generally be happy, pleasant, and nurturing. Children need their caregivers to be basically the same people each day and not have mood swings.

Sense of Trust

Both caregivers and children need a sense

Figure 14-13: Positive interaction is shared by both people.

Figure 14-14: Comforting helps the child to develop a sense of trust.

of trust. This is established by consistency within the classroom, fairness, and genuine concern for others. By showing *empathy* (knowing how another feels) and *sympathy* (sharing another's sorrow or trouble), caregivers model appropriate emotional behavior.

During periods of sadness, caregivers allow children to express themselves by listening to them and offering a gentle shoulder. After the child calms down, caregivers may suggest a remedy to the situation. At times of happiness, caregivers are again good lis-

teners. They show enthusiasm for the child's accomplishments.

Trust is also built when children know that they are free to express their feelings, whether positive or negative. They are sure that the caregivers will not allow their feelings to get out of control during these times. Children know appropriate expression of feelings, such as using words instead of hands. They also know that the caregivers will support and guide them during moments of stress.

Anger is an acceptable emotion, but

Case Study #2:
Michelle and Susie

Michelle is feeling angry and frustrated waiting for her turn on a bicycle. It seems that each time she wants a turn, somebody else is using the bike. Finally, she runs over and grabs the bike handles, forcing Susie to stop. She pulls and pulls at the bike, saying, "It's my turn! Get off!"

Miss Betty walks over to help solve the problem. "Michelle, you seem very angry. Tell me about the problem." Michelle, in tears, says, "I've been waiting for a turn, and Susie won't give me one!" Susie, also crying and angry at being stopped, says "I'm not done yet! I had it first!"

Miss Betty gently comforts both girls and then asks them, "How can we make sure that each of you gets a turn?"

Susie answers, "I'll ride the bike two more times around the path and then let Michelle have a turn."

Miss Betty asks Michelle, "Is that all right with you?" Michelle nods yes. Miss Betty states, "That seems to be a good solution." Michelle waits patiently and is ready to take possession of the bike as Susie completes her second time around the path.

children often need to be guided in the proper expression. Caregivers may again listen to the children, not belittling their anger. They must reassure angry children and then discuss with them a means to solve the problem. They may even give the children the vocabulary, stand beside them as they tell a friend why they are angry, and offer encouragement during the solution.

Strength of Character

Caregivers' morals, their views of right and wrong, and their convictions are parts of their strength of character. Since they are role models for the children, they need to demonstrate the principles they feel are important.

Therefore, caregivers must be aware of the unspoken messages they send to the children and be able to defend their principles.

Case study #2 shows how the caregiver, Miss Betty, remained calm, understanding, and supportive of both Michelle and Susie. She allowed them to mutually assume responsibility for solving the problem. She treated each with fairness and respect. Miss Betty did not condemn Michelle for being angry or rough with Susie. Rather, she identified the emotion and helped to reduce the frustration level of the situation.

She enabled the girls to learn an acceptable method of problem solving. This method can be carried over to many stressful or frustrating situations that the girls may encounter. They learned that by discussing the problem, a solution is possible.

Caregivers need to possess the special qualities and characteristics to enhance the emotional atmosphere of their classroom. By establishing a climate of fairness, cooperation, and warmth, they allow the children to express their emotions within acceptable limits. Children, looking to the caregivers for information, learn by their example.

SUMMARY

Emotions are the feelings that each of us possess. We express our feelings through words and actions. Some emotions are fear, anger, jealousy, sadness, disgust, affection, love, happiness, joy, and curiosity.

The personality of individuals is influenced by sex, temperament, heredity, and environment. Stereotyping of individuals is caused by predisposed notions of girl (pink, lovable, cute, pretty, sweet) and boy (blue, rough, tough, hardy). It is important to not reinforce these stereotypes. Let each child perform at his or her own interest level.

Caregivers need to be consistent in establishing their expectations for the classroom This helps to build a sense of trust in the children. By showing empathy and sympathy as children work at solving emotional problems, caregivers allow them to grow in security and confidence.

As role models for the children, caregivers demonstrate their morals, philosophies, and principles. The children are then able to emulate the behaviors and establish strength of character themselves.

Review Questions

1. How can caregivers help the child to understand emotions?

2. What is sibling rivalry?

3. How do children learn about fears?

4. What is the difference between assertiveness and aggression?

5. At what age is jealousy the strongest?

6. When is the beginning of a sense of trust established?

7. What is the difference between love and affection?

8. Why must stereotyping be avoided?

9. What is meant by anti-bias curriculum?

10. How does temperament play a role in the development of the personality?

11. Which is the most important to the development of the personality: heredity or environment?

Things to Do and Discuss

1. Observe a kindergarten classroom. Are the children displaying healthy emotional attitudes? Are they solving problems on their own, or is the teacher intervening? Is the teacher supportive of emotions displayed by the children?

2. Role play an emotional situation that may occur in a child's school.

Possibilities are sharing toys, snack time, the first day of school, separating from parents, and not wanting to go home. Demonstrate various solutions to the situation you choose.

3. Devise a curriculum specifically to ease a child during a crisis. Possibilities are divorce; death of a friend, pet, or family member; a new baby in the family; and step-families.

4. Describe your temperament and how it affects you in social situations, such as school, the family, and the community.

5. Write a brief description of a time in your life when you experienced negative emotions and a time when you experienced positive emotions. Who was the caregiver that influenced you at this time?

6. Observe a group of children on several occasions for fifteen to twenty minutes. Look for examples of positive and negative emotions. Record your observations and share them with the class.

CHAPTER 15
Intellectual Development

School-age children need many opportunities for cognitive growth.

KEY TERMS

auditory
classification
cognition
cognitive
   development
conservation
dyslexia
envision
expressive language

initiate
innate
intelligence
receptive language
reversibility
self-correct
seriation
spatial relationships
temporal relationships

OBJECTIVES

After completing this chapter, you will be able to:
   1. define and explain the differences between intellectual and cognitive development;
   2. demonstrate means to enhance problem-solving and creative abilities;
   3. demonstrate examples of classification and seriation, as well as spatial and temporal relationships activities.

INTRODUCTION

Julie, age one, is playing with blocks; Mark, age four, is playing shape bingo with classmates; and Susan, age five, is dictating a story to her caregiver. These are some of the activities that demonstrate *innate* (inborn) intelligence and *cognitive development* (the acquiring of knowledge). Children engage in learning experiences from the moment of birth. They continue to learn throughout their lives.

Intelligence encompasses a large range of learning abilities including the senses, language development, concept development, eye-hand coordination, reasoning, and creativity. All of these factors contribute to the cognitive growth of young children.

Intelligence is defined as the ability to learn and to know using the mind. Intelligence is an innate capacity to learn. It is often measured by intelligence testing to determine IQ (intelligence quotient). Alfred Binet developed an IQ test in 1905. This test was refined by Dr. Lewis M. Terman of Stanford University in 1916. The test is now known as the Stanford-Binet. The Stanford-Binet tests children from age two through age sixteen. It uses a mathematical formula designed to establish 100 as the average IQ at any given age.

The disadvantages of the IQ test include that it is not entirely accurate. It can give only an estimate of intelligence. Emotional stability, reaction to the test giver, physical condition (whether healthy or ill), understanding of language, and experiences can affect the results. Therefore, the test is only an indicator of the approximate intelligence level.

The mind can be stimulated by the environment and a variety of instructional activities. As we know, all children develop at their own rate; therefore, each child must be treated as an individual.

Jerome S. Bruner (1915-   ) is an American psychologist who determined that infants show intellectual development at birth. Intelligence can be demonstrated as infants interact to satisfy their basic needs, such as nourishment, by signaling (crying) to the caregiver. Bruner also felt that children must be encouraged and motivated to interact with the materials. Children *initiate* (begin) the interaction by showing an interest.

Figure 15-1: This student is taking an IQ test with an adult present.

Figure 15-2: Infant demonstrating cognitive development by observing himself in a mirror.

As caregivers plan the activities and environment, they should include methods of motivation. Children must be able to *envision* (to picture mentally) a reason to use and learn from the materials. Materials and activities must have meaning to them.

Cognition is the act of learning, perceiving, and acquiring knowledge. Caregivers must provide many different materials to encourage and challenge cognitive development.

The ability to reason and solve problems gives immense pleasure to children as they learn to deal with the world around them. Because of their natural curiosity, they enjoy experimenting and exploring to understand relationships. Thinking encourages language, as questions and ideas arise.

Jean Piaget was the theorist who established the concept of cognitive development in young children. He identified a series of stages by which caregivers can evaluate the maturation of children. His areas of concern were how children learn, what they learn, and how they use this information in their daily lives. He divided cognitive development into four major steps—sensorimotor (infancy), preoperational (ages two to seven), concrete operations (ages six to twelve), and formal operations (age twelve to adult). (See Chapter 11 for further details.)

CONCEPT RELATIONSHIP DEVELOPMENT

During Piaget's studies of how young children learn, he isolated four major areas of concept development. He identified these as classification skills, seriation skills, spatial relationships, and temporal relationships. Success in each of these areas begins in the first seven years of development. Children acquire these skills by acting on their environment and through play.

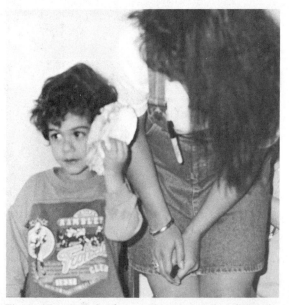

Figure 15-3: Preschooler experimenting and exploring the science center.

Classification

Classification is putting like or similar objects into groupings. Children may choose color, shape, or size to use as their classifying means. Children usually begin by using only one concept (such as color—red) to learn classification. They may put all the red objects in one pile and all objects of other colors in another pile. Classification is the beginning of math and science skills in later years.

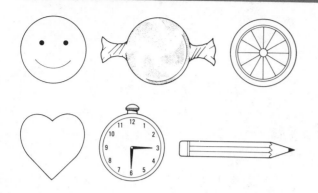

Find all the circles.

Figure 15-4: Classification game.

Equal amounts of liquid in different-sized containers demonstrate the theory of conservation.

Figure 15-5: The theory of conservation.

Children learn classification by using their senses. Taste, touch, smell, sight, and hearing activities and experiences stimulate learning.

Conservation is the ability to determine amounts, such as more, less, or the same, regardless of how the objects are arranged. This is another property of classification. Usually from about age seven through age twelve, children grasp this concept. Ten buttons are ten buttons regardless of how they are arranged—in a straight line, stacked on top of one another, or placed in separate groups of five. Ten buttons still remain.

Conservation also may be shown by using a glass of water. The water can be poured into a larger container and then poured back into the original glass. Children can demonstrate that regardless of the size of the container, the amount of water remains the same. Another term for this example is *reversibility*—the awareness that a situation can return to its original status.

Seriation Skills

Seriation (or ordering) is putting objects in a graduated order according to size, number, or shape. Children begin with comparisons between two objects, such as which is the larger and which is the smaller. Then they progress to three objects and determine which is the middle size. Again, as they increase their understanding, children build on this concept, adding more and more size differentiations.

Remembering the alphabet and numbering are seriation skills for school-age children. As children begin math and reading skills, they need to know how these symbols relate to the objects in their environment. The word *apple* stands for the object, apple, that we eat. Ten apples can be cut in half to serve twenty children.

Matching and sorting are also included in seriation. By practicing these skills, children learn to place like objects together. Matching and sorting are also the beginning of reading

Case Study #1:
Julie

Julie, a toddler, is playing in her classroom. The theme for February is the color red. Wall hangings, pictures on the wall, and snacks all include the color red. The children in the classroom are asked to wear red to school.

Julie is interested in the large toddler beads. She enjoys putting them together and pulling them apart. The caregiver asks Julie to find a red one just like the valentine on the wall. Julie quickly hands her one red bead. The caregiver tells her, "Julie, you found the red bead. Can you find another?" Julie, feeling good about her success, hands her another one. Together they attach it to the other bead.

They continue to play the game until they have all the red beads joined to make a necklace. Julie proudly marches around the room, showing the other children and caregivers her necklace. Julie has learned to classify all the red beads, has enjoyed playing the game, and has enjoyed the interaction with her caregiver.

Figure 15-6: The caregiver helps the children classify beads to string.

Case Study #2: *Jonny*

Jonny, a toddler, is intrigued by the smell of the applesauce he sees in his dish. He sticks his fingers into the bowl and feels the chunks of apples. As he tastes it, his caregiver exclaims, "Mmmm, this is good applesauce!" Jonny has been able to experience several concepts, such as chunky (texture), cold (temperature), name of the food (applesauce), and pleasure (good) in this one eating activity.

Case Study #3: *Mark*

Mark, age four, is playing with the nesting circles. He is trying to stack all six pieces inside each other. He cannot get them in the right order.

Mr. Wilson notices that Mark is becoming frustrated. He sits down on the floor next to Mark. Then he asks Mark to line up the six pieces according to size, starting with the smallest circle. Mark is able to accomplish this task.

Mr. Wilson then asks, "Which is the smallest? In which circle does it fit tightly?" He continues, "You found the next to the smallest circle, Mark. Can you put these two circles into another circle tightly?"

Mark and Mr. Wilson work together until all the circles are in the proper order. Mark feels successful, so he immediately turns the circles over and starts the game again.

readiness skills. Usually choosing a specific property, such as color, size, shape, or number, children can distinguish similarities and discriminate between differences. This process is often accomplished by trial and error. Children can learn to *self-correct* (correct without intervention or help).

Spatial Relationships

Spatial relationships are concerned with objects in space and how they relate to others. Spatial relationships also deal with the body and how it moves or occupies space.

Children need to have experiences that allow them to feel how their bodies move in space. Dancing, creative movement, climbing structures, and swinging give them chances to experiment with different kinds of locomotion.

Infants begin to develop spatial relationships by visually tracking objects and by trying to reach and grasp them. Toddlers increase their skills by beginning to manipulate their bodies around objects in their paths. The preschooler practices putting smaller items inside larger containers and rearranging objects such as furniture and toys. Spatial relationships and language development are enhanced as children try to describe what they see from different viewpoints—in, out, over, under, on, in front of, and behind.

Temporal Relationships

Temporal relationships are concerned with time and how it passes. Young children need to be able to internalize time. This is probably the most difficult of the concepts to learn. Routines and activities that children experience enable them to have a sense of time. Television programs, dinner, and sleeping have significant value to children. They learn to identify these times first.

As children mature and have more experiences, they can understand specific time segments, starting with minutes and progressing to hours or days. Repeated exposure to the statements that in ten minutes it will be pickup time or tomorrow they are going to the park helps to give children an internal sense of time.

Caregivers should plan activities that help children experience temporal relationships. They should establish a daily routine to allow children to anticipate what will happen during their time at the school or center. Calendar activities, songs, and finger plays about the days of the week, and flannel stories concerning the weather or seasons help children to learn about the passage of time.

LANGUAGE DEVELOPMENT

Children learn language by listening to the sounds around them. Even though infants are unable to talk, they learn by listening to the cooing and talking of their caregivers. The understanding of language precedes the ability to express language. For example, infants learn to recognize their principal caregiver and show pleasure at the caregiver's arrival before they are able to give a name to that person, such as mother. Mothers often refer to themselves as ma-ma, and soon children learn that the sound stands for this important person in their lives. They practice using sounds by cooing and gurgling back to their mothers as they "talk" to each other.

Sequence cards—Place the tepees in order from smallest to largest.

Figure 15-7: Seriation game.

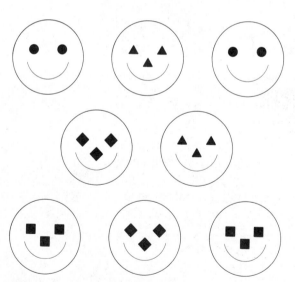

Find the faces that match.
Look carefully at the eyes, noses, and mouths.

Figure 15-8: Matching game.

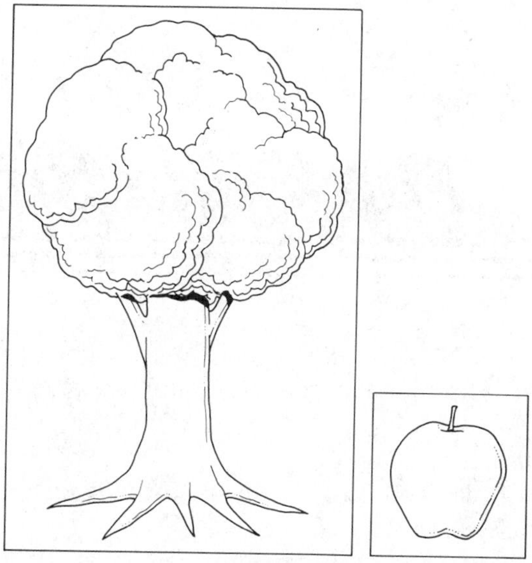

Place the apple over, under, on, left of, and right of the tree.

Figure 15-9: Spatial relationships.

Case Study #4:
Susan

Susan and her classmates are enjoying the obstacle course that their caregiver has set up for them. They start by walking along the balance beam. They crawl through the tunnel, climb over the geometric dome, climb up the cargo net, slide down the pole, and run to the gate. The children take turns following the course, enjoying the feel of their bodies as they practice physical skills. There is much talking and giggling among the children while they complete the activity.

Case Study #5:
Mark and Susan

Mark and Susan need to get up at 6:30 each morning for school. Because it is routine, they are able to wake up without the aid of an alarm clock. They even get up at 6:30 on Saturday and Sunday, much to the dismay of their parents.

While Dad fixes breakfast, they watch the morning children's program on television. They know that when the program is over, it will be time to eat, brush their teeth, and get dressed for school. They have until the news program is finished to be ready.

At night, after spending the day at school, their mother reminds them that they have half an hour until dinner. They decide they have enough time to play one computer game. After dinner, it is time for baths, a story, and then to bed.

The next day begins again at 6:30 A.M., with the children knowing what is expected of them. Routines help to establish a sense of time for children.

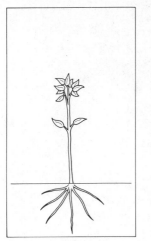

Sequence cards—How do trees grow?
Place them in order.

Figure 15-10: Temporal relationships.

Figure 15-11: *Pat and his friends are interested in all of the tricks his new truck can perform.*

Figure 15-12: An obstacle course challenges gross motor skills of school-age children.

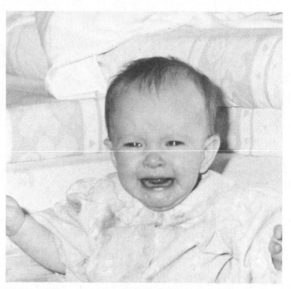

Figure 15-13: Infants and toddlers express fear by crying.

Baby's Cries and What They Mean

Cry	Means	Parent Should
1. An angry howl with sucking in between	hunger	feed baby
2. Low moans with yawns and sighs	sleepiness	rock, soothe, let baby sleep
3. Low moaning cries and feverish look	sickness	call doctor
4. Angry howls that stop when baby sees parent	wants attention	talk, sing, give toy
5. Short, sharp piercing screams or cries. The same screams with a swollen tummy or stiff, pulled-up legs. High-pitched shrill wails with whimpering and moaning.	pain	call doctor

Figure 15-14: Reprinted from Children in Your Life by Radeloff & Zechman. Copyright 1981 by Delmar Publishers. Used with permission.

Caregivers can quickly distinguish the needs of newborns. An angry howl can signal frustration, while a low moaning cry can mean sleepiness. This the way that infants communicate and is the beginning of language development.

Soon they add other sounds to their vocabulary. They add sounds until they are able to reproduce a sound that is recognizable. The pleased reaction of their mothers to that sound stimulates and encourages them to practice other sounds, thus building more words into their vocabulary.

Infants and toddlers also discriminate between tones. Tones can denote either pleasure or displeasure. Sounds displaying calmness and warmth represent security and happiness, while loud voices displaying anger can cause children to cry or be frightened. Language often expresses emotions as well as content.

Language Development

Age	Spoken Vocabulary
1 year	10 words
1½ years	50 words
2 years	200 words (can combine 2 or 3 words into short sentences
2½ years	450 words (start to learn the rules of grammar)
3 to 6 years	900 to 2,500 words (understand meaning of 20,000 words)

Figure 15-15: Language Development chart.

Case Study #6: Susan and Marie

Susan, age five, is busy in the housekeeping corner. She enjoys being the mother. The housekeeping corner is well-equipped. It has a refrigerator, a stove, a sink, tables and chairs, cradles, and dress-up clothes. Susan carefully surveys her area and decides that the cradle with the baby is too close to the stove. "The baby needs to sleep in a quiet place," says Susan. She struggles to move the cradle and doll to the other side of the table.

Marie, Susan's friend, notices her struggles and quickly comes over to help her. They discuss the problems of raising children (mimicking conversations overheard from their own parents) as they work together.

Sensory experiences enable children to learn language. By actually interacting with objects, children develop a need to be able to describe what they are experiencing. Learning must have meaning to children. It must affect them in some way. In order for children to express language, they must first decide what it is they wish to express (think). Sensory experiences establish order to thinking. Thoughts are processed and stored for future use.

Caregivers should spend a large portion of every day encouraging language development. They must constantly be aware of listening and talking as children participate. Caregivers can take advantage of individual and group times to introduce new ideas and vocabulary. They should foster the innate curiosity of children.

Children learn various methods of communication. *Expressive language* is the use of speech. *Receptive language* deals with understanding. Language can be expressed verbally, manually (sign language), or through body actions (facial expressions, hand gestures, and body position). Language delays and disorders can occur when there is a problem with either expressive or receptive language.

Dyslexia is a learning disability associated with an inability to learn the basic language skills (reading, writing, and spelling). Dyslexia sometimes also affects listening and speaking skills. It may involve visual problems, *auditory* (hearing) problems, or both. Following are some characteristics of dyslexia. Watch for:

- difficulty in reading with comprehension
- difficulty in writing
- handwriting that is difficult to read
- inability to correctly name a letter (*b* is seen as *p*). Children often try to guess the correct name
- lack of spelling skills
- reversing letters or sequences of letters that make up a word (water may be perceived as mate)
- spoken language delayed until a later age
- trouble remembering spoken and printed words

Dyslexics are sometimes mistakenly labeled slow or mentally retarded. However, they are often highly intelligent. Famous people diagnosed as dyslexic include Albert Einstein (Nobel Price winner, scientist), Nelson Rockefeller (governor of New York State, United States senator, and United States Vice President), and Bruce Jenner (Olympic Gold Medal winner).

The cause of dyslexia is not known. Some physicians theorize that there is damage to the brain during the fifteenth to seventeenth week of life. There is also evidence that heredity is involved. Several children in a family may be affected.

Although dyslexia cannot be cured, children can learn skills to help cope with or to overcome the learning disability. Repeated lessons of basic skills, taped versions of books, and an understanding of the problems help children to achieve their potential.

Dyslexia is only one learning disorder associated with language. By being observant, caregivers can distinguish possible language disorders or delays. They can then refer parents to community resources that help children with their problem.

Enhancing Language

Suggestions for enhancing language development include:

- Talk directly to the child.
- Give simple, short, and clear directions.
- Encourage the child to use complete sentences.

Figure 15-16: Enhancing Language chart.

ACTIVITIES

It takes a great deal of planning on the part of caregivers to structure activities for each child's development. Good planning is an essential ingredient for intellectual growth.

There are several methods to intellectually stimulate children. Simple activities for infants and toddlers enable them to build on their knowledge and to acquire new information.

Language Arts

Language arts may use books, puppets, flannel stories, finger plays, poetry, prose, drama, spelling, and discussions to encourage practice in language development. When planning the curriculum, use various methods to stimulate language in an enjoyable, positive, and non-threatening manner.

Science

Science may use experiments, displays, field trips, gardening, and walks to encourage the asking of questions and the discovering of answers about the world.

Math

Math may use numbers, colors, shapes, measurement, quantitative words (small, big, all, some), groups (sets), temperature, weather, time, and weight. A variety of activities encourage rational thinking and the ability to draw conclusions.

Music

Movement activities, rhythm band instruments, finger plays, and recall of familiar songs and dances encourage children to develop memory skills.

Arts and Crafts

Following directions, learning the nature of materials, solving problems, using creativity, and using perception encourage children to explore and learn new techniques of expression.

Social Studies

Learning about self, family, school, city, state, country, world, and universe encourages children to understand different cultures and habitats. Holiday celebrations are also important learning activities.

VALUE OF PLAY

"I don't pay good money to have my child just play all day at school." "What learning activities are offered beside play time?" "Why should I send my child to a day care home just to play; he can do that at home for free." Often phrases such as these are heard by caregivers. Parents are unaware many times of the developmental values and personal satisfaction a child encounters when playing. As stated in Chapter 12, play is the work of young children. It is during play that children often learn how to adapt to different environments and to different social behaviors. They are able to satisfy their emotional needs through forms of imitation, role playing, releasing frustration and negative feelings, and problem solving.

Children, as adults, enjoy play most when it is free of many rules, enjoyable to all members, and focused on the process of play more than the final product or goal. Play should be fun as well as a learning experience. Through play children learn about themselves, others, and their environment. With each curriculum activity planned, caregivers should be aware of ways to encourage play as an important part of the learning process.

The following is a possible theme that both the caregiver and the children can build their play activities around.

Cars and Trucks

- cutting and painting large appliance boxes into the forms of cars and trucks
- making directional signs, traffic lights, stop signs, becoming familiar with common street signs
- mapping out roads, crosswalks
- learning to follow directions, north, south, east, and west
- setting up car washes, gas stations
- introducing tools and equipment used to fix cars
- role playing gas station attendants, mechanics, truck drivers, ambulance drivers
- discussing and role playing car and street safety rules

Water Play

Water play is always fun! Children enjoy this sometimes forbidden, yet pleasurable activity of splashing, pouring, and mudpie making. Water play may be promoted by setting up water tables, small ringed pools, buckets, hoses, or sinks. At all times water play must be supervised! As children engage in water play, they learn to share space, water toys, and time with each other. They learn to problem solve, and experiment with pouring and measuring different sizes of objects. They become aware of quantity, volume, weight, and temperature of the water as well as different ways to move and store water.

Dramatic Play

What fun it is to dress up like a police officer, waitress, or queen! Dramatic play takes the child out of reality and into the world of make-believe. It is at this time that children can act out dreams, aggressions, or just become creative. Although dramatic play is most often found in the housekeeping corner, the caregiver can offer the opportunity of this form of play most anywhere in the classroom or play yard. Large furniture boxes can be painted to depict most anything; houses, caves, automobiles, or a grocery checkout counter.

Caregivers can encourage children to pretend that the play yard is a trip to their favorite amusement park. The balance beam can be used as an exciting high wire act. Even a plain chain link fence can be transformed into a hitching post for a team of horses. The opportunities for dramatic play are endless, yet these activities and environments can be successfully planned by both the children and caregiver.

SUMMARY

Children begin learning at birth, and they continue to learn throughout their lives. Intelligence is the innate capacity to learn, while cognition is the act of learning. IQ tests cannot be depended upon to give entirely accurate measurements of intelligence.

Jerome S. Bruner, a psychologist, felt that children's interests need to be stimulated in order for meaningful learning to occur. Jean Piaget, a theorist, developed the concept of cognitive development. He was interested in how children learn and assimilate information into their lives. He identified four principal periods of learning—sensorimotor, preoperational, concrete operations, and formal operations.

Piaget's studies also determined four major areas of concept development—classification skills, seriation skills, spatial relationships, and temporal relationships. Piaget felt that children need to interact with the environment through play in order to learn these skills and relationships.

Language development is an important part of intellectual development. Children begin to develop language by hearing sounds around them. Soon they begin to equate sounds and meaning. Then they practice speaking. Children can understand many more words than they can express.

Plan daily activities to present opportunities to express and practice language. These activities should include language arts, science, music, arts and crafts, math, and social studies. Positive attitudes toward children's attempts at language encourage them to use language creatively, ask questions, and feel responsible. Positive attitudes build self-confidence and help children feel comfortable in their surroundings.

Review Questions

1. What factors contribute to the cognitive growth of children?

2. What are the advantages and disadvantages of the IQ test?

3. What theorist determined that children must show an interest in order to learn?

4. How do children acquire concept development?

5. Who was the theorist who established the Theory of Cognitive Development?

6. What are sensorimotor experiences?

7. Match the definition with the term:

Classification Skill   Temporal Skill
Conservation Skill   Reversibility
Seriation Skill   Spatial Skill

   a. Objects in space and how they relate to others
   b. The ability to determine amounts
   c. Putting like or similar objects in groupings
   d. The awareness that a situation can return to its original state
   e. Concerned with time and how it passes
   f. Putting objects in a graduated order

8. What is the first step in learning language?

9. What is the difference between expressive and receptive language?

10. How can caregivers help children with the learning disability, dyslexia?

11. What is the value of play for the young child?

Things to Do and Discuss

1. Read the description of the following activities and decide which skill is being demonstrated in each one. The skills include spatial relationship, matching, conservation, seriation, classification, and temporal relationship.

   a. A basket of multicolored buttons is given to a child. She is asked to find all the green buttons, then to find all the black buttons.
   b. The same basket of buttons is given to another child. He is asked to line them up from smallest to largest.
   c. The children join in a scarf dance.
   d. The children play games such as follow-the-leader and Simon says.
   e. A child is given a ball of clay. First she makes a long, thin snake, then she remakes her clay into a snowman.
   f. A game is given to the children. They are asked to find which objects go together. The game has mother animals and baby animals, such as the cow and her calf and the cat and her kitten.

2. Make or plan one of the above activities and present it for a preschool classroom. During the presentation, be sure to keep in mind the skill to be learned. Write down your observations and report to your class.

3. Observe a toddler and record all that toddler's language and communication skills (words, sounds, and actions) demonstrated during a fifteen-minute period.

4. Report on one of the following areas
   in which to intellectually stimulate a
   child of a specific age:

   - language arts

   - science

   - math

   - music

   - arts and crafts

   - social studies

CHAPTER 16
Observations

To observe is to watch, listen, and record.

KEY TERMS

anecdotal record
charting
checklist
cubby
ethics

event sampling
home visits
narrative
observe
time sample

OBJECTIVES

After completing this chapter, you will be able to:

1. record observations of the children, staff, school, or center;
2. identify several characteristics of good relationships between staff and children;
3. evaluate what elements help to create a good school or center environment.

INTRODUCTION

Who? What? Why? When? Where? How? These are the questions you need to ask yourself when you are doing observations. To *observe* is to watch, listen, and record what is happening around you or with a particular subject. Observing is a task that all caregivers need to learn and practice. It requires more than just watching children. You will need to be able to recall events with understanding and knowledge of each child's development and history. Observations allow you to organize your thoughts and to plan for future action. Written observations also provide important documentation. You will need a pencil, a clipboard, forms, and extra paper for your observation.

General guidelines for observers include:

1. Be aware of the total situation.

2. Be objective and sensitive. Deal with facts, not feelings.

3. Concentrate on listening and seeing.

4. Do not laugh aloud at things children do.

5. Do not sit on children's equipment.

6. Do not talk to other observers.

7. File observations as directed.

8. Identify the child by name and age.

9. If a child talks to you, answer briefly and then go back to work.

10. Include your name, the date, the time, and the place of observation.

11. Observe professional *ethics* (the standards that establish right and wrong behavior). Remember the confidential nature of records.

12. Record accurately.

13. Record your feelings separately from the observation.

14. Remain inconspicuous while recording.

15. Use observations to improve aid to the child.

16. Write the why and what of the observation.

TYPES OF OBSERVATIONS

There are several ways to perform observations. Recording may be done by writing notes, using a tape recorder, video taping, or

Figure 16-1: A director conducts an event sample of a teacher during outside play.

taking pictures. You need also to familiarize yourself with all styles of observations in order to find the best type to fit your needs.

Anecdotal Notes

An *anecdotal record* is a brief *narrative* (story) of your impressions of a child, staff member, school, or center. It may include an area of concern, behavior patterns, moods, achievement of skills, and plans for the developmental future. These are continuing observation notes, allowing caregivers to chart progress.

Time Sample

A *time sample* is a brief description at timed intervals, such as every five minutes during a specific time frame. Record just the facts, being careful not to interject your emotions or interpretations into the situation.

Event Sampling

An *event sampling* is an observation to understand a particular problem or event. The caregivers watch closely in order to analyze the situation. Then they write down what happened, what happened immediately preceding the action, and the results. This enables them to determine if there is a pattern.

Checklist

A *checklist* is a form on which appear appropriate questions for each child, staff member, school, or center. This is a quick guide to evaluation.

CHILDREN

Who

Caregivers observe each child, separately as an individual, and with other children in a group. Every age of childhood has special needs and responsibilities. Children are interesting and fun as you watch them develop.

What

The importance of observing children is to first familiarize yourself with their behavior and personality patterns. Are they developing

Figure 16-2: *The caregiver observes a child playing alone as the child experiments with paint.*

at appropriate stages physically, socially, emotionally, and intellectually? How is their general appearance in regard to health and nutrition? Are they interacting with others cooperatively? Are they becoming independent by solving problems effectively? Are they able to perform self-help tasks such as toileting and tying shoes?

Why

Understanding each child's development and personality enables you to formulate lesson plans to increase learning and exploration. By observation, you will be able to determine if the child is functioning within the standards for his or her age and development. Observation provides documentation necessary for decisions concerning the child. Does the child need help socially, emotionally, physically, or intellectually? Is the child developing acceptable behavior patterns? Is the information obtained by observation necessary for parent conferences?

People working with infants and toddlers observe their daily patterns and developmental needs. *Charting* (writing a record of daily happenings concerning each child) is a requirement in most day care centers. Most charts are designed to require only a minimum amount of effort on the part of caregivers, yet they can be

Child Observations

Anecdotal Notes (usually done on 3" × 5" cards)

Name: Michelle Todd
Age: 3 years, 2 months
Recorder: Miss Betty

9/12 — M. arrived with mother. Hangs on to mother's skirt for several minutes before saying good-bye. Stays by door for 3 minutes, observing the room. Wanders slowly around room watching various groups. Ten minutes later is interacting with Cindy at puzzle table. At end of day, expressed to mother she wanted to stay longer at school and wasn't ready to go home. Promised family puzzle for 9/13.

10/1 — M. adjusted to school routines. She readily shares her toys. Peer group expanding to include Billy and Susie. Today interacted in block corner, building roads with B. Discuss transportation 10/2.

Time Sample (usually done on a preprinted form)

Child: Trisha
Age: 19 months
Date: 12/2
Observer: Miss Lynn Chin Ho
8:00 A.M. Arrives at school
8:10 Eats breakfast — pancakes, butter, orange juice, banana
8:20 Talks with caregiver, asks for seconds
8:30 Throws cup in trash, carries plates to washbasin on low table, washes hands with caregiver's help, giggles while water tickles hands
8:40 Joins other children on carpet, takes car from Sarah and runs
8:50 Throws car at others as Sarah wants it back and cries
9:00 T. snuggles in caregiver's lap to listen to story

Event Sample (can be done on notepad kept in pocket)

Name: Leo
Age: 8 years old (3rd grade)
Date: 1/3
Recorder: Mr. Juan

L. & G. are arguing about whose turn it is during a four square game. They begin to push, shove, and yell at each other. Sally steps in to settle argument. Neither boy is able to listen. Caregiver intervenes and discusses problem with boys. Unable to reach acceptable solution. Both boys given time out in order to reach a mutual solution. Boys decide to play separately.

Figure 16-3: Child Observations chart.

Checklist — Observation Checklist for Preschool Child

Name: Miguel
Date: 3/23
Time: 2:15 P.M.
Observer: Miss Sonia

Carefully read each question. Mark the appropriate box with 1 (the lowest) to 3 (the highest). Add your comments on the back.

Physical Development

_____ 1. Is the child walking and running in the appropriate manner for age?

_____ 2. Is the child able to do puzzles with skill?

_____ 3. Is the child able to build a tower with five blocks?

_____ 4. Is the child clean and neat?

_____ 5. Does the child eat the foods served?

Social Development

_____ 1. Does the child get along with peers?

_____ 2. Does the child seem self-confident when relating to others?

_____ 3. Does the child follow daily routine with cooperation?

_____ 4. Does the child express ideas openly?

_____ 5. Does the child participate in group activities?

Emotional Development

_____ 1. Does the child express feelings?

_____ 2. Does the child recover quickly from disappointments?

_____ 3. Is the child's self-esteem high?

_____ 4. Is the child concerned with the feelings of others?

_____ 5. Is the child aggressive?

Intellectual or Cognitive Development

_____ 1. Is the child's attention span appropriate for the age?

_____ 2. Is the child able to listen to stories?

_____ 3. Is the child able to recall events in the story?

_____ 4. Is the child able to concentrate on manipulatives?

_____ 5. Does the child finish what he/she starts?

Figure 16-4: Caregivers chart infants' and toddlers' daily routines for the knowledge of the parents and the facility.

very detailed. These records are readily available to the parents at the end of the day.

The developmental patterns of small children change rapidly. It is essential that all adults involved with children be kept advised on a regular basis of their progress. Are the children toileting at a regular time each day? Are they eating the appropriate amounts of food? Are they eating at the proper times? Do they seem cranky or happy? Are they crawling or beginning to walk at an appropriate age?

Preschool caregivers need to be aware of any aspects of children's development that may require special help. Caregivers should notice if the children are displaying passive or active behavior. Are their personalities or moods consistent each day? Or do their moods swing from one extreme to the other?

Caregivers must also observe for school readiness. Will the children be able to function in a normal kindergarten setting? Are they able to write their names? Can they interact, communicate, and cooperate in a group?

Caregivers of school-age children are concerned with the children's reading, writing, and math skills. They also observe physical development, as well as social and emotional maturation. Are the children able to get along with peers? Can they do their homework without becoming frustrated or bored? Do they seen capable of handling added stress at the next grade level? Again, observations are a means of updating information about developmental traits. This information can be shared in a parent conference.

When

Children are observed at all times during the day. From the moment they are greeted in the morning, caregivers observe their general appearance and attitude. They listen carefully to the children's news and notice any changes from the normal routines. They are consistently aware of participation at quiet, group, and play times. At the end of the day, have the children had a successful time? What activities tomorrow would enhance their development?

Where

Children are observed at home during visits and at school or the center each day as they interact with peers and adults. Extracurricular activities, such as plays, scouts, sports, and musical exhibitions, are other opportunities for observations.

How

Caregivers are careful not to include their expectations and feelings concerning the subject being evaluated. They need to record only the actions, language, feelings, and behaviors of the subject. They must be objective when performing observations.

STAFF

Every staff member, whether it be the director, teacher, aide, cook, or janitor, comes

Figure 16-5: Observations must be taken for school readiness.

Figure 16-6: Children and their families may be observed during home visits.

Figure 16-7: *This school cook interacts with children daily and allows them to fix the snack.*

into contact with the children. All members play an important part in their daily interactions. Staff personnel should be able to relate to the children in a warm, pleasant, understanding, and loving manner.

Who

While you are visiting schools, observe all the staff members. These will include the director, teachers, aides, office personnel, maintenance people, and the cook. The principal caregiver in a family day care setting should be included in this category. All of these people come in contact with the children at some point in the day. Are they professional in early childhood education? Have they had previous experience working with children?

Staff qualifications are usually regulated by state and local guidelines. In order to be hired at a facility, staff members must meet these laws. Proper staff is necessary in order for the school, center, or home to be licensed. Is there a sufficient staff to children ratio? Does the staff meet the education, experience, and health requirements of your state?

What

As you observe the staff members, notice

Figure 16-8: The caregiver observes a group of children in an infant-toddler center.

the characteristics or qualities that influence the children. Caregivers have a responsibility to nurture children, providing an atmosphere that is pleasing and inviting. The environment must enhance discovery and creativity on the part of children.

The class and routines should be organized with a daily lesson plan. Materials should be within easy reach. Are the planned activities appropriate for the age of the children? Are the staff members good role models? Are they clean and neat? Are they warm and receptive to the children? Do they take the time to listen? Do they smile easily? Would you want your children to interact with these people?

It is also important to notice staff relationships. Staff members must be able to cooperate with each other, working together to provide for the children's needs. Can the staff interact and communicate freely? Are materials and activities shared? Are there regularly scheduled staff meetings? Are meetings productive?

Why

We observe staff members in order to determine the quality of the school or day care home. The interaction of the staff with the children can make the difference between an

Staff Observations

Anecdotal Notes

Observer: Mr. G. Johnson, school board member
Name: Miss Ho, teacher of the 3-year-old class
Date: 9/25
Time: 9:30 to 10:00 A.M.

Miss Ho reads story, *Fireman Small*, to group. Reads with expression and ease. Holds book so that all children can see pictures. Children appear attentive and relaxed. At end of story, Miss Ho checks comprehension by asking pertinent questions.

Allows children easy transition to snack preparation by first telling them the procedure. She sings simple songs with group as aide helps with toileting and hand washing of a couple of children at a time. Jimmy is setting the table with cups and napkins.

As children are dismissed to go to the snack table, she thanks Jimmy for a job well done. Children obviously know the routine, and their behavior is satisfactory. Snack consists of bananas, crackers, and milk. Miss Ho encourages quiet conversation among the group. When finished, they know to take their cups and napkins to the trash.

Time Sample — Family Day Care Provider

Name: Margaret Beecher
Address: 1046 Placer Square, Los Angeles, CA
Date: 10/21
Observer: Mrs. Mary Rodriguez, supervisor

2:30 P.M.　M. greets students as she arrives to pick them up from school.

2:40　M. walks them to her home, listens about their day and activities.

2:50　M. and children arrive home. She begins to prepare snack as children wash up.

3:00　Serves snack of milk and cookies. Children still discussing day. Speaker had come to discuss earthquake safety. M. joins into conversation, discusses procedure to take if earthquake happens while at her home.

3:10　Children help clean up and prepare to do homework.

3:20　M. helps explain math assignment to Kenny.

3:30　M. sits with Julie, age eight, to review reading.

Figure 16-9: Staff Observations chart.

Event Sample

Name: Mr. Juan, teacher of 3rd grade class
Date: 10/21
Time: 10:20 A.M. recess.
Observer: Mrs. Wang, assistant principal

Mr. J. has play yard duty. He observes Leo and George begin pushing and shoving during a game of four square. He walks over quickly in time to notice Sally trying to stop fight. Boys stop fighting physically but are still arguing. Mr. J. stops them and questions them about their behavior. He listens to both boys calmly and decides on time out until they are able to reach a solution. He resumes play yard duty. He keeps a watchful eye on boys. Returns to boys in five minutes, discusses their solution to play separately and dismisses boys.

Checklist — Staff Observation

Name: Westworld Children's Center
Date: 10/21
Time: 9:30 A.M.
Observer: Ms. Moresaki, parent

In the blank to the left of each item, place a check (√) if the item applies.

_____ 1. Do the staff members seem interested and relaxed but busy?

_____ 2. Does there appear to be mutual trust and respect among staff members and children?

_____ 3. Do the staff members have plenty of physical contact (hugging, holding) with children?

_____ 4. Do the staff members encourage the children to ask questions?

_____ 5. Do the staff members foster the children's interest in new ideas?

_____ 6. Are the staff members respectful of children who are different?

_____ 7. Do the staff members value each child?

_____ 8. Are the staff members sufficiently firm and flexible?

_____ 9. Do the staff members appear prepared and organized?

_____ 10. Do the staff members demonstrate positive interaction with each other?

Figure 16-10: A parent meeting is an excellent opportunity to observe school and staff.

excellent experience or a poor one. Children deserve to have staff members who can nurture and respect them as individuals.

A carefully thought-out lesson plan that allows each child room for growth and development is another aspect of a quality program. Does the program provide for each child? Do the staff members appear to respect and value each child? Is the discipline policy fair and understood by each child?

When

The staff can be observed at all times during the school day. Observation also is possible during conferences, parent meetings, and community functions. Staff members are role models for not only the children but also the parents and the community. They represent the facility. Do they appear friendly and organized? Do they seem knowledgeable concerning the policies? Do they represent the center well?

Where

During a visit to a school or center, we see the staff interacting. Other opportunities for observation include *home visits* (teachers visiting the child at home with the parents

Figure 16-11: Parachute play is a fun activity for school-age children.

present), meetings, school socials, and sports events. Do the teachers appear interested in the group? Do they appear professional?

How

Interacting, talking, listening, and writing notes are all methods of observing staff members. Staff members can be observed individually and in group situations with both children and other adults.

The staff is an important factor in the daily operation of the school or center. Because they interact continuously with the children it is necessary that they exhibit outstanding characteristics.

THE SCHOOL OR CHILD CARE CENTER

Who

The school or center, as a whole, is made up of the staff, the children, the equipment, the buildings, and the grounds. As we observe a facility, it matters little if the building is new or old if it is clean and safe. Each facility has its own personality and style, depending on the philosophy and imagination of the staff.

What

Good health, safety conditions, and

Figure 16-12: The caregiver is helping a child with a problem.

general upkeep are major concerns. Traffic patterns should permit easy access to the outside, as well as to the learning centers. Are the floors washed and polished? Is the trash disposed of daily? Are the walls and doors washed free of grime? Are the carpets vacuumed? Are the windows shiny? Is the equipment disinfected? Are washing and drinking water readily available?

Maintenance of inside as well as outside equipment is vitally important to a successful center. Are puzzles and games complete (with all pieces)? Is the furniture free of sharp corners? Does the furniture have smooth surfaces? Is the furniture sturdily built? Is the furniture appropriate? Is the equipment appropriate? Does each child have a personal *cubby* (generally a box or container used to keep belongings) and napping equipment? Have you looked behind doors, in corners, and around

Figure 16-13: Old and new school facilities.

Figure 16-14: This classroom demonstrates sufficient space and appropriate learning centers.

large pieces of equipment to ensure health and safety?

Most classrooms have learning centers set up to encourage discovery. Are there enough centers for all the children to have a choice of activities? Is there a variety of centers, including arts and crafts, cooking, science, manipulatives, language arts, blocks, concepts (numbers, shapes, and colors), housekeeping, creative movement, and music?

The amount of space available depends on the state guidelines per number of children enrolled and the design of the building. In California, thirty-five square feet are mandatory per child, and stationary cupboards are not included in the measurements (Title XXII). The states of Ohio and New York have the same provision (Ohio Day Care Licensing Law and New York Day Care Center Licensing Regulations). In Florida, twenty square feet per child of usable floor space is mandatory (Florida Child Day Care Standards, Chapter 10M-12). Are there too many children for the size of the classroom? Can the children move comfortably

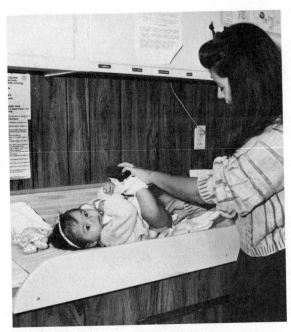

Figure 16-15: Here are a kitchen and changing table at an infant and toddler center.

from one center to another? Does the arrangement of the classroom include both noisy and quiet areas?

A quiet area may be a separate section of the room for manipulatives, a record player, or a tape recorder with earphones. Books, a soft or comfortable sitting chair, a table and chairs for writing, and shelves for display should be included in an area to form a language arts center. An aquarium with fish or plants, calm colors (blue, green, pink), and pictures or posters also add to a relaxed atmosphere.

Blocks, cars, trucks, games, and housekeeping materials would occupy the noisy area, where conversation and vigorous play are encouraged. Are noisy areas provided in the classroom? Are the children motivated to participate in all the centers?

A pleasing atmosphere helps to set the mood of the classroom. Bulletin boards encourage the children to learn concepts and develop self-esteem if their work is displayed. Mobiles, door decorations, wall decorations, window displays, and arrangements on shelves add to the aesthetics of the room. Is the room attractive and inviting? Do the bulletin boards display teacher work, children's work, or both? Is the noise level appropriate for the learning involved?

Proper supervision is vital for safety. Proper supervision can also encourage the children to use all areas of the room. Caregivers should plan the environment so that every area is easily observed. Large pieces of equipment should be placed along the walls to avoid obstructions to supervision. Can you observe all areas of the room? Are the furniture and equipment placed to allow supervision? In case of emergency, will evacuation be easy?

The bathroom and kitchen facilities are separate from the classroom, but they are equally important to observe. Once again, are these areas clean, maintained, and safe? Does the staff practice good health and safety measures? Are these rooms supervised when children are present? Is there easy access from the classroom? Is there a fire extinguisher in the kitchen?

After completing your observations inside, check the play yard. Look outside to determine its cleanliness and maintenance. Again, observe safety, atmosphere, availability of drinking water, and supervision. Is there a variety of equipment? Are there various surfaces, such as sand, grass, and cement? Is

Figure 16-16: Describe the play yard environment; include equipment, surfaces, sun, and shade areas.

there adequate space for the children using the area at one time? Are the play structures built to accommodate the age and size of the children? Is the yard aesthetically pleasing? Is it clean? It is free of debris?

Many child care centers enjoy the addition of pets to their school population. Pets, however, need special care and attention. Are they adequately housed? Are their cages cleaned and maintained daily?

Why

We observe schools and centers in order to determine if the physical plant meets high standards. We want the children to be learning in an atmosphere that encourages and stimulates discovery. State requirements are established to ensure that the children are cared for in a safe and healthy environment. Licensing guarantees that the child care centers or schools meet professional standards. Caregivers should feel at ease that their school is following state, county, and city guidelines.

When

Observations may be made at any location and at any time that the center is in operation. Besides during the daily routine, we can

School and Center Observations

Anecdotal Notes

Name: Crestview Day Care
Date: November 12
Class: Room 6
Time: 9:00 A.M.
Observer: Mrs. Marquez, principal

Room appears clean—corners free of dirt, walls newly painted, no debris behind doors and cabinets. Well equipped, plenty of interesting learning centers. Especially liked reading corner. Equipment well maintained, all pieces to games intact, specific areas on shelves for games.

Room attractive, bulletin boards have both teacher and children's work displayed with imagination. Windows decorated with Thanksgiving turkeys. Traffic patterns show planning. Children able to move freely. Emergency plan posted by front door.

Time Sample

Name: Sixth Street Extended Day School
Date: December 16
Teacher: Mrs. Jones
Observer: Mr. Nguyen

3:30 P.M. Children help prepare snack—mini-pizzas.

3:40   Aide prepares juice.

3:50   Children eat snack, conversing with energy.

4:00   Cleanup time. Fifth grade in charge of washing tables, sweeping floor, taking trash to bin.

4:10   Large motor activity outside.

4:20   Game of soccer on playing field. Girls talking under tree. Children using swings and jump rope. Game of catch.

4:30   Preparation for homework time.

Event Sample

Name: Pine Tree Infant Center
Date: September 20
Event: Orientation
Time: 7:30 P.M.
Observer: Mr. G. Johnson, school board member

O. held in large classroom. Chairs placed in semicircle, podium placed in easy viewing. Refreshment table at back of room (cookies, punch, coffee) next to kitchen.

R. is decorated colorfully. Birthday chart displayed at children's eye level. Toys are clean and placed on shelves (new toys prominently displayed). Charting area is easily accessible. Bulletin boards have fall theme. Ceiling has rainbow-colored

Figure 16-17: School and Center Observations chart.

material hung (bright). Rocking chairs and cribs are in their daily position.

During meeting, parents are able to hear and see well; therefore, participation is lively. Refreshments are easily attainable and enjoyed.

Meeting is 1-1/2 hours long. Parent handbook, bylaws, emergency procedure information, and handout of developmental stages of infants and toddlers are given to participants.

Parents appeared interested. Questions were answered. September 28 was arranged to build outside playhouse.

Checklist

Name: Crestview Child Care Center
Date: September 20
Observer: Mrs. Marquez, principal

In the blank to the left of each item, place a check (√) if the item applies.

School Environment — Classroom

_____ 1. Is the classroom clean, warm, and inviting?

_____ 2. Are there various learning centers?

_____ 3. Are the materials offered appropriate to age of children?

_____ 4. Are the bulletin boards stimulating and attractive?

_____ 5. Is children's work displayed?

_____ 6. Does the atmosphere encourage participation?

School Environment — Play Yard

_____ 1. Is the yard clean, well maintained, and inviting?

_____ 2. Is there a variety of outdoor equipment?

_____ 3. Does the play yard meet safety standards?

_____ 4. Does the play yard have a variety of surfaces?

_____ 5. Does the play yard have a covering for different weather conditions?

Curriculum

_____ 1. Does the program seem well planned and balanced?

_____ 2. Does the program encourage the development of curiosity?

_____ 3. Are there opportunities for freedom of choice in learning activities?

_____ 4. Are the children free to ask questions?

_____ 5. Is plenty of time allotted for working with learning materials?

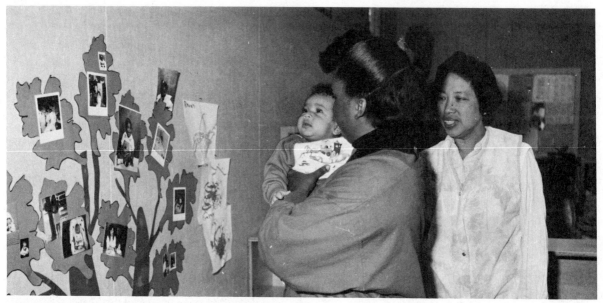

Figure 16-18: At Open House, the teacher and parent can communicate with each other.

observe the school at open house, conferences, programs, sports events, and parent meetings. Are there any limitations to the time and availability of observations?

Where

Child care centers, family day care centers, extended day centers, and elementary schools are places at which we observe. By gaining knowledge of the different programs available in our area, we can distinguish between a quality school and an inadequate school. Is this a school at which you would want to seek employment? Is the facility licensed?

How

Following the guidelines outlined in the beginning of the chapter, place yourself in an inconspicuous location. Take notes carefully so that you do not disturb either the teachers or the children. Refrain from talking with anyone busy with the children. Ask questions when caregivers are free.

SUMMARY

Observation is used to take a close look at, to listen to, and to record the actions of children, staff members, centers, or schools. Observation enables you to recall events and helps you to become more organized. You can also use observations to plan for meeting children's needs.

By following the general guidelines, you can become efficient in performing observations. It is important to have all materials readily available—pencil, clipboard, forms, and extra paper.

There are four types of observation. Anecdotal notes are a brief narrative of your impressions. A time sample is a timed interval description. An event sample is an analysis of a particular behavior of a person or a specific event. A checklist is used for quick evaluation in a preprinted format.

Review Questions

1. Why is it important for caregivers to do observations?

2. Define the following types of observations: anecdotal notes, time sample, event sample, and checklist.

3. Why is it important to do observations?

4. Why do we need to observe children?

5. Why do we observe staff members?

6. Why do we observe facilities?

Things to Do and Discuss

1. Following the general guidelines in the chapter, observe a teacher at a children's center using the anecdotal notes method for one hour. Include in your observation the teacher's attitude, organizational abilities, and professionalism.

2. Following the general guidelines in this chapter, observe a child at an elementary school using the time sample method for half an hour at five-minute intervals. Remember to remain objective.

3. Using the general guidelines in this chapter, observe a school facility using the checklist in this chapter. Add your own comments at the end.

4. Attend an extracurricular event at your school. Using the general guidelines, write an event sample observation over a period of one hour.

5. Obtain a copy of the form used by your local or state licensing agency for inspecting child care center facilities. Inspect a child care center for compliance with health, safety, space, and nutrition standards.

SECTION IV

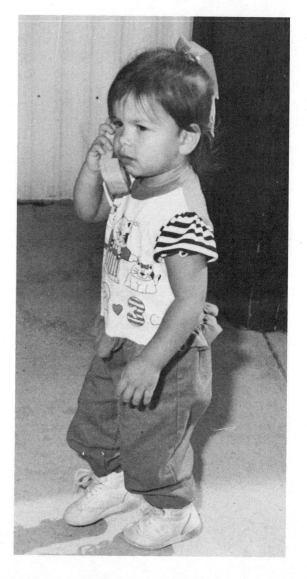

The Ages of Child Development

This section gives you an understanding of the specific focus of each stage of child development. As you have already discovered, the role of child care workers is very important. In child care centers, the caregivers are the principal nurturers to the children in their group. They must be aware of developmental needs and must know when to encourage future development, and how to stimulate children.

It is important that caregivers understand the normal expectations for the group of children for which they are responsible. Caregivers constantly observe the children, as a group and individually, to determine the next step in development or to help with a lag or area of concern. This section discusses each age group in detail and defines the specific role of caregivers in each situation.

CHAPTER 17
Prenatal Care

OBJECTIVES

After completing this chapter, you will be able to:
1. explain the necessity of pregnant women to maintain good health during this period;
2. explain the concept of fertilization;
3. list the developmental stages during the prenatal period.

KEY TERMS

amniotic sac	lanugo
cell	menstrual cycle
cesarean birth	ovum
chromosomes	palate
conception	perinatal
ejaculate	placenta
embryo	prenatal
fertilization	puberty
fetus	quickenings
fontanels	sperm
genetic	trimester
hormones	umbilical cord
incubator	vernix

INTRODUCTION

The beginning of child development starts at *conception* (the joining of cells which later become a baby). It is important to understand how adults influence the embryo's progression to birth as well as after birth. How well the mother takes care of herself by obtaining prenatal care from a doctor, as soon as she realizes that she is pregnant, by refraining from ingesting harmful chemicals, by eating nutritious meals, by getting plenty of rest and exercise, and by striving to be free of stress and tension, help to increase the chances of having a healthy baby.

REPRODUCTION

Cells

All living beings, whether plant or animal, begin as a single *cell* (the smallest structural unit of plant and animal life). Every cell contains forty-six *chromosomes* (threadlike bodies contained in the cell nucleus or center). Each parent donates half or twenty-three chromosomes. Each chromosome contains all the *genetic* (hereditary) information for a new being.

In humans the genetic code or *DNA* determines whether the child will be a boy or a girl, tall or short, fair- or dark-skinned, blond or brunette, blue or brown eyes, and the tendencies for temperament and intelligence. It also contains information pertaining to predisposition of health problems or diseases. The male sex cell (*sperm*) establishes the sex of the child.

Fertilization

From the onset of *puberty* (when a person is first capable of reproduction), the female and male together are capable of creating a child. Both parties contribute the same quantity of genetic information for a new life. The determination of which genes in the chromosomes will be dominant is different for each individual, except in the case of identical twins.

Each month, in four-week intervals, the female's body produces an egg or a single cell, approximately the size of the smallest dot that is visible to the eye. The egg is called an *ovum* During the first two weeks of the cycle, the pituitary gland, which is located at the base of the brain, produces *hormones* (internally secreted compounds that affect the functions of the body) and prepares the egg for *fertilization* (the union of the male and female sex cells). At this time, the ovum is released by the ovary and travels through the Fallopian tube. The lining of the uterus also prepares for fertilization. If the ovum is not fertilized, the lining is shed during the *menstrual cycle*

The male's body is constantly capable of producing and discharging three to five centimeters of seminal fluid containing hundreds of millions of sperm. It would take 2500 sperm to cover the period at the end of this sentence. The sperm is produced in the testicles and travels through a series of ducts until it passes through the urethra. The sperm swim vigorously through the penis and *ejaculate* (to eject suddenly) into the vagina. Only one of the many sperm is used for the fertilization of the ovum. The sperm has the capability to live for several days and can cause fertilization at any point during this time.

As the ovum is released from the ovary and travels towards the Fallopian tube, fertilization occurs when the male's sperm approaches the opening of the female's Fallopian tube. The sperm then penetrates the ovum and proceeds to the nucleus of the female cell. The ovum, after fertilization, spends the first week moving along the approximately four and one-half-inch long tube. After the first twenty-four hours, the cells begin to divide and later become implanted into the prepared lining of the uterus.

PREGNANCY

The First Trimester

At approximately two weeks, the *embryo* (an organism in the early stages of development) has been firmly established into the lining of the uterus. A primitive *placenta* (an organ that provides protection, nourishment, and allows for elimination of waste) is being formed along with the *amniotic sac* (sack that contains fluid in which the embryo is suspended) and the *umbilical cord* (a cord connecting the placenta of the mother to the navel of the embryo through which nourishment is passed). The embryo now begins to grow rapidly.

At this time usually the mother will notice that the menstrual cycle has stopped. (Sometimes the menstrual cycle will continue during the pregnancy.) She may not be sure that she is pregnant, but precautions should be taken as soon as she suspects that it may be a possibility. She may be very hungry, tired, and may experience morning sickness or nausea. She may have some soreness in her breasts and feel the frequent need to urinate.

The embryo is extremely vulnerable during the first three months of rapid cell growth to chemicals and illnesses of the mother. It is important for the pregnant woman to avoid any usage of medications (any drugs, even the common aspirin), X-rays, caffeine (coffee, tea, sodas, chocolate), cigarettes, alcohol, and salt. She must eat balanced, nutritious meals; do nonstrenuous exercises; and get plenty of rest to help ensure a healthy infant. Anything that the mother ingests will pass through the umbilical cord and into the embryo. For example, if the mother has even one alcoholic drink, it passes to the fetus. The mother may not feel intoxicated because her liver and kidneys can easily filter the alcohol and pass it out of the body through the urine. The embryo's organs, however, are very immature and inefficient. Its body cannot filter the alcohol out of its system, and the embryo retains the alcohol for a much longer time. As the brain cells are developing during this time, the alcohol causes the brain cells to die and can cause permanent brain damage to the developing baby. The pregnant woman must be careful of anything that she ingests as it passes directly to the baby.

At four weeks the embryo is approximately one-third of an inch long. The one-chamber heart is already beating and the circulation of blood has started. Head, trunk, tail, arm, and leg buds, as well as the nervous systems and brain, have begun to be formed. Outlines of a skeleton and internal organs, which are beginning to function, can be seen. Facial features and the neck are taking shape. Through careful examination, it is also possible to determine the sex of the embryo at this time.

By the seventh week the embryo begins to look like a very small baby, with all the facial characteristics of eyes spread widely apart on either side of the head, ears, mouth, tongue, lips, and tooth buds. All the internal organs that it will have as it grows into an adult are now formed. The heart beats, the brain sends messages, and the stomach, kidneys, and liver are beginning to function. Arms, hands, fingers, legs, feet, and toes are beginning to be recognizable. The body is becoming fuller as the muscles and tissues develop. It is about one inch long and weighs one-third of an ounce.

At about the eighth week bone cells appear and thus begins the *fetus* (Latin term for "young one") period of gestation. Now the mother probably has a good idea that she is pregnant as she approaches the time of her second regular cycle. She should visit a doctor or maternity clinic for a pregnancy test and to get answers to questions about both her health and the fetus'. If the mother is in her teen years or over thirty-five, special precautions need to be taken.

By the end of the first *trimester* (third month), the fetus becomes energetic. It can now move its legs, hands, toes, frown, squint, and turn its head as it gains strength in the muscles. The nerves and muscles are increasing their connections and the fetus is able to move separate parts of its body. For example, it can now move its thumb separate from the fingers.

Facial characteristics now are individual as determined by the genes. The eyes have moved closer to the nose bridge and now have eyelids that seal the eyes until the sixth month. The ears have now moved upward on the head to become level with the eyes. It is easy to identify the sex of the fetus during the third month as the reproductive organs are refined.

The beginnings of ovum and sperm cells for future generations are also being formed.

The fetus also swallows substantial amounts of amniotic fluid as the lungs develop. As it receives all the oxygen necessary for growth through the umbilical cord, the fetus does not use its lungs for breathing yet. Although the vocal cords are formed, it cannot produce sounds due to the lack of oxygen.

Some of the early bone cells are now becoming solid; the ribs and vertebrae, and the *palate* (the roof of the mouth). Fingernails and toenails are now forming and will soon harden. The lips are very sensitive and the cheek muscles are developing. These are both necessary as the fetus prepares for sucking after birth. The stomach digestive glands are now functioning and some urine is passed into the amniotic fluid.

The Second Trimester

As the fetus enters its fourth month in the womb, the mother will often feel "*quickenings*" (small sensations of movement). It is also easily apparent by looking at the mother that she is pregnant; clothes fit tighter and her waist is now thicker. Her stomach now has a slight bulge or roundness. Her breasts are fuller and may become very sensitive or sore as the mammary glands are preparing for breast-feeding.

The fetus now has grown considerably in length (approximately ten to eleven inches) and has half of its birth height. Weight gain also increases rapidly during this period. It weighs about six ounces. As it gains strength and control of its muscles, the fetus becomes very active. The doctor can now listen to the heart as it pumps at about one-sixth of its birth capacity or about fifty pints of blood a day. Additional food, oxygen, and water are essential for this period of speedy growth. This is obtained from the mother through the placenta and the umbilical cord. The placenta performs all the duties that the internal organs will accomplish after the birth of the baby. It helps to purify the blood and oxygen, prevent infections by producing antibodies, filter the urine out of the blood, and to process or digest nutrients necessary for growth.

Although both the mother's and fetus' blood systems are separate, the walls of the veins are so thin that they easily allow for the transference of substances from one body to the other. Most items that the mother digests are effortlessly passed from the placenta through the umbilical cord and into the fetus. If the mother drinks an alcoholic beverage, the fetus drinks too. If the mother smokes a cigarette, the fetus smokes too. If the mother eats too much salt, caffeine, and sugar; the fetus eats too much salt, caffeine, and sugar. Because of the inefficiency of the fetus' organs, it retains the substances for a much longer time than the mother.

During the fifth month the fetus adds considerable weight and now has the appearance of a small, but well-formed baby. It is about twelve inches long and weighs about one pound. The doctor can now identify, by examination, different parts of the fetus' body. The fetus may develop hiccups, kick its legs, stretch its arms, turn head-over-heels, and show a startled reflex when it hears a sudden loud noise. The fetus has periods of being awake and of being asleep. There is also evidence that it can cry and suck. Fine soft baby hair begins to grow on the head, eyebrows, and eyelashes. Nipples and mammary ducts are now noticeable.

By the sixth month the fetus starts to add a padding of fat under the skin, and although it still looks skinny, begins to get the rounded effect of a healthy looking baby. The body now has a waxy, creamy covering called a *vernix*. (This will later help the baby move through the birth canal.) The back and arms also have a covering of fine hair called *lanugo*. Most of the lanugo will disappear before birth.

It now weighs one and half pounds and has added two inches to its height. The tooth buds are now formed under the gums. Eyes can now open and shut and it can move its eyes in order to see. A grasping reflex is now developed. This will enable the newborn to hold on to its mother.

The fetus is now capable of breathing on its own and could survive being born prematurely. Twenty-four hour special care by *perinatal* (after birth) personnel in the hospital is necessary. The baby would be placed in an *incubator* (a specially designed enclosed crib that maintains constant heat, oxygen, and nutrition).

The Third Trimester

During the last three months of pregnancy the baby gains most of its weight; approximately five more pounds. A thick padding of fat will help to keep the baby warm after birth. In the seventh month the mother may experience soreness in her ribs and back as the fetus' movements become stronger. Thumb sucking occurs during this time and the baby may be born with a definite mark on its thumb.

The fetus also receives immunities against diseases and illness from its mother during this period. The immunities usually last for the first six months of life. A baby being born during the seventh month has a good chance of survival, although special care is still necessary.

As the fetus nears the term for birth, the space in the womb becomes very crowded. It is unable to move freely due to the lack of space. The mother may feel signs of pressure as her body prepares for the birth of the child. She may feel pains or aches in the uterus and in her back. Frequent urinating is necessary as the fetus presses on the bladder.

THE BIRTH

As the time for the birth of the baby becomes near, (towards the end of the eighth month) the wall of the mother's uterus stretches and the fetus' head drops into position. The fetus is now firmly held in place until the time to be born. The placenta's usefulness is now ending and the walls of the sac are thin.

Within eleven days, before or after the expected birth date, the mother will experience small sensations or tightness in her stomach. This may last for several days before the actual birth. As these feelings or contractions get stronger they will gradually settle into a pattern. When the contractions are ten to fifteen minutes apart labor is said to have started. Other signs of the beginning of labor are when the mother's water breaks (amniotic sac begins to leak) or when the mother notices a 'show' of blood (blood-stained mucus) when the uterus begins to dilate (get larger).

The parents are often very excited that the labor has begun and are anxious for the birth of their child. It is best to try to remain as calm as possible during this stage. Often labor will last for many hours as the head of the baby pushes against the closed cervix of the mother. Mothers often nap between the early contractions.

Usually the baby's head is pointed downward towards the birth canal. This is the normal position. If, however, the head is pointed upward, the baby will be born in a breech or bottom position. Often the doctor will attempt to turn the baby to the normal position. If this is not possible, the doctor may determine that a *cesarean birth* (an operation to remove the baby through the uterine wall) is necessary.

The five plates or bones of the skull are still pliable with spaces in between each plate. These spaces are called *fontanels* (or soft spots). The brain does not fill the skull cavity. This allows the skull to compress during birth. The measurement of the circumference of the head is about equal to that of the baby's shoulders. As the head of the baby presses towards the birth canal, it helps to prepare the way for the body to move towards the opening.

As the contractions become stronger the head continues to press against the cervix until it is fully dilated. At this point the labor has entered the second stage. The baby's head is now entering the birth canal and it can now be seen by the doctor. The mother does experience a great deal of pressure on the muscles of the pelvis and will continue to push until the baby's body slips out. The parents will hear the baby's cry and the mother is given her baby to hold for the first time.

The third stage of labor occurs as the uterus contracts once again and the placenta is expelled. This generally happens very easily in about twenty minutes after the birth.

Both mother and baby are checked by the doctor to ensure that everything is fine and normal. Both are allowed to rest after all their hard work.

SUMMARY

The birth of a baby is an exciting and special time. Conception begins with the joining of ovum and sperm. Each parent donates twenty-three chromosomes, which include all the heredity information for the newborn. Each child is unique. The dominant characteristics determine the physical structure, predisposition of disease, temperament, and intellect of the child.

During the first trimester the embryo establishes its place in the uterus and begins to rapidly develop its basic structure. The placenta, amniotic sac, and umbilical cord are also established. The embryo is very vulnerable and must be protected from illness and substance abuse. The mother must take good care of herself and the baby by eating nutritious meals, exercising, and resting.

The mother often will feel movement at the beginning of the second trimester. The fetus' body is refining its organs, muscles, and bones. Its appearance now more closely resembles an infant. Hiccupping and thumb sucking occurs during this period.

During the third trimester the fetus is adding weight and length. It is preparing for birth as the space in the womb becomes scarce.

The head points downward and begins to move into position.

The birth process begins as the mother feels a tightness in her stomach muscles. This may last for several days. As the contractions become stronger the head moves into the birth canal. The uterus stretches to allow for the baby to move through the canal, to the cervix, and the baby is born. Soon afterwards, the placenta is expelled. This is a moment of great excitement and relief.

7. How does the fetus obtain nourishment?

8. At what age can the fetus survive premature birth?

9. What is the 'show'?

10. What is meant by the baby being in the 'breech' position?

11. When does labor begin the second stage?

Review Questions

1. How many chromosomes does each parent contribute to the embryo?

2. Where is the genetic information stored?

3. When does cell division begin?

4. Why is it important that the pregnant woman avoid harmful substances?

5. When does the heart begin to beat?

6. At what stage does the embryo become a fetus?

Things to Do and Discuss

1. What type of diet should a pregnant woman eat?

2. What are the reasons for maintaining good health during pregnancy?

3. Discuss the dangers of substance abuse during pregnancy.

4. Research and discuss the science of genetic engineering.

5. Research and discuss the different methods of giving birth.

CHAPTER 18
Infants and Toddlers

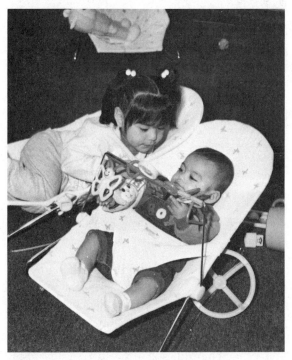

Infant David enjoys toddler Crystal's attention.

KEY TERMS

egocentric behavior   rooting reflex
Moro reflex   self-help skills
object permanency

OBJECTIVES

After completing this chapter, you will be able to:

1. identify and give examples of four developmental stages of infants and toddlers;
2. discuss the caregiver's role in enhancing and developmental stages of infants and toddlers;
3. give three exampless of daily routines that caregivers perform with infants and with toddlers.

INTRODUCTION

Many authorities disagree as to the exact time span for infants and toddlers. In this book, we define the infant stage from birth to walking (approximately one year) and the toddler age from walking to potty training (approximately ages one to two and a half years). The most rapid growth of children's entire lives happens during their first year of life.

Infants and toddlers develop in a common sequence. They all perform the same skills and tasks, but the time when they perform them differs with the individual child. Each child should progress at his or her own rate. Growth and progress appear in spurts as the child concentrates on one area of development. One child may appear to be focusing on grasping a toy (physical development) while another may be interested in practicing repetitive sounds (language development). This is a natural pattern for young children.

NORMAL DEVELOPMENT OF INFANTS

As you have learned, children develop in four areas—physical, social, emotional, and intellectual. The following material breaks down the normal developmental sequence of infants and toddlers by age. Remember that normal varies widely, depending on the environment and the heritage of the child. Included are sample materials that you can use to encourage children's development and your role as facilitator.

Birth

At birth, infants normally have a *rooting reflex*, which permits them to get nourishment from a bottle or breast. In addition, they have a reflex called the *Moro reflex*, or startle reflex, which causes them to respond with whole body motion to loud noises.

One Month

Physical Development

At one month, infants normally begin lifting their chins and holding their heads up-

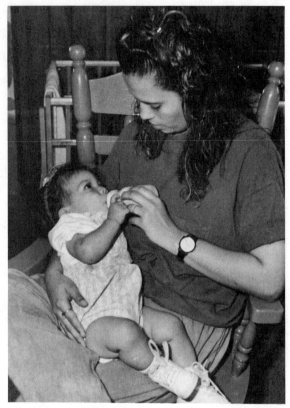

Figure 18-1: Infant demonstrating rooting reflex.

right with support. Placing the infants in a variety of positions (on the back, stomach, and side) and providing a mirror encourage development.

Infants also have a reflex to grasp when their palms are stimulated. Place toys (rattles and other colorful, soft toys) to the side, over, and in front of infants.

Social Development

Infants enjoy cuddling and motion. They quiet down when being held or rocked. It is important that caregivers continually talk to, sing to, and make eye contact with infants as part of the bonding process. Consistent care is crucial. Infants are developing familiarity with one caregiver. Relax, smile, and make your time together pleasurable.

Emotional Development

One-month-old infants show a variety of emotions — excitement, distress, enjoyment, anger, and fear. Quickly meeting children's needs (feeding, changing diapers, checking for discomfort) and providing companionship (using a calm soothing voice, playing soft music, or singing) reassure children and help them to develop a sense of trust.

Intellectual Development

At one month, infants are in the sensorimotor stage and need to exercise certain reflex actions — grasping, eye movement, and sucking. Therefore, provide mobiles and pictures (hung at eight inches from the children's eyes), teething rings, and colorful and small toys with which the infants can practice skills. Playing simple games such as peekaboo and passing colorful objects across an infant's line of vision also help to strengthen the eye muscles. Repeat the games often.

Language skills are also beginning, as infants enjoy listening to the caregiver. Crying to signal needs, cooing with pleasure, and imitating their caregiver's facial expressions, the infants are learning to communicate.

Three Months

Physical Development

At three months, infants are progressing rapidly. They can lift their chests upright, support their weights on the elbows, turn from side to back, and sit when propped with pillows. They can easily follow objects with their eyes and look from object to object. Continue to play the game of moving objects slowly across the line of vision.

Infants at three months respond eagerly to sounds and enjoy musical toys, music, and rattles. Caregivers can talk, whisper, sing, laugh, and play music boxes, records, or tapes to stimulate the sense of hearing.

Infants also enjoy playing with their hands and grasping nearby objects. Bumpy toys, toys that fit easily into their hands, small toys to push and pull, and a teether with a variety of surfaces help to develop the senses of touch and taste as well as develop their muscles.

Social Development

Infants recognize the voice of their principal caregiver and will produce a different cry when they see the caregiver. A general decrease in crying is evident. Three-month-old infants begin smiling with pleasure and show an interest in other family members. They coo and gurgle in response to others. Caregivers should provide a variety of places and people for the infants to observe. Holding an infant in front of a mirror and talking about the infant encourages self-concept.

Emotional Development

Infants at three months display the positive emotions of pleasure and happiness. Introduce new toys and opportunities to enhance pleasure. Express your happy feelings and play silly games to encourage laughter and joy.

The negative emotions also occur. Fear of strangers can be reduced if caregivers introduce new people slowly and wait until the infant feels secure. Comfort infants if they become frightened.

Frustration and anger are also expressed by infants. Caregivers must take care not to overstimulate infants with too many toys or people at one time. A quiet time and cuddling can calm infants.

Intellectual Development

At three months, infants practice actions that are of interest to them. They look and reach for a favorite toy, object, or person. They enjoy looking at large picture books. They also repeat the same action, such as banging on the side of the crib with a rattle.

Infants are more actively responding to sounds by cooing and smiling. They try to reproduce sounds that they hear and enjoy communicating with their caregivers.

Six Months
Physical Development

At six months, infants can sit alone, roll over, and begin scooting, rocking, and falling. Provide soft surfaces. Chairs should have backs and safety straps.

These infants enjoy grasping objects with the whole hand and objects with a variety of shapes and textures. Introduce objects that are too large to be swallowed. Infants also can hold their own bottles, but they still need to be held and cuddled during feedings.

Infants at this age are able to focus their eyes on appealing objects. They can distinguish color and distance. An unbreakable mirror, colorful pictures, ribbons, toys, and mobiles (which are changed frequently) help to develop vision. In addition, these infants can recognize their own voices, and they enjoy entertaining themselves by talking.

Social Development

Infants at six months are able to show affection for family members but may cry around an unfamiliar person. They are becoming very observant. They enjoy playing imitative games such as clapping.

These infants are now seeking independence from the influence of others and should be allowed to initiate and complete tasks such as scooting for a toy. But they also crave attention and will perform movements or make sounds in order to achieve their goals.

Emotional Development

Fears of unfamiliar surroundings prevail at six months. Introduce new environments gradually and in a positive manner. At six months, infants may also display anger and begin temper tantrums. Caregivers should try to determine the reason for the anger and remove the situation if possible. These infants often show displeasure by rejecting objects, situations, or people. Allow infants to make choices by offering several toys or opportunities. Choices help to dispel feelings of displeasure.

The positive emotions of happiness and joy are also expressed. Caregivers can encourage positive emotions by modeling a happy, pleasureful attitude.

Intellectual Development

At six months, infants are becoming proficient at imitating others' actions and sounds.

They enjoy playing copycat games and try to reproduce sounds that they hear. Books with familiar objects are favorites.

Nine Months

Physical Development

Nine-month-old infants can crawl. They need a large area and a variety of surfaces (dirt, grass, carpet, linoleum, and cement) that are free of obstacles. Caregivers should supervise them as they crawl over, under, around, and up steps. These infants can pull themselves up and stand while holding on to a sturdy object (be careful of sharp edges and breakable objects). They can also sit unsupported for long periods of time.

Grasping objects with the thumb and first two fingers delights these infants. They enjoy reaching, picking up, and holding objects and controlling their arm movements. They practice eye-hand coordination while playing with blocks and other toys. Drinking from an infant cup with handles is another new achievement.

Social Development

Nine month olds are very possessive of favorite people and toys. They may appear shy and cling to caregivers. Offering reassurance of your whereabouts helps to dispel these concerns.

Emotional Development

Infants at nine months relish displaying affection to others. Caregivers can enhance this behavior by accepting affection happily and by exhibiting a loving attitude whenever possible. Hug and talk calmly and warmly to infants.

Self-esteem is beginning to develop at this time. By showing a nurturing attitude and treating infants as wanted and special, caregivers help to enhance this feeling. Infants at this age desire more independence, so offer many opportunities for them to practice skills and tasks.

Intellectual Development

Object permanency, or knowing that an object removed from sight still exists, is being developed at nine months. Playing hiding games, such as hiding a toy under a blanket or behind the back and permitting infants to find it, allows infants to practice this knowledge.

At nine months, infants also enjoy showing off and repeating actions if encouraged. They will scribble with crayons and paint with roller bottles on large pieces of paper. They practice language by imitating sounds and listening to conversations. They will name objects in books. They appreciate hearing short stories. They know the meaning of *no* and will respond accordingly. Games such as pat-a-cake and Simon says are enjoyed.

NORMAL DEVELOPMENT OF TODDLERS

Twelve Months

Physical Development

It is important to provide a safe environment, sturdy furniture, and push and pull toys as toddlers begin to walk. They can also pick up large objects with two hands. Provide balls, unbreakable toys, and soft objects. Tod-

Figure 18-2: The twelve month old shows affection with her caregiver.

Social Development

At twelve months, toddlers exhibit *egocentric behavior* (understanding only one's viewpoint without regard for the viewpoint of others). This is the period of autonomy when toddlers are establishing their sense of self or of being independent of others. They often display negativism and defiance by refusing to eat or nap. They frequently tell their caregiver "No!" and may have tantrums. They are practicing different modes of behavior in order to gain attention. Caregivers can use positive reinforcement to encourage acceptable behavior.

Competition for toys of siblings or friends is demonstrated by grabbing the desired item. Toddlers enjoy company, however, and engage in parallel play. Caregivers can diminish competition by providing enough toys.

Emotional Development

Toddlers at twelve months are very affectionate. They express their emotions through language and behavior. They respond to nurturing and an accepting attitude on the part of caregivers.

Toddlers are also developing a sense of humor. They enjoy opportunities to perform silly actions. Standing on their heads, making faces, and wearing funny clothes are examples. Toddlers continue to perform as long as they have an audience.

Intellectual Development

At twelve months, toddlers are extremely curious. They often experiment with cause and effect to determine the results of their actions. A safe environment and freedom to explore are essential to encourage intellectual development.

dlers delight in rolling the ball and playing catch. Large targets can be used to practice throwing to improve eye-hand coordination. At twelve months, toddlers are able to build a tower with three blocks.

Introduce a variety of table foods in small amounts to toddlers. Toddlers can distinguish between food likes and dislikes. Ask if the food is hot, cold, hard, soft, sweet, or sour. Allow toddlers to differentiate between temperatures and textures. Let them feed themselves.

Toddlers copy the behaviors, sounds, and words of others. They also are able to follow directions given by words or gestures. Caregivers can help to increase the toddler's knowledge by:

- naming body parts while bathing and dressing
- naming common objects
- naming common sounds such as the lawn mower and water running
- playing word games
- saying nursery rhymes with body actions
- singing simple songs

Eighteen Months

Physical Development

At eighteen months toddlers take pleasure in their ability to walk forward, backward, and sideways. They can jump with both feet, climb, run with frequent stops and starts, and kick and throw awkwardly. They need large, unobstructed areas and games in order to practice movements (naming the action encourages language and increases knowledge). Toddlers also enjoy dancing to records, tapes, musical toys, and instruments that are played at different tempos. Clapping hands to the rhythm and using scarves, ribbons, or streamers add to the experience.

Toddlers also can carry several objects at one time. They enjoy putting small objects into small containers such as pockets and purses. They like to show off their many possessions. They begin fine motor skills by using a variety of manipulatives, such as blocks, thick pencils, crayons, touch and feel games, simple puzzles, books, and plastic jars with screw-on lids. Supply the name of each object.

Toddlers are also learning self-help skills, such as undressing (before learning to dress), and pulling up and down zippers. Clothes that are easy to take off and put on encourage success.

Social Development

Toddlers demand attention and want to help with adult activities, such as washing dishes and wiping tables. Encourage participation with such simple tasks as washing unbreakable dishes, clearing the table, and putting away toys. Present each chore as fun instead of demanding action. Word requests in a positive and inviting manner. Sharing the activity makes it more fun.

At eighteen months, toddlers are becoming more independent. They have great difficulty sharing either toys or people. However, they begin to be aware of others' feelings and are becoming very social. Plenty of toys, books on feelings, and short explanations help them to understand others.

Emotional Development

Emotions during this period last for only a short time. Toddlers quickly move from happiness to anger to sadness and back to happiness. They often express their emotions through play. A housekeeping area with dolls and dress-up clothes allows them to play out feelings using props. Caregivers can help toddlers understand emotions by labeling the emotion and modeling the acceptable behavior.

Toddlers want the approval of adults. They need security and routine as they practice handling emotions. They have many fears about any unfamiliar situation. Reassure them that they are safe and provide consistent guidelines and schedules.

Intellectual Development

Toddlers at eighteen months are beginning to solve problems through trial and error. They are often called "Water Babies" as they enjoy experimenting and playing in water. Both conservation skills and reversibility are being learned at this time. Caregivers can provide many simple games and tasks. By asking open-ended questions, caregivers encourage independent thinking. Say, for example, "The doll is cold. What should we do?"

Eighteen-month-old toddlers use language to express thoughts and to name objects. By reading books, describing pictures, and looking at photographs, toddlers learn about past, present, and future events (temporal skills). This is the age for caregivers to stress and role model the use of manners as they learn social skills. Terms such as *please, excuse me*, and *thank you* are important. When responding to toddlers' needs, use complete sentences, "Here is the milk that you wanted." Use specific, descriptive words.

Twenty-Four Months

Physical Development

Twenty-four-month-old toddlers can run, but they fall when taking sudden turns. They can stand on one foot briefly, climb up and down stairs using two feet per step, and bend at the waist when picking up objects. As their fine motor skills improve, they enjoy filling, emptying, twisting, and picking up small objects. Large plastic nuts and bolts, plastic jars with lids, large pegs and a board, and small cars enhance their play. Caregivers should provide more water experiences at this age. They derive great pleasure and gain eye-hand coordination from playing in water.

These toddlers are developing an awareness of different textures and temperatures. Placing a variety of objects in feely boxes helps to develop the sense of touch.

Self-help skills include using a fork, beginning toilet training, and brushing their teeth. Assist and praise the toddler for attempts. Positive reinforcement helps to establish these tasks as worthwhile.

Social Development

At two years, toddlers are possessive, but they enjoy helping others. They are beginning cooperative play. Instruction on sharing is appropriate at this stage. Following guidelines with nurturing caregivers reinforces appropriate behavior.

Emotional Development

Twenty-four-month-old toddlers have both positive and negative feelings about themselves. Stress the positive aspects at every opportunity, and present toddlers with a clear picture of themselves.

Intellectual Development

Toddlers at two years recognize and use symbols in language and drawings. They need many opportunities to use a housekeeping area, dress-up clothes, paper, crayons, pencils, and books. They are interested in symbolic play and need playmates to practice interaction and problem solving.

Matching and sorting games provide opportunities for the toddler to label classes of objects; to understand quantitative words such as *big, some,* and *more*; and to understand spatial words such as *over, under,* and *through.* Repeat terms often, introduce new materials, and play creative movement games to keep the toddler stimulated.

Thirty Months

Physical Development

Thirty-month-old toddlers can walk and run smoothly with many stops, starts, and turns. They need uncluttered floor and yard space in order to participate in running and relay games. They have all twenty baby teeth. They can hold a glass with one hand and begin to wash themselves during baths. They can now learn about dental hygiene and good nutrition.

Social Development

Toddlers have a very cooperative attitude during this stage. They want to please adults. Caregivers can give positive reinforcement by expressing pleasure at toddlers' efforts. Toddlers need to feel that they are vital members of home and school.

Emotional Development

Toddlers at thirty months react strongly to most situations or criticism. Allow them to express their emotions in appropriate manners;

for example, let them pound on clay to release anger.

Intellectual Development

Thirty-month-old toddlers can think symbolically; speak in sentences; and use verbs, pronouns, prepositions, and adjectives. Storybooks, finger plays, flannel stories, records, and toys encourage toddlers to learn new words and proper sentence structures. At thirty months, toddlers will pretend to read a book by themselves.

These toddlers enjoy exploring how things are put together and how they work. Therefore, they are soon adept at taking things apart. Allow them to have free expression with a variety of materials, such as paints, paper, crayons, and glue. Allow them to create their own projects. Print the name of each toddler in the upper left-hand corner of a paper to help to train the eyes for reading. Display toddlers' projects prominently to enlarge their sense of worth.

Easy-to-put-together toys, puzzles, and games help to increase eye-hand coordination. Be sure to discuss work with toddlers to further their language development.

PLAY

Infants and toddlers are busy working by accomplishing tasks which may appear as play. However, focusing on a colorful rattle and attempting to grasp it, practicing turning over from stomach to back, and creeping on the

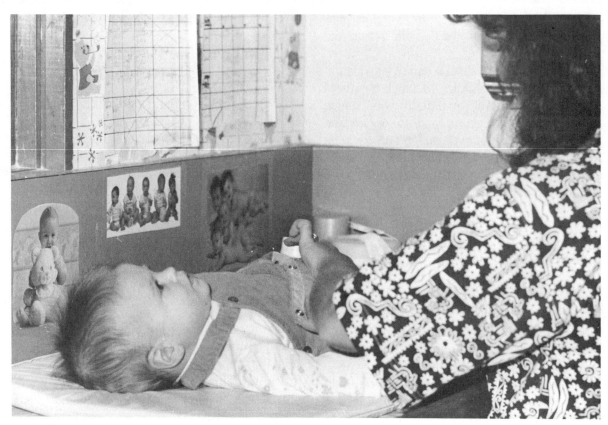

Figure 18-3: *The caregiver keeps one hand on the infant at all times when diapering.*

stomach and knees are major accomplishments in development.

Play is children's work. It is important for growth and development. Infants play independently (solitary play) with their hands, toes, toys, and caregivers. They show little interest in interacting with peers. Their free time consists of watching, listening, and discovering new information.

Toddlers can enjoy other peers (parallel play) and play with concept-building materials and toys. During play, toddlers begin to discover the world and their place in it.

DAILY ROUTINES

Physical Care

When caring for infants and toddlers, the facility must provide the proper equipment and materials. Many states regulate the specific size and numbers of equipment. Depending on the policy of the center, food and diapers are either provided or supplied by the parents. Centers funded federally and by the state usually provide diapers. They may also include social services such as checkups and immunizations.

Figure 18-4: *"Three Speckled Frogs" is a favorite flannel story for toddlers.*

All children should have a complete change of their own clothes, labeled with their name, at the facility in a separate cubicle or cubbyhole. Wardrobe items provided by the parents for infants should include:

- hat
- overshirt
- pair of booties
- pair of long pants
- pair of plastic pants (if cloth diapers are used)

- pair of socks
- receiving blanket
- sacque or nightie
- sweater
- undershirt

Wardrobe items provided by parents for toddlers should include:

- 1 hat
- 1 overshirt

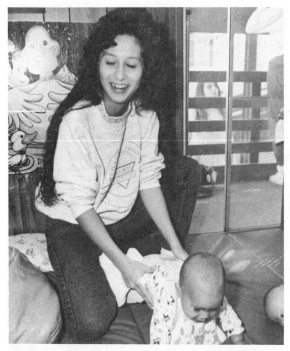

Figure 18-5: This caregiver is exercising with an infant.

Figure 18-6: The parent looks forward to picking up his child each day.

- 1 pair of long pants
- 3 pairs of socks
- 6 pairs of training pants
- 1 sweater
- 1 undershirt

Upon arrival of infants to the center or family day care home for the first time, caregivers should receive as much information about the children as possible. The daily schedule, eating habits, sleeping patterns, allergies (if any), immunizations, and physical examination information should be included. Caregivers should set up a similar schedule to avoid upsetting the routine of the child. The application, emergency information, and physical and immunization records must be kept in a file for ready access.

Figure 18–19, a sample infant schedule, is provided to give an understanding of the type of center routines necessary to furnish quality care for infants. Figure 18–20, a sample toddler schedule, is provided to give an understanding of the type of center routines necessary to furnish quality care for toddlers. Any schedule should fit the individual needs and ages of the children being given care.

SELF-HELP SKILLS

Toddlers are at the stage of development where they begin to assert their independence. From the time that they become mobile, children want to do what they want and to do it their own ways. This is an excellent time for caregivers to begin teaching self-help skills.

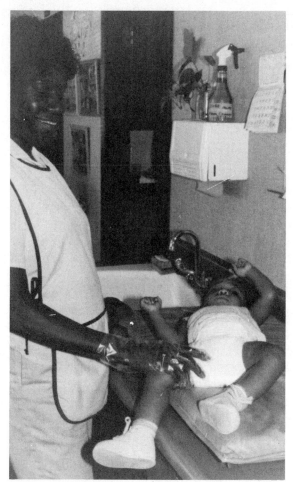

Figure 18-7: While changing diapers, caregivers and infants enjoy talking together.

Figure 18-9: Infants enjoy playing and developing fine motor skills.

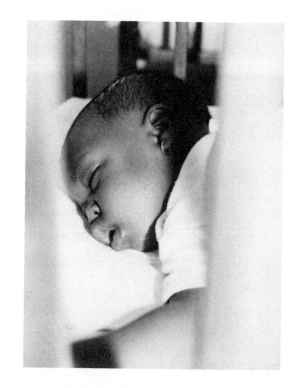

Figure 18-8: Make nap times peaceful.

Self-help skills are skills that allow people to do everyday tasks for themselves. Since efforts can be slow, messy, and unsuccessful at first, show patience and understanding when the children are practicing these skills. Following is a list of self-help tasks that caregivers can reinforce—toileting, washing hands and face, brushing teeth, hanging up coats, selecting and picking up toys, eating and cleaning up, undressing and dressing, and helping in the classroom.

Toileting

Toddlers are ready to toilet train when they gain control of the bladder and bowel muscles. This occurs usually between eighteen months and twenty-four months. They will first indicate discomfort by coming to the caregiver after having wet their diaper. This is the time to explain to the child about using the toilet. If the caregiver remains calm and patient, changing diapers as needed; toilet training can be accomplished with ease.

Washing Hands and Face

Teach proper hand washing methods. Use warm water or a cloth. Point the fingertips downward. Rub vigorously. Scrub between fingers and on wrists. Dry hands with a paper towel and dispose of it in the trash.

Brushing Teeth

Some centers have facilities to keep individual toothbrushes and paste. After meals, provide children with the opportunity to brush their teeth. Explain the importance of good dental hygiene.

Hanging Up Coats

As the child is welcomed to school each morning and after outside play, assist removal of the child's coat and putting it in the proper place.

Selecting and Picking Up Toys

Inside, allow children to remove a toy from the shelf on their own, but also encourage them to replace items when they finish. Outside, encourage children to return sand toys, scooters, and tricycles to the proper place.

Eating and Cleaning Up

Most toddlers can eat finger foods or easy-to-manage table food from a plate. Provide small, bite-size foods, a bib, a plate, a cup, a spoon, and a napkin to enable toddlers to eat by themselves and at their own paces. When they finish, encourage toddlers to throw away their disposable cups and napkins, place dishes and utensils in a dishpan, and help to wash the table.

Undressing and Dressing

Toddlers begin to discover how to take off (first step) and then put on their own clothing. Assist the removal of pants while toilet training. Teach children how to unbutton buttons, unzip zippers, and unsnap snaps. Show children how to match heel of sock to foot, how to buckle shoes, and how to close velcro closures. Teach young children how to take off their shoes and socks for naps and to place them under or beside their cots.

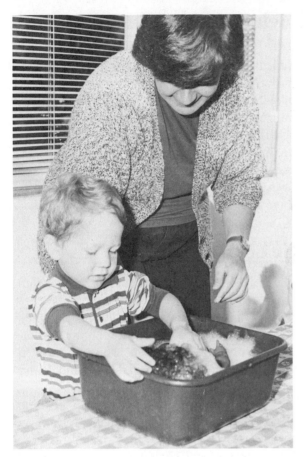

Figure 18-10: Caregiver and toddler enjoy water play.

Figure 18-11: Do you like my picture?

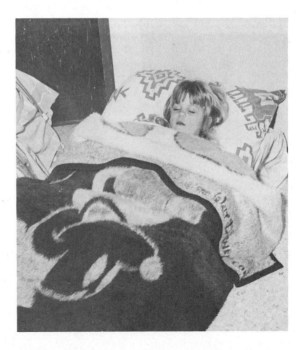

Figure 18-12: Toddler taking a nap at the children's center.

Figure 18-13: *Toddlers enjoy musical activities.*

Figure 18-14: *Picking up toys is an important self-help task.*

Helping in the Classroom

Give toddlers chores that are not too difficult yet foster a positive self-image. Depending on the maturation level, these chores may include passing out snack cups and napkins, passing out paper or art supplies, feeding fish, watering plants, wiping up spills, and picking up trash in the play yard. Remember to constantly supervise each activity. Encourage and be patient when children are in doubt. Praise them for their efforts.

SELF-ESTEEM

Feeling good about oneself is the beginning step to successful growth and development. When toddlers succeed at their assigned tasks and are praised for their efforts, they develop positive self-esteem. This results in a willingness to please the caregiver and to try new tasks.

Positive interaction between caregivers and young children (such as infants relying on their caregivers to meet their needs of food, clean diapers, and comfort) fosters a sense of trust and nurturance. Erik Erikson's first stage of personality development is formation of trust and security. Infants and toddlers form their sense of trust and security from how they interact with the world. Children who do not have their basic needs met and do not receive warmth and tender responses from caregivers often develop a sense of mistrust.

Erikson's second stage, autonomy versus shame and doubt, is formed in the later toddler stage, around the toilet training period. At this time, children are independent and assertive in making decisions and choices. They

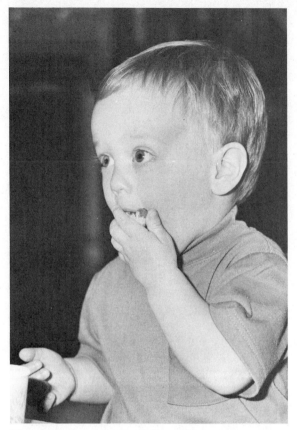

Figure 18-15: Self feeding is fun and increases autonomy.

learn about the world around them. When caregivers overregulate the activities of toddlers and deprive them of making decisions and establishing their independence, they cause the children to feel shame and doubt about their actions and worth.

Providing a variety of learning opportunities and teaching self-help skills in the classroom help children establish a positive attitude toward learning, about other people and about themselves. Enabling children to feel competent in their achievements and praising them

honestly for their efforts also build self-esteem. Plan sufficient amounts of time to practice challenging skills (appropriate for the level). Use your initiative and creativity to enable children to develop in their individual manners.

THE CAREGIVER'S ROLE

Infants and toddlers are demanding. They require much individual attention and a caregiver who can nurture them. The special care and guidance given to young children determine their sense of trust and self-concept in the years to come.

Safety

The largest percentage of deaths in young children are caused by accidents. Falls, poisonings, and drowning are the most common. When a situation demands immediate attention, caregivers need to respond quickly and accurately to help prevent accidents and to ensure a successful day for all.

The first priority is to keep the children safe and healthy. Caregivers are responsible for providing an environment free of dangers, one in which children can grow without fear of being hurt. Infants are totally dependent. They need protection from unsafe obstacles. Toddlers, however, are more independent. They can move quickly into small, dangerous places. Therefore, safety rules for both staff and children must be enforced.

Caregivers should enable children to interact in a safe manner. They must know each child well, including physical capabilities and curiosity. Use the following list to check

Figure 18-16: Caregiver and infant enjoying a quiet moment.

safety precautions in an infant and toddler center.

Because small children tend to place many small objects into their mouths, follow these guidelines to prevent choking and inability to breathe:

1. Are carpets and floors cleaned daily?

2. Do toys have large pieces that cannot be swallowed?

3. Are pins, buttons, coins, and filmy plastic out of reach?

4. Are all cleaning supplies in a locked cabinet? (Prevents accidental burns and poisoning.)

5. Are all medicines in a locked cabinet? (Prevents accidental overdoses and poisoning.)

6. Are purses and backpacks out of reach?

7. Are all plants out of reach? (Many plants are poisonous if swallowed or rubbed on the skin.)

To prevent accidents from occurring, follow these safety guidelines:

1. Are toys and equipment maintained and repaired regularly? A classroom of small children causes the equipment to be used constantly and to have parts that wear out. Children can be hurt on broken articles.

2. Are bars and railings no more than two and half to three inches apart? Children may get their head and limbs stuck between the bars.

3. Are the sides of cribs always in the up position? (Prevents children from falling.)

4. Are toys constructed well, with no sharp points or pull-apart pieces? (Prevents poking, cutting, and choking of children.)

5. Do caregivers always keep one hand on children when bathing or changing diapers? Children tend to wiggle and they can drown in two inches of water.

6. Is the water temperature checked to be sure it is not too hot or too cold? (Prevents children from being scalded or chilled.)

7. Are there screens around hot radiators, floor furnaces, and stoves? (Prevents accidental burning.)

Figure 18-17: The toddler looks over the safety gate at the doorway.

8. Are all stairways fenced at top and bottom? (Prevents children from falling.)

9. Are all unused electrical outlets covered to prevent accidental shock?

10. Are all electrical cords out of reach and do plugs have safety covers? (Prevents children from tripping, pulling down appliances, and unplugging equipment.)

11. Are children kept away from hot surfaces? (Prevents accidental burns or fires.)

12. Are all flammable materials out of children's reach? (Prevents accidental burns and fires.)

13. Are children securely fastened in a car seat when traveling in a car?

14. Are all large pieces of furniture securely anchored? Is all play yard equipment anchored or cemented into the ground?

In addition, follow these safety rules:

1. Do not use pillows for infants. (They can smother.)

2. Never leave children unattended. (They are able to get into almost anything.)

Communication

It is important that caregivers be available daily to communicate with the parents. Sharing information is imperative to the well-being of the children. Sharing information also enables parents to feel more comfortable about leaving their children with another person each day. Giving information about everyday events helps to maintain ties between the center and home. Remember to tell parents about happy and successful events as well as negative behaviors.

Charting is a valid method of letting parents know toileting, eating, and napping routines as well as special interests. Charts usually denote times and amounts of food, sleep, and toileting. Caregivers can initiate attractive and interesting charts. Examples of charts are shown in Figure 18–18.

Communication concerning children's needs must be encouraged among staff members. Most infant and toddler staff members

a)

Daily Activity

Name _____ Date _____

Diapering _____

Sleep time _____

Meals & Snacks _____

Bottles _____

Moods _____

Comments, Behavior, Etc. _____

_____

Caregiver _____ Hours _____

_____ Hours _____

b)

Name _____

Today _____. I was diapered by _____.

I slept _____.

I ate at _____.

I felt _____.

Figure 18-18: Examples of charts. Which chart is more thorough? Which is more interesting and cheerful? Which would you feel more comfortable receiving?

work in shift hours and care for the same children at different times of the day. It is imperative to relate important developmental growth or changes to the next caregiver in charge.

For example, Stacy had a bad evening trying to cut a new tooth and the parents told the caregiver in the morning upon arrival. The continuing staff members should be made aware of it. Then they are prepared to give Stacy the extra understanding, comfort, and napping necessary to provide her with a more pleasant day at the center. The evening caregiver can then relate to the parents how Stacy managed throughout the day. Some centers find it helpful to maintain a daily log of important information.

Communication is the key to a successful classroom. When caregivers feel free to talk to other staff members, the parents, and to interact with the children, they ensure an environment that allows each child, parent, and caregiver to grow.

IN THE HOME CARE

Many times the nanny or family day care provider has more than one child to care for in the home. Therefore, it would be difficult to design one schedule to be used as an appropriate model. That task should be left up to the caregiver.

It is necessary although, to set a daily routine that best meets the needs of all the children in your care. The effective caregiver should allow each child to:

Grow	Feel	Cry	Eat healthy	Speak	Wonder
Create	See	Challenge	Get dirty	Yell	Question
Explore	Listen	Crawl	Think	Smile	BE A CHILD!

Infant Day Care Schedule

Child's Age: 6 months
Time: 8:00 A.M.
Activity: Arrival
Materials: Clean clothes, diapers, bottles, foods, comfort item

Greet child and parent cheerfully. Check diaper bag for daily supplies. Ask parent questions about any problems or changes in the schedule since the child's last visit to the center. Provide a quick but thorough health check. Provide several minutes of holding and talking to the child in order to give reassurance and an easy separation from the parents. Nurture the parent as well as the child.

Time: 8:15 A.M.
Activity: Diaper change
Materials: Diapers, sink with hot and cold water, liquid soap, changing table, wash cloth, or disposable wipeups, plastic bag to dispose of diaper, lotion if needed, antiseptic spray, disposable towels to protect the changing table

Wash your hands thoroughly. Be sure to have all articles needed nearby. *Do not leave the infant unattended at any time.* Talk to the infant to give reassurance. Gently exercise the arms and legs. Make the time together enjoyable.

Lay the infant on his or her back on the changing table. Keep one hand on the infant at all times. Carefully undress or pull up the clothing to easily remove the soiled diaper. If using cloth diapers, remove the pins and stick them into soap or a container away from the infant's view. Place the soiled diaper in a plastic bag away from the infant.

Gently wipe the infant's bottom with a clean, damp cloth or wipeup to remove all bowel movement or urine. Wipe from front to back. Separate the folds of the skin around the genitals to thoroughly clean. Rinse the cloth or use a new wipeup and clean the area again. Apply lotion if needed.

Put on a clean diaper. If cloth, place your fingers between the pin and the infant to prevent the pin from sticking or pinching the infant. If disposable, tape it snugly to fit but not bind or hurt the infant's stomach. Redress the infant, wash the infant's hands, and place in a secure area.

Disinfect the table in preparation for the next infant. Dispose of the soiled diaper. Wash your hands thoroughly.

Provide talking and smiling opportunities each time you diaper an infant. Explain your actions and play the body parts game. Ask, "Where is your tummy?" Let the infant know how sweet he or she smells with a new diaper and how comfortable the clean diaper will be.

Figure 18-19: Infant Day Care Schedule.

Time: 8:30 A.M.
Activity: Breakfast
Materials: Infant plate, spoon, bottle or covered cup, food, bib

Hold the infant securely. Check that the food is not too hot. Place the dish in an easy-to-reach area. Make meals enjoyable by talking to the infant about what he or she is eating. Talk about the color and texture of the food.

If bottle-feeding, hold the infant upright in your arms. Never put infants or toddlers to bed with a bottle. Always keep the neck and nipple of the bottle filled to eliminate getting air into the infant's stomach. Talk to and nurture the infant. Chart the amounts of food and drink consumed each time.

Remember, when feeding infants:

1. Always mark the bottles with the name of the infant when they are brought into the children's center.

2. Never save an unfinished bottle until the next day.

3. Sterilize all feeding equipment or put it into disposable pouches before use.

4. Do not feed an infant at same counter or table where diapers are changed.

5. Never force an infant to eat more than he or she wants.

6. Be sure to burp the infant. Place him or her over your shoulder or sit him or her up on your lap bending slightly forward. Rub the infant's back in an upward motion. Do this after each few ounces of bottle feeding.

Time: 8:45 A.M.
Activity: Cleanup
Materials: Wash cloth, paper towels

Wash the hands of the infant with warm, sudsy water. Make certain to wash between the fingers. Wash the backs of the hands, the wrists and around the fingernails. Rinse and dry with a disposable paper towel.

Time: 9:00 A.M.
Activity: Inside play
Materials: Soft, light toys with rounded edges; cloth picture books; musical mobiles and boxes; large, padded cushions; a large floor space

(continued on next page)

While the infant is awake, present a variety of stimuli to enhance curiosity and to develop the senses. Provide colorful toys to look at, touch, taste, smell, and hear. For the crawling infant, provide a large carpeted area with safe toys to climb over, under, and around.

At story time, include a large book with colorful pictures and few words. Be sure to let the infant enjoy each picture.

Interact with the infant by playing an imitation game, visual reaching game, or hide and seek. Do not overstimulate or overtire the infant.

Time: 9:30 A.M.
Activity: Diaper change
Materials: See 8:15 A.M. above

Time: 9:45 A.M.
Activities: Bottle-feeding, morning nap
Materials: Formula or juice; clean crib
               sheet and blanket; quiet,
               darkened room; soft music;
               rocking chair

The length of nap depends on the age of the infant. Some children nap for hours at a time, while others catnap, sleeping only twenty minutes to half an hour. Sleeping patterns may be irregular. One child may fall asleep immediately when put into the crib, while another child may be restless, thrash, and cry.

Provide ample time to soothe, caress, rock, sing, and rub or pat the infant's back to enable the child acquire peaceful rest.

Clean sheets, a warm blanket, and a quiet, darkened room invite a longer and more relaxing sleep.

Time: 11:00 A.M.
Activity: Diaper change
Materials: See 8:15 A.M. above

Time: 11:05 A.M.
Activity: Outside play
Materials: Outside equipment and
               materials: push and pull toys;
               large, colorful balls; playpens;
               large blankets or pads; strollers
               with safety belts; grassy, cement,
               sun, and shade areas; proper
               clothing for weather conditions

Provide opportunities outside whenever weather permits. Encourage gross motor skills—crawling, standing, pushing, pulling, rolling, and walking. Encourage spatial awareness skills like climbing and sliding. Allow the infant to safely explore all areas and surfaces of the yard.

If the infant is very young, place in an infant seat or stroller. Interact with the child by talking and singing. Watch carefully to be sure that the infant does not put objects from the ground into his or her mouth.

Time: 11:45 A.M.
Activities: Hand washing, lunch feeding
Materials: See 8:30 A.M. above

Figure 18-19 continued

Time: 12:30 P.M.
Activities: Cleanup from lunch, diaper change, afternoon nap
Materials: See 8:15 A.M. and 9:45 A.M. on page 324 and 326, respectively.

Spend nap time checking each infant's supply of formula and diapers for the day, preparing new activities and opportunities for the afternoon play, and updating each chart on feeding, toileting, and attitude. Write any additional notes to the parents at this time.

Time: 2:30 P.M.
Activities: Wakeup, diaper change, washing and cleaning infant
Materials: Clean diapers, clean clothes (if wet), warm wash cloth

Encourage a warm, slow wakeup. Greet the infant in a happy, soft, and positive tone. Allow plenty of time for the infant to adjust to the light, the noise, and the surroundings. Hold, cuddle, and talk to each infant for several minutes before changing the diaper.

Provide warm, dry clothes. Gently wash the infant's hands and face with a warm wash cloth. Comb the infant's hair, if necessary.

Time: 2:45 P.M.
Activity: Bottle or snack
Materials: Formula, juice, or water; cracker or biscuit (if older infant)

Hold the infant in your arms if feeding a bottle. Sit the infant in an infant seat, in a high chair, or on your lap when feeding a cracker. Talk or sing to the infant.

Time: 3:00 P.M.
Activity: Inside play
Materials: Toys, soft balls, rattles, colorful objects and pictures, push and pull toys, large plastic crates, blocks for climbing

Provide a variety of play opportunities to enhance all the children in the group. Play simple interaction games (imitating, peekaboo, pat-a-cake).

Encourage language by labeling, explaining what you are doing, and repeating sounds. Provide sensory experiences (sight, hearing, touch, smell, and taste). Tell and read stories and nursery rhymes.

Provide music experiences through singing, movement of body parts, or slow dancing with the infant in your arms. Provide records, radios, and musical toys.

Time: 4:00 P.M.
Activity: Diaper change
Materials: See 8:15 A.M. above

Time: 5:00 P.M.
Activity: Departure
Materials: Diaper bag, chart for the day, dirty clothes

Provide parents with information of the infant's day (it can be observed from chart). Be sure that all articles of the infant's go home daily (clothes, bottles, favorite toy). Leave the infant with a positive, warm feeling to encourage an eager return.

Toddler Day Care Schedule

Time: 8:00 A.M.
Activity: Arrival
Materials: Training pants, change of clothes, favorite toy

Greet the toddler, using his or her name. Perform daily health check. Reassure the child as the parents leave. Introduce the child to activities and other children in room.

Time: 8:15 A.M.
Activity: Wash hands and eat breakfast
Materials: Small chairs and low table, bib, plate, spoon, and cup

The toddler will be learning to self-feed, yet a caregiver should always be present for safety, guidance, and socialization. Provide foods that are easy to digest, enjoyable to see and touch, yet nutritious. Introduce self-help skills, including serving oneself, eating with a spoon, and cleaning up. Introduce and expect manners, such as using the words *please* and *thank you*.

Time: 8:45 A.M.
Activities: Cleanup and toileting or diapering. For diapering instructions see the infant chart.
Materials: Training pants, potty chair or adapter seat, loose clothes

Provide ample time and patience for the children to toilet train. Help them to remove clothes, wait several minutes for the child to go, teach them to wipe their bottoms from front to back, and help them to pull up their clothes. Praise them for each attempt and consistently remind them throughout the day about using the toilet.

When the children are finished toileting, have them wash their hands with soap and water. Then disinfect the seat and wash out the container.

Time: 9:00 A.M.
Activity: Inside group play
Materials: Music, records, rhythm band, storybook, flannel stories, art materials, manipulatives

Provide interesting group activities to motivate children and give them enjoyment. Vary the activities each day and keep them within a reasonable amount of time to avoid boring the children.

Time: 9:30 A.M.
Activities: Washing hands, eating morning snack
Materials: Drink, cup, nutritious snack, napkin

Provide liquid soap and warm paper towels for washing hands and faces. Have the children put the towels in the trash.

Provide the children the opportunity of passing out the napkins and cups. Keep the juice or milk in small cups, which are easy to handle. Encourage tasting new foods.

Figure 18-20: Toddler Day Care Schedule.

Discuss what you are eating and possibly from what it is made, for example, tuna is a fish. Remind children of manners. Let the children help clean up when they are finished.

Time: 9:45 A.M.
Activity: Toileting or diapering
Materials: See 8:45 A.M.

Time: 10:00 A.M.
Activity: Outside play
Materials: Gross motor equipment—
            scooters, balls, small slide,
            small climbing structures,
            push and pull toys, sandbox;
            proper clothing for the weather

Supervise all equipment. Provide enough equipment and opportunities for physical development. Include running games and exercise for variety. Present different surfaces—grass, concrete, and sand. A quiet area, possibly under a shady tree, provides the quiet or warm child a place to relax.

In warm weather, introduce water play in washbasins or water tables. Constantly supervise this activity.

Time: 10:30 A.M.
Activities: Washup, rest
Materials: Cribs, mats, or cots; sheets and
            blankets; quiet, darkened room;
            short story book or soft music

Upon arrival back into the classroom, help the children remove their coats. Have them put the coats where they belong. Provide liquid soap and warm paper towels for washing hands and faces. Have the children put the used towels in the trash.

Older toddlers can help lay out their mats and blankets. Prepare the children for rest by reading a short story or playing a record of soothing songs. Rub the backs of the children to relax them. Some children may fall asleep, while others may just lie quietly with a doll or stuffed animal.

Time: 11:15 A.M.
Activities: Awakening, toileting or
            diapering
Materials: See 8:45 A.M. for toileting and
            diapering

Awaken the children slowly and easily. Allow them to get up and join the group when they are ready.

Time: 11:30 A.M.
Activity: Lunch
Materials: See 8:00 A.M. breakfast

Time: 12:00 A.M.
Activity: Free inside play
Materials: Toys, blocks, housekeeping
            corner, push and pull toys,
            books

(continued on next page)

Provide time between lunch and nap for free inside activities. Encourage children to play with a toy of their choice and then put it away when finished. Explain skills necessary for pleasant group activities, such as sharing, waiting for a turn, the rights of others, and gentleness.

Time: 12:30 P.M.
Activities: Toileting or diaper check, nap
Materials: See 10:30 A.M. rest

Time: 2:30 P.M.
Activities: Awakening, toileting or diaper change, free play inside
Materials: See 11:15 A.M. above

Awaken children slowly and easily. Let children move at their own paces, giving them time to lie quietly and get used to the noise and lights.

Diaper the children or place each one on a toilet seat. Assist with washing hands and face, combing hair, and putting on shoes. Allow each child to comfortably move to the toys or play corner while you care for another child.

Time: 3:00 P.M.
Activity: Snack
Materials: See 9:30 A.M. snack

Time: 3:15 P.M.
Activity: Story
Materials: Picture books, flannel story, or puppets

Immediately following the snack, have toddlers sit in a group. Read a picture book or tell a flannel story. This provides enough time for the food to settle before they go outside.

Time: 3:30 P.M.
Activity: Outside play
Materials: See 10:00 A.M. outside play

Time: 4:15 P.M.
Activity: Inside play
Materials: Art materials—crayons, paints, paper, clay and cookie cutters; inside toys, music, books

Supervise art activities, letting children use their imaginations. Play activity records and encourage children to participate. Read books to children who need quiet activities.

Time: 5:00 P.M.
Activity: Departure
Materials: Dirty clothes and training pants, favorite toys, any art creations

Communicate with parents concerning the children's day (notes or daily log may be helpful when more than one caregiver works with each child during the day). Tell the children that you will see them tomorrow.

Figure 18-20 continued

Toddler Curriculum

Theme: Touch

Arts and Crafts

1. Toddlers can explore the different sensations of finger painting with shaving cream, liquid starch, soap suds, and sprinkled sand. The list is endless.

2. Finger painting can be experimented on different surfaces such as: table tops, glass, wood, metal, and cardboard.

3. The toddlers can explore the feeling of glue and paste. They may paste something hard such as small sticks or stones, and something soft such as leaves or cotton balls.

4. Play dough and glob, (cornstarch and water mixture), is both fun for toddlers and caregivers to play with.

Language

The caregivers and children may discuss the way the fingerpaint feels on the different surfaces. The questions that may be explored are: Is the paint or surface hard or soft? What is the color? Is it cold or hot? Scratchy? Smooth?

Books

"Loving Touches" Lory Freeman
"Ooopps" Suzy Kline
Touch and feel books, and pop-up books are great for story time.

Finger Plays

Touch
Touch your nose
Touch your chin
That's the way this game begins.
Touch your eyes
Touch your knees
Now pretend you're going to sneeze.
Touch your hair
Touch one ear
Touch two red lips right here.
Touch your elbows
Where they bend
That's the way this touch game ends.

Open, Shut Them
Open, shut them
Open, shut them
Give a little clap.
Open, shut them
Open, shut them
Lay them on your lap.

Songs

Head, shoulders, knees, and toes.
This is the way we...
Wash our hands
Comb our hair   (To the tune of
Brush our teeth   Mulberry Bush)
Shine our shoes
Go to school

(continued on next page)

"Getting to Know Myself" by Hap Palmer
"Ideas, Thoughts and Feelings" by Hap Palmer

Flannel Stories

Prepare any flannel story that may have pieces with unusual materials for the children to touch. A good example is "Tommy Turkey." (See instructor's guide for the story.) Each turkey can be decorated differently with colorful sequins, beads, feathers, buttons, tissue, crepe paper, and yarn, to name a few. The children will enjoy holding the pieces and sharing the story.

Games and Activities

1. Take each toddler on a touch tour, both of your home or school, and of the outside world. Encourage the child to touch different surfaces: cement, glass, sand, brick, metal, and glass. Walk with the child and emphasize what you feel as you both touch a tree trunk, leaves, the doorbell, a sign post.

2. To introduce the toddler to a variety of textures make a "Touch Me" book or board. Cut small samples of different textured materials and glue them to the pages or board. Textures may include: carpet squares, cotton, silk, fur, corduroy, metal, sandpaper, or wood.

Science

1. Present the toddlers with two bowls

of water, one warm and one ice cold. Allow them to put their fingers in the bowls as you emphasize the difference between hot and cold. You could follow this activity with a nutritious snack of something warm (soup, muffins), and something cold (apple juice,, popsicles).

2. On a warm day allow the toddlers to experiment with dry and wet sand. Provide a sandbox or small tub of clean sand. Pour some water into the sand, making it moist. Encourage the children to explore with their hands and feet.

Math

1. Simple counting can be so enjoyable when children use everyday items such as cups, napkins, blocks, toys, flannel pieces, and fingers.

Nutrition

1. Encourage toddlers to feel raw fruits and vegetables, measuring spoons, bowls, pots and pans, wooden spoons, and canned foods.

2. Allow the toddlers to help prepare a simple snack such as sugarless chocolate pudding. With the caregivers help they can open the package, pour the milk, and stir the pudding. Upon completion, the best task is to eat the pudding.

Theme: Touch continued

SUMMARY

Infants are children from birth to walking (age one). Toddlers are children from walking to potty training (ages one to two and a half). Children all develop in a common sequence, yet they progress at their own rates of maturation. As defined by a developmental chart, the infants and toddler years are times of great growth and learning.

Children learn best when routines are based on sensorimotor experiences that are fun and enjoyable. Play is the child's work. Scheduling for infants and toddlers must include flexibility and initiative on the part of the caregiver. Proper diapering, feeding, and nurturing techniques are equally important.

In order for infants and toddlers to feel self-confident, caregivers teach self-help skills. Easy skills, such as picking up toys, toileting, hand and face washing, dressing, and eating, allow children to become independent and to increase their self-esteem. Positive reinforcement of children's efforts encourages them to practice and to become proficient.

By preparing the environment before the children arrive, communicating with other staff members and parents, and practicing safety precautions, caregivers can plan a successful day. Providing an atmosphere that encourages fun, learning, and positive self-esteem is a goal toward which caregivers should strive.

Review Questions

1. What are the rooting reflex, grasp reflex, and the Moro reflex?

2. What games can be played with the one-month-old infant to stimulate intellectual growth?

3. When does the infant begin smiling?

4. At what age does the infant show a fear of unfamiliar surroundings?

5. When is the infant able to drink from a cup?

6. When do toddlers develop a sense of humor?

7. At what age is it important to stress manners?

8. When does the toddler begin cooperative play?

9. Symbolic thinking begins at what age?

10. Describe the self-help tasks that toddlers are capable of performing.

11. What is charting?

Things to Do and Discuss

1. Observe an infant and toddler classroom. Use the safety checklist from this chapter to determine whether or not the environment is safe.

   Choose one child and observe the developmental level. Does the child's maturation level match that of the developmental description for the age?

3. Following the routine chart, practice diapering and feeding an infant and a toddler. How do they differ?

4. Observe a toddler, and list the toddler's self-help skills. Which ones are still being practiced?

5. Develop a creative chart that could be used for infants. Develop one for toddlers. Remember to include sections for feeding, diapering, napping, moods, and special events for the day.

6. Assist in an infant or toddler setting. Practice changing diapers, feeding, bathing, dressing, supervising play, handling activities, and communicating with children, staff, and parents.

CHAPTER 19
Preschoolers

Children listen intently during the morning circle time.

KEY TERMS

consistent
defiant

phonetics
pincer hold

OBJECTIVES

After completing this chapter, you will be able to:

1. list and give examples of the four developmental stages for the preschooler;
2. define the caregiver's role when working with the preschooler;
3. identify three daily routines for the preschooler.

INTRODUCTION

The preschool years, approximately ages two and a half through five years, are for learning through exploration, experimentation, and observation. This is a time when play is work and children can be successful. It is a time for children to discover themselves and the world. Challenge is exciting. Children form new ideas and express themselves freely.

Preschoolers have become independent. They can walk, run, talk, and manipulate objects. They are perfecting their self-help skills, such as toileting, dressing, and eating. They are also practicing adult roles through symbolic play. They are eager to help and proud of their accomplishments.

Figure 19-1: Jon (four years old) sits with Ken (eighteen months).

NORMAL DEVELOPMENT OF PRESCHOOLERS

The following sections give an overview of the developmental stages of the preschooler. They also provide the caregiver with activities to enhance each child's growth.

Two and a Half Year Olds

Children often overlap in their development as they progress from stage to stage. Two and a half year olds in preschools are usually potty trained and often have slightly better skills than those in infant and toddler programs. They learn by observing and imitating the older children in the school environment.

Physical Development

Walking and running smoothly are taken for granted by two and a half year olds. They enjoy using their large muscles with ease, and they eagerly show off their skills. Small muscle control is improving with practice. These children are able to perform many self-help tasks, such as pouring small amounts of a drink, holding a cup with one hand, bathing with supervision, and going to the potty themselves. They have all twenty baby teeth and are able to learn about good dental hygiene and nutrition.

Social Development

Showing a more cooperative attitude, two and a half year olds want to please the adults and other people around them. Although their attention spans are still short, these children enjoy being a part of the group and interacting with peers in a school setting. Positive reinforcement of their efforts and nurturing encourage the young preschoolers to participate and learn school structure.

Emotional Development

Two and a half year olds are beginning to learn appropriate methods of handling emotions and solving problems. They often react strongly to situations, laughing heartily or having temper tantrums. Caregivers need to help them learn alternative actions when they feel frustrated. Pounding clay and hitting a punching bag (made from a pillowcase stuffed with newspapers) are positive ways to release negative feelings.

Intellectual Development

Two and a half year olds are eager to learn. They delight in listening to stories. They enjoy books, flannel stories, puppets, records, tapes, or finger plays. They often pretend to read books to themselves and others. They can think symbolically, communicate in sentences, learn proper sentence structure, and carry on intense conversations.

Their fine motor skills are also improving. Two and a half year olds now have a *pincer hold* (ability to hold object between thumb and index finger) and can use blunt scissors to cut around pictures. They will spend time working puzzles and other easy manipulatives. They also will experiment with craft materials—fringe cut with scissors, pasting and gluing to make collages, rolling out play dough, and finger painting. Their self-esteem increases when their efforts are frequently displayed and are appreciated by their caregivers.

Three Year Olds

Physical Development

Three year olds can walk, run, kick, jump from an eight-inch elevation with both feet together, alternate feet as they climb stairs, balance momentarily on one foot, catch a large ball or bean bag, and pedal wheel toys with proficiency. They need many opportunities to practice gross motor skills. By providing large, unobstructed areas, climbing structures, wheeled toys, traffic signs, obstacle courses, balls, and bean bags, caregivers encourage development. Preschoolers also can follow directions on exercise records and play follow the leader and Simon says.

Their fine motor skills are also improving. They can create their own projects by using paper, pencils, crayons, markers, glue, paste, collage materials, and scissors. They enjoy manipulatives such as beads to string, puzzles, small blocks, sewing cards, pegs and board, and matching and sorting games as they practice eye-hand coordination. Be sure that manipulatives are appropriate for the age. They should be challenging yet not too difficult. Have a variety of items to stimulate each child's interest.

At three years, preschoolers can self-feed using a spoon and fork with easy-to-manage foods. They take great pride in dressing and undressing themselves and can manage most items except those with ties and other difficult fasteners. Encourage efforts in self-help and allow plenty of time for preschoolers to practice.

Social Development

Three year olds enjoy playing in groups and can engage in cooperative play. They are learning about the rights of others, and they can share easily. Provide sufficient time each day to encourage group activities in the house-keeping area, in the block area, and at learning centers. A sharing time allows preschoolers to talk about a favorite item or family trip. Introduce group games. Examples include farmer in the dell; duck, duck, goose; and the hokey pokey.

Symbolic play is important, as three year olds imitate adult actions. Dress-up clothes, costumes of community workers, and house-keeping areas allow these children to demonstrate concerns and solve problems.

Emotional Development

Preschoolers at three are beginning to show self-control, develop independence, and become predictable and reliable. They enjoy performing simple tasks in the classroom, such as passing out snacks, cleaning the table, sponging chairs, watering plants, feeding pets, picking up in the play areas, and taking care of their own possessions.

Negative emotions may be exhibited by bad dreams and fears of parents leaving, the dark, animals, loud noises, and burglars. Caregivers should permit discussions of fears and provide opportunities for these children to share how they feel—angry, happy, or sad. Help children work through their feelings and solve problems. Three year olds may also develop feelings of jealousy. They may dislike sharing caregivers' time with other children. To reinforce self-esteem, praise each child's efforts and encourage abilities. Allow time each day to interact with children both individually and in a group setting.

Intellectual Development

Three year olds are intrigued with new words and with *phonetics* (the study of the combination of letter sounds to form words). They can use nouns, verbs, adjectives, and adverbs as they relate experiences or retell stories. They ask many questions, such as, "Where do babies come from?" They enjoy listening to stories (both imaginary and true), records, and tapes. It is important to allow plenty of time for talking and listening in groups and sharing new words and their meanings. Provide entertaining language arts activities.

Three year olds are developing interest in numbers and can count to three with ease. Provide number cards and games. Play counting activities, such as how many children are present, day of the month, and birthdays. Recognizing colors also fascinates these children, and they take pride in being able to match colors. Asking what colors they are wearing, what color the paint is, and if they can find the color red are ways to encourage color identity.

Four Year Olds

Physical Development

At four, gross motor skills have improved to the point where children can throw overhand, hop on one foot, climb easily, and walk across a balance beam. Provide many outdoor games to increase skill level. Provide a low basketball hoop and toss boards. Plan creative movement and balance beam activities.

Fine motor skills are also improving. Four year olds can color. They paint realistic objects. They can use one hand to cut on a line and the other to turn the paper. They can make representative objects out of clay and play dough, and they enjoy working and building with wood and styrofoam. Provide wood and styrofoam pieces, hammers, nails, scissors, glue, and paint. Supervise carpentry and teach the proper use and care of tools.

At this age, manipulative skills are increasing. Four year olds are able to pour from a pitcher into a glass. They can lace shoes. Old shoes, sewing cards, and doll clothes encourage children to practice this task.

Social Development

Four year olds like to play with others (cooperative play), engage in dramatic play (symbolic play), and to use their imaginations. They spend large amounts of time in pretend activities. Using stage props of various occupations and dramatizing well-known stories become favorite undertakings.

The behavior of four year olds is bossy and talkative. They learn that words are effective means of hurting other people's feelings. They say things such as, "I won't invite you to my birthday party," or "Let's not play with him." They delight in shocking adults by using bathroom words or inappropriate language. Tall tales or wishful thinking also occur. Model proper behavior and language, explain how words can hurt feelings, and label tall tales as using imagination. Telling and reading stories and using puppets help preschoolers to solve social problems.

As four year olds experiment with social interaction, they need routines and schedules to feel secure. Positive, firm, and *consistent* (always following the same principles, courses,

Figure 19-2: Preschool children must learn to play cooperatively.

or forms) guidelines let them understand the limits to their behavior. (Keeping to a familiar schedule also helps to build temporal skills.) Be ready to intervene when necessary to ensure the well-being of all children.

Emotional Development

Four year olds may be *defiant* (go against authority), independent, and assertive. They also can be sensitive to others' feelings. They are learning to express sympathy. Demonstrate appropriate methods of exhibiting emotions,

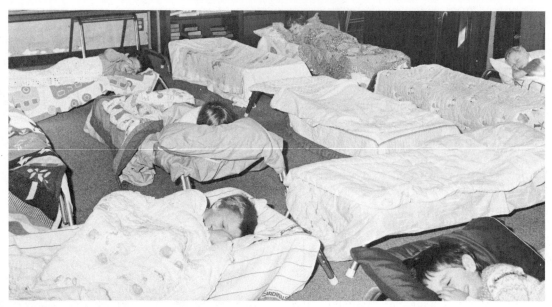

Figure 19-3: Preschoolers are trying to settle down for a nap.

Figure 19-4: The four year old is playing a classification game.

and allow many opportunities for making choices within safe limits.

Four year olds fear death, old people, the dark, parental separation, animals, and bodily harm. They have dreams about monsters and therefore may be afraid to go asleep. They are trying to understand death. Encourage preschoolers to share their feelings without belittling or punishing them. Reassure them about safety precautions and your protection.

Intellectual Development

Four year olds can perform classification tasks (distinguishing colors, as well as matching and sorting items), seriation tasks (arranging sizes and numbers), and temporal tasks (understanding past and future events). Color, number, and shape activities including counting calendar days, recalling what they did last weekend, and telling what they plan to do on their birthdays allow them to practice these skills.

Preschoolers have many why and how questions. They want true answers. Learning centers that provide for discovery experiments encourage cognitive development. Four year olds also enjoy singing, making up stories and jokes, reading books, and learning riddles and rhyming games. Furnish musical instruments, art materials, records, and books to allow these children opportunities to be creative and to use their imaginations. They find pleasure in combining activities such as singing and coloring.

Five Year Olds

Physical Development

At five years, preschoolers are busy refining their gross and fine motor skills. They are learning to distinguish left from right. They are self-sufficient in personal care such as tying shoes. They can ride a two-wheeled bicycle with training wheels, can skip with ease, and are practicing jumping rope.

Social Development

Five year olds enjoy other children, take turns easily, play organized games (but make up their own rules), want to please, and understand right from wrong. Give plenty of opportunities and positive reinforcement for proper peer interaction and helping others. Establish firm and consistent guidelines.

Emotional Development

Five year olds have a strong attachment to their mothers and need frequent approval.

They are developing pride in their accomplishments. They also are sensitive to scolding and criticism. Their feelings are hurt easily. Caregivers can provide a nurturing environment by commenting on children's good characteristics and by displaying their projects.

Intellectual Development

The attention span of the five year old has increased from twenty to forty minutes. These children are developing an interest in telling time (temporal skill), learning their addresses and phone numbers, and expanding their vocabularies to 2,000 to 2,500 words. They like stories about real things, such as when they were younger, and about family members. They are developing an interest in how people live in other countries.

Figure 19-5: Reading quietly is relaxing.

Case Study #1:
Mrs. Ho

At 8:30 A.M. is the scheduled morning group. The children arrange themselves comfortably on the rug, facing the caregiver, Mrs. Ho.

Mrs. Ho greets each child by singing a song containing the child's name and the color of the child's shirt (social and intellectual development). As the children are singled out, they stand in front of the group (self-esteem). Then they share something special that excites them (social, language, and listening skill development).

Juan Rodriquez is introduced to the children. This is his first day at school. Juan is reluctant and shy. He is allowed to remain seated until he feels comfortable with the group (emotional development). Mrs. Ho asks Peter to be Juan's special friend today.

Mrs. Ho shows birds' nests of different sizes and construction to the class. The class looks at and discusses the different materials that birds use to construct their nests (intellectual and language development).

Mrs. Ho places an activity record about pretending to be baby birds on the record player. The children gather around her and nestle close in the nest. They practice flying and chirping for food until they are old enough to leave the nest and fly around the room (physical development and science).

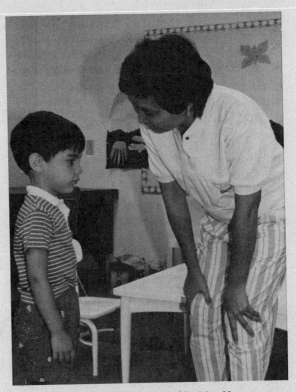

Figure 19-6: Juan is being greeted by Mrs. Ho.

After the children have enjoyed the activity record, they fly out the door as birds to enjoy outside free play.

Activities should include playing with manipulatives, playing science and math games, reading books, looking at photo albums and videos, and discussing customs and cultural heritages. Introduce the five year old to watches and clocks, a world globe, and foods, customs, and items from different countries.

DAILY ROUTINES

Preschoolers accomplish developmental tasks through daily routines and activities. Caregivers must carefully plan group-enhancing tasks as well as individual growth tasks.

Figure 19–17 is an example of a daily routine that encompasses many developmental stages and allows children to participate in a group and individually. The preschool routine enables the caregiver to plan activities to meet the needs of all the children.

SELF-HELP SKILLS

Teaching self-help skills is a way to prepare preschoolers to become independent and to develop a positive self-concept. Preschool children expect and want to practice helping in the classroom. They feel great satisfaction when helping others, pleasing adults, and successfully completing tasks.

Following is a list of self-help skills that the preschooler can accomplish in the classroom or at home. Allow preschoolers sufficient time and practice to feel successful. Encourage efforts and honestly praise good intentions. Mistakes and mishaps will occur, so handle them diplomatically.

Figure 19-7: Preschoolers must learn to take turns on the play equipment.

Figure 19-8: Michelle has had a good day at preschool and looks forward to tomorrow.

Personal Hygiene

Preschoolers can learn to properly wash their hands and face, brush their teeth, and comb their hair. Four and five year olds can also bathe themselves with supervision. By modeling appropriate methods and behaviors, caregivers allow the children to learn what is expected.

Dressing and Undressing

Preschoolers are able to put on and take off easy pieces of clothing. They can be encouraged to put on and take off their paint shirts, their shoes at nap time, and their outdoor clothing, and to pull their pants down and up when they go to the bathroom. Buttoning, zippering, and tying are still difficult for some children. Provide opportunities to work on such skills during the day. Practice boards, dolls' clothing, and helping another child can increase skill levels.

Picking Up or Cleaning Up the Play Areas

As children complete their play, encourage and expect them to replace toys and books on the appropriate shelves and throw all unnecessary trash in the wastebasket. Define specific places for all items. Outlines of the toys glued on the shelves help children find the places for items.

Preparing for Meals

Provide opportunities for preschoolers

Figure 19-9: The boys are learning responsibility by helping to clean the table after the snack.

Figure 19-10: Preschoolers helping to put away the tricycles.

to count the number of children being served and to pass out cups, napkins, plates, and utensils. Let them help prepare the food. This is an excellent way to introduce new foods. Children are more likely to try something different if they help to prepare and cook the meal (adult supervision is necessary when using cooking appliances). They can also serve themselves from large bowls, pour their own drinks from small containers, and feed themselves.

Cleanup After Meals

Upon finishing snacks or meals, expect children to properly dispose of all uneaten food and paper products in the wastebasket. Have them wash their tables and chairs with wet sponges, dry the areas, and replace the chairs. Provide damp sponges and supervise the area.

Figure 19-11: These preschoolers are cleaning up the playhouse area.

Washing Equipment and Toys

Give the children sponges, wet cloths, and buckets of water to help wash tables, chairs, toys, dolls, cupboards, and outdoor equipment such as bicycles (have a "car wash"). This not only helps the children feel pride in their accomplishments and in their environment but also helps to keep the area clean.

Keeping Possessions Orderly

Expect children to keep track of their belongings in a designated cubbyhole. It is their responsibility to keep the cubbyhole clean (without trash) and to take home their daily work and special share items, as well as any extra clothes.

Classroom Chores

Chores such as feeding pets, cleaning cages, feeding and watering plants, taking out equipment and supplies, erasing boards, putting dates on the calendar, leading the flag salute, sweeping sidewalks, and raking leaves encourage participation and increase self-esteem. Join in activities, and make them fun. They can become games that all enjoy and anticipate. It helps to keep a chart or other system to ensure a turn for each child.

SELF-ESTEEM

Helping children to feel good about themselves throughout the preschool years is an important responsibility of the caregiver. During this time, children formulate a sense of self (autonomy), form their own opinions, and share their feelings with others. They also make friends with peers and interact, learning and patterning their behavior after adults.

By describing the children's accomplishments, praising their efforts, and encouraging them to try new endeavors, caregivers help to increase the self-esteem of each child.

Guiding preschoolers gently with areas of difficulty allows them the opportunity to practice new skills without a sense of failure. To encourage self-esteem:

Figure 19-12: This caregiver is proud to hang up her children's artwork.

1. Greet each child by name and use the name frequently throughout the day.

2. Talk in a positive manner to children.

3. Encourage children to complete the projects they begin.

4. Display projects. Place the child's name prominently in the upper left-hand corner.

5. Encourage self-help skills.

6. Nurture each child daily by touching, holding, and hugging.

7. Compliment children on their appearance and behavior when appropriate.

8. Give children chances to participate in helping, even with difficult tasks.

9. Be fair and consistent with all children.

THE CAREGIVER'S ROLE

Caregivers evaluate each child's level of self-esteem, developmental progress, and range of activity. After observing each child, they can determine interest and skill areas and arrange lesson plans to help the child progress to the next level of development.

Firm and consistent discipline techniques, understanding, and a nurturing environment help children learn to get along in a group. By providing varied experiences that allow exploration, caregivers enhance social, emotional, physical, and intellectual development. Exploration is work for the young, and success enables them to feel confident.

Figure 19-13: Mother and preschooler saying "Goodbye."

Safety

Preschool children possess a high energy level. They are beginning to learn coordination. They are very physical. They enjoy exploration and take risks when playing on outside equipment, especially in symbolic play (role playing). Jumping off the highest rung of the climbing dome may be the only way that monster man may leave his home. Although caregivers should encourage vigorous activities, they need to remember that some preschoolers have no fear and do not anticipate danger when experiment-

Figure 19-14: Gross motor skills are enhanced by the balance beam.

ing with new ideas. This combination can cause young children to suffer accidents.

Providing an atmosphere for young children to work and grow safely is the responsibility of all the staff members in a facility. Every caregiver must see that his or her room is clean, free of broken toys and equipment, includes enough activities and materials to enhance growth, and has equipment that is age-appropriate.

Below are some safety rules that are particularly designed for preschoolers:

1. Discuss safety rules concerning climbing structures. Rules may include beware of others playing on or near the structure, take turns going down poles or jumping from the structure, and climb using both hands.

2. Discuss safety rules concerning riding bicycles. Rules may include being a careful driver to avoid accidents, using the designated bike path, sitting on the bike seats when riding, and only one person to a bike at a time.

3. Discuss safety rules concerning slides. Rules may include walk up the ladder, slide down the slide feet first; one child on the slide at a time; and be sure no one is in front of the slide when you come down.

4. Discuss safety rules concerning swings. Rules may include sit on your bottom, hold on with two hands, watch for others walking near swings, swing forward and backward only.

5. Instruct children to use walking feet and inside voices in the building. This will eliminate a high noise level and confusion.

6. Provide sufficient adult supervision. Staffing ratios that surpass state requirements will eliminate most accidents.

7. Provide supervision of all cooking projects to protect children from all sharp utensils, hot appliances, hot pans and pots, and hot liquids. Teach safety rules to the children concerning fire and electricity.

8. Supervise the use of scissors, staplers, and any sharp objects designated for use with an art project.

Communication

Caregivers and parents should work together to provide the best environment and education for children; therefore, it is vital to have open communications between all involved. When communicating with parents, remember:

1. Welcome parents each day and help them to feel comfortable with leaving their children.

2. Be a conscientious listener with parents. Use the parent's name. Answer in a friendly manner to show respect for the parent.

3. Encourage parents to participate in school activities. Hold parent meetings and social functions. Praise parents' contributions to the program.

4. Send out regular newsletters to keep parents informed about upcoming and past events. Include interesting

handouts on discipline (parents can help reinforce rules at home), units of study, and favorite finger plays or songs. Encourage parents to enjoy these activities with their children.

5. Be ready to offer suggestions to help the parents interact with their children. Share with parents the positive actions of the child as well as areas that need improvement.

6. Ask parents to visit the classroom on any day or at any time that they are free. They may discuss and share with the children their occupation, cultural background and customs, or special talents. Sometimes parents feel more comfortable when given a specific task when visiting.

7. Include parents on field trips.

8. Keep a specific bulletin board near the sign-in sheet for parent news and updated articles of interest.

9. Remind parents that this is a time of rapid language development and it is necessary to provide good adult language role models.

Remember these points when talking with parents to help them feel that everyone is concerned with their children and that you are working together. This gives a sense of security and continuity to children's lives.

Figure 19-15: Caregiver and child communicating.

Figure 19-16: An information board helps to keep parents updated.

Preschool Day Care Schedule

Time: 7:15 A.M.
Activities: Arrival, greeting, health check, inside play
Materials: Manipulatives, learning centers, art supplies

Arrange the learning centers: housekeeping corner with dress-ups, play dough table, large block area, manipulatives, and art table with crayons, paper, scissors, glue, and markers. These tasks and activities should be able to be accomplished by the child with little help from the teacher.

Time: 7:45 A.M.
Activities: Cleaning up room, using bathroom, washing hands
Materials: Specific places for each item

Help children put toys and books on the proper shelves. Urge each child to use the bathroom. Have the children wash their hands for breakfast.

Time: 8:00 A.M.
Activity: Breakfast
Materials: Plates or bowls, spoons, cups, napkins, place mats

Help the children set the table, pass the food, use proper manners, try new foods, carry on appropriate conversations, and clean up after breakfast, throwing away the trash and wiping the table.

Time: 8:30 A.M.
Activity: Sharing
Materials: Articles belonging to unit of study, materials for music or songs

Greet each child by name. Allow a sharing time. Introduce new people or visitors. Explain the plans for the day. Show articles of special interest.

Time: 9:00 A.M.
Activity: Outside free choice of learning centers
Materials: Gross motor equipment — tricycles, swings, sand, climbing structures, water table, outside paint easel, obstacle course

Encourage participation in all areas of yard. Vary equipment and learning centers frequently. Other centers might include a science area, woodworking area, books, and music. Be aware and ready to offer help with socialization problems and problem solving opportunities if needed.

Time: 9:45 A.M.
Activity: Cleanup
Materials: See 7:45 A.M. above

Time: 10:00 A.M.
Activities: Hand washing, snack
Materials: See 8:00 A.M. above

Figure 19-17: Preschool Day Care Schedule.

Time: 10:15 A.M.
Activity: Inside learning centers
Materials: Vary each day or week depending on the unit of study — include manipulatives, blocks, housekeeping materials, and arts and crafts materials for language, music, science, math, and nutrition study.

Plan a variety of activities to allow children to pursue their own areas of interest. Be ready to encourage children to explore all centers and to assist them when they need help.

Time: 11:00 A.M.
Activity: Cleanup
Materials: See 7:45 A.M. above

Time: 11:15 A.M.
Activities: Group language development, creative movement, music
Materials: Books, flannel stories, puppets, finger plays, records, record player, musical instruments

Provide time for language development as well as listening skills. Vary activities each day. Encourage questions, discussion, and recall skills for both the group and the individual. Introduce new activities, but leave time for favorites.

Time: 11:45 A.M.
Activities: Toileting, hand washing, lunch
Materials: See 8:00 A.M. above

Time: 12:15 P.M.
Activity: Preparation for naps
Materials: Separate cots or mats, sheets, blankets

Allow children to practice self-help skills — toileting, washing hands, arranging cots, taking off shoes.

Time: 12:30 P.M.
Activity: Nap
Materials: Records, record player

Provide a quiet, darkened room for peaceful sleep. Play soft music, rub the backs of restless children, and keep the room temperature at a comfortable level.

Time: 2:30 P.M.
Activities: Awakening from nap, toileting, washing up
Materials: Wet paper towels or wipeups

Allow children to wake up slowly, adjusting to the lights and noise level gently. Welcome them cheerfully. Encourage self-help skills — folding blankets and sheets, putting cots away,

(continued on next page)

putting shoes on, toileting, washing face and hands, brushing hair. Plan quiet inside activities until all children are awake.

Time: 3:00 P.M.
Activity: Snack
Materials: See 8:00 A.M. above.

Time: 3:30 P.M.
Activities: Outside free play, washing hands
Materials: See 9:00 A.M. above

Time: 4:30 P.M.
Activity: Inside free play
Materials: See 7:15 A.M. above

These tasks and activities should be able to be accomplished by the child with little help from the teacher. Activities and learning center materials may be used the next day as the children arrive.

Time: 5:15 P.M.
Activity: Departure for home
Materials: Daily work, notes, soiled clothes, sharing items

Communicate with parents about each child's day. Explain projects. Briefly describe plans for tomorrow (to allow children to anticipate tomorrow's activities). Say good-bye to each child, and mention something positive that happened that day.

Figure 19-17 continued

Preschool

Theme: Bears

Arts and Crafts

1. Have the children cut the bear out of brown construction paper. They can draw facial features or cut them out of the construction paper and glue them on. They may also color clothes on their bear or glue on corduroy overalls.

2. Let the children finger paint with brown paint and fill in a bear shape.

3. Sponge-paint brown and white "Bear Prints" on paper. The teacher can cut these prints out when they dry and tape to the floor and walls throughout the room. The children can then go on a bear hunt.

Language Arts
Finger Plays

This Little Bear

This little bear has a fur suit. (*thumb*)
This little bear acts so very cute. (*pointer*)
This little bear is so bold and cross. (*middle*)
This little bear says, "You're not boss." (*ring*)
This little bear likes bacon and honey,
   (*little finger*)
But he can't buy them, he has no money!

Five Little Polar Bears

Five little Polar bears
Playing on the shore;

One fell in the water,
And then there were four.

Four little Polar bears
Swimming out to sea;
One got lost,
And then there were three.

Three little Polar bears said,
"What shall we do?"
One climbed an iceberg,
Then there were two.

Two little Polar bears
Playing in the sun;
One went for food,
Then there was one.

One little Polar bear
Didn't want to stay
He said, "I'm Lonesome."
And swam far away.

Flannel Story

**Brown Bear, Brown Bear,
What Can You See?**

1. Cut each piece from flannel and demonstrate on the flannel board.

Books

"Are You There, Bear" Ron Maris
"Ask Mister Bear" Marjorie Flask
"Beady Bear" Don Freeman, (Viking Press, 1954)
"Bearymore" Don Freeman, (Viking Press, 1976)
"Berenstain Bears Books" Stan & Jan Berenstain
"Blueberries For Sal" Robert McClasky
"Corduroy" Don Freeman, (Viking Press, 1968)
"Corduroy's Busy Street" Don Freeman
"Goldilocks and the Three Bears"
"Happy Birthday Moon" Frank Asch
"He Bear, She Bear" Stan & Jan Berenstain
"Ira Sleeps Over" Bernard Waker
"Jessie Bear What Will You Wear?" Nancy White Carlstrom
"The Lazy Bear" Frank Asch
"A Pocket For Corduroy" Don Freeman, (Viking Press, 1978)
"Sleepy Bear" Lydia Dabkovich
"The Teddy Bears' Picnic" Jimmy Kennedy
"The Velveteen Rabbit" Margery Williams
"What Next, Baby Bear" Jill Murphy
"Winnie the Pooh"

Puppetry

1. Teacher shares a bear puppet with the classroom. Ask the children questions about the bear, such as: "What color is the bear?" "Is the bear wearing any clothes?" "How many eyes does the bear have?" "Can this bear talk to you?"

Math

1. Graph the answers to yes or no questions. "Do you have a teddy bear?" "Is your bear old?" "Is your bear brown?" "Is your bear white?"

(continued on next page)

2. Arrange the bears in a row from shortest to tallest.

3. Group the bears in different ways according to size, color, clothing, material, eye color, etc.

4. Tell the story of "The Three Bears" on the flannel board. Ask the children to count the beds, bears, bowls of porridge, and the chairs.

Science

Discuss where a bear lives in the summer and in the winter. Show pictures of different types of bears, (grizzly, polar bear). If possible, take a field trip to the zoo and observe the bears at play.

Nutrition

1. Allow children to cut bread with bear-shaped cookie cutters. They can then spread honey butter on the bear cutouts.

2. Make gingerbear cookies using the same recipe as gingerbread cookies.

3. **Honey Balls**
   1 cup peanut butter
   1 cup nonfat dry milk
   ¼ cup honey
   Mix together; form into balls; and EAT!

Theme: Bears continued

SUMMARY

The ages of two and a half through five years are usually associated with the preschool child. Preschool children are making discoveries about themselves and the world around them. Plan a wide range of activities to stimulate children in their physical, social, emotional, and intellectual growth.

The rate of growth differs for each child. Caregivers must know the skill level of each child and plan accordingly to challenge abilities while increasing self-esteem. Routines help to establish a sense of independence as well as a secure knowledge of the environment.

By allowing children to develop self-help skills, caregivers again assure children that they are worthwhile, capable of making decisions and accomplishing tasks. Learning to get along in groups, handling emotions, and growing physically and intellectually take firm and nurturing guidance.

Arrange the classroom environment to allow room for activities, including safety. Communicate daily with parents and guardians to assure a successful program for all involved. Young children are eager to learn. They work hard to gain the approval of people for whom they care.

Review Questions

1. What are the ages of the preschool child?

2. Describe several methods to help the two and a half year old handle frustration.

3. Describe four self-help tasks that can be done by the preschooler.

4. Why is the preschooler sometimes referred to as "defiant"?

5. Why does the four year old have dreams about monsters?

6. Why are learning centers considered appropriate cognitive activities for the preschooler?

7. What is the approximate vocabulary of the five year old?

8. What elements need to be included when planning a daily routine?

9. Name three safety guidelines that should be taught to the preschooler.

10. Why is it vital to have good communication with parents?

Things to Do and Discuss

1. Observe a preschool classroom.

Carefully note learning centers, safety precautions, daily schedule, and discipline techniques.

2. Divide the students in the classroom into groups to discuss methods of communicating with parents. This may include newsletters, outlines of parent meetings, colorful parent information bulletin boards, or creative ideas of your own.

3. List the steps necessary for teaching children the self-help skills of personal hygiene, cleaning up, preparing for meals, and specific classroom chores. Share ideas with others in the classroom.

4. Explore methods of building self-esteem other than those listed in chapter. Examples are making books about personal likes and dislikes and providing mirrors for self-image. Many other methods can be used.

5. Assist in a preschool classroom.

CHAPTER 20
School-age Children

This is my best friend at age eleven.

KEY TERMS

abstract

academic learning

adolescence

concrete

extracurricular events

peer pressure

peers

OBJECTIVES

After completing this chapter, you will be able to:

1. define and give examples of the developmental areas of school-age children;

2. explain the caregiver's role when dealing with school-age children;

3. identify three daily routines established for children that attend an extended day care program.

INTRODUCTION

School-age children, ages six to twelve years, attend a regular school schedule of kindergarten through sixth grade. The school day usually lasts from three to six hours. This environment is often structured with a planned curriculum.

Many children in today's society also use a form of day care before and after school called extended day programs or latchkey programs. This child care is offered to the children of working parents. The program is established to provide these children with a secure, unstructured, homelike environment. Afterschool activities such as help with homework, crafts, drama, games, nutrition, and gross motor exercises are offered. *Extracurricular events* (activities that are not part of the everyday routine) including scouts, clubs, music lessons, gymnastics, and field trips are also planned. The children are allowed to choose the activities that interest them.

Children also establish their identities, peer relationships, and likes and dislikes (Erikson's third stage of development) during these middle years. School and home life help children to obtain information about themselves and their world. They expand their learning capacity. They build on their reading skills and learn complex math, science, and social studies. Children in this age group also develop physically at a steady pace with defined signs of maturity. This time in life bridges childhood and young adulthood (*adolescence*).

Figure 20-1: Weekly field trips to the library encourage reading and making choices.

NORMAL DEVELOPMENT OF SCHOOL-AGE CHILDREN

The following sections describe the developmental stages of school-age children. It is important to remember that children grow at individual rates and that many of the descriptions below may fall anywhere in the six-year age span.

Physical Development

Long arms and legs, boniness, and large hands and feet give school-age children an awkward appearance. These children often are clumsy as they perform fine and gross motor tasks. They may bump into, knock over, or trip over objects in their way. They need understanding caregivers, positive reinforcement, time and experience to adjust to the growth.

Thirty-two permanent teeth are now replacing baby teeth. Explain the importance of good dental hygiene and take a field trip to a local dentist's office. An eye examination is also advisable, as vision is fully developed by age seven.

Girls are entering puberty at approximately ten to twelve years of age. Boys enter puberty at approximately age fourteen to sixteen. School-age children become modest as their bodies mature. It is important to discuss personal hygiene and care as well as the changes that are occurring in their bodies.

Social Development

School-age children enjoy time to themselves and spend a great deal of time daydreaming, so allow opportunities for quiet activities. They also enjoy performing in dramas or musical recitals and writing original material.

Friends are of paramount importance, and they have much more influence over children than do families. *Peers* are generally of the same sex, age, interest, and intellectual level. School-age children often imitate others

to be part of a group. Fads, idols (musicians, movie stars, sports heroes), and collections are common interests. Television and movies provide models for behavior. Girls usually initiate boy-girl activities. Social clubs, scouts, and sports are meaningful. Providing positive role models and firm and consistent guidance helps children to form a sense of identity as they learn about themselves as individuals.

Girls' interest areas can include sports, games, dress-up dolls, homemaking, reading, interacting with young children, slumber parties, dancing, talking on the phone, telling secrets, and keeping diaries. Boys' interest areas can

Figure 20-3: School-age girls solve problems while playing with dolls.

Figure 20-2: Young children spend time daydreaming.

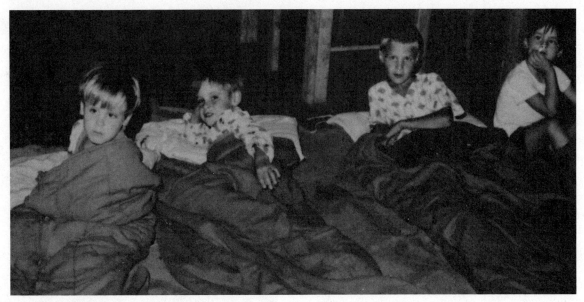

Figure 20-4: Boys enjoying a "night out" camping.

include sports, games, daring feats, homemaking, reading, playing with young children, sleepovers, outdoor adventures, and nature.

Emotional Development

Because school-age children are going through puberty and the hormonal balance in their bodies is changing, they are very sensitive to both approval and criticism. They can easily get their feelings hurt and often feel they are ugly or that they have few friends. Other times they feel very happy and successful. They have a need to be liked and therefore are generous and cooperative. Positive reinforcement helps to encourage children to behave in an appropriate manner. Enhance the development of positive self-esteem.

School-age children fear appearing different, and are influenced by their peers (*peer pressure*). Other fears include failure in school, spooky tales, bodily injury, and death of a parent, friend, or themselves. Allow these children to express their fears. Be reassuring of efforts and successes. Validate the use of imagination. Teach safety precautions concerning sex, drugs, and gangs.

At this age, children consider shows of affection childish and embarrassing. Respect and follow their lead. Do not force them to display affection either when alone or in a group.

Bickering with siblings or friends, threatening to beat up someone, throwing rocks, calling names, and threatening to run away are expressions of anger. Children need to develop self-control and to acquire problem-solving skills. Caregivers can provide positive role models in handling anger. Redirect anger. Using punching bags and throwing objects at a target are positive ways to release negative emotions.

Reassure children that it is all right to be angry but let them know that they need to express their emotions in words and explain what occurred to make them feel that way. Reassure them that they are loved.

Intellectual Development

School-age children are very curious. They seek adventure and want to learn about the outside world. They actively accumulate information through reading. These children enjoy reading fairy tales, comic books, and stories about animals, adventures, the supernatural, and heroes.

School-age children need both *concrete* (real) and *abstract* (existing only as an idea) experiences. They engage in *academic learning* (learning in areas such as language arts, mathematics, science, and social studies) during the school day and are interested in crafts and hobbies in their free time. Plan trips to the library and other community sites to help increase knowledge in academic and nonacademic areas.

Such children are becoming independent, and they enjoy determining, planning, doing, and cleaning up their own activities. They are developing a sense of accomplishment. Provide materials and guidance, but encourage children to do for themselves.

DAILY ROUTINES

As they do for younger children, daily routines help school-age children establish a sense of continuity. A schedule allows children to plan and anticipate the daily activities, to

Figure 20-5: These school-age children are interacting in the child care center.

plan for exceptions to the routine, and to function at a high level of efficiency.

Because so much of school-age children's daily schedule is structured in an official classroom, the day care center often tries to relieve the stress by planning unstructured activities. A relaxed and homelike area is created to be different from the normal school climate. Out go desks and orderly rows, and in come couches and easy chairs. Out goes quiet talking, and in comes conversation. Out go quiet, structured activities, and in come more active participation and freedom of choice. Figure 20–11 is a sample schedule for a school-age care center.

Figure 20-6: School-age children enjoy socializing at snack time.

SELF-HELP SKILLS

By the time children reach school age, they are able to take care of most of their physical needs and communicate their wants easily and loudly. They can dress and feed themselves and keep their belongings in order. Proper reinforcement of these skills at school and the center enables children to acquire pride and satisfaction.

Helping to Set Up Learning Centers

Help students determine areas of inter-est. Help them make lists of materials needed, acquire materials, do the projects, and clean up the area.

Maintaining Order at the Center

Help children rotate tasks necessary to the maintenance of the center. This can be accomplished by assigning duties, establishing checklists of responsibilities, and supervising all areas. Keeping track of personal belongings and center equipment also helps to maintain order. Provide proper storage areas.

Figure 20-7: Homework is an important task for school-age children.

Figure 20-8: Games with rules are a favorite activity for school-age children.

Preparing Snacks and Meals

Children can help to plan menus that are fun, nutritious, and easy. They can also make shopping lists, go on a field trip to the store, and decorate the table for their enjoyment. Cleanup is also part of the fun.

Managing Time

Help children to plan their schedules to include the necessities as well as fun. Teach children to tell time and to keep appointments.

SELF-ESTEEM

For children, this is a time of changing emotions and changing friends. Children figure out and question values, and they come to decisions about who they may be as adults.

The self-esteem of school-age children is often either very high or very low. It can change within a matter of moments. Self-esteem is fragile, and children can misinterpret what is told to them. Caregivers need to be sensitive to feelings and be careful and nurturing when children appear injured by what they view as criticism from either adults or peers.

Children need to have positive reinforcement as they practice new skills. (Remember, they are going through awkwardness as their bodies change physically.) Often they are unsure of how to act, and they need guidance to expected behavior. Boys become important to girls, and these relationships can cause much concern and stress.

Role models are extremely important. Children watch the adults in their lives for clues to solving problems. Firm and consistent guidelines help children to know the limits and expectations. Guidelines add security to their behavior and help them to know they are loved and valued (although children often test limits and disagree loudly about situations affecting them). A feeling of worth and importance to others helps to build self-esteem.

Fads, clothes, and idols are parts of belonging to a group. Peer pressure can be extreme at this age. Children feel more comfortable being like the others in their group of friends. Fear of being different often concerns them. Girls will all wear the same hairstyle or type of clothing. Boys will all admire the same sports hero or team.

Being aware of areas of growth and change affecting school-age children is a significant part of caregivers' responsibility. Being diplomatic when discussing problems or areas of concern is essential. Children's self-esteem must always be considered.

THE CAREGIVER'S ROLE

School-age child care is an extension of both the home and the school. It is a bridge between the two environments. As such, it must meet the needs of the families it serves. Caregivers should arrange activities to reach the interests of a variety of children of different ages. Creativity, encouragement, and an accepting attitude are essential.

Communication

Caregivers are very important people in the lives of school-age children. They allow children the freedom to grow and experiment, yet they guide in a gentle manner toward accepted behavior. Below are some communication guidelines for caregivers to use to help children grow in programs before and after school:

1. Be a good listener.

Figure 20-9: Caregiver and children work together at meal time.

2. Be firm when necessary.

3. Be friendly.

4. Be nurturing.

5. Exhibit good habits of speech by using language correctly.

6. Guide with positive reinforcement and consistency.

7. Have realistic expectations for individuals and groups.

8. Offer emotional support.

9. Show understanding.

10. Take time to talk with children individually.

Safety

Alertness to the protection of children is a prime responsibility of caregiving. Teaching safety skills to school-age children is necessary so that they can protect themselves. They

Figure 20-10: School-age children like to dress in similar ways.

are often without adult supervision when they leave the security of home, school, or the care center. Children need to practice safety skills and be able to think for themselves when danger appears.

School-age children like to explore and experiment; therefore, it is important to teach them about the hazards of electricity, fire, and gas. Children should learn how to use appliances in the proper way. They must be informed of the dangers of frayed electric cords, broken plugs, exposed wires, and the use of electrical appliances near water.

An important rule to remember is to stay clam in case of an emergency (do not panic). Panic prevents clear thinking and skillful action. If an accident should occur, children should be instructed to dial 0 or 911 for immediate help if they are at home. At the center, they should notify the caregiver.

Fire safety can be taught by an experienced supervisor who demonstrates the harm and destruction of fire and explosives. Allow children to become aware that oils and grease burn rapidly; grass fires spread quickly; and gasoline, many cleaning fluids, and chemicals can explode and cause fire. School-age children should be taught the stop, drop, and roll method in case they become inflamed. They also should participate in the center's safety drills.

The uses and dangers of medicines, drugs, alcohol, and poisons can be taught at the center. School-age children may be curious about mind-altering substances or just interesting-looking chemicals. They should be made aware of the consequences of chemicals not professionally prescribed.

Safety rules should be made and enforced for the playgrounds, the classroom, and field trips. Equipment and materials must be used, not abused. They should be shared by all children. They also should be appropriate for the age. School-age children play roughly and vigorously, so they may need to have a separate play area or be taught to be careful around younger children.

Although youngsters spend much of their day in the confinement of a school, they need instruction on safety in the street. Following are street safety rules:

1. Bicycles are to follow all traffic laws.

2. Cross the street at the corner.

3. Keep away from dumps, construction areas, quarries, steep ravines, abandoned refrigerators or buildings, creeks, and pools.

4. Never run into the street to fetch a lost ball or Frisbee.

5. Respect private property and no-trespassing signs.

Children are intrigued by water, whether it is a fountain, puddle, or pool. It is essential for them to learn water and swimming safety early in life. Children should be made aware of water rules. Following are water safety rules:

1. Never dunk or wrestle with someone in or around water.

2. Never rock an inner tube or small boat. It might cause someone to fall overboard.

3. Nonswimmers should wear a life jacket whenever in or near water.

4. Swim in pairs, never alone.

5. Swim only in familiar areas with a lifeguard.

Caregivers need to teach personal safety. Although it is important not to frighten children, they must be warned about dangers such as child abuse, rape, and kidnapping. To prevent these actions, children can learn to refuse gifts or rides unless they have permission from caregivers or parents, come home before dark, stay in groups, and stay in public places. If children are made to feel uncomfortable or are touched in an inappropriate area (parts of body covered by the bathing suit), encourage them to tell an adult immediately.

When safety rules are exchanged in a serious yet informative manner, children understand and remember them better. Remind young children that police officers are here for their protection and well-being.

School-age Day Care Schedule

Time: 7:00 A.M.
Activities: Arrival at the extended day care center, free choice of inside activities
Materials: Learning centers — book and magazine corner, computer center, table games, study corner

Provide warm relationships with all of the children. Provide a calm, relaxed, and homelike atmosphere. Prepare enough interesting learning centers without structuring too many activities or time limits. Offer a variety of learning materials, and allow the children to choose from their interest areas.

Time: 7:20 A.M.
Activities: Hand washing, preparation for breakfast
Materials: Water, liquid soap, paper towels, plates, cups, napkins, utensils

Have all children wash their hands and help set the table for the meal. Given the time and proper supervision, children may also help to prepare their meals.

(continued on next page)

Figure 20-11: School-age Schedule.

Time: 7:30 A.M.
Activity: Breakfast
Materials: Plenty of food and room for
            active eaters

This should be a time for socialization, enjoyable conversation, and table manners. New foods may depict different cultures or be seasonal, with distinct tastes and flavors.

Time: 8:00 A.M.
Activity: Cleanup
Materials: Trash basket, sponges, basin
            for dirty dishes

Encourage the children to dispose of their trash, place their dishes in the basin for washing, and wipe their places at the table or their trays with a sponge.

Time: 8:15 A.M.
Activity: Preparation for departure to
            classroom or school
Materials: Individual books, book bags,
            lunches, coats, homework,
            notes from home, special items

Wish each child a good day. Walk kindergarteners to class.

Time: 11:30 A.M.
Activity: Kindergarteners return from
            morning class
Materials: See 8:00 A.M. above

Welcome children individually. Listen to their news of the day. Set aside a short amount of time for students to share with the group.

Time: 12:00 P.M.
Activity: Lunch
Materials: See 7:30 A.M. above

Time: 12:30 P.M.
Activity: Rest
Materials: Cots or mats, blankets, sheets

Help the children prepare for rest by helping them set out their mats, sheets, and blankets. Encourage them to use the toilet. Let them remove their shoes and carefully place them near their mats.

Children of this age sometimes resist napping; therefore, it is important to provide a quiet, dimly lit, serene atmosphere to encourage resting. If a child cannot fall asleep, provide quiet activities such as books to read at the mat.

Time: 2:00 P.M.
Activities: Getting up from rest, putting
            away mats, putting on shoes
            and socks, washing, toileting
Materials: A standard place in the room
            to replace the resting equipment

The caregiver should arrange an easy awakening time. Leave enough time for the children to awaken slowly and take care of their personal needs.

Figure 20-11 continued

Time: 2:15 P.M.
Activity: Snack for kindergarteners
Materials: See 7:30 A.M. above

Time: 2:30 P.M.
Activity: Older afterschool children arrive at the center
Materials: See 11:30 A.M. above

Time: 2:45 P.M.
Activities: Hand washing, snack
Materials: Cups, napkins, food

Time: 3:15 P.M.
Activities: Homework, quiet activities
Materials: Tables, chairs, homework assignments, reference materials, books, paper, pencils

Provide enough time for the children to complete their homework before leaving for home. This allows the student to get tutoring and extra help from teachers.

If a child doesn't have homework or is finished early, allow reading or quiet activities. An incentive reading club or badge system can be started for enjoyment.

Time: 3:45 P.M.
Activities: Outside and inside free play

Materials: Play yard and equipment, hobby materials, craft supplies

School-age children need plenty of free time to exercise their large muscles and use their abundant energy. Give children freedom to explore and create within an unstructured setting with a variety of equipment and materials. Organize team sports and group games, if children are interested.

Inside time can be used to learn new skills or handicrafts. Gymnastic, drama, and art materials may also be supplied. Arrange field trips to areas of interest, scout meetings, and music lessons.

Time: 5:00 P.M.
Activities: Washing, toileting, departure
Materials: Learning center with art and craft materials, books, writing supplies, games, computer, videocassette players, television

Encourage children to try new activities. Check that their belongings are ready to go home. Let children relax after strenuous activities outside. Say good-bye to each child and parent, mentioning an activity to be presented or continued tomorrow.

School-Age

Theme: Literature-based Curriculum

"Caps For Sale" by Esphyr Slobodkina

Classroom Activities

1. Ask each child to bring in a special hat. Identify the hat's shape, color, size, and use.

2. Put all of the hats in a line on the shelf. After the children close their eyes, the teacher removes one hat. The children must decide which hat has disappeared.

3. Prepare a "hat store" center. Include several mannequin heads for display, a cash register, mirrors, and price tags for each hat.

4. Make a surprise box having the children discuss the use of each item within. Include fireman's hat, chef's hat, cowboy hat, ski cap, visor, nurse's cap, hard hat, sailor's cap, engineer's hat, baseball cap, etc.

Language Development

Books:
"A Three Hat Day" Laura Geringer;
"Jennie's Hat" Ezra Jack Keats
"Old Hat New Hat" Stan & Jan Berenstain

Read "Caps For Sale" several days in a row.

Encourage the children to listen carefully the first few times. Ask specific questions:

1. How many caps did the peddler have?

2. Did he sell any on his way to the country?

3. How much were the peddler's caps?

4. What did the peddler shout when selling his caps?

5. What were the monkeys doing in the tree?

6. Where did the peddler fall asleep?

7. What happened to the caps when he fell asleep?

8. What color was the peddler's own cap?

9. How many monkeys were in the tree?

10. What did the peddler say to get his hats back from the monkeys?

11. How did the monkeys respond to the peddler?

12. How do you think the peddler was feeling when the monkeys had his caps?

13. What words could describe how the monkeys were feeling as they wore the caps?

14. How did the peddler acquire his hats from the monkeys?

15. Would it be easier to sell caps in a store or walking in the village? Why?

By asking these questions the teacher reinforces their listening and comprehension skills.

After several readings, encourage the children to read along from their books.

New words to add to a vocabulary list may be:

- peddler
- checked
- wares
- ordinary
- cap
- disturb

After returning their books to the shelf, play the "What did you see?" game. This reinforces observation and visual awareness skills. Ask the children:

1. "Did you see any houses in the village?"

2. "How many?"

3. "Did you see any people other than the peddler?"

4. "Did you see a church steeple?"

5. "Were there any flowers on the ground; any grass; cobblestones in the path?"

6. "What color was the tree that the peddler napped next to?"

7. "How many caps did you see?"

8. "What color were the caps?"

9. "Were there any lakes, rivers, or pools in the story?"

10. "Did the sun have a face?"

11. "Was it happy, sad, or angry?"

12. "What color were the monkeys?"

13. "What color was the peddlers' hair; pants; jacket?"

Introduce other words used to define a hat, such as: cap, fedora, chapeau, mantilla, helmet, etc.

The Writing Process

1. Ask the children to look carefully at all of the hats in the "hat store" corner for five to ten minutes. Once they have returned to their desks ask them to draw a picture of their favorite hat and print the name of the hat below the picture. (Be sure all of the hats are labeled in the "hat store.")

(continued on next page)

2. If the group is age-appropriate, ask them to write their own ending to the story, different than what happened in the book. They may do this assignment alone or in groups.

Finger Plays, Songs, and Flannel Stories

The children may enjoy reciting and acting out the following:

- "Five Little Monkeys"
- Create the "Caps For Sale" story with flannel pieces allowing each child to take time setting the pieces on the flannel board.

Math and Science

1. Have sets of caps, monkeys, and trees that match. For example, the shape of one monkey will match the shape of another monkey. You may want to mix colors and shapes to intermatch objects. For example, a monkey with a cap. This can be done in degrees of difficulty. The matching patterns can match colors, numbers, shapes, sequencing objects, words to their pictures, partner alphabet letters, addition, or subtraction. The list is endless.

2. Reinforce the concept of balance. Allow children to balance hats on their heads, balance blocks, balance small objects such as paper clips, coins, toothpicks, or cotton balls.

3. Introduce weights and balance. Have the children guess the weight of different hats. Practice using a scale.

4. Explore the world of the monkey. Display and discuss a variety of pictures of different types of monkeys, gorillas, chimpanzees, and apes. Discover where they live, the foods they eat, their similarities and differences.

5. If possible, arrange for a real monkey to visit the class from your local zoo, or visit the zoo on a field trip.

Cooking

1. Bake banana bread.

2. Dip banana chunks into warm chocolate fudge sauce.

3. Make peanut butter and banana sandwiches.

Crafts

1. Provide colorful paper, glue, buttons, glitter, crepe paper, yarn, flowers, and

Theme: Literature-based Curriculum continued

scraps of material. Let the children use their imagination making their own original hats.

2. Allow the children to cut pictures out of magazines of people wearing hats. Discuss their pictures when completed.

3. Have the children color and cut caps in each color of brown, grey, blue, red, and don't forget checked. When that is complete, put all of the hats together to use in a number game.

4. The children can all have monkey faces. The children will cut out a mask, including the center section, reinforce one hole at each ear, and attach strings.

Fine and Gross Motor Activities

1. Obtain a good selection of bottle caps. The children can utilize these in many ways: sorting according to size, color, name, patterning, classifying, and graphing.

SUMMARY

School-age children are defined as being from six to twelve years of age and from kindergarten through sixth grade. Their school day is often structured with academic subjects, so child care centers and latchkey programs or extended day programs are planned to include an unstructured environment. Freedom of choice, large homelike areas, and many enjoyable activities are planned around their interests.

Children in this age group are establishing their identities and forming peer relationships. Idols, heroes, movie stars, and sports figures are important role models. Fads in clothing and hairstyles are important as school-age children try to find places within groups. Self-esteem fluctuates frequently. School-age children need an understanding and caring caregiver. Such children are very sensitive to what they perceive as criticism. They want approval from peers and important adults.

These children are growing at a rapid pace physically. Their extremities become large and lanky at the onset of puberty. This results in awkwardness, which can cause embarrassment when accidents occur.

Review Questions

1. Name the three types of care offered for school-age children.

2. Identify Erikson's third stage of development and explain how this stage relates to the school-age child.

3. At what age is vision fully developed?

4. At what age do boys and girls enter puberty?

5. Identify three interests that are common to girls and three interests that are common to boys during puberty.

6. Describe the difference between concrete and abstract learning experiences.

7. Identify three extracurricular activities that may be offered at an extended-day program.

8. Why is it necessary to be a good role model when working with school-age children?

9. Why is peer pressure so important for school-age children?

10. What three safety rules would you enforce if you were the caregiver?

Things to Do and Discuss

1. Observe a structured classroom and an unstructured afterschool program. Name the differences. Note the activities accomplished in both settings.

2. Discover the interest areas of groups of boys and groups of girls. What activities were similar? What activities were different?

3. Discuss the peer pressures you experienced during this age span. Do school-age children today have the same pressures?

4. Bring in pictures of your school-age years. Discuss how you have changed socially, emotionally, physically, and intellectually since that period.

5. Assist in a before- and afterschool program.

CHAPTER 21
Exceptional Children

Mainstreaming places an exceptional child in a regular child care center.

KEY TERMS

allergies
autism
blindness
cerebral palsy
deafness
delayed, or impaired
  children

digestive impairment
epilepsy
exceptional children
gifted children
mainstreaming
respiratory
  impairments

OBJECTIVES

After completing this chapter, you will be able to:
  1. define the characteristics of the gifted child;
  2. explain the characteristics of the impaired child.

INTRODUCTION

Children who exhibit development outside the normal range are considered *exceptional children*. These can be either *gifted children* (who display physical, social, emotional, or intellectual progress that exceeds or is superior to that of normal children) or *delayed, or impaired children* (whose developmental levels are below the normal range). Such children can be found in all social, economic, and cultural backgrounds. Since no two children are the same, individualized programs are needed.

Caregivers are in a unique position to recognize children with exceptional needs. They have studied normal developmental patterns and see large numbers of children of the same age. The earlier the age at which exceptional children are identified, the sooner appropriate educational programs can be started, and the better the children can be helped to reach their potential. Caregivers can also maintain a list of specialists in their community to which they can refer the parents.

GIFTED CHILDREN

Children with exceptionally high achievement levels for their age or maturation are considered gifted. They may be advanced in one or more particular areas, such as math, drama, music, science, baseball, or the ability to get along with others.

Gifted children are often labeled geniuses, prodigies, or brains. Evidence supports the theory that an excellent genetic makeup and an enriched environment encourage the development of gifted children. There is often additional pressure by adults on these children to succeed or to perform at a high skill level. Stress and emotional problems can result. Caregivers must endeavor to reduce areas of concern and allow the children to experience a full range of development to achieve a sense of worth.

Characteristics of gifted children include:

- advanced creative and imagination skills
- advanced fine and gross motor skills
- advanced memory and recall skills
- curiosity for additional information
- eagerness to learn
- excellent problem solving abilities
- extreme language development and vocabulary for age
- extremely empathetic (ability to understand how others feel)
- high motivation levels
- long attention spans
- unprompted reading ability at an early age

Gifted children require additional support and guidance in order to stimulate their progress. They often can become bored with the average curriculum and are in danger of becoming drop-outs unless encouraged and motivated to further their learning. The capacity of a child can vary in degree from borderline to highly gifted.

IMPAIRMENTS

Although all children at one time or another may have problems in a particular area of development, some children have prolonged or extended needs in one or more areas. Such a child needs special help in order to develop to full potential. An exceptional child requires specific guidance and lesson plans to progress to the next level of competency.

Impairments may develop as the result of genetic or hereditary elements, illness or substance abuse by the pregnant mother, or an illness of or accident to the child after birth.

Many times, exceptional children are referred to as "bad," "slow," "lazy," "trouble," or "disruptive." However, these behaviors may be an indication of physical, social, emotional, or intellectual impairments.

Behaviors or conditions that may indicate impairments or learning disabilities include:

- chronic illness

- delayed language or reading development

- frequent clumsiness or lack of coordination in fine motor skills (such as writing, drawing, cutting), gross motor skills (such as running, hopping, throwing), or eye-hand coordination

- frequent confusion

- frequent extreme emotional reactions

- frequent inability to follow directions or routines

- frequent inability to get along with others

- hesitancy to enter into activities

- hyperactivity or hypoactivity

- impaired discrimination of perceptual motor functions, such as size, right-left, space, distance, time, or reversals of figures or letters

- inadequate motivation

- irregular school attendance

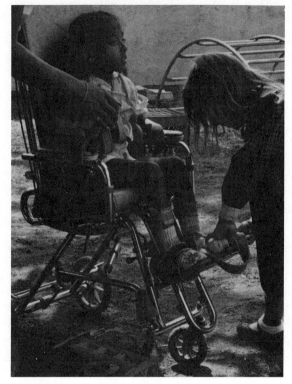

Figure 21-1: A cerebral palsy child.

- lack of cultural and environmental stimulation

- malnutrition

- mental impairments, such as poor ability to perform abstract thinking, disorganized thinking, poor short- and long-term memory, *autism* (a condition where the individual withdraws from reality), or retardation

- neurological impairments such as *cerebral palsy* (a condition with speech difficulties and a lack of coordination caused by brain damage before or during birth) or *epilepsy* (a condition usually causing convulsions)

● physical impairments in vision, hearing, or brain damage

● short attention span

● specific learning disabilities in such areas as reading (slowness, inaccuracy, or reversing letters or words), mathematics (poor understanding and ability to perform), writing (scribbled or unreadable handwriting), or spelling (absent, additional, or reversed letters)

Physical Impairments

Children with physical impairments often need special care. Caregivers should consult with parents and their specialists in order to follow the prescribed methods of management. Physical impairments vary in degree of intensity from mild to severe.

Physical impairments include:

● *blindness* (loss of vision)

● *deafness* (loss of hearing)

● deformities such as those of the arm, leg, hand, foot, cleft lip and palate, or internal organs

● diseases or illnesses that result in continual impairment, such as cerebral palsy, arthritis, heart disease, sickle cell anemia, muscular dystrophy, and diabetes

● internal impairments such as heart, *respiratory impairments* (breathing difficulties such as asthma), anemia, *digestive impairments* (inability of the

body to utilize nourishment), and *allergies* (the body's negative reactions to certain substances)

Children with physical impairments should be encouraged to be as independent as possible. The ability to perform self-help skills allows the children to obtain a sense of worth. Since these impairments often interfere with everyday life and performance, special equipment, physical therapy, and understanding caregivers are necessary to enable these children to develop to their potential and to increase their fine and gross motor skills.

Mental Impairments

Children with mental impairments may develop physically as other children do. However, their all-around development is slower and may stop completely at a younger age. Behavior is often disruptive, so guidelines must be simple, firm, and consistent. Establishing daily routines helps these children to perform at acceptable levels.

Figure 21-2: A Down's syndrome child.

Figure 21-3: These exceptional and normal children are enjoying an art project.

Mental impairments may take the form of dyslexia and other learning disabilities, brain dysfunction (malfunction), or mental retardation. Following are levels of retardation (from *Pediatric Nursing,* by Lisner, Albany, NY: Delmar Publishers, 1983):

- Mild—IQ of 51 to 68. Functions at approximately sixth-grade level. Considered educable. Can perform repetitive tasks. Able to be relatively independent and implement life support tasks. Has frequent behavior disorders. Easily influenced by peers.

- Moderate—IQ of 36 to 51. Functions at approximately second-grade level. Considered trainable when supervised. Can manage most self-help tasks. Has low tolerance for frustration. Seeks immediate gratification. Can usually get along with others.

- Severe—IQ of 20 to 35. Functions at toddler level. Severe sensorimotor dysfunction. Inability to perform self-help tasks. Total dependency. May need custodial nursing care.

MAINSTREAMING

Allowing exceptional children to attend centers or schools with other children is called *mainstreaming*. There are multiple advantages for all involved. The normal or nonimpaired children learn to accept and understand differences in others, while the gifted or impaired children learn appropriate behavior by modeling the behavior of the other children. As each group helps and learns from the other, feelings of self-esteem and worth are increased.

Caregivers must plan carefully when integrating exceptional children into the center or school. Consulting with parents and specialists, special training, and understanding the special requirements are necessary to help the children progress. A nurturing and accepting attitude also helps to make mainstreaming successful.

SUMMARY

Exceptional children may be gifted, impaired, or both. Because caregivers see large numbers of children of similar ages and have studied child development, they are more likely to be able to distinguish or recognize children who exhibit exceptional behaviors.

Gifted children have high achievement levels in one or more area of development. Special planning and encouragement are necessary to stimulate these children to progress or reach their potential.

Children may have social, emotional, physical, or intellectual impairments that cause disruptive behavior or delay learning. Specialized therapy or treatment is often indicated. Impairments vary in degree from mild to severe.

Mainstreaming exceptional children into the classroom with other children has advantages, as each group is able to learn and accept the other. Caregivers need to plan carefully for mainstreaming to be beneficial for all concerned.

Review Questions

1. Define "exceptional children."

2. Why is it important to identify exceptional children as early as possible?

3. What aspects encourage the development of gifted children?

4. Impairments may develop as the result of what elements?

5. Define the condition of autism.

6. Why should children with physical impairments be encouraged to be as independent as possible?

7. In what forms does mental impairment reveal itself?

8. Define and describe the three levels of mental retardation?

9. Why is mainstreaming encouraged in many states?

Things to Do and Discuss

1. Observe and report on a classroom or center that uses mainstreaming.

2. Report on the causes and effects of one of the following physical impairments:

- allergies
- arthritis
- asthma
- blindness
- cerebral palsy
- cleft palate
- cystic fibrosis
- deafness
- diabetes
- Down's syndrome
- epilepsy
- heart disease
- hemophilia
- muscular dystrophy

- sickle cell anemia
- stuttering

3. Report on the causes and effects of one of the following mental impairments:

   - autism
   - brain dysfunction
   - brain injury
   - Down's syndrome
   - dyslexia
   - hyperactivity
   - hypoactivity
   - learning disabilities
   - mental retardation
   - psychosis

SECTION V

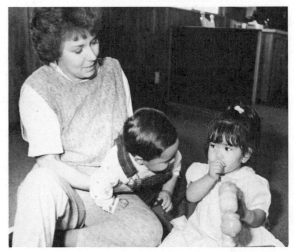

Classroom Management

CHAPTER 22
Classroom Management

The caregiver is comforting a distressed child.

KEY TERMS

discipline
punishment

OBJECTIVES

After completing this chapter, you will be able to:

1. discuss methods of communicating effectively with young children;
2. demonstrate an understanding of various classroom discipline techniques;
3. describe the difference between discipline and punishment;
4. identify and utilize appropriate methods in meeting the needs of individual children.

INTRODUCTION

This chapter focuses on how to communicate with and gain the cooperation of children. It discusses what to do when conflicts arise between children's desires and the rights of others in the classroom. The chapter also analyzes the use of discipline techniques that allow choice and learning. The last aspect is the importance of discipline that fosters self-esteem while meeting the needs of the individual children and the needs of the group.

The challenge that confronts most caregivers is how to have a successful classroom. Caregivers envision a program that permits each child to grow socially, emotionally, physically, and intellectually; runs with few conflicts; and is a source of enjoyment for all involved. On most days, all of these hopes can be accomplished with knowledge, practice, patience, planning, and understanding on the part of the caregiver.

SETTING GUIDELINES

Classroom and center management include limited rules or guidelines for behavior and routines. Children feel comfortable when they know what is expected of them. When children first arrive at a center, it is important to allow them enough time to learn and understand the guidelines. Caregivers can gently demonstrate and explain guidelines to help ease children through this adjustment period.

Most guidelines should concern safety and the proper use of equipment. These are necessary to prevent accidents and to limit the disagreements. When children understand the logic or reason for a direction, they are more likely to cooperate.

When setting guidelines, consider safety, fairness, the maturation level of the children, and the type and amount of equipment available. Are the guidelines too stringent? Do they allow freedom of choice? Do they allow explor-

ation? Do they allow experimentation? Sample guidelines follow.

In general:

1. Everyone helps to pick up and clean up.
2. Hands are for holding.
3. Treat each other with respect.
4. Use chairs and benches for sitting.
5. Use supplies and equipment carefully.
6. Use words to describe problems or feelings.

In the classroom:

1. Keep all four feet of the chair on the floor.
2. Use inside voices.
3. Walk.

Figure 22-1: Playing in the sandbox is fun.

Figure 22-2: *A caregiver can help children take turns on the slide.*

In the play yard:

1. Be careful drivers on wheel toys.

2. Check for others in the way before jumping or sliding.

3. Keep sand close to the ground or in the sandbox.

4. Sit on swings.

5. Use two hands while climbing.

6. Walk up the ladder and go down the slide feet-first.

Did you notice that the rules and guidelines *told children what to do* instead of using a negative instruction, such as "Don't do that" or "I told you no"? Children need to know what you want them to do. Give directions in a calm and pleasing voice. Be specific (for example, "The square blocks go on the top shelf.") and anticipate that the children will do what is expected. When instructions are stated in a positive manner, children are more cooperative.

It is also important to model the appropriate behavior. Remember that children learn best by observing people in their environment. If the guideline is "sit on chairs and benches," then you do not sit on tables or the tops of low shelves and do not stand on chairs or benches. If the guideline is "hands are for holding," then you need to be gentle when dealing with children.

Remember that children's safety is your first responsibility. Secondly, you are there to interact with the children. Steps to effective supervision include:

1. Keep discussions with other caregivers to a minimum.

2. Never leave your designated area without informing another caregiver.

3. Position yourself so that you can always supervise a large segment of the room or yard.

4. Remain alert to possible problems and react quickly to redirect children to appropriate behavior.

5. Spread caregivers around the room or yard to make sure that all areas are properly supervised.

When planning to introduce a popular activity, have enough supplies and equipment to allow a turn for all the children who wish one. Make sure there are sufficient caregivers to supervise all other activities in the room. Plan only one special activity during a particular time. Other choices should require little supervision. (Finger painting takes one caregiver in attendance at all times; another adult supervise the other activities.)

DISCIPLINE VERSUS PUNISHMENT

Discipline is defined as "training to act in accordance with rules,...[or] instruction and practice designed to train to proper conduct or action" (*Random House Dictionary*, New York: Random House, 1984). Positive discipline is effective. It encourages a change of behavior that is acceptable. When caregivers make positive comments about behavior that is appropriate and appreciated, children learn to function in a satisfactory manner.

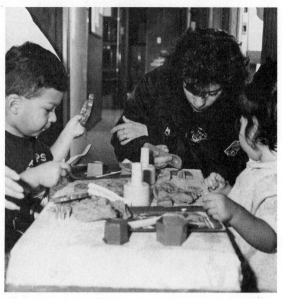

Figure 22-3: The caregiver is supervising the play dough activity.

A main goal is for children to learn how to solve problems in a manner that respects the rights of others. Other important objectives are for children to feel confident and secure, to have a good self-concept, and to have high self-esteem. Effective and positive discipline is the means to accomplish these objectives.

Punishment is defined as "a penalty inflicted for an offense,...[or] severe handling or treatment" (*Random House Dictionary*, New York: Random House, 1984). Punishment may be physical, emotional, or both. Name-calling, sarcastic remarks, threats, and lectures reinforce a negative self-image. When punishment is imposed on children, their attention is removed from the problem. Instead it focuses on revenge and feelings of unworthiness. It also removes the opportunity to make amends.

Case Study #1:
Ken and Scott

Ken is playing in the sandbox with several other children. They are digging a tunnel and making roads for their cars. Scott wants to use the tractor, but Ken is using it to smooth the roads. Scott, getting impatient for his turn, runs across the roads, scuffing them up. Ken takes a handful of sand and throws it at Scott, yelling, "Leave my roads alone! You messed them all up!" Scott starts to cry because he has sand all over his clothes. He hits Ken. Ken starts to cry, too.

Miss Hahn, hearing the dispute, goes quickly to the sandbox. Both boys begin to tell her what happened at the same time. Since both are crying, it is hard to distinguish what is being said.

Miss Hahn bends down to be on the children's level. First she checks to see if either is hurt. Noticing the sand on Scott's clothes, she brushes him off, checks to make sure he does not have sand in his eyes, and comforts him. Next she checks Ken to make sure he is all right and comforts him.

When both boys calm down, she asks Scott what has happened. Scott tells her that he wants a turn with the tractor and Ken won't share. Next, she asks Ken what happened. He tells her that Scott ruined the roads that he was making for the cars. She reminds Ken that the sand must stay close to the ground and Scott that we are careful with others' work.

Figure 22-4: *Ken and Scott are playing in the sandbox.*

She then describes the problem by saying, "Ken was using the tractor to make roads and Scott wants to have a turn with the tractor, too. How can we solve this problem?"

Both boys give suggestions. Scott says, "You've had the tractor for a long time."

Ken says, "I'll give you a turn when I'm finished."

Scott asks Miss Hahn, "Are there any more tractors?"

Miss Hahn asks Scott if he has looked in the toy shed. Scott and Ken run to check and do find another one. "I like the way you both worked to solve the problem. Now you are ready to work together to build roads," says Miss Hahn.

When rules or guidelines are broken, the caregiver needs to remind the children of expected behavior and redirect them to an acceptable activity. This can be done in a manner that encourages their cooperation. It is important to state the situation so that the child's self-esteem is not attacked. The problem or action may not be acceptable, but the child is always respected and accepted.

In Case Study #1, the boys practiced using words to describe feelings and wishes, reaching a conclusion that was acceptable to both of them to solve the problem. The caregiver remained close to the children and gave them reassurance. Miss Hahn did not make a judgment as to who was right and who was wrong, nor did she solve the problem for them. Rather, she allowed the boys the time to practice problem-solving skills. She stated the expected behavior and remained calm throughout the discussion.

In order for children to reach a successful conclusion to a problem, they must first be taught the necessary skills. Caregivers must plan situations in order for children to gain the necessary experience.

Often caregivers have expectations that are too high for children. They expect children to know how to share. However, children must be given time to practice and to learn that others also have rights. Steps to teaching problem solving and sharing include role modeling acceptable behavior, giving specific directions, and allowing children to make choices on their own. Examples of each step are given below:

1. Caregivers do the actual dividing of the equipment among the children (instead of just placing a box of the equipment in the middle of the table). This eliminates arguments about who has too much or too little. It also encourages sharing and a sense of fairness.

2. Caregivers give direct instructions by using positive statements such as, "Ken is using this tractor. You may get another one from the shed," or "Jose, you may use the blue and yellow beads to string. Maria is using the red and green beads." This helps children to look for alternatives when sharing is necessary.

3. Caregivers may ask questions or make statements that let the children make a choice about the division of equipment or toys. "Which shape of block do you want to use?" or "Divide the blocks between you."

The above techniques can be used in many situations. First, demonstrate or do the desired task. Next, give a specific direction, and let the children accomplish the task. Finally, permit the children to make a choice and expect them to complete the task with little help. Caregivers sometimes presume that children will be able to complete the last step without first learning the necessary techniques. This is often unrealistic.

Giving Choices

Giving children choices allows them practice in decision making. Often we use questions when we really want children to comply or follow an instruction. When giving direc-

Figure 22-5: Caregiver demonstrates how to play the game.

Problem Solving

1. Keep the discussion short and to the point.
2. Describe the problem.
3. Give children a chance to solve the problem or offer suggestions for possible solutions.
4. Make positive statements.
5. Tell the children what to do (the expected behavior).
6. Remain calm.

Figure 22-7: Problem Solving chart.

Figure 22-6: Caregivers teach sharing by demonstrating how to divide toys among children.

tions which are meant to be followed, use a firm, pleasant tone of voice and phrase the direction in a statement. Examples follow:

1. "It is time to clean up now" instead of a question, "Is it time to clean up?"

2. "We always wash our hands after using the toilet" instead of a question, "Do you want to wash your hands now?"

3. "You need to put your jacket on before going outside" instead of a question. "Do you want to put your jacket on?"

Making statements when giving directions leaves little doubt in the minds of children about what behavior is expected. It is reassuring to them to understand exactly what the guidelines and expectations are in any particular situation.

When children fail to complete a direction, the caregiver must follow through by helping until the task is finished. The children and the caregiver may work together (I'll pick up the rectangular blocks; you pick up the square ones) or the caregiver may offer suggestions as to how to complete the task (The large rectangular blocks go on the bottom shelf). A positive reinforcement statement that describes the finished accomplishment helps the child to remember the task next time and increases the child's self-esteem. "All the blocks are now on the shelves. Thank you for helping."

Handling Discipline Problems

When misbehavior does occur, it is helpful if the caregiver can understand what is motivating the child. By asking yourself several questions, you can determine the appropriate course of action. Remember, there is always

Figure 22-8: The caregiver demonstrates how to divide the beads equally.

Figure 22-9: This caregiver and children pick up the playhouse area together.

Figure 22-10: Toy shelves with toys neatly put away.

a reason why children misbehave. The following questions address possible reasons for misbehavior:

1. Are expectations too high for the child? Does the child have a sense of failure or frustration?

2. Are expectations too low for the child? Does the child seem bored or disinterested?

3. Are there too many people around? Does the child need some time to be alone?

4. Does the child need more attention or nurturing?

5. Has there been an emotional disturbance or a change at home—divorce, separation, new baby, death, new home, or visitors?

6. Has there been an emotional distur-bance or a change at their school—a close friend that moved away, a close friend that is playing with someone else, a new classroom, or a new teacher?

7. Is the child becoming ill?

8. Is the child experimenting with or testing new behavior? Is the child asking for more choices and responsibility?

9. Is the child lacking in self-esteem?

10. Is the child tired?

As we strive to accept and understand children's feelings, we show respect and consid-eration. When children know that we care, their behavior improves.

Caregivers have several choices of the type of discipline to use for misbehavior. They can use humor. They can ignore small offenses. They can state their expectations. They can redirect to another activity. They can model acceptable behavior. Or they can remove the child from the situation.

The use of time out may be effective for repeated occurrences of misbehavior. Time out allows the child to be removed from a situation and to sit quietly until ready to return to the group. There should be no specific amount of time imposed. The caregiver should calmly state that obviously the child needs a few minutes to relax and be alone. This quiet time allows the child to calm down and to think about problem-solving methods. Time out should not be used as a threat, nor should it be used for every situ-ation. This method can be overused, thereby losing its effectiveness.

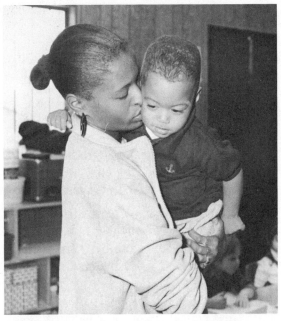

Figure 22-11: Caregiver comforting a tired child.

Sometimes children may need to be denied a privilege, such as when they refuse to cooperate or repeatedly break a rule. Parents may need to be consulted so that all caregivers are cooperating to help change the misbehavior.

Common problems and possible solu-tions include:

1. *A child hurts another child.* Separate the children and make sure both chil-dren are all right. If an object was used for hurting, remove it. If the child hit another child, remind the first child that hands are for holding and that we use words when we are angry or frustrated. Have children practice telling each other how they feel. State your expectations

and redirect children to a safe activity. Never force a child to say "I'm sorry!" Usually children are not sorry at that moment, and you are only teaching the child to lie about his or her feelings.

2. *A child refuses to eat.* Determine if the child is really hungry. Suggest taking one bite of the food. Remove the food if the child is uninterested. Do not offer alternative food; the child will eat when hungry at the next mealtime.

3. *A child refuses to share.* State your expectations calmly and firmly, "The toys at school are to be shared with all the children." Help the children reach an acceptable solution. You may need to suggest a time limit or to divide the toys equally. Help the children to follow through on the solution.

4. *A child runs away from you.* Do not chase after the child unless he or she is in danger. Wait calmly for the child and then listen to his or her explanation for the behavior. State your expectations and help the child to follow through with the appropriate behavior.

5. *A child uses bad language.* Calmly and firmly state that the child is using inappropriate (do not be afraid to use big words when talking to children) language for school. State your expectations and offer an alternate or silly (using humor) word to say when frustrated or angry. Often children use words that they have heard without understanding the meaning. The word may also be acceptable language at home.

6. *A child willfully destroys an item.* State calmly that we are careful with the supplies and equipment at school. Have the child make amends by replacing or fixing the item. Listen to the explanation and redirect the child to alternative activity that will allow for venting of the child's emotions. Examples are pounding clay, hitting a punching bag, or tearing newspaper and putting it in a bag.

Remaining calm, fitting the discipline to the problem, determining the maturity of the child, and using creative discipline techniques are important skills for the caregiver. Remember that children need to learn how to behave appropriately and to solve problems in our crowded society.

Chart of Discipline Techniques

Stating Expectations

State expectations in a clear, positive manner to reinforce expected behavior of students. This establishes guidelines. Examples include:

1. Chairs are for sitting.

2. Sand stays close to the ground.

3. Use your quiet voice.

Positive Reinforcement

Making a positive statement about appropriate behavior (ignoring or giving little attention to inappropriate behavior) provides positive reinforcement. Examples include:

1. I like the way you shared with Juan.
2. Lyhn will show you how to solve the equation.
3. Thank you for helping.

Role Modeling

Children observe caregivers demonstrating appropriate behavior to learn appropriate behavior. This is called role modeling. Examples include:

1. Caregivers following guidelines.
2. Caregivers treating children and others with respect.
3. Caregivers using correct language.

Problem-Solving Techniques

Demonstrating how to use words to reach a compromise or solution to a mutual problem is called problem-solving techniques. Examples include:

1. Reach a mutually acceptable solution.
2. State the problem.
3. Write down or talk about solutions.

Natural Consequences

When children decide to break or go against a guideline, there is a consequence for the behavior. All children get one reminder and then the caregiver must follow through with the consequence. Examples include:

1. I'm sorry you decided to talk instead of studying for the test. Now you must stay in at recess and study for the test.
2. I'm sorry you forgot to keep the sand close to the ground. Now you must find somewhere else to play.

Appropriate Time Out

Allowing a child time in order to change ongoing behavior is called appropriate time out. This method is usually used for repeated offenses. However, a time limit should not be given; rather, the child is allowed to determine when it is time to rejoin the group. A Time Out Chair should not be used. Caregivers need to be sensitive to the emotional state of the child. By being gentle and understanding, the child will realize that you are helping him to regain control and the child's behavior will be corrected. Always end your statements with the expectation that the child will behave in the appropriate manner when he or she comes back to the group. Examples include:

1. Let's sit down and read a story for a while.
2. Mercedes, you are having a bad day.
3. Ralph, you are having trouble listening to directions. You need some time to yourself. When you are ready, you may come back.
4. Scott, you are very angry. You need to sit at the play dough table for a while. When you are ready, you may rejoin the group.

REMEMBER: Say what you mean, mean what you say, and follow through!

MEETING INDIVIDUAL NEEDS

Recognizing that children are individuals, with unique personalities and positive and negative aspects, enables you to treat them with respect and acceptance. Children have their own thoughts, temperaments, tastes, feelings, desires, and dreams.

Autonomy

Autonomy, or sense of self, is reaffirmed when caregivers:

1. Allow sufficient time and opportunities for children to practice and do tasks for themselves;

2. permit children to use problem-solving techniques;

3. allow children to learn from their mistakes.

Caregivers often step in and help children accomplish a task by offering suggestions or solutions before giving children a chance to practice or attempt the task on their own. This course of action helps to keep children dependent on adults. It also leads to children having feelings of being incapable, helpless, or unworthy.

By not hurrying to give children the correct answer to their problems, we allow them the opportunity to first discover their own knowledge and to explore their imaginations. For example, we first state the problem and then ask an open-ended question; "I can see that you both want to use the game. How can we solve this problem?" or, "You want to make sure that your answer is correct. Where can you check your answer?" Using another source (such as library books or a specialist) to check theories stimulates curiosity and provides chances to learn new skills. By implementing this procedure, children and caregivers are free to discuss several possible conclusions.

To encourage independence, caregivers need to admire the amount of effort demonstrated by the children as they struggle to learn new skills. As caregivers show respect for children's endeavors, children gather determination to keep trying. Describing efforts by saying "It's hard work to write your name," "Adding three columns of numbers is difficult," or "You are really learning to share," shows an understanding of the problems that children are attempting to solve.

By using these methods, caregivers can help children to feel that their attempts to learn new skills or to gain knowledge are positive endeavors. They encourage children to keep trying. They help to establish the fact that problems and questions have value. These methods also help children see themselves as independent, responsible, and competent people.

Individual Differences

Another area of individuality is genetic and ethnic backgrounds. Teaching children about other heritages (all through the year, instead of just during holidays) or about physical and mental impairments, leads to an understanding that all people need to be treated equally and with respect.

Children require an opportunity to learn about the special qualities that each culture

Figure 22-12: Students and children working together in a Laboratory School.

has to offer. Foods, customs, clothing, art, literature, government, geography, and sports are just a few of the subjects that may be discussed. Pride in one's own culture is established as learning progresses.

Caregivers have to be aware of cultural differences that may affect the classroom. For example, some cultures have specific instructions as to the food to be eaten or the types of clothing to be worn. It is important to make adjustments that allow these children to feel comfortable following the directives of their own culture.

Many states now require that children with impairments or from different countries be mainstreamed into the normal classroom.

Figure 22-13: These girls are using a resource to find the answer to their question together.

Figure 22-14: These caregivers and children are from different ethnic backgrounds.

Some of these children may need help to learn to communicate. Speaking slowly, using simple terms, and using gestures help to demonstrate meanings of directions or words. Patience and understanding on the part of caregivers and the other children is important as individual differences are assimilated or mainstreamed into the classroom.

SUMMARY

Effective classroom management includes well-defined guidelines and rules while allowing freedom for exploration and experimentation. Children are comfortable when they understand and are able to exhibit acceptable behavior. Safety factors are a prime consideration when establishing guidelines.

Specific instructions tell children what

to do instead of what not to do. They help to foster a cooperative attitude. When caregivers plan the environment, model expected behavior, and treat children with respect, they enable children to feel secure and confident.

Punishment is a penalty inflicted for unacceptable behavior or conduct. Discipline, on the other hand, is training in how to act within acceptable limits. It provides for instruction in proper conduct and action. Positive discipline methods set guidelines for children to follow that allow them to retain their self-esteem and feelings of worthiness.

Problem-solving techniques help children learn to settle conflicts and differences of opinion. The manner in which caregivers encourage compliance with instructions, such as making positive statements, leads children to understand what action is expected. Reinforcement is given when a task is completed.

Several methods can be used when misbehavior occurs. Deciding what motivated the behavior helps caregivers understand the problem and determine the proper method of discipline. Remaining calm, ignoring small offenses, using humor, redirecting children to new activities, stating expectations, and removing children from the situation are ways to encourage proper behavior. Time out is used for repeated offenses.

Meeting the individual needs of children is an aspect of caregiving that is essential to children's self-esteem. By encouraging pride in their cultures, we allow children to feel good about their heritages. When we incorporate cultural differences in the lesson plan, we help children learn that all people are important.

Review Questions

1. Why is it important to set guidelines?

2. Change the following into a positive statement:
   a. "Stop hitting!"
   b. "Don't run in the classroom!"
   c. "Stop playing!"
   d. "Don't yell!"
   e. "You are a bad girl! If you don't stop this minute, I'm going to tell your mother!"

3. Why is it better to discipline rather than to punish?

4. How do you role-model sharing?

5. Why is it important to not force a child to say "I'm sorry!"?

6. Why is it important to make a statement, rather than ask a question, when giving directions?

7. When do you give children a choice?

8. What are the seven discipline techniques?

9. How can the caregiver encourage autonomy when dealing with children?

10. What does the child learn when allowed to be creative?

11. Why is it important to remember the cultural backgrounds of the children when planning activities?

Things to Do and Discuss

1. While observing a classroom of school-age children, add any other appropriate rules to the list under Setting Guidelines. Explain your reasons for including these rules.

2. While observing that classroom, notice what problem-solving techniques are used by the teacher. How would you solve problems differently?

3. Make a list of common positive responses when talking to young children. Problems that warrant these replies are running in front of swings, loud voices in the classroom, throwing objects at another child, and tantrums.

4. Research aspects of the different heritages of the students in your class.

SECTION VI

OBJECTIVES

After completing this section, you will be able to:

1. prepare a lesson plan;
2. discuss areas of study;
3. plan activities for specific age groups.

Curriculum

Previously, you have learned the background information concerning child caregiving—job descriptions, types of programs, health and safety rules, and the ages and areas of child development. You should now have an idea about the group of children with whom you would like to work.

Now is the time to begin learning what to teach or how to provide a meaningful experience for young children. The enjoyment, creativity, and challenge of planning activities that stimulate learning are fun.

This section defines and discusses curriculum planning and ideas to help you prepare a creative atmosphere to enhance children physically, socially, emotionally, and intellectually. It points out to you the importance of appropriate materials and activities, easy ways to plan a lesson, ideas for specific occasions, and activities that will enable children and caregivers alike to have a sense of satisfaction and enjoyment of learning.

CHAPTER 23
Curriculum Areas

School-age children in an afterschool setting enjoying outdoor activities.

KEY TERMS

cadence
creative movement
creativity
fictional
language arts

music
nonfictional
pantomime
physical movement
social studies

OBJECTIVES

After completing this chapter, you will be able to:
1. describe the elements in the curriculum areas of arts and crafts, language arts, physical and creative movement, music, math, science, nutrition, and social studies;
2. plan activities in each area for a specific age group—infants and toddlers, preschoolers, and school-age children.

INTRODUCTION

This chapter includes a description of each curriculum area as it pertains to the separate age groups. When choosing curriculum materials, keep in mind the specific goals being taught.

THE IMPORTANCE OF CREATIVITY

Each child has the capacity to be creative. *Creativity* is defined as the act of bringing something into existence; to be inventive or imaginative. It can be displayed in any area of learning such as cognitive (art, music, language, math, science, social studies), physical (movement, exercising of muscles), social (role playing, cooperative play), or emotional (problem solving, dealing with feelings). The caregiver must define and encourage each child's innate creative talent while at the same time provide ample opportunities to expose the child to other areas of using the imagination. Listed below are some ways that the caregiver can use to encourage creativity:

1. Allow opportunities for the child to be a discoverer and inventor. Provide plenty of time and supplies in order for the child to experiment redesigning a new play corner, discovering a new game, or to collage a unique picture.

2. Allow the child the freedom of making decisions and of exploring the environment and materials provided. A child may decide to paint the cow green and the grass black, may construct a unique structure from blocks, or use a manipulative in a different manner than anticipated by the caregiver. If the creativity is safe and the child is not in danger, it is important that caregivers reinforce to the child that the work and the creativity accomplished is acceptable and has value.

3. Allow the child to make mistakes. The child learns other methods of problem solving when allowed to make mistakes without being criticized or misjudged ("You should have known better than to do it that way!" or "That was stupid!").

Rather, caregivers can encourage the child to recognize the mistake and then discuss together other ways to continue the project successfully ("How else could you construct the blocks?" or "Maybe you could try this method?").

4. Allow the child to set and attempt to fulfill self-setting goals. Goal setting can be fun and is a means of increasing the child's self-esteem. Any age child can be encouraged to try a new skill. A toddler may be invited to build a tower of four blocks. A preschooler may be asked to complete a craft project for Mother's Day that takes three days to accomplish. A school-age child might set a goal of learning the multiplication table. Caregivers help to enable the child to reach his goal by using positive reinforcement and describing their efforts; "You are working hard. You have written your five multiplication tables ten times."

5. Allow the child to be challenged. Caregivers can plan and initiate some activities that may be a little more difficult, thought provoking, or just plain tricky. Motivate the child to try the new task, but state that the task is challenging and may not be completed on the first attempt. "You almost did it. Keep trying!" "How else could you do the task?"

6. Allow time for questions and answers from both the caregiver and the child. Ask open-ended questions to encourage the child to be creative, to use imagination, and to expand his own knowledge. "What would happen if _____?," "Why

do you think it happened that way?," "In how many different ways can we do it?," or "Where could we find the answer to that question?" Actively listening to and answering the child's questions in an honest and concise manner gives the child a sense that the questions are important. Remember, one of the best ways for children to learn is by asking questions and discovering the answers. This method challenges the child to use his own mind and leads to building self-esteem.

7. Allow the child sufficient time to think and to share thoughts, feelings, or experiences. Often caregivers set aside a specific time to share, usually only fifteen minutes each day, and for the child to talk about experiences or something special brought from home. Although this is a great opportunity to learn language and to speak in front of a group, it should not take the place of active conversation throughout the day. During each activity, the child should be invited to talk about feelings concerning the project, suggestions on how we can make the project better, or similar experiences. It is important that caregivers watch, listen, and include the suggestions into the project when doing any creative activity. Allow children to experiment with new and different methods. When attempts of providing information are belittled or ignored, the child becomes discouraged, gives up trying, and will learn to just follow others' directions. This leads to lowering of self-esteem and feelings of unworthiness.

Creativity is fun. It allows the child to feel excitement and encourages self-discovery as each new task is learned and completed. The atmosphere and environment is enriched as one child's experiences are shared by others. It motivates the child to attempt other new tasks. Caregivers are also motivated to provide new and more challenging experiences for the child. Everyone grows and everyone learns.

ARTS AND CRAFTS

Art activities include projects that are imaginative, creative, self-expressive, and aesthetic. Art can be distinguished from crafts by how much personal thought and creativity are put into the project once the materials are presented.

Art

Infant and toddler art projects are kept very simple, with much repetition, such as making a picture using glue and paper. Preschoolers and school-age children may be involved in an art experience that includes many different materials and tools such as scissors, paper, glue, staples, paint, and painting implements.

In order to provide an art experience that is beneficial to children, caregivers should remember the following guidelines:

1. Allow children to do their own work. Do not complete or add to their art project.

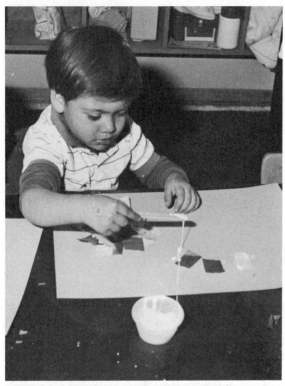

Figure 23-1: Different textures increase the enjoyment of making collages.

Figure 23-2: Toddlers enjoying a gross motor activity.

2. Allow sufficient time for the children to accomplish their goals so they can realize a sense of completion.

3. Be ready to lend support, interest, and praise for the work being done, but be careful not to interfere.

4. Display art projects frequently in order to give the children a sense that their efforts have value.

5. Eliminate the use of patterns for examples. Permit children to use their own imaginations and to be creative.

6. Experiment with the project and materials beforehand. This will allow you to become organized and help to solve any potential problems.

7. Gather all materials and equipment ahead of time. Childrens' attention spans are short and they get impatient if they are made to wait while you get ready.

8. Permit interested children to make more than one project.

9. Remember, the processes or the skills learned are more important than how the project looks when finished.

A variety of materials enhances creativity. Recyclable materials are inexpensive and fun to use. Listed below are basic art materials and examples of their uses:

- *Dough and clay.* See Figure 23-4 for dough and clay recipes. Variations include snow, sand, sawdust, wood chips, and mud. Children enjoy the feels and textures of natural and different materials. Allow them the pleasure of shaping and making snow figures, sand castles, and mud pies.

- *Drawing materials:* chalk (large and standard size), crayons, pencils, pens, and felt markers. Variations include chalk used on wet paper; wet chalk used on dry paper and sprayed with liquid starch; broken and different colored crayons that have been melted and poured into a variety of shapes, cooled, and used as rainbow crayons; crayon shavings sprinkled on waxed paper, covered with another layer of waxed paper and ironed carefully (crayons melt); paper placed on a warming tray (use the crayons carefully to color a picture (the crayons melt); different colored pencils, pens, or felt markers used while listening to a variety of music tempos, and crayon rubbings of items with interesting shapes or textures.

- *Paint:* watercolors, tempera, acrylics, oils, enamels. Variations include finger painting, sponge painting, object painting, drip painting, string painting, marble painting, easel painting, blot painting, soap suds painting, foot and hand painting, glitter painting, spatter painting, shaving cream painting, glue painting, straw painting, Q-tip painting, brush painting, cookie cutter painting, eyedropper painting, vegetable and fruit painting, squeeze bottle painting, roll-on deodorant bottle painting, salt or sand painting, printing with paint, and painting completed craft projects.

- *Paper:* computer, newsprint, wallpaper, cardboard, sticky, butcher, easel, construction, tissue, manila art paper, paper plates, coffee filters, poster board, paper bags, waxed paper, carbon.

Figure 23-3: This child is concentrating on her play dough activity.

Dough and Clay Recipes

Goal: The child will be able to experience tactile and sensory awareness to aid in the development of physical, social, emotional, and cognitive skills.

Basic Play Dough Recipe

4 cups flour
1 cup salt
6 tablespoons powdered paint tempera, or a
    few drops of food coloring
6 tablespoons oil
1 3/4 cups water

Mix together the flour and salt. In a separate container, mix together the oil and water. Add either the powdered paint tempera to the dry mixture or food coloring to the wet mixture.

Add the water mixture slowly to the dry mixture and knead it in with your fingers until it feels like bread dough and does not stick to your fingers. During wet weather, less water may be needed; during dry weather, more water may be needed.

Velvet or Cooked Play Dough

4 cups flour
2 cups salt
8 tablespoons cream of tartar
1/4 cup oil
4 cups water
several drops of food coloring

(Velvet or cooked play dough continued)

Mix together the flour, salt, and cream of tartar. In a separate container, mix together the oil, water, and food coloring. Add the wet mixture to the dry mixture.

Cook over low heat, stirring constantly, until the mixture is the right consistency and shiny (about two minutes). This may be cooked in an electric skillet or on the stove.

Glob

1 cup cornstarch
1/4 cup water

Mix them together and enjoy the feel!

Silly Putty

white glue
liquid starch

Mix together equal parts of white glue and liquid starch. Store the mixture in an airtight container. Children enjoy the fun of stretching and pulling this mixture.

Figure 23-4: Dough and Clay Recipes.

Figure 23-5: Toddlers enjoy finger painting with shaving creme.

Figure 23-6: Gluing a collage together can be fun and creative.

Collage

This is a self-expressive art medium. It is a technique of pasting or gluing a variety of materials onto a single surface. Young children can become aware of and combine innumerable materials together to produce a final product. These materials help to build recognition of colors, textures, substance, and design. They are often free and found around the school or home. Following are examples of some of these materials:

- aluminum pie pans
- boxes
- buttons, beads

- construction paper scraps
- different types of paper—cards, labels, gift wrappings, cardboard, paper plates
- eggshells
- fabric materials, trimmings, notions
- magazines
- natural materials—bark, cones, leaves, dried flowers, seeds
- newspapers
- packing materials

- plastic bottles
- rug scraps
- soda straws
- string, ribbon, yarn, wire
- styrofoam trays
- toilet paper rolls, paper towel rolls
- toothpicks
- wood shavings, scraps

Woodworking

Woodworking can be introduced when working with older children (preschool and school-age) provided the area is well-supervised. Basic woodworking tools should be child size (not toy replicas) and include hammers, cross-cut saws, coping saws, screwdrivers, nails, screws, C clamps, rulers, and pencils. It is also important that a sturdy table or workbench be provided. Enough elbow room for each child is necessary to prevent crowding and accidents. Wood scraps from the local lumber yard can often be obtained free of charge.

Children enjoy hammering into styrofoam, plasterboard, or wood chunks and making their own creations. This exercise provides good eye-hand coordination as well as a chance to experiment with tools.

Crafts

Crafts are usually teacher-oriented projects. These items have a specific set of instructions and a specific product. Crafts are often initiated for holiday gifts and household items. There is less self-expression and creativity on the part of the children.

Figure 23-7: Girls enjoying their painting projects.

Figure 23-8: School-age children sometimes need assistance with craft projects.

Art Samples

Goal: The children will learn to use their imaginations to develop their creative skills and to make decisions.

Toddlers

Art: Paper collage
Materials: Glue, colorful paper

Allow the children to tear paper into different shapes and sizes, then glue pieces onto another paper. This sheet can be of a particular color or shape, depending on your goal for the lesson. The project is good for eye-hand coordination, small motor skills, following directions, feeling different textures, shape or color recognition, and self-esteem building.

Preschoolers

Art: Patriotic finger painting
Materials: Red, white, and blue paint; liquid starch; large piece of butcher paper; record of patriotic songs

Children are to finger paint with one or all of the colors onto the paper as they listen to the different tempos of the music.

Observe if they paint fast, slow, hard, or easy as they listen to the record. This project teaches listening skills, rhythm, touch, and colors, and it builds self-esteem. If the children all paint together on one large sheet of butcher paper, the activity can also teach social skills.

School-Age Children

Art: Wood sculpture
Materials: Wood blocks of different sizes, hammers, nails, saws, rulers, pencils

Children are to create their own designs by using the materials provided. This project teaches eye-hand coordination, creativity, social skills, and proper use of tools and materials. Children may be asked to first design their projects on paper, as well as list the materials needed and the procedures that will be used. This additional step will teach organizational and writing skills.

Figure 23-9: Art Samples.

Craft Samples

Goal: The children will be able to increase listening skills, improve fine motor skills, and to follow specific directions.

Toddlers

Craft: Child's handprint
Materials: Plaster of Paris, water, pie tin, ribbon or yarn, pencil

To make handprints of children, mix together the plaster of Paris and water to a stiff consistency. The amount of water

(continued on next page)

depends on the weather. Less water is needed on wet days than on dry days.

Pour the mixture into an aluminum pie plate and have a child press a hand into the mixture. Use a thick pencil to make a hole at the top of the plate (this will allow a ribbon to be threaded through the hole after the plaster has dried). Let the children choose the color of ribbon. This is an ideal Mother's or Father's Day gift. Children are learning to follow directions, listen, make decisions, feel a different texture, and think of others.

Preschoolers

Craft: See-through screen
Materials: Twenty-four-inch long pieces of waxed paper, collage materials, a warm iron, liquid starch, construction paper strips about three inches wide, stapler, and eighteen inches of string, yarn, or ribbon

Children may collect flowers, tear tissue paper, or do something that is visual from two sides. Have the children fold the whole piece of waxed paper in half (the paper is now twelve inches long) and arrange their items as they please. Drizzle a small amount of liquid starch (about two tablespoons) around the items. Place an eighteen-inch piece of yarn across the top and tie a knot.

Staple the construction strips to top and bottom of the screen. Iron with a warm iron. Place the screen in a window. Children will learn to listen, follow directions, make decisions and enjoy creating something to give to others.

School-age Children

Craft: Wind chimes
Materials: Plastic container (from butter or sour cream) or small shoe box, heavy string or fine wire (one piece that is two feet long and several ten-inch pieces), scissors, masking tape, assorted small metal pieces (bottle caps, nails, screws, washers, juice can lids, etc.), marking pens, stickers, glitter, construction paper, and glue for decoration

Poke four holes in the bottom of the container equal distances from the sides and each other. Thread two feet of string through the holes, tying the ends together at the top.

Allow the children to decorate the sides of the container as they please. Poke as many holes as there are small metal pieces around the open end of the container (equal distances from each other). Tie a ten-inch piece of string in each hole. Tape or tie small metal pieces to the other end of the string. Pieces should be balanced by weight so that they will hit each other. Hang where the wind will gently blow. Enjoy the sound!

Figure 23-10: Craft Samples.

Figure 23-11: *Looking at books is a favorite pasttime of the preschooler.*

Figure 23-12: *Dressing up and acting out dramas stimulate school-age children.*

LANGUAGE ARTS

Language arts is defined in this text as any means of communication through speech, reading, story telling, and sign or body language. Language arts can be used to teach concepts such as numbers, shapes, letters, and phonics or for problem solving and enjoyment.

Storytelling

The art of storytelling is one way of communicating with children. Telling a story to children, *fictional* (invented) or *nonfictional* (true), using details about them to add suspense, animation, and interest, is an enjoyable method of teaching. Pictures or other materials can enhance the experience.

For example, on a rainy day caregivers can begin a story with one or two sentences, "One morning, a boy named Tino fell into a puddle on his way to school." Let each child add a unique response to the narrative. The same story can always have a different ending —silly, sad, or happy. The caregiver can then highlight aspects of the story that relate directly to the children's own lives. This exercise helps to develop memory, listening, sequencing, grammatical, imaginative, and creative skills.

School-age children especially enjoy creating their own stories. They may be given a theme such as bees swarming, or paper airplanes, or a trip to the zoo and be asked to write a story with a beginning, a middle, and a conclusion. Additionally, caregivers can provide important, relative words to be included (perhaps spelling words). Pictures may also be drawn (in place of words) for a variation.

When telling or reading a story to young children, remember:

1. Choose a story or book according to the unit of study whenever possible.

2. Prepare the story or read the book beforehand to familiarize yourself with the plot.

3. Position the children on the floor or in chairs in front of you, making sure that all can see before you begin to tell or read the story.

4. Explain to the children that we look with our eyes, listen with our ears, and keep our mouths quiet so as to not bother others during a story.

5. Hold the book upright, with the pages facing the group to ensure clear visibility for the children.

6. Read and talk clearly, loud enough to be heard, and with expression (use different voices for each character and emotions when appropriate).

7. Appear interested in the plot, the pictures, and the outcome of the story.

8. Include children's names and belongings to add personal interest.

9. Ask simple questions at the end of the story to check recall and understanding.

10. Do not be discouraged if the story is not well received by the children. The best of stories can sometimes flop. Cut short a poorly received story and try it again later using a revised edition.

Figure 23-13: A picture story.

Setting goals when choosing a story is important. What is the purpose of the story? What will the children learn? When telling the story, keep in mind the goals that were set. At the conclusion, did the story accomplish the goals expected?

An example of goal setting has been done for the story *The Big, Big, Turnip*. Possible goals include:

- acting out the pulling up of the turnip

- identifying animals and sounds

- identifying the turnip as a vegetable

- memorizing the sequence of the story (recall skills)

- reciting as a group

- understanding that everyone working together helps to accomplish a common goal

Books

The selection of books is fun. Today, books are pleasing to the eye, plentiful, and varied. They fit all age groups and interest areas. When choosing books for the classroom, be aware of the age and developmental level of the children in the group. Avoid books that stereotype people and events or depict idealistic and unrealistic daily activities. Books must be of interest, relate to normal circumstances, and allow for imagination and fantasy. They must also be available at any time of the day.

Books for Infants and Toddlers

Books are a welcome addition to the daily curriculum for infants and toddlers. Their attention span is short, so books with very few words, few pages, and large, colorful illustrations are most appropriate. Telling the story instead of reading the words captures the children's attention more readily. It is wise to have a small group (one to five children) when reading so that you will not disrupt others who are busy.

Stories about items with which children are familiar are best. Children enjoy naming the items and talking about their own possessions that are similar. A sample of an infant or toddler book is shown in Figure 23-15.

Listed below are books that infants and toddlers enjoy:

- *Babies, Babies, Babies* by Kathy Welburn, Golden Press
- *Egg in the Hole Book* by Richard Scarry, A Golden Book
- *The Five Senses: A Tasting Party, What Your Nose Knows, The Look Book, Sounds All Around, The Touch Book* by Jane Belk Moncure, Children's Press
- *Friends* by Helen Oxenbury, Wonder Books
- *Goodnight Moon* by Margaret Wise Brown, Harper & Row
- *I Am a Little Cat* by Helmut Spanner, Barron's Press
- *Once Upon a Potty* by Alona Frankel, Barron's Press
- *1, 2, 3 to the Zoo* by Eric Carle, Philomel Books
- *Play with Me* by Mercer Mayer, Golden Press
- *Teddy Bear Plays in Water* by Helmut Spanner, Price/Stern/Sloan

Books for Preschoolers

Children between the ages of two and five are beginning to enjoy actual stories with characters. Because their attention span has increased, they need books that are longer. A story time can average ten to twenty minutes. Illustrations that are clear and easy to see are best for group reading. One or more books may be read, depending on the interest of the children.

Preschoolers tend to have favorite stories and may request the same book several days in a row. Repetition is important, as children are beginning their prereading skills. Checking children's understanding and recall skills at the end of the book should be part of story reading.

Listed below books that are appropriate to read and discuss with preschool children:

- *A Book of Seasons* by Alice and Martin Provensen
- *Chickens Aren't the Only Ones* by Ruth Heller, Grosset & Dunlap
- *Dinosaurs—A True Book Series* by Mary Lou Clark, Children's Press
- *Dreams* by Peter Spier, Doubleday
- *For Sale: One Sister—Cheap!* by Katie Alder and Rachael McBride, Children's Press
- *The Four Elements: Air, Earth, Fire, Water* by Maria Rius and J. M. Parramon, Barron's Press
- *I Was So Mad!* by Norma Simon, Albert Whitman & Co.
- *The Honeybee and the Robber, The Very Busy Bee* by Eric Carle, Philomel Books
- *Make Way for Ducklings* by Robert McCloskey, Puffin Books
- *The Land of Colors* retold by Margaretta Lundell, Grosset & Dunlap
- *Peter's Chair* by Ezra Jack Keats, Harper & Row
- *Sleepy Bear* by Linda Dabcovich
- *Thomas' Snowsuit* by Robert Munsch
- *The Trouble with Mom, The Trouble with Dad* by Babette Cole, Coward-McCann, Inc.

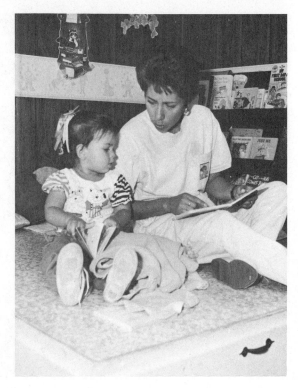

Figure 23-14: The caregiver is reading to a toddler.

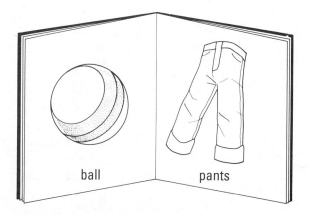

ball   pants

Figure 23-15: Infant and toddler picture book.

Figure 23-16: Reading together is fun and exciting for school-age children.

Books for School-age Children

These children are capable of reading to themselves, but they enjoy group reading occasionally. Caregivers can read chapters or selections from a long book, carrying over portions to another day, or each child can take a turn at reading a section to the rest of the children.

Older children enjoy stories with a plot, characters, and a firm conclusion. They like to read both fiction and nonfiction. Caregivers can display reading materials that are varied in subject matter and appropriate for the age. Children can then make their own selections for the classroom. Reading ability improves when children are interested in the subject. Comprehension, spelling, vocabulary, and listening skills are increased with reading competence.

Caregivers can provide reading time and materials in a program before and after school. Weekly trips to the local library and

Figure 23-17: Young children enjoy looking at the pictures in a book.

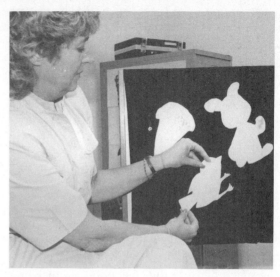

Figure 23-18: A flannel story is a fun method of encouraging recall skills.

challenging projects such as reading awards, book clubs, and word games can induce children to find and share good reading materials.

Books that will interest school-age children are:

- *Charlie and the Chocolate Factory* by Roald Dahl, Knopf

- *Charlotte's Web* by E. B. White, Harper & Row

- *The Happy Lion* by Louise Satio, McGraw-Hill

- *Huckleberry Finn* by Samuel Clemens, Raintree

- *It's Like This, Cat* by Emily Cheney Neville, Harper & Row

- *Johnny-Cake* by Joseph Jacobs, Viking Press

- *Little Bear's Visit—An I Can Read Book* by Else Holmelund Minarik, Harper & Row

- *One Fine Day* by Nancy Hogrogian, Macmillan

- *Stone Soup* by Marsha Brown, Scribner

- *The Velveteen Rabbit* by Margery Bianca, Holt, Rinehart & Winston

- *Where the Red Fern Grows* by Wilson Rawls, Doubleday

- *Why Does It Rain?* by National Geographic

Flannel Board Stories

Another interesting way to tell stories is to use the flannel board. Familiar stories such as nursery tales or special stories made for the flannel board can be used. Individual pieces of material depicting characters or scenery are made of felt, poplin, pellon, scraps of material, or construction paper. They are placed on a board that is covered by flannel. The pieces can be colored and detailed or can be silhouettes. Flannel and pellon will stick to the board, but other materials are often backed with small pieces of flannel or sandpaper to allow them to adhere to the board.

Children can participate in the story by holding a piece until it is time to place it on the board. This allows children to become a part of the story. It can help to increase their self-esteem because they feel good about being given a portion or piece of the story. Depending on the story, children often recite rhythmic lyrics, make sounds like the animals, or change the endings to suit themselves.

The learning possibilities from one flannel story are numerous. The children can see and hear the story, feel the pieces, speak the words, memorize the story line, and discuss their feelings about the outcome of the story. They can increase their vocabulary, enjoy the repetition, practice the rhythm, recall the sequence of characters and events, and be creative when they use the pieces to develop their own story line.

Stories for Infants and Toddlers

When presenting a flannel story to very young children, remember to keep it simple. Use very few pieces, tell the story instead of reading it from a book, and let the children participate by placing the pieces onto the board. Instead of a story, simple shapes, colors, or objects can be placed on the board and caregivers can discuss each piece with the children.

An example story for toddlers may be farm animals—mothers and babies. Caregivers can explain the animal names, food, sounds, and homes. The discussion can lead to talking about their own families and homes.

Stories for Preschoolers

As with books, preschool children enjoy a longer story, with characters, action, and more vocabulary. They often become involved with the theme and sometimes interject their own feelings about the characters and the conclusion.

Several excellent flannel stories for preschoolers are *The Big, Big Turnip, It Looks Like Spilt Milk,* and *The Runaway Cookies.* These are not only fun to share but they also can be told repeatedly without boring the children.

Stories for School-age Children

Children at this age would rather make and tell their own stories than listen to one that is already prepared. This lesson plan can be included in arts and crafts projects. Let children plan and make the pieces to be used on the flannel board. Often two or three children can work together to prepare one story. This encourages the sharing of ideas. When each child plays a specific character, the quieter child participates.

Finger Plays

A language arts activity that is usually performed for infants, toddlers, and preschoolers is the finger play. With the use of words

Figure 23-19: Child enjoying finger plays.

and actions together, the caregiver can tell a short story by using hand and body motions. These stories are customarily done in a rhyme format that is easy for children to remember. Finger plays are created to increase vocabulary, develop a positive self-concept, learn repetition, teach facts, develop gross and fine motor skills, and to release energy as the children participate in the story. Finger plays can be set to music, and they are fun to sing.

Caregivers need to practice and learn the finger plays well before attempting them with the children. It is best to have them memorized for maximum enjoyment and learning to occur. Since most are short, this is easily accomplished. Children often like to have the finger plays repeated many times, and this helps to increase their recall.

Finger Plays

Goal: The children will increase math and science concepts, recall skills, and fine motor development.

Ten Red Apples (Math and Science Concepts)

Ten red apples grow on a tree (both hands high),
Five for you and five for me (dangle one hand and then the other).
Let us shake the tree just so (shake body),
And then the red apples will fall below (hands fall).
1, 2, 3, 4, 5, 6, 7, 8, 9, 10, (count each finger).

Little Brown Seed (Science Concept)

I'm a little brown seed in the ground,
Rolled up in a tiny ball! (sitting on heels on the floor, drop head over knees).
I'll wait for the rain and sunshine (in the same position, place arms over head and wiggle fingers downward for rain, then place both hands in large circle overhead for sun)
To make me big and tall (stand straight, stretching hands over head).

(continued on next page)

Figure 23-20: Finger plays.

Here Is the Beehive (Math and Science Concepts)

Here is the beehive (make a fist).
Where are the bees?
They're hiding away so nobody sees.
Soon they'll come creeping out of their hive,
One, two, three, four, five. Bzzzzzzzzz
(draw fingers out of fist on each count, have
all fingers bzzz in circle in front of the child).

Five Little Monkeys Sitting in a Tree (Math and Science Concepts)

Five little monkeys sitting in a tree (hold
up hand with fingers spread),
Teasing Mr. Crocodile, "You can't catch me!
You can't catch me!" (shake finger back
and forth to say no).
Along came Mr. Crocodile as quietly as can
be (use other hand, fingers become mouth
of crocodile).
Snap that monkey right out of that tree (have
crocodile grab one finger, bend finger down)!

Four little monkeys sitting in a tree (hold
up four fingers),
Teasing Mr. Crocodile, "You can't catch me!
You can't catch me!"

(Five Little Monkeys continued)

Along came Mr. Crocodile as quietly as
can be.
Snap that monkey right out of that tree!
Three little monkeys sitting in a tree (hold
up three fingers),
Teasing Mr. Crocodile, "You can't catch me!
You can't catch me!"
Along came Mr. Crocodile as quietly as
can be.
Snap that monkey right out of that tree!

Two little monkeys sitting in a tree (hold
up two fingers),
Teasing Mr. Crocodile, "You can't catch me!
You can't catch me!"
Along came Mr. Crocodile as quietly as
can be.
Snap that monkey right out of that tree!

One little monkey sitting in a tree (hold up
one finger),
Teasing Mr. Crocodile, "You can't catch me!
You can't catch me!"
Along came Mr. Crocodile as quietly as
can be.
Snap that monkey right out of that tree!

No more monkeys sitting in a tree.
Along came Mr. Crocodile as full as he could
be (put arms in circle in front of stomach).

Figure 23-20   continued

Finger plays can be found in many books, created from nursery rhymes, or made up by creative caregivers. Figure 23-20 contains some of the favorites for children.

Puppets

Puppets are another visual way of expressing oneself and of telling a story. Children who are too timid, shy, or fearful to express themselves generally feel more comfortable talking to or with a puppet. They may be willing to let the puppet say and do things that they would not do themselves. (They often forget that the adult is nearby and talk directly to the puppet itself.)

By making the puppets, children frequently feel more closely involved. Puppets are generally divided into three large groups—shadow, string, and hand puppets.

Hand or Glove Puppets

The hand or glove puppet is the simplest and most easily manipulated by young children. It can be made into any type of character or animal. The hand can readily slip inside the puppet constructed of materials to form a head and body. This allows freedom of movement and creativity. The puppet may assume any position or attitude that the children and caregivers desire.

Shadow Puppets

The shadow puppet is made of translucent materials such as thin leather or paper and then mounted on a stick. The puppet is held close behind a transparent screen, and a light behind throws the shadow onto the screen.

Figure 23-21: Puppets are another form of storytelling.

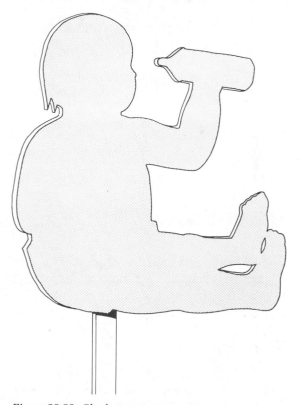

Figure 23-22: Shadow puppet.

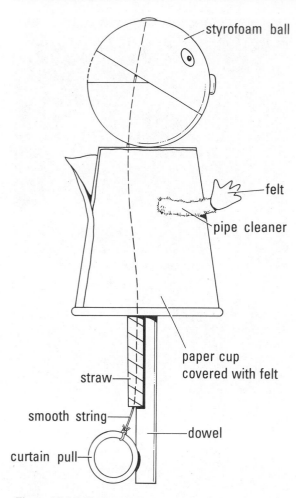

Figure 23-23: String puppet.

The audience sees only the shadow. This type of puppet is limited in movement, being able to move only from left to right and right to left across the stage.

String Puppets

The string puppet, or marionette, is a doll joined together with movable head, arms, and legs. It is manipulated by strings mounted to a board and controlled by one person. This is a good puppet for older children to work with, but it takes considerable practice. Care must be taken that the strings do not become entangled or break.

Puppets to Make

Children of all ages from infants through school age enjoy puppetry. They can create their own simple puppets. Several examples of easy-to-make puppets follow:

- *Finger puppets.* Cut construction paper or material approximately three inches long. Put it around a finger and tape it on. Draw a figure or face. Let the fingers be used as legs.

- *Paper bag puppets.* Draw or cut out a figure or face from paper and glue it to the bottom of the bag. Turn the bag so that the fold is at the top. Use the fold as the mouth of the puppet.

- *Sock puppets.* Use an old, thick sock. Turn it inside out and cut around the edges of the toe (about three inches on each side). This will become the mouth. Fold the material inside the open part of the sock and sew each section, one to the top and the other to the bottom. Turn the sock right side out and sew on the features.

- *Stick puppets.* Attach a picture or an object to a stick.

Role-Playing

Children role-play when they act out fantasies, emotional situations, and use their imaginations to solve problems. Role-playing

Figure 23-24: Hand puppet.

Figure 23-25: Paper bag puppet.

Figure 23-27: Stick puppets.

a)

b)

c)

d)

e)

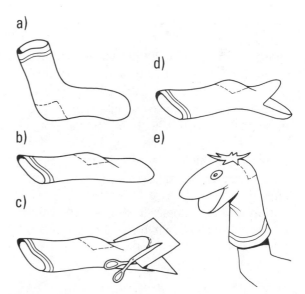

Figure 23-26: Sock puppet.

Figure 23-28: Finger puppets.

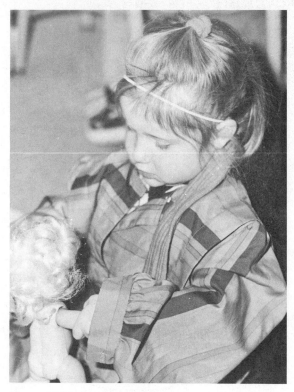

Figure 23-29: Preschool child engaging in symbolic play.

can be performed in the housekeeping corner, in the block area, on the playground, or anywhere in the classroom. Caregivers can observe children when role-playing in order to learn more about how they feel and think.

Role-playing is also a good opportunity to introduce children to new situations. Setting up a restaurant or office in the housekeeping area, transforming a large box into a fire engine, or transforming a dome climbing structure into a teepee allows children to be creative and practice how it feels to be a part of a new environment.

Drama

Plays, skits, *pantomime* (a play where performers express themselves without words), and dramatic readings are all under the title of drama. Drama can be as simple as preschoolers acting out a flannel story or as involved as school-age children putting on a play with props, costumes, and lines to memorize.

Drama is as effective way to work through emotions, dispel shyness, and encourage imagination. It also helps children to develop speech, think creatively, listen, memorize, make decisions, and interact.

Caregivers can promote opportunities for drama by keeping the following guidelines in mind:

1. Accept all imaginative acts. Remain

close, yet do not interfere except when necessary.

2. Encourage all children to participate.

3. Encourage children for their efforts and participation, yet do not tease or belittle them when they are reluctant to join. There will always be another drama in which they may feel like participating.

4. Familiarize children with the story so that they are aware of what happens in the beginning, middle, and end.

5. Keep props and scenery simple. Let the children create props and scenery.

Some familiar classics that are enjoyable to act out are *The Three Little Pigs, Little Red Riding Hood, Three Billy Goats Gruff, Goldilocks and the Three Bears, The Gingerbread Man,* and *The Big, Big, Turnip.*

PHYSICAL AND CREATIVE MOVEMENT

Physical movement is the use of the body as it moves either in place or from one area to another. How the child moves his body, gross and fine motor skills combined with imagination, is *creative movement*

Movement is the way young children express themselves before their ability to use words is fully developed. Infants and toddlers learn about space and movement as they creep and crawl around a room searching for objects that attract them. Preschoolers progress to walking, balancing, kicking, skipping, hopping, running, and climbing as they gain confidence about their abilities. School-age children develop more sophisticated movements as they refine the physical skills they learned earlier.

Within every curriculum area (arts and crafts, language arts, music, math, science, social studies), there is a degree of movement involved. When planning physical activities, establish primary goals (body awareness, spatial awareness, gross and fine motor development, and creative movement), while keeping in mind the other areas of development.

Games that encourage concept learning combined with physical activity include name it games, Simon says, and the hokey pokey, all of which may include the naming of body parts. These games are fun and still provide opportunities to practice different movements of each

Figure 23-30: Children engaging in a creative movement activity.

part of the body. Other games can encourage the children to use their imaginations as they demonstrate how they would move if asked, for example, "Show me what part of your body you would use if you were a bird flying. How does it feel to fly? Close your eyes and pretend you are flying."

Some games to play with children to encourage cooperation, to wait for turns, and to practice gross motor activities include:

- *For Infants and Toddlers:* Doggy, doggy, where's your bone?, ring around the rosies, follow the leader, and who's got the button?

- *For Preschoolers:* Duck, duck, goose; musical chairs; Mother, may I?; Simon says; red light, green light; cookie jar; tisket, tasket, green and yellow basket; bean bag toss; and hot potato.

- *For School-age Children:* Hide and seek, relay races, snake in the grass, leapfrog, twenty questions, concentration, tag, twister, heads up, 7-up, statue, jump rope, and organized sports.

Movement in a Confined Space

Games in which the children remain fairly stationary or move just in place can include exercises such as bending, stretching, pushing, pulling, turning, twisting, shaking, balancing, and bouncing. Ask questions of the children as they practice gross and fine motor activities:

1. Can you add another small part and move them both at the same time?

2. Can you make just one small part of you move?

3. Can you rub your tummy and pat your head?

4. Can you touch the sky?

5. How does a dog settle down to sleep?

6. How does your body move when the wind blows?

7. How would you pick up something that is very heavy? Very light? Very big? Very delicate?

You may wish to add the dimension of partners or small groups to the activities in the lesson.

Movement from Place to Place

Within a given space, children can do creative movement activities that help them follow directions (forward, backward, sideways, up and down), pathways (zigzag, straight, curved), and tempo (fast, medium, slow). Demonstrating force (light, strong), and spatial awareness (near, far, in front of, behind, over, under, next to, between) are other activities. Music can be added for additional enjoyment. Movement can be stimulated by the following types of questions:

1. As you travel around the room, can you move very high? very low? very fast? very slow?

2. Can you move like a bunny? bear? elephant? kangaroo? frog?

3. How do you move in the rain?

4. How do you move when you are angry? happy? scared? sad?

5. How does a pony gallop? trot? prance?

MUSIC

Songs, dance, rhythm, creative movement, and instruments are all included under the curriculum area of music. *Music* can be defined as a sequence of sounds that are pleasing to the ear and satisfying to the emotions. In the classroom, music is shared for creative expression, singing, group activities, relaxation, socialization, and enjoyment. Caregivers can freely adapt music to fit most daily situations. Figure 23-33 illustrates several musical activities. Music can also be included at meals, at rest time, for gaining the class's attention, or for any indoor or outdoor activity.

Rhythm

Rhythmic experiences provide opportunities for children to express themselves through the use of their bodies. Rhythmic experiences help to develop coordination and listening skills. As children begin to recognize a pattern or order to the music, they can clap their hands, play instruments, or move their bodies in time to the music.

Include variations in music, such as fast, slow, soft, and loud. Vary the *cadence* (beat) to encourage body movements that suggest leaping, hopping, skipping or tiptoeing. Use different instruments (drum, bell, triangle) to inspire the children to use gross or fine motor skills.

It is fun to be creative with these exercises and allow the children to add their own ideas. They can use their bodies as instruments by clapping, snapping fingers, tapping feet, whistling, and patting legs.

Figure 23-31: The toddlers are enjoying their musical instruments.

Songs

Songs to sing or to be heard on a record or tape aid listening and memory, repetition, language, and movement skills. Songs should be chosen with care, performed in a comfortable singing range, be appropriate for the age, and have easily remembered words and melodies. Children often like to create their own songs, and they should be encouraged to do so. This helps to stimulate creative abilities and free expression.

Songs that are generally enjoyed by children are listed below. Remember that repetition of favorites and the addition of new verses increase the pleasure.

Figure 23-32: Toddlers enjoy using instruments.

Songs for Infants and Toddlers

Infants and toddlers enjoy the following songs:

- How Much Is That Doggy in the Window?
- Hush, Little Baby
- Itzy Bitzy Spider
- London Bridge's Falling Down
- Mary Had a Little Lamb
- Patty Cake
- Ring Around the Rosies
- This Little Piggy
- This Old Man
- Where Is Thumbkin?

Songs for Preschoolers

Preschoolers enjoy the following songs:

- Alphabet Song
- B.I.N.G.O.
- Farmer in the Dell
- Hokey Pokey
- If You're Happy and You Know It

Music Activities

Goal: The children will be able to increase recall skills, language, rhythm, rhyming, movement, and motor skills.

For Taking Attendance

Caregiver: Where is Michael? Where is Michael?

Child: Here I am. Here I am.

Caregiver: How are you today, sir?

Child: Very well. I thank you.

Caregiver: I'm glad you're here. I'm glad you're here.

For Introducing a New Student

Caregiver: My name is Mrs. Jones, and what's your name?

Child: My name is Victoria, and what's your name?

Next Child: My name is Tino, and what's your name?

Continue until everyone has had a turn to say their name.

Figure 23-33: Music Activities chart.

- Oh, Suzanna
- Old MacDonald Had a Farm
- People on the Bus
- Pop! Goes the Weasel
- Ten Little Indians
- You Are My Sunshine

Figure 23-34: Children enjoy clapping and marching to their favorite tunes.

Figure 23-35: A child paints to music.

Songs for School-age Children

School-age children enjoy the following songs:

- America
- Bringing Home a Baby Bumble Bee
- Do Your Ears Hang Low
- John Jacob Jingleheimer Smith
- I've Been Working on the Railroad
- Home, Home on the Range
- Let's Go on a Bear Hunt
- My Bonnie Lies over the Ocean
- The Old Lady Who Ate the Fly
- She'll Be Coming Around the Mountain
- When the Animals Get up in the Morning

Instruments

Simple instruments can be used to accompany music time. These may be either bought or handmade. Drums, triangles, shakers, rhythm sticks, bells, tambourines, and sandpaper blocks lend themselves to the enjoyment and learning of young children.

Depending on the ability of the caregiver, piano, guitar, or autoharp can be used to supply the melody and the beat of the music. Children may pick up the rhythm or beat using their own instruments. If desired, creative movements may be added.

Records and Tapes

There are many excellent records and

Figure 23-36: Dancing is a fun and healthy activity for school-age children.

tapes that can be played to encourage musical ability, concept learning, creative movement, or gross and fine motor development. Records and tapes also can be played to fit the mood of the classroom. Not only activity and singing records and tapes should be played but also classical music to enhance the children's appreciation. Children's records are available through catalogues and in music and school supply stores.

Records and Tapes for Infants and Toddlers

Infants and toddlers enjoy the following records and tapes:

- "Babysong," "Learning Basic Skills Through Music" (Volume 1), and "Ticky Toodle" by Hap Palmer
- "I'm Not Small" by Marcia Berman and Patty Zetlin

- "We All Live Together" (Volume 1) by Steve Millang and Greg Scelsa

Records and Tapes for Preschoolers

Preschoolers enjoy the following records and tapes:

- "Dance-a-Story, Sing-a-Song" by Anne Lief Barlin and Marcia Berman

- "Everybody Cries Sometimes," "Won't You Be My Friend," and "Spin, Spider, Spin" by Marcia Berman and Patty Zetlin

- "Free to Be You and Me" by Marlo Thomas and Friends

- "I Know the Colors in the Rainbow" and "Early, Early Childhood Songs" by Ella Jenkins

- "Learning Basic Skills Through Music" (Volume II—Health and Safety—and Volume V—Building Vocabulary) "Sea Gulls," "Pretend," "Getting to Know Myself," "The Feel of Music," "Movin'," and "Easy Does it" by Hap Palmer

- "Rainy Day Dances, Rainy Day Songs" by Marcia Berman and Patty Zetlin with Anne Barlin

Records and Tapes for School-age Children

School-age children enjoy listening to the following records and tapes:

- All current pop rock, folk music, and square dance records. (Listen to the words on the record or tape to ensure acceptable language.)

- "Dancing Words" (Reinforcing Reading and Language Skills Through Music and Movement) by Rosemary Hallum, Ph.D., and Henry Glass, with Edith Hom Newhart

- "Hopping Around from Place to Place" (Volumes 1 and 2) by Ella Jenkins

- "Math Readiness—Addition and Subtraction" and "Singing Multiplication Tables" (from the twos through the twelves) by Hap Palmer

MATH

Is it realistic to teach math concepts to infants and toddlers? If you said yes, your answer is correct. They begin to learn math skills as they touch a round ball, lift a heavy toy, and watch a shape mobile dance in the air.

As children grow and develop concepts such as matching, sorting, sequencing, space, and time, the concepts become a natural part of their day. Matching one shoe with its mate after naps, sorting toy cars and tucks, counting fingers while doing finger plays, crawling around and under the table, and becoming aware that snacks come after outside play are math concepts.

By providing simple games and manipulatives, caregivers help encourage these skills. Pegboards, counting beads, matching cards, and toys of different colors, sizes, and shapes also add practice and reinforcement. Ask how many and what shape it is. Use words that depict size and quantity, such as *big, little, some, more,* or *less.* Following are some examples of math curriculum found in the classroom.

Math for Infants and Toddlers

Infants and toddlers enjoy:

- counting napkins for snacks
- finger plays that include numbers
- matching shapes
- sorting colored blocks into separate piles

Math for Preschoolers

Preschoolers enjoy:

- *Counting Cards.* Using two pieces of rectangular tagboard, write the numeral 4 on one and draw four colored dots on the other (a third piece could be added later with the word *four* printed). Make a set for numbers 0 through 9. Have the children match the appropriate cards.

- Cutting food servings in halves, fourths, and eighths

- Making shapes with pegs on pegboards or with rubber bands on a nail board

- *Matching the Numbers.* Using an 8½″ × 11″ piece of tagboard, draw numbers and pictures of articles to match. Tie shoe laces to the left side next to the numbers and punch holes into the board next to the pictures on the right side. Children thread the lace next to the appropriate picture.

- Playing color, shape, or number bingo

- Putting together puzzles with shaped pieces

Figure 23-37: The children are concentrating as they try their skills at a matching game.

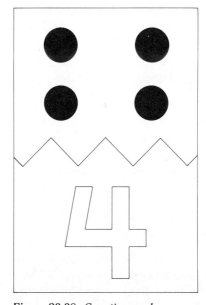

Figure 23-38: Counting cards.

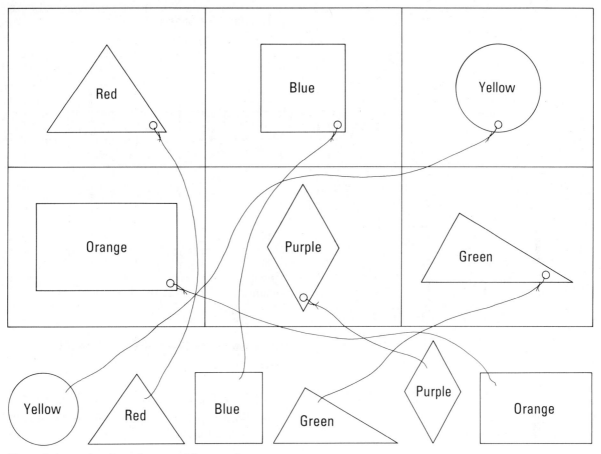

Thread the string into the matching card.

Figure 23-39: Matching game.

Math for School-age Children

School-age children enjoy:

- Algebra
- The apple tree game. Each apple tree has a numeral on its trunk. Students make an many addition, subtraction, multiplication, and division combinations as they can to match the answer on the trunk.

- Geometry
- *Graphs.* Place one thermometer inside the classroom and one outside the door. Have each child graph the daily temperature. What is the difference from one day to the next? What is the difference between the temperatures inside and outside? What is the difference between Fahrenheit and Celsius temperatures?

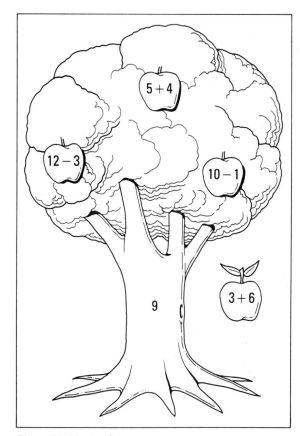

Figure 23-40: Apple tree game.

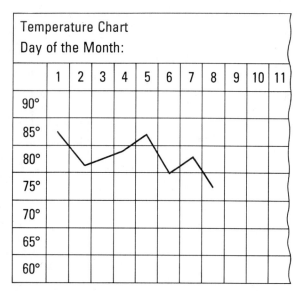

Figure 23-41: Temperature graph.

- *Measurement.* Have students measure with a ruler or tape measure various objects in the classroom—desk, trash can, circumference of globe, chalkboard, or each other.

SCIENCE

Children are very curious. They have many questions about the world around them. They are eager and excited when they discover the answers for themselves. Children learn best when science learning centers are set up to encourage their exploration and experimentation. Learning may occur in the classroom, on the playground, on a field trip, or on a walk around the block.

The theme seashore could include a variety of seashells, different types of sand from around the world, driftwood, seaweed, rocks smooth from wave action, and a wave bottle (made from vegetable oil and blue food coloring placed in a small plastic jar). Pictures and books of sea animals and fish may complement the center. The water table outside can be filled with different types of boats available for sailing. A special day, beach party, may be planned and the children asked to wear their swimsuits and sunglasses to school. Lunch or snack can include tuna sandwiches. A field trip to the beach may be an alternative.

The more firsthand or hands-on materials presented, the more that children will be encouraged to explore and discover aspects of the subject. Learning centers should have a touch and do area, where children feel welcome to work. Enthusiasm shown by the caregivers is important to stimulate the interest of the children.

Equipment for the science learning center does not have to be extravagant or expensive. Magnifying glasses, a balancing scale for weight measurement, rulers, and labeled specimen boxes are basic equipment. Aquariums for fish or an ant farm can be added when needed.

Centers should be changed periodically to stimulate interest and awareness. Projects should be kept simple, relate to the children personally, be adaptable to the developmental level, and stimulate curiosity.

Weather, for example, provokes questions of what makes the wind, why does it rain, and why does it snow when it gets cold? To show how air moves and has substance blow up a balloon or make a wind sock and hang it up outside. Water experiments can exhibit water frozen to make ice and ice melting over heat to produce the original state of water. Such experiments help to depict how cold weather freezes water to form ice and snow.

It is important to use the appropriate vocabulary when explaining aspects of science projects. Children are eager to learn the words and enjoy trying to use them in their own explanations. When discussing different types of animals and their homes, children can be introduced to terms such as *nest, burrow, jungle,* and *cave.* Discovering that some animals hibernate or go underground for the winter (rabbits) can create opportunities for questions

Figure 23-42: Michael is examining the tadpoles in the fish bowl.

and answers about life-styles of other animals.

We can recognize and define our senses by simple, everyday experiences at the child care center. Children can touch textures that are hard, soft, cold, warm, smooth, and rough. Feeling the rough cement in the play yard, the soft sand, the cool bricks of the building, the brittle leaves of the tree, and the smoothness of the metal on the climbing dome lets children use their senses to become aware of their surroundings.

Children distinguish different foods by their taste, touch, smell, and sight. Some foods may look alike (salt and sugar) but taste different. Strong, familiar food odors (fried bacon, onion, and coffee) help to develop the sense of smell.

Simple Science Experiments

Goal: The children will be able to self-discover their environment through exploration and experimentation.

For Infants and Toddlers

- *Hot and cold.* Fill two bowls with water, one with ice-cold water and the other with warm water. Let the children feel the difference.

- *Feely board.* Using a large piece of cardboard (such as a packing case from a washing machine or refrigerator), attach carpet pieces, cotton batting, sponges, leather, sandpaper, silk, metal, or any other textures. Lay the board on the floor and let children walk over it with their feet, or place it next to a wall and let them touch it with their hands.

- *Matching game.* Find or draw pictures of baby animals and their parents. Glue the pictures on a long piece of tagboard and cut the board into a puzzle form. You can use a cow, calf, horse, pony, chicken, chick, cat, kitten, dog, puppy, sheep, lamb, pig, and piglet.

For Preschoolers

- *Fruits and Seeds.* Let children help cut up a variety of fruits. Take out the seeds. How are the fruits alike and how are they different? Which have seeds? Which seeds can be eaten? Which cannot? How do the different fruits taste? Where do they grow? How do they travel? What types of protective coverings do they have? You can use oranges, apples, bananas, cherries, watermelon, peaches, plums, lemons, cantaloupe, and grapes.

- *Nature walk.* Go on a nature walk around the school or the park. Observe different trees, flowers, plants, animals, insects, and water. Collect specimens to take back to school if possible.

  Wear old socks as you walk across the grass. What kinds of seeds stuck to your socks? Take the seeds back to school. Fill a planter with planting mixture. Plant the seeds. Water them and place the planter in sunny window. Watch and see what grows.

For School-age Children

- *Bees.* Read books on the life habits of bees. Bring into class a piece of honeycomb. Ask a beekeeper to visit if possible. Discuss what is made from the wax. Make wax candles. Let children taste honey from the comb and from a jar. Discuss why bees are necessary for plant life. Where do they live? Why do bees sting?

- *Compass.* Stroke a pin forty to fifty times with a magnet, always in the same direction. This will magnetize the pin. Put the pin into a cork and float it in water. (Magnets always point north due to the large mineral deposits found there.) Why do we use compasses? What minerals attract magnets?

Figure 23-43: Simple Science Experiments.

NUTRITION

Learning about nutrition and cooking in the classroom can be fun and rewarding for both the children and the caregivers. The children learn to follow directions, develop the math and science skills of measuring, and discover the causes and effects of physical changes. By allowing children to pour, cut, open jars, measure, dump, beat, and stir, the caregiver is giving them practice in fine motor and manipulation skills.

Working with others on a cooperative venture teaches children about team effort. The pride and accomplishment felt while eating the food prepared in the lesson develops a sense of worth. These firsthand experiences provide time for children to compare textures, colors, sizes, and shapes and to use all of their senses.

Setting up a cooking center and practicing health and safety rules will allow everyone to have a comfortable and enjoyable experience. When cooking, remember the following simple guidelines:

1. Allow plenty of time.

2. Avoid overcrowding at the table.

3. Choose recipes that are simple, pretested, easy enough to encourage participation by children, and pleasant to the senses.

4. Ensure the safety of children when working with hot appliances, utensils, and food.

5. Encourage cleanup as an integral part of cooking. Allow children to wash dishes in hot, soapy water and to

Figure 23-44: Mandy enjoys a baking project.

rinse, dry, and put away all cooking materials.

6. Everyone washes hands before cooking.

7. Let everyone have a turn.

Remember, try to eat the final product the same day as preparation. This prevents a loss of interest on the part of the children. Eating new foods is an adventure when you have helped in the preparation.

When cooking, you will need the following supplies and equipment:

- blender
- cake pans

- cooking utensils
- cutting board
- dishcloths and dish towels
- graduated set of bowls
- hot pads
- measuring spoons and cups
- oven, stove, hot plate, or electric skillet
- paper towels
- paring knives
- plastic wrap, waxed paper, and aluminum foil
- refrigerator
- rolling pin
- saucepans
- sifter
- table and enough chairs for each participant
- timer
- water
- wooden spoons and spatulas

SOCIAL STUDIES

Social studies is the study of people and places; past, present, and future. They include the relationships of people to each other and their environment. Children enjoy learning about other cultures as well as their own. They begin to recognize societal rules and acceptable behaviors.

Simple Recipes

Goal: The children will increase nutritional, mathematical, scientific, and fine motor skills.

For Infants and Toddlers

Sandwiches

Spread peanut butter, butter, or cheese on crackers or half a slice of bread.

Banana Milk Shake

3 cups milk
1 cup vanilla ice cream
2 cut bananas

Pour the ingredients together in a blender. Mix them on high. Drink the milk shake.

For Preschoolers

Granola Peanut Butter Bars

1/2 cup honey
2/3 cup peanut butter
3   cups granola

Heat the honey to boiling. Boil it for one minute. Remove it from the heat. Mix it with the peanut butter until they are well-blended. Add the granola. Press the bars into a buttered 9″ × 9″ pan. Let them cool, and cut them into squares.

Figure 23-45: Simple Recipes.

Pizza Burgers

6 English muffins
1 can pizza sauce
6–8 ounces pizza cheese

Split the muffins in half. Spread pizza sauce on each half. Sprinkle cheese on the top. Bake, broil, or put the pizzas in an electric skillet with a cover until the cheese melts.

For School-age Children

Gazpacho

1   cup chopped tomatoes
1/2 cup green pepper
1/2 cup celery
1/2 cup cucumber
1/4 cup green onion
2   cups tomato juice
2   tablespoons parsley
1/2 tablespoon olive oil
1   teaspoon salt (optional)
1/2 teaspoon Worcestershire sauce

Chop all the vegetables. Combine all the ingredients. Chill the mixture, and serve it cold as soup.

Since family, friends, and community play important roles in children's lives, children enjoy learning about their history. Looking at family pictures and discussing past experiences and the occupations of family members expand children's understanding of the world. Parents, grandparents, and other relatives may share their backgrounds with the class. Field trips to community workplaces may show children how our food is grown, transported, and sold at the grocery store. Trips to local museums may invite questions about the community—how it started, how it had developed, and its plans for the future.

Topics of interest that encourage social studies are listed below. Each area can provide an extensive curriculum. Caregivers should identify which is appropriate to their group of children and when to integrate these subjects into the lesson plan.

- *Career awareness:* doctor, dentist, nurse, cosmetologist, secretary, teacher, carpenter, construction worker, banker, postal worker, fire fighter, police officer, chef (nontraditional roles should be emphasized)

- *Civics:* government and national history

- *Community:* grocery store, farm, stables, library, restaurant, pet shop, florist, radio and television station, newspaper, museum, zoo, and fire and police stations

- *Ethnic backgrounds:* dress, language, food, traditions, customs, arts and crafts, and history

Social Studies Activities

Goal: The children will increase their knowledge of people in their environment.

For Infants and Toddlers

- *Similarities and Differences.* Let children cut pictures of people from magazines and paste them onto construction paper. Discuss similarities and differences — girl, boy, baby, brown hair, blond hair, etc.

- *Self-Image.* Place each child in front of mirror and point to the child's hair, eyes, mouth, nose, teeth, and ears. Name and discuss each part.

For Preschoolers

- *Occupations.* Make people and their jobs puzzle cards. Match the picture of person dressed for an occupation with a picture of the tools used in the job.

- *Holidays.* Celebrate Cinco de Mayo. Share the Mexican holiday by dressing in Mexican native costumes, eating burritos for lunch, breaking a piñata, studying a map of Mexico, and asking Mexican parents to share experiences and customs with the class.

For School-age Children

- *Elections.* Set up a mock election booth in class during a local election in government. Let the children elect a president, vice president, secretary, and treasurer from the class. Provide ballots for secret voting. Appoint several students to count ballots.

  This is a good time to invite a local politician to visit the room. Discuss the importance of free elections and the electoral process.

- *Occupations.* Allow each child to pick a career that is most interesting to him or her. Have each child research and write a report on the career chosen. Include the education needed, skills needed, labor market, pay, and advancement opportunities. Encourage the children to interview someone from that field. Have the children read their reports to the class.

Figure 23-46: Social Studies Activities.

Figure 23-47: Grandparents help children have a sense of family history.

Figure 23-48: Occupation cards.

- *Family:* in home, outside home, similarities and differences to other members, traditions, and ethnic backgrounds

- *Friends:* schoolmates and neighbors

- *Geography:* cities, states, countries, world and topography

- *History:* family, community, county, parish, state, nation, and world

- *Self:* personal data, home, pets, emotions, likes, and dislikes

CONCLUSION

From the preceding curriculum area descriptions, caregivers can plan a variety of learning experiences that are meaningful to children. The same teaching or learning goal may be presented in many different ways in order to stimulate discovery. An open mind to new learning adventures is necessary for creative caregivers and eager students.

In some classrooms, curriculum areas are divided into learning centers. These can include a gross motor area (blocks, cars and trucks, dancing, musical instruments); a library area (books, tapes, records); a dramatic area (housekeeping, dress-up, mirror); a manipulative area (puzzles, tabletop games such as matching, small blocks); a science area (experiments and hands-on, self-discovery projects); and an arts and crafts area (painting, glue, scissors, crayons). By dividing the room, the caregiver can keep similar activities together and allow the children freedom of choosing the task in which they are interested. Caregivers need to ensure that all children eventually investigate all of the learning centers.

SUMMARY

Curriculum areas enhance the learning of young children. Deciding on a goal to be taught and the best method of teaching that goal are prime responsibilities of the caregiver. Many concepts can be taught in an enjoyable manner.

Children of all ages can experience learning through a variety of curriculum methods. Arts and crafts provide children with aesthetic, imaginative, and creative experiences. By using materials for free expression in an art project or by following specific instructions in a craft project, children practice fine motor skills. Caregivers can provide a variety of stimulating materials.

Language arts can be presented in a variety of forms—storytelling, books, flannel board stories, finger plays, puppets, role playing, and dramas. These methods encourage creative thinking, problem solving, vocabulary building, and reading and writing skills. Language arts should be a part of each day's curriculum.

Physical movement activities provide experiences that promote the body's motor development. Children can move in place or move from one place to another. Both activities involve practice of the gross and fine motor skills. How children choose to move their bodies is creative movement.

Music may be presented in a variety of forms—songs, dances, rhythmic exercises, creative movement, instruments, records, and tapes. Children enjoy adding their own verses and variations. Music may set the mood of the classroom or be used during other curriculum activities. The enjoyment and participation experienced by children makes music a pleasing addition to the lesson plan.

Math is included in every aspect of our daily lives. When caregivers discuss quantity, size, shape, and amounts of objects, they are using basic math concepts. Classification, seriation, spatial relationships, and temporal skills may be developed through simple games and manipulatives. Formal math instruction (addition, subtraction, multiplication, and division) can be presented in ways that have meaning to children and encourage learning.

Science, too, surrounds children in their normal routines. It inspires their curiosity and invites exploration for answers. The effective caregiver provides many opportunities for discovery. By arranging learning centers and activities to promote learning and use the senses, caregivers encourage experiences that give children firsthand knowledge.

Nutrition provides a way to learn to follow directions and to develop math and science skills. Cause and effect of physical changes, use of the senses, health and safety procedures, fine motor and manipulative skills, as well as socialization are also learned. Eating the product is positive reinforcement of a well-accomplished project.

Social studies stimulate children to acquire knowledge about themselves, family members, friends, the community, and other cultures. Social studies gives information about historic events, present conditions, and future endeavors. The studies allow children to gain an understanding of others and how they live.

By being creative, caregivers sanction learning as an enjoyable experience. Children should feel free to explore their environment and extend their knowledge.

Review Questions

14. What is social studies?

1. Why is it important not to provide an example or pattern of an art activity?

2. Why is it necessary to provide a variety of materials for collages?

3. What physical skill is increased when doing woodworking?

4. What is the difference between art activities and craft projects?

5. Why is it necessary to ask questions at the end of a story?

6. When telling a flannel story, pieces are given to the children to hold until it is time to place them on the flannel board. Why is this a good practice?

7. What is learned by the children when participating in finger plays?

8. How do puppets help the timid child?

9. Why is it important to include creative movement in the curriculum?

10. What skills are increased as children practice rhythmic activities?

11. What concepts are learned through math activities?

12. How should the science learning center be set up?

13. Many skills are stimulated when you do nutrition experiences with children. What are they?

Things to Do and Discuss

1. Plan one art lesson and one craft lesson for a group of school-age children. Prepare a list of materials, directions to follow, and a written report on its success.

2. Create your own flannel board story chosen from a children's storybook. Decide the main characters and scenery that will be used to tell the story. Remember to keep the story short and interesting.

3. Make a set of matching shape and color cards. Include squares, circles, triangles, rectangles, and diamonds using red, blue, yellow, orange, purple, and green colors.

4. Review the list of songs in the music curriculum section. Make your own list of favorite children's songs and research ten new songs that could be added.

5. Picking one theme from the following list, choose a recipe to share with a group of preschoolers. Remember to follow the simple rules in the nutrition curriculum section when cooking. Possible themes are the circus, winter, Thanksgiving, the farm, and colors.

CHAPTER 24
Lesson Planning

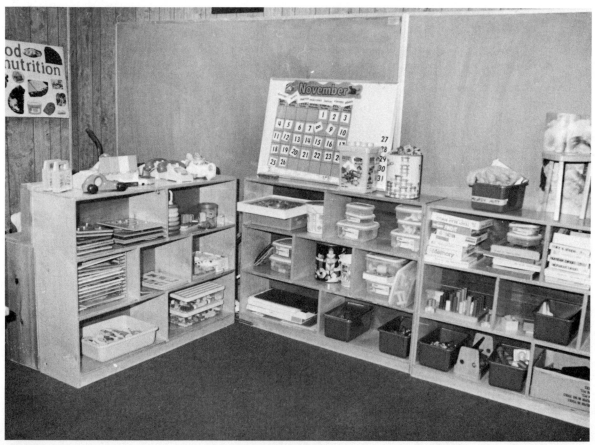

An organized classroom.

KEY TERMS

brainstorming
calendar method
cognitive web
comprehension level

firsthand or hands-on
experience
senses
themes

OBJECTIVES

After completing this chapter, you will be able to:
1. discuss the necessity of lesson planning;
2. arrange a balanced daily schedule;
3. define three specific curriculum areas that should be included in a daily schedule;
4. explain methods of preparing a lesson plan including the areas of child development.

BEGINNING PLANS

The first two case studies in this chapter are good examples of *why* it is necessary to prepare a daily lesson plan when working with young children. Imagination, exploration, and creativity are elements of children who need challenge and stimulation whenever possible. Children grow and learn from the adults, peers, and experiences within their environment.

Why

Caregivers need to plan activities and routines that encourage learning about oneself and others. Organizing the thoughts, activities, and interests of young children helps to create a more enjoyable and successful environment. Each day learning centers should be arranged, toys displayed, and visual aids presented to foster learning in a planned manner. Each portion of the day should provide a learning opportunity with the goals clearly defined.

Planned activities often enhance more than one area of development. Caregivers should choose the area of development they want to emphasize in a particular lesson (this becomes the goal for that lesson) but realize that other areas should also be included.

Caregivers should plan their daily schedules to best meet the children's needs. Obviously, the ages and abilities of the group must be considered during this stage. Caregivers must first list the important routines to be met for the general health and safety of the children—meals, toileting, rest, and hygiene requirements. Routines in the classroom help to reassure children and let them anticipate what is happening next in their day. From this starting point, caregivers can next decide on the best times for inside and outside activities.

Caregivers should try to provide a balanced day. A basic formula of one-third of the time for inside learning, one-third of the time for outside learning, and one-third of the time for routine activities can be a guideline when planning for infants, toddlers, and preschoolers. School-age children should have a longer inside learning time.

All classrooms should be organized so all the children can participate in a variety of activities. At the same time, schedules must be flexible enough to consider individual differences, thus allowing children the freedom to choose the activities that interest them. Decision making is an important part of maturation.

Case Study #1:
Mrs. Williams

The children are arriving at the center. They have to wait outside the door with their mothers until Mrs. Williams arrives five minutes later. She quickly turns on the lights, tells the children to come in, and says good-bye to the mothers. Chairs are still up on the table and cabinets and materials are locked up.

The children push and shove as they try to hang up their coats and show items they brought to school to each other. Several children try to talk to Mrs. Williams at the same time. Jose and Thomas are hitting and yelling at each other because Jose bumped Thomas as he was trying to take the chairs down. Several chairs have slid off the table, one hitting Charlene on the head (she is now crying).

Health checks are forgotten, and chaos prevails as Mrs. Williams struggles to bring the class to order. She must yell in order to be heard over the confusion. She tells the children to sit down while she gets materials and activities arranged. It takes a great amount of effort to get the children settled. Now they must wait for what seems a long time as Mrs. Williams unlocks the cabinets and hurries to get some materials out. Meanwhile, the children are squirming, pushing others, or retreating to comfort habits such as twisting hair or sucking thumbs.

By the time Mrs. Williams is ready, the children rush to the table, several trying to get in the same chair to play with the few manipulatives she has arranged. Seth takes one look and decides that these are "baby toys." He's tired of using the same games every day. Besides, yesterday the children were allowed to go directly outside when they first came to school. He decides instead to dump all the puzzles onto the floor.

There appears to be no planning or organization to each day's activities. The children feel a lack of structure and consistency. This causes insecurity and lack of direction.

What

Whether preparing the lesson for a day, week, or month, *what* topics can be used? It is wise to choose *themes* (subjects or topics) or units of study that interest the children with whom you are working. Most three year olds are not interested in nor do they understand entomology, although scaling that idea down to basics, they may easily understand and enjoy the study of insects.

Keeping the unit of study relatively close to the children's *comprehension level* (ability to understand) challenges their cognitive skills by introducing new vocabulary and ideas. Allowing children to experiment and explore through the use of their *senses* (sight, touch, smell, hear-

Case Study #2:
Miss Jones

Miss Jones, in the room next door to Mrs. Williams, has the door open when the children arrive for the day. They and their parents are welcomed leisurely. There is time for a brief conversation with each person. Miss Jones is able to assess the general health condition of the children as she listens to their news.

As the children enter, the lights are on, the chairs are placed around the tables, and manipulatives pertaining to the lesson and maturity level of the children are already placed on the tables. There are choices of activities.

Some activities are familiar to the children but there are also new games to challenge their abilities. The beginning routine is the same each day; therefore, the children know that they are free to select the activity that interests them, and they quickly become busy.

The general atmosphere of Miss Jones' room is conducive to proper and acceptable behavior. There is a feeling of calmness, order, and security. The children enter knowing the room is ready for them to begin work and play.

ing, and taste) is the easiest and most enjoyable method to teach children about a specific subject. Allowing children to learn by doing is known as *firsthand* or *hands-on experience.*

Imagine how learning can be enhanced by using the children's senses. For example, in Case Study #3, Mrs. Williams could have shown large, glossy pictures of different types and colors of fire trucks; brought in toy fire trucks and let the children play with the ladder, hose, and bell; made a large fire truck out of packing boxes for the children to paint and use outside; included toy plastic fire hats for dramatic play; and had the children use lengths of hose to put out imaginary fires.

Plan a field trip to your local fire station or call and ask if a fire truck could visit your school. Allow the children to hear the

siren, touch the truck, sit in the cab and see the controls, squirt the hose, and see the lights flash. Trying on the heavy, waterproof coat and putting their feet in the big boots is fun as well as educational. Seeing where the fire fighters live while on duty is also interesting.

This would be an appropriate opportunity to discuss fire safety (the stop, drop, and roll technique), playing with matches, and emergency phone numbers. Smokey the Bear may be available in your area to encourage fire safety. Materials passed out at this time foster reinforcement at home.

At school, the children can make art projects depicting fire trucks, can do science projects, read storybooks, and listen to flannel stories encompassing the fire theme. When children are able to enjoy the activities provided

Case Study #3:
Mrs. Williams Revisited

Mrs. Williams decides to tell the group of three year olds in her preschool class about her trip to the fire station. She begins by describing the fire truck she observed. She begins, "Yesterday I went to the fire station, and I saw a great big, white fire truck!" Jimmy can only imagine his grandpa's white pickup truck.

"And at the top of this truck is a red object, round like a ball, that flashes lights when the truck is going to a fire." Jimmy visualizes that red beach ball that he has at home.

"And when the lights flash, a siren or bell makes a loud sound to alert the traffic that the truck is coming quickly and to get out of the way." The only bell that Jimmy can identify with is the school bell.

Figure 24-1: What Jimmy imagines.

The picture that Jimmy has in his mind is Grandpa's white pickup truck with a red beach ball on top, sounding like the school bell ringing as it goes quickly down the street. Is this an accurate picture of a fire truck?

and understand the information presented, they begin to learn.

When working with toddlers, the unit of study may be transportation. It may be kept at a superficial level. Trucks, cars, and buses have wheels and go. In a classroom of first graders, the unit can develop information concerning vehicles with two, four, or more wheels. Aeronautical, nautical, and land vehicles can be discussed. Talk about how they operate and whom they serve. Different types of engines and how they perform can also be included.

Following is a list of units of study for young children. Depending on the interest and maturation level of the class, each of the themes may be used for infants and toddlers, preschoolers, and school-age children.

- *Alphabet:* letters, spelling, reading, writing
- *Amphibians:* frogs, turtles, salamanders
- *Animals:* circus, farm, pets, wild, sea, zoo, prehistoric

Figure 24-2: A male caregiver shares a few moments with some students.

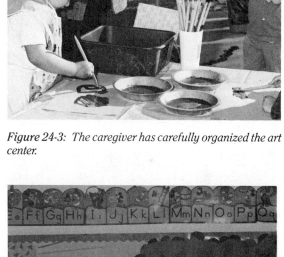

Figure 24-3: The caregiver has carefully organized the art center.

- *Beach:* water, sand, fish, mammals, boats
- *Birthdays:* numbers, calendars
- *Circus:* people, animals, food
- *Colors:* primary, secondary, tints, shades
- *Christmas:* religious beliefs, families, Santa Claus, Christmas trees, reindeer, foods, customs, and culture
- *Communication:* television, records, tape cassette players, radio, satellites, movies, books

Figure 24-4: This bulletin board has insects, flowers, and a tree made by the children.

Developmental Goals

Event	Goal for Development			
	Social	Emotional	Physical	Intellectual
Morning greeting and health check	X	—	X	—
Group sharing	X	X	—	X
Outside time	X	X	X	X
Music	X	—	X	X
Nature walk around neighborhood	X	—	X	X
Hygiene	—	—	X	X
Snack or meal	X	—	X	X
Arts and crafts	—	—	X	X
Naps	—	X	X	—
Manipulative play	X	X	X	X
Concept games	X	—	—	X
Visiting police officer	X	—	—	X

Figure 24-5: Developmental Goals chart.

- *Community helpers:* fire fighters, police officers, teachers, librarians, postal workers, restaurant workers, sanitation workers

- *Easter:* religious beliefs, families, bunny, ducks, chicks, eggs, candy, customs, culture

- *Farms:* farmers, animals, barns, vegetables, fruits, flowers, equipment

- *Geography:* neighborhood, city, states, countries, people, cultures, topography (volcanoes, mountains, rivers, oceans, glaciers)

- *Halloween:* trick or treat, Jack-o' lanterns, pumpkins, costumes, witches, ghosts, goblins, cats, safety, orange, black

- *Health:* doctors, nurses, hospitals, dentists, veterinarians, basic food groups, exercise, self-help skills, life cycles, sex education, hygiene

- *History:* city, state, nation, world
- *Independence Day:* freedom, family, picnics, fireworks, safety, history, red, white, blue, flag
- *Insects:* kinds, ecology
- *Martin Luther King Day:* freedom, history, culture
- *Nature:* flowers, plants, animals, birds, moths, butterflies, life cycles
- *Numerals:* counting, shapes, mathematics, fractions, algebra, geometry, money, economics
- *Occupations:* housewife, construction worker, office worker, factory worker, public official, movie star, musician, writer, sports figure, teacher, computer technician, union workers
- *Parents' Days:* Mother's Day, Father's Day, Grandparents' Day, families
- *Patriotism:* city, state, nation, armed forces, president, legislature, judicial system, history, Fourth of July, independence
- *Presidents' Day:* Washington, Lincoln, history
- *Recreation:* parks, sports, vacations
- *Religious observances:* Jewish, Christian, Buddhist, Moslem
- *Reptiles:* lizards, snakes
- *Safety:* fire, electricity, poisons, kitchen, water, street, natural disasters, drug awareness, sex education, first aid, emergency services, emergency phone numbers

- *Saint Patrick's Day:* leprechauns, rainbows, gold, green, Ireland, snakes, clover, customs
- *Seasons:* fall, winter, spring, summer, weather, safety, sports, recreation, dress, temperature, nature, planting, harvesting
- *Self:* features, personality, family, home, friends, address, name, phone number, pets, principles, likes, dislikes
- *Space:* planets, astronauts, space travel, satellites, meteors, astronomy, communication
- *Sports:* players, large motor skills, Olympics, track, ball games, gymnastics, skating, bowling
- *Thanksgiving:* food, Pilgrims, Indians, customs, families, thankfulness
- *Transportation:* cars, buses, trains, planes, hot air balloons, bicycles, skateboards, skates, feet
- *Vacations:* trips, mountains, rivers, lakes, seashores, deserts, geography, other lands
- *Valentine's Day:* hearts, flowers, friends, families, red, love, cupids
- *Zoo:* animals, keepers, food, geography

As you can see, there are many subjects that are of interest to young children. These topics can be simplified for infants and toddlers or expanded to relate to older, school-age children. Basic skills, such as reading, math, and science, can be built around a specific topic.

Figure 24-6: *"Sports Day" at preschool.*

Special Days and Events

Planning a special day curriculum can be an enjoyable addition to a lesson plan. Special days are usually very interesting for young children. Field trips, special visitors, or a party can be added to the regularly structured day.

Preparing for these special days can be a source of enjoyment for everyone involved — caregivers, children, parents, and invited guests. Planning, sending invitations, setting up a different environment, dressing to fit the theme, bringing in special items, reading or initiating a story specific to the theme, and appropriate foods can also add to the festivities.

Occasionally a special event for an evening or weekend can include family members. Children are proud to show off their school, room, class, work, and teachers to their families and friends. This opportunity can also help to establish a bond between home and school. It is another form of communication. Establishing a relaxed atmosphere can allow parents to interact with the staff and other families. They can enjoy this special time with their children. Possible special events include:

- *Baby Day:* dressing as a baby and bringing a favorite doll

- *Backwards Day:* wearing clothes backwards and following the day's schedule backwards

- *Beach Day:* dressing for the beach, eating typical beach foods, engaging in water and sand play

- *Christmas in July Day:* giving presents for charities in creating a Christmas environment

- *Clown or Circus Day:* dressing in circus clothes, performing circus acts, and eating circus-type foods

- *Color Day:* dressing in the appropriate color, decorating the room in that color, eating food of that color

- *Computer Day:* playing computer games appropriate for age, making computer paper crafts, making robots

- *Gingerbread Day:* making gingerbread and reading stories and plays

- *Kite Day:* making and flying kites, studying the weather

- *Numbers and Shapes Day:* reading and telling stories, dressing as shapes, finding shapes in the room, hiding and seeking numbers

- *Pajama Day:* wearing pajamas to school, bringing special stuffed toys, playing soft music

- *Pet Day:* bringing pictures or pets to school, bringing favorite stuffed animal, writing stories, discussing the care and feeding of pets

- *Record Breaking Day:* practicing large and small motor activities, playing physical and intellectual games

- *Science Fair Day:* making individual projects and classroom projects

- *Spelling Bees:* learning phonics, rhyming words, spelling words, similar meanings

- *Sports Day:* playing games and dressing in a favorite sport outfit

- *Teddy Bear Day:* bringing a bear to school, having a teddy bear picnic or tea, making cookies

- *Western Day:* panning for gold, dressing in western outfits, going on a hay ride, and having a rodeo with stick horses

- *Winter Picnic Day:* having a picnic on the floor, playing inside games

Traditional Special Events

- Back to School Open House
- Ethnic Fair
- Family Picnic
- Holiday Productions
- Parents and Me Breakfast
- Potluck Dinner

ORGANIZATION OF LESSON PLANS

How

When choosing a theme or unit of study, consider the time of year, the interests of the children, and their level of comprehension. Areas to include when doing a lesson plan are arts, crafts, language, science, math, gross and fine motor development or physical development, creative movement, spatial awareness, nutrition, social studies, and music. The theme must then be organized into a lesson plan that enhances the four developmental areas of the children.

It appears to be a monumental task to try to include all of these areas into a concise format to fit into a limited amount of time. Practice *brainstorming* (a technique for coming up with ideas), researching ideas, developing new learning materials to make lesson planning exciting and challenging.

Keep in mind that several activities can be included into one large subject area. An example for the theme metamorphosis follows:

1. Explain that metamorphosis is the change that occurs as a caterpillar becomes a butterfly. Show large glossy pictures to illustrate and clarify the definition. Read a book concerning the life cycle of butterflies, such as *The Very Hungry Caterpillar* by Eric Carle (science and language).

2. Next, teach a song about an ugly caterpillar transforming into a beautiful butterfly or play an activity record during which the children act out the life cycle (music and physical movement).

The total lesson time may be only twenty minutes to half an hour, but it can be repeated several times for the enjoyment of the children. Repetition is necessary to reinforce learning and instill the facts into children's minds.

Plan the lesson using the following steps:

1. Define important topics or goals relative to that unit.

2. Determine the overall learning goals (what type of learning is to occur) for students.

3. Establish a unit of study or theme.

4. Have a daily schedule of events or time frame established to teach each curriculum area.

5. Research interesting yet challenging activities to enhance growth and development and to meet goals.

Styles of Plan

Two types of lesson plans are explained below in order to let caregivers choose the style that is best for them.

The *cognitive web* is a method of organizing thoughts, then formulating a lesson plan around a central theme. When the subjects for each week are established, then the goals, activities, equipment, speakers, and trips can be defined. A lesson plan for a weather unit, using the web, may look like that in Figure 24-7.

The *calendar method* is simple and concise. It depicts areas of learning by day. Caregivers can keep this calendar in a lesson book or posted on a bulletin board for parents and other staff members to observe. An example of a calendar lesson plan is shown in Figure 24-8.

One of the above styles of lesson plans may be used to organize curriculum areas and materials. By practicing the styles you may find one that is best for you. Remember, establishing goals, organizing, planning, and acquiring needed materials beforehand will allow the classroom day to be smoother and more efficient.

Flexibility is another important element in developing lesson plans. Sometimes children become deeply interested in one aspect of the lesson plan and their enthusiasm carries over into the time allotted for another subject. You may have to revise your plan accordingly and allow for extra discussion or activity time.

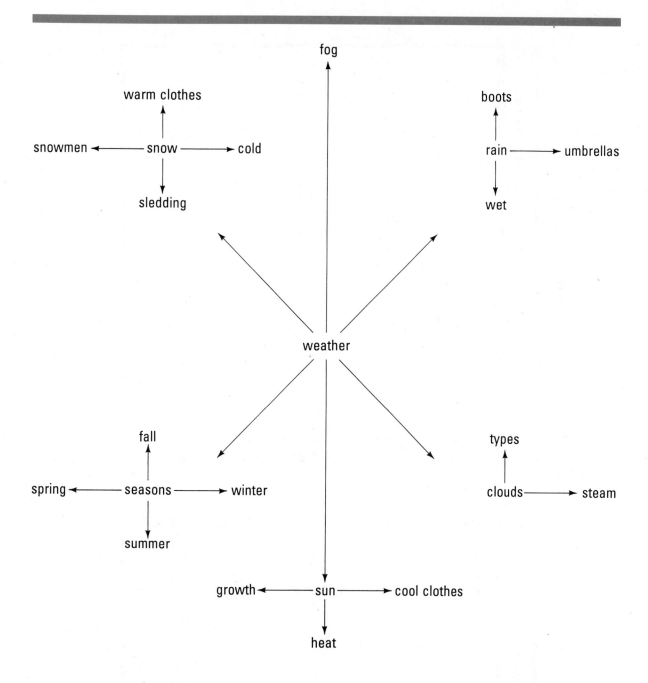

Figure 24-7: A cognitive web.

Subject—Weather	Arts/Crafts	Science and Math—Concept Learning	Story Time	Music—Creative Movement	Physical Development
Monday—wind	Make kites with pasteboard, markers, string, and rags.	Discuss weather, the days getting longer, and the clothes we wear in different weather.	*Book: January Brings the Snow.* Finger *play:* "The Wind."	Sing "The Wind Song." Sway back and forth in rhythm.	*Manipulatives:* Pegs and blocks, sewing cards. Outside, fly real kites.
Tuesday—rain	Cut out magazine pictures of things that are wet.	Look at pictures of the seasons and weather. Discuss things to do on a rainy day.	*Book: Why Does It Rain?* Flannel *story:* "The Rainbow."	*Activity record:* "Rainy Day Dances, Rainy Day Songs."	*Manipulatives:* Pour beans on the water table.
Wednesday—clouds	Finger paint with black and white paints.	Look at pictures of different types of clouds. Experiment with steam to form clouds.	*Finger play:* "The Wind." *Flannel story:* "Spilt Milk."	Play instruments in time with a record. March outside around the play yard and building.	*Manipulatives:* large and small blocks. Outside, water play.
Thursday—sun	Sponge paint flowers on butcher paper.	Discuss some of the things we can do on a sunny day. *Film strip:* "Fall, Winter, Spring, and Summer."	*Flannel story:* "Sleepy Mr. Sun." *Book: Sun Cat—A Book About Weather.*	Sing "You Are My Sunshine." Do simple exercises.	*Manipulatives:* Use play dough.
Friday—weather	Use play dough.	Reinforce all types of weather. Show different clothes worn on sunny, rainy, cold, and hot days.	*Finger play:* "The Wind." *Book: Seasons.*	Sing children's favorite songs.	Color and cut. Have outdoor relay races.

Figure 24-8: Calendar lesson plan.

SUMMARY

Careful planning of activities and daily routines enables caregivers to organize their thoughts in a constructive manner to stimulate learning in young children. Goals for the group and the individual child must be considered when preparing lesson plans.

Remember, all areas of development (physical, social, emotional, and intellectual) must be included within the plan. A variety of stimulating activities can be arranged to allow maximum participation on the part of the children. Using the senses for learning, firsthand knowledge is accomplished. Large pictures, field trips, costumes, nutrition, and arts and crafts projects add to the learning process.

Choosing a theme or unit of study that is interesting to the children is the next priority. Use one of the lesson plan styles—cognitive web or the calendar—to organize your thoughts. Begin to develop activities in the specific curriculum areas—language arts, arts and crafts, science, math, nutrition, music, social studies, and physical movement. This planning allows for a smooth operation of your classroom.

Review Questions

1. Why is it necessary to have a daily lesson plan?
2. What elements must you take into consideration when making the daily lesson plan?
3. What routines must be included in the lesson plan?
4. What is the basic formula for the day?
5. Why is it necessary to have a flexible schedule?
6. Define themes and describe their value to the lesson plan.
7. Who could you invite on a "special day"?
8. Why is it important to plan repetitions of activities?
9. What are the two styles of lesson plans and how do they differ?

Things to Do and Discuss

1. Visit a classroom and observe the lesson plan in action. Is the lesson plan posted? Does there appear to be organization or structure to the class? Are the learning centers reinforcing the lesson plan? Are the classroom bulletin boards pertinent to the theme?
2. Interview the teacher in a classroom. What method id the teacher use to formulate the lesson plan?
3. Make a cognitive web using a subject from the theme list (pages 446–449).
4. Arrange the subjects chosen for the cognitive web in outline form.
5. Using the same theme as above, make a calendar lesson plan for one week, covering all the curriculum areas.

SELECTED REFERENCES

Chapter 1

Kutner, Laurence, "Searching for the Best in Day Care," *New York Times*, February 4, 1988, P.CI

Chapter 2

American Broadcasting Company News Department documentary, "After the Sexual Revolution," (1986).

Carlson, H., and Stenmalm-Sjoblom, L. (1989). "A Cross-cultural Study of Parent's Perceptions of Early Childhood Programs." *Early Childhood Research Quarterly*, 4, 505–522.

Education Week, 1987.

Fugua, R.W. and Shieck, R., (1989). "Child Care Resource and Referral Program and Parent's Search for Quality Child Care." *Early Childhood Research Quarterly*, 4, 357–365.

Galinsky, 1989.

Chapter 5

Gardephe, C., (1989). "Hear! Hear!" *Healthy Kids*, Cahners Publication. p. 8.

White, B.L. and Shelov, S. (1990). "Is Your Baby's Hearing Normal?" *Healthy Kids*, Cahners Publication. p. 8.

Chapter 8

Wilson, L. (1990). *Infants and Toddlers*. p. 7 NY: Delmar Publishers.

Chapter 9

Child Abuse Prevention/Intervention/Education Program, 1986.

Jackson, *CTA ACTION*, "Crack babies are here! Can you help them learn?" California Teachers Association, November 1990.

State of California, San Bernardino Sheriff's Department, 1987.

Chapter 10

Rothlein, *Young Children*, "Nutrition Tips Revisited...," 1989.

US Department of Agriculture, *Eating Right*, 1989.

Chapter 12

Random House College Dictionary, 1984.

Chapter 14

Derman-Sparks, 1987.

Chapter 21

Lisner, (1983). *Pediatric Nursing*. NY: Delmar Publishers.

Chapter 22

Random House Dictionary, (1984). New York: Random House.

GLOSSARY

abandonment—the leaving of a child to fend alone at too young an age or the leaving of a child in a potentially dangerous situation

abrasions—wounds made by rubbing or scraping the skin

absenteeism—not being present on the job

abstract—existing only as an idea

abuse—to hurt or to treat badly

academic learning—learning in areas such as language arts, mathematics, science, and social studies

acute—having severe and sudden symptoms

administers—gives out, applies, or dispenses

adolescence—the time in life that bridges childhood and young adulthood, encompassed by many physical, emotional and intellectual changes

aggression—combative behavior

allergies—the body's negative reactions to certain substances

ambidextrous—being able to use both hands equally well

amblyopia—lazy eye

amino acids—components that aid the heart, dilate the air passages, and are essential in living cells

amniotic sac—sack that contains fluid in which the embryo is suspended

anaphylactic shock—usually caused by an allergen reaction from bee stings, insect bites, or penicillin; this generally produces sudden, excessive swelling and requires immediate emergency treatment

anecdotal record—a brief narrative of your impressions of a child, staff member, school, or center

anemia—lack of iron in the red blood cells

appropriate—suitable for particular persons, occasions, or places

assertive—standing up for one's rights

auditory—hearing

autism—a condition where the individual withdraws from reality

autonomy—independence

bacteria—microorganisms that can cause illness

beriberi—a disease of the nervous system

blindness—loss of sight

bonding—interacting with another for a warm, secure closeness *brachial pressure*—pressure on the brachial artery (between the biceps and triceps) to stop bleeding in the arms or hands

brachial pulse—pulse found on the upper arm

brainstorming—a technique for coming up with ideas

cadence—rhythmic flow of a sequence of sounds or words; beat

calendar method—a method that plans by the day

calories—units of food energy

carbohydrates—substances that provide living things with much of the energy needed to operate muscles and nerves and to maintain optimum performance of plant and body tissues. Found in rice, wheat, beets, vegetables, fruits, and juices

cardiac arrest—the condition when the heart has stopped beating and circulation of the blood has ceased

cardiopulmonary resuscitation—to restart breathing and blood circulation by artificial means (usually another person providing breaths and heart compressions to the victim)

carotid pulse—pulse found on the side of the neck

cell—a small unit of protoplasm, usually with a nucleus and a membrane (wall); the smallest structural unit of plant and animal life

cerebral palsy—a condition with speech difficulties and a lack of coordination caused by brain damage before or during birth

cesarean birth—operation to remove the baby through the uterine wall

characteristics—qualities that define a person or thing

charting—writing a record of activities or behaviors

checklist—a form on which appears appropriate questions; a quick guide for evaluation

chemical burns—burns caused by either acids or alkalis

child abuse—the lack of an act or the incorporation of an act that endangers a child's development either physically or mentally

child molestation—the use of force or coercion to induce a child into sexual actions that are physically or socially inappropriate

child neglect—failure to provide the care, love, and support necessary for a healthy and nurturing existence

cholesterol—a substance that can line the blood vessels

chromosomes—threadlike bodies contained in the cell nucleus

chronological age—the age of the child/person counted in years

classification—putting like or similar objects into groupings

coercion—making one do something against one's will

cognition—the act of learning, perceiving, and acquiring knowledge

cognitive development—the acquiring of knowledge

cognitive web—a method of organizing thoughts

comminuted fracture—several breaks in a bone

communicable—capable of being transmitted or spread

communicable illness—an illness spread either directly or indirectly from person to person

communication—an open dialogue between people to keep everyone informed

compound comminuted fracture—several breaks in a bone, one or more of which sticks through the skin

compound fracture—a break in the bone that also breaks through the skin

comprehension level—ability to understand

comprehensive care—a combination of custodial and developmental care plus many specialized services

conception—the joining of the female ovum and the male sperm

concrete—real

concussion—type of head injury usually caused by a violent blow or impact

conducive—contributing

connective tissue—tissues that bind the body together to support it

coordination—muscles working together

conservation—the ability to determine amounts, such as more, less, or the same, regardless of how the objects are arranged

consistent—always following the same principles, courses, or forms

contagious—communicable

contagious illnesses—illnesses spread by contact, such as colds and flu

convulsions—the onset of unconsciousness, characterized by paleness, high body temperature, salivation, and violent jerky movements of the body

cooperative play—playing with someone else

CPR—cardiopulmonary resuscitation—a method used to help restore breathing and heartbeat

creative movement—the combination of gross motor skills, fine motor skills, and imagination

creativity—the act of bringing something into existence, to be inventive or imaginative

cruel and unusual punishment—inappropriate or extreme punishment for an action

cubby—generally a box or container used to keep belongings

curriculum—planned program of activities to promote growth and development

deafness—loss of hearing

defiant—going against authority

deficiency—lack of something needed or required

deformity—abnormal formation or shape

dehydration—the loss of body fluids

delayed or impaired children—children whose developmental levels are below the normal range

development—progressive growth

developmental care—a program formulated to stimulate growth

deviant behavior—behavior different from normal

diaper gait—movement with the legs spread for comfort and balance *digestive impairments*—inability of the body to utilize nourishment

dilated—wider or larger than normal

direct pressure—method to stop severe bleeding by placing a hand over a clean cloth directly over the wound and applying firm, constant pressure

direct transmission—spreading disease by contact with another person

discipline—training to act in accordance with rules; instruction and practice designed to train to proper conduct or action

disposition—emotional attitudes

DNA—chemical found in the genes and dealing with heredity

dosage—the correct amount of medicine given to a patient

dyslexia—a learning disability associated with inability to learn the basic language skills (reading, writing, and spelling)

ego—the part of the personality associated with reason and common sense

egocentric behavior—understanding only one's own viewpoint without regard for the viewpoint of others

ejaculate—to eject suddenly

elevate—raise

embryo—an organism in the early stages of development

emotional neglect—any action that negatively affects a child's sense of self

emotions—inner feelings

empathy—knowing how another feels

energy—the ability of the body to do work

enrichment—exposing children to new ideas and knowledge

environment—surroundings; a variation of experiences with different people, places, and things combine to make up the environmental process

envision—picture mentally

epilepsy—a condition of the central nervous system usually indicated by convulsions

epithelial tissues—covering tissues such as skin and lungs

ethics—the standards that establish right from wrong behavior

evacuation plan—a plan to empty a room or area of people

event sampling—an observation to understand a particular problem or event

exceptional children—children who exhibit development outside the normal range

excessive physical punishment—any physical punishment that results in injuries to the child

expressive language—the use of speech

extracurricular events—activities that are not part of the everyday routine

facilitator—provider of the methods of instruction

failure to thrive—not showing normal development

fainting—short-term loss of consciousness due to a lack of blood to the brain

fat soluble vitamins—vitamins that can be dissolved in fat *fatigue* —tiredness

fats —substances that furnish twice as much fuel and energy for the body as the same amount of proteins or carbohydrates. Found in meats and dairy products

feces —waste by-products that are expelled from the bowels (bowel movements or stools)

femoral pressure —pressure on the femoral artery (between the groin and leg) to stop bleeding in the legs and feet

fertilization —the union of the male and female sex cells

fetus —the baby before birth

fictional —invented, not necessarily based on fact

fine motor development —developing the small muscles and eye-hand coordination

first-aid —the immediate and temporary care given to the victim of an accident or sudden illness before the services of a physician can be obtained

first-hand or hands-on experience —to learn by doing

fondling —handling in a caressing manner

fontanels —the soft spots or spaces between the five plates of the skull that are still pliable in babies

fracture —a break in a bone

frostbite —a condition caused by extended exposure to the cold

full-day care centers —facilities open more than six hours but fewer than twenty-four hours each day

fungicide —medication to kill fungus infections

games with rules —any games with specific sets of rules; team games, relays, baseball, soccer

genetic —heredity characteristics passed from the parents to offspring

genitals —male and female reproductive organs

gifted children —children who display physical, social, emotional, or intellectual progress exceeding that of normal children

goiter —a condition of the thyroid gland

greenstick fracture —a chip or break on one side of a bone caused by a bend on the other side

gross motor development —developing the large muscles, such as those in the arms, legs, and torso

growth —the physical change that occurs as children mature

half-day care centers —facilities that operate for six hours or less per day

handedness —dominant use of one hand over the other

health —physical and mental well-being; freedom from pain, defect, or disease

heat exhaustion —a condition caused by the lack of water in the body to replace fluids lost by perspiring

heat stroke —a condition caused by higher than normal body temperature and disruption of the cooling properties of the body (perspiring)

hemorrhage —excessive bleeding

heredity —qualities and traits transmitted from parent to offspring *home visits*—teachers visiting the child at home with the parents present

hormones—internally secreted compounds that affect the functions of the body

hygiene—the science of health and maintenance

hyperactivity—a condition characterized by a short attention span and behavior disorders, including restlessness, impulsive behavior, and disruptive behavior

hyperextension—wide-spread and stiff

hypervigilant—always twitching or staring

hypoactivity—a condition characterized by passive and complacent behavior, including a low activity level

hypothermia—a condition caused by a drop in the body temperature below 98.6 degrees Farenheit

id—the part of the personality concerned with pleasure

imitative—copying the actions of others

immersion—placing or plunging into a liquid, such as water

incest—sexual relations between close relatives

incubation—period from infection to the onset of symptoms for a specific illness

incubator—a specially designed enclosed crib that maintains constant heat, oxygen, and nutrition

incisions—sharp cuts that tend to bleed freely

incoherence—inability to answer questions logically

indirect pressure—applying brachial or femoral pressure when an artery appears to be affected by a wound, thereby slowing down or stopping blood flow to the wound

indirect transmission—spreading disease by contracting infected materials

inflammation—a diseased condition that includes redness, pain, heat, or swelling

initiate—begin

initiative—the ability to start something or motivate oneself

innate—inborn

intelligence—the ability to learn and to know using the mind

integrated movement—use of the small and large muscles together; the combination of primary and secondary movements for activities such as running and jumping to catch the ball in an organized game of baseball

internalize—feel from within

isolation—separation from the group

jaundice—yellow appearance to the skin and eyes

kinesthetic sense—sensation of movement

knock-knee—knees close together

lacerations—jagged or irregular wounds

lactation—nursing

language arts—any means of communication through speech, reading, storytelling, and sign or body language

lanugo—covering of fine hair during second trimester

learning centers—areas of the classroom designated for a particular learning environment

lesions—sores

lethargy—abnormal drowsiness, laziness, or indifference; lack of enthusiasm

liable—legally responsible

low resistance—susceptibility to illness

mainstreaming—allowing exceptional children to attend centers or schools with other children

malaise—vague feeling of discomfort or uneasiness before an illness

manipulatives—materials for activities that provide opportunities to increase small muscle control

masturbation—handling one's own genitals for sexual gratification

maturation level—the stage of development as the child progresses and learns

menstrual cycle—monthly shedding of uterus lining when ovum not fertilized by sperm

mental abuse—verbal barbs used to damage self-esteem

metabolism—how much energy we use and store; the breakdown of nutrients to supply the body with energy to grow, develop, provide heat, and engage in physical activity

model curriculum—a program where the latest theories and techniques are explored

Moro reflex—a reflex that causes infants to respond with the whole body to loud noises; startle reflex

motor development—physical movement and control of the body

motor skill—ability to use muscles to control movement

muscular tissue—tissue made of cells that can contract and relax again

music—a sequence of sounds that are pleasing to the ear and satisfying to the emotions

narrative—story; written account

nausea—a sense of needing to vomit

negative emotions—feelings that make children unhappy or dissatisfied

neonatal care unit—special department of the hospital for infants at risk

nonfictional—factual, true

nucleus—the central portion of a cell; responsible for growth and division of cells

nutrition—the taking in and using of food for growth and energy

object permanency—knowing that an object removed from sight still exists

observe—watch, listen, and record

observing—watching and recording actions or behaviors

open classroom—a classroom where children are free to choose among learning centers

ovum—female sex cell

palate—roof of the mouth

pantomime—a play or movement where performers express themselves through gestures without words

parallel play—playing next to someone else with little interaction

pediatricians—doctors who treat children

peers—others of equal maturity generally with the same sex, interests, and intellectual level *peer pressure*—the fears of appearing or acting differently that are usually influenced by one's peers

pellagra—a chronic disease causing gastrointestinal disturbances, acne, and nervous disorders

perforation—hole

perinatal—the month after birth

personnel—people employed by the facility

philosophy—teachings and beliefs

phobias—fears

phonetics—the study of the combination of letter sounds to form words

physical abuse—any physical action that injures, such a hitting, pushing, biting, punching, slapping, or burning

physical movement—the use of the body as it moves either in place or from one area to another

physical neglect—the withholding of physical necessities to a degree that endangers health or well-being

pincer hold—the correct way to hold an object between the thumb and index finger, such as a pencil

placenta—an organ that provides protection, nourishment, and allows for the elimination of waste for the fetus

poison—a substance causing illness or death when eaten, inhaled, drunk, or absorbed in relatively small quantities

pornographic materials—materials that depict sexual actions of the type considered unacceptable by the community

positive reinforcement—saying what should be done instead of what should not be done

postnatal—after birth

posture—alignment of the body

premature birth—birth before maturity

prenatal—the period from conception to birth

prescribed—ordered in written instructions by a doctor

primary movement—the use of large muscles for gross motor activities, such as walking, running, and jumping

professionalism—education, ethics, and experience in a specific field

proprietors—owners

proteins—chemical compounds that are an essential part of every cell. Found in lean meat, fish, cheese, nuts, eggs, legumes, vegetables, and poultry

protoplasm—a mixture of proteins, fats, and other complexes suspended in water and providing the living materials of cells

puberty—when a person is first capable of reproduction

punctures—deep, small holes, such as those from a splinter or nail

punishment—a penalty inflicted for an offense; severe handling or treatment

quickenings—small sensations of movement in the womb often felt by pregnant women *receptive language*—understanding

resilient—flexible

respiratory impairments—breathing difficulties such as asthma

reversibility—the awareness that a situation can return to its original status

rickets—a disease that causes bone malformation

RNA—chemical in the cells

role models—people whom others can copy or emulate

rooting reflex—a reflex that permits infants to get nourishment from a bottle or breast

scurvy—a disease causing bleeding of the gums

secondary movement—the use of small muscles for fine motor activities, such as writing, stringing beads, and buttoning

self-concept—how one views oneself

self-correct—correct without intervention or help

self-esteem—feeling good about oneself and having confidence in one's abilities; self-respect

self-fulfilling prophecy—something that happens because it was expected to happen

self-help skills—skills that allow people to do everyday tasks for themselves

senses—sight, touch, smell, hearing, and taste

sensorimotor activity—an activity that combines the use of the senses and the muscles

seriation—ordering

shock—a depressed condition of many of the body functions due to failure of enough blood to circulate through the body following an injury or trauma

sibling rivalry—competition among children in a family

simple fracture—a closed fracture that does not go through the skin

sliding fee scale—a rate schedule where families pay what they can afford, based on income and number of dependents

social development—the process of interacting with others

social studies—the study of people and places; past, present, and future

solitary play—playing by oneself

spatial awareness—awareness of the relationship of the body to other objects

spatial relationships—awareness of the relationship of objects in space; also refers to the body and how it moves or occupies space

sperm—male sex cell

sprain—any injury to the ligaments around a joint

stamina—ability to withstand hardship or stress

stereotypes—cultural expectations of role

stop, drop, and roll technique—method used to put out clothes that are on fire: stop moving immediately, drop to the ground, and roll until the flames are put out

strabismus—crossed eyes

stress—mental pressure or physical strain

structured classroom—a classroom where all children follow a set schedule

subconscious mind—mental processes of which the individual is not aware

superego—conscience; the part of the personality associated with morals and identification with the parent of the same sex

supervision—watching over the work and performance of others

symbolic play—imitation or role-playing

sympathy—sharing another's sorrow or trouble

synthesizes—combines parts to make a whole

teacher—someone who guides, instructs, and trains students, providing knowledge and insight

temporal relationships—awareness of relationships with time and how it passes

themes—subjects or topics

theorists—experts who develop theories by observation and reasoning. They do extensive testing to confirm an original assumption

theory of cognitive development—the theory that children think differently from adults

time sample—a brief description at timed intervals

tooth buds—teeth below the gums

trimester—three-month period during pregnancy

umbilical cord—a cord connecting the placenta of the mother to the navel of the fetus

ventilation—air circulation

venting—getting rid of or expressing emotions

vernix—waxy, creamy covering of the skin during the second trimester

versatile—usable in more than one way

vitamins—complex substances that are essential to the human body for health and growth

water soluble vitamins—vitamins that can be dissolved in water

INDEX